Silence and the Rest

SRLT

Northwestern University Press
Studies in Russian Literature and Theory

Silence and the Rest

Verbal Skepticism in Russian Poetry

Sofya Khagi

NORTHWESTERN UNIVERSITY PRESS / EVANSTON, ILLINOIS

Northwestern University Press
www.nupress.northwestern.edu

This book has been published with the support of the Andrew W. Mellon Foundation.

Printed in the United States of America

ISBN 978-0-8101-4319-7

10 9 8 7 6 5 4 3 2 1

The Library of Congress has catalogued the original, hardcover edition as follows:

Khagi, Sofya.
Silence and the rest : verbal akepticism in Russian poetry / Sofya Khagi.
p. cm. — (Northwestern University Press studies in Russian literature and theory)
Includes bibliographical references.
ISBN 978-0-8101-2920-7 (cloth : alk. paper)
1. Russian poetry—History and criticism. 2. Language and languages—Philosophy. I. Title. II. Series: Studies in Russian literature and theory.
PG3041.K43 2013
891.7109—dc23

2013004711

Contents

Acknowledgments

This book took many years of work, and many people contributed to it along the way.

I would like to thank my dissertation advisor, Svetlana Evdokimova of Brown University, and the members of my dissertation committee, Alexander Levitsky of Brown University and Stephanie Sandler of Harvard University, for their expertise and help with the project in its initial stages.

I owe an immense debt of gratitude to Stephanie Sandler. Throughout all these years and all the stages of the project's development, Stephanie has tirelessly and generously guided me—reading multiple drafts of the manuscript, providing thorough and stimulating commentary on them, encouraging me to push on with my work and develop it in novel and enriching ways, and always being by my side with astute advice and staunch support.

I would like to express my warm appreciation to all my colleagues at the Department of Slavic Languages and Literatures at the University of Michigan, Ann Arbor, for their endorsement of this project. I am especially grateful to my mentor Herbert Eagle for his great advice on later chapter drafts; to Michael Makin for his numerous valuable insights on the manuscript; to Mikhail Krutikov for his recommendations on the book's completion; and to Olga Maiorova and Jindrich Toman for their helpful comments at various stages.

The book benefitted much from the manuscript workshop that took place at the University of Michigan in October 2010. I am indebted to Michael Makin for his thorough, insightful, and encouraging comments at the workshop; to Michael Wachtel of Princeton University for his advice and encouragement; to Sarah Pratt of the University of Southern California for her insightful critique; and to Herbert Eagle for organizing this very helpful event.

I owe much to Michael Wachtel for his attentive reading and astute comments on the manuscript, not only at the workshop stage but earlier as well. His suggestions were instrumental in shaping my work as it evolved from a doctoral thesis into a book project, and his enthusiasm for the project was heartening. Irene Masing-Delic of Ohio State University and Gerald Janecek of the University of Kentucky gave helpful feedback on the sections of early chapter versions published in *The Russian Review* and *The SEEJ*, respectively; Irene also contributed to this study in the course of our many friendly conversations and through e-mail exchange. Kathleen Parthé of the University of Rochester and Barry Scherr of Dartmouth College both took time to read the manuscript and share their thoughts on it; Kathleen, my undergraduate teacher of Russian literature and a source of inspiration, provided many helpful editing suggestions.

At Northwestern University Press, I am indebted to Gary Saul Morson for his endorsement of the project, to Mike Levine for guiding me through the intricacies of the publication process, and to my anonymous reviewers for suggesting ways of enriching my work.

This book is dedicated to my parents, Khaya and Kasriyel Khagi. I admire their decency and strength—they did what only they could do under circumstances only they know.

Silence and the Rest

Introduction

Silence and the Rest

IN 1882 IVAN TURGENEV composed a prose poem entitled "The Russian Language" ("Russkii iazyk"):

> In days of doubt, in days of grim reflection on the fate of my motherland, you alone are my support and pillar—the great, powerful, truthful, and free Russian language! Were it not for you, how could one not fall into despair at the sight of what is taking place at home? But one cannot believe that such a language was not given to a great people![1]

This poem, memorized by generations of Russian schoolchildren, epitomizes the culture's mythologizing of its logos. Alexander Pushkin's classic transposition of Horace's "Exegi Monumentum" (book 3, ode 30), "I have wrought a monument not made by hand" ("Ia pamiatnik sebe vozdvig nerukotvornyi," 1836), and scores of other pronouncements also claim an exceptional status for the Russian word. Few, if any, cultures have been as persistent or as moving in endorsing their languages in ethical and even religious terms.

For some time now this idealization of logos has been entrenched in critical and secular consciousness as a master narrative of Russian culture. My goal is to put this approach in perspective by charting a divergent tradition—one that distrusts language and verbal art. The very strength of the tradition mythologizing the Russian logos has meant that examinations of the antiverbal view have been cursory at best. Yet this view is also deeply felt. Though it has been richly investigated in the West, the antiverbal topos has received less attention in the context of Russian literature—a lacuna I seek to remedy.

This study investigates articulations of verbal skepticism—the notion that language is unable to furnish a full expression of the human and the world—in Russian poetry and argues that this skepticism informs the work of many of the greatest poets in the Russian tradition. I trace its development from the age of romanticism to contemporary poetic culture and demonstrate the continuity of the antiverbal philosophical preoccupation.

Essential facets of the antiverbal paradigm introduced during the romantic period continued to haunt twentieth-century poetry.

Verbal skepticism in fact occupies a key place in Russian culture. Russian philosophy, theology, and belles letters all offer fertile ground for exploring the antiverbal paradigm. As opposed to the more verbally oriented Western theology, Russian Orthodoxy distrusts theological debates and emphasizes practice over scholastic argumentation. Hesychasm exercised a major influence on Russian spiritual life in the Middle Ages and further reinforced Orthodoxy's bent toward inexpressibility and silence. Russia's early philosophical thought, as manifested in the writings of the Slavophiles, defined itself as a critique of the Western exaltation of conceptual knowledge. The flowering of Russian philosophical culture during the early twentieth century was distinguished by its concentration on ineffability. Important theorists such as Mikhail Bakhtin, Roman Jakobson, and Yuri Lotman focused on the problems of the word. The works of Nikolai Gogol, Fyodor Dostoevsky, Leo Tolstoy, and Anton Chekhov contain a wealth of material on verbal inadequacy.

In this book I focus on the most powerful and influential expressions of verbal skepticism in poetry, where experience of the word is at its most intense. Poets' prowess in deploying linguistic resources not only allows them to appreciate the richness of language, but also to perceive its limits and foibles. It is no accident that in the poetic milieu we find especially emphatic complaints about the limitations of language. Thus poetry provides a particularly fruitful sphere for the study of verbal skepticism. Moreover, Russian antiverbal lyrics address larger philosophical issues in astute and unorthodox ways.

No attempt has previously been made to undertake an in-depth study of Russian antiverbal poetry, or to situate it within the broader context of word devaluation in Western and Russian philosophy, theology, and literary theory.[2] My goal is to lift the topos of verbal skepticism out of the arcane category to which it is often consigned and demonstrate that it permeates the work of many of the greatest Russian poets. Although the mythologization of the Russian logos has marginalized the antiverbal view, this view is far from marginal: the majority of the texts under consideration in this work belong to the core of the Russian poetic canon. To a significant extent, these poems and their antiverbal thrust determined the canon itself. By investigating major poetic texts of verbal skepticism, I hope to introduce a new analytical perspective on the Russian poetic tradition —a perspective that has the power to change our readings of major poems and poets.

This study acknowledges the centrality of the verbal–idealist paradigm to Russian letters but at the same time challenges the clichés of logocentrism as a largely exclusive way of approaching the Russian poetic tradition. Russian verbal idealism stands in need of qualification, as one part of a key antinomy. The antiverbal agenda, as opposed to veneration of the word, constitutes the other crucial, if under-studied, tradition within Russian culture and Russian poetry in particular. In other words, my objective is not to argue that the notion of Russian culture dominated by veneration of the word is a misconception, but rather to show that verbal skepticism is also important to that culture—much more than is often assumed.

My stress here on Russian logophobia, motivated by the traditional emphasis on Russian logocentrism, in no way dismisses the latter inasmuch as verbal skepticism and verbal idealism stand in a dialectical relation to each other. In a loop, Russian verbal idealism reinforces Russian verbal skepticism, and vice versa. The unique social and spiritual associations of the poet in Russia do not act as a barrier to antiverbal thought but, once brought into contact with it, ignite a powerful reaction. Certain periods (e.g., the romantic period) produce a concurrent intensification of logocentric and logophobic discourses. As logocentrics postulate the vatic role of poetry, claiming its transformative power to be equal to Logos, the high demands put on the word also prompt the flourishing of antiverbal attitudes advanced by those who believe that language has not risen to the occasion. The extreme form of verbal idealism—Christ as Logos, the poet as prophet—sets up an unattainable ideal. The messianic-sacral understanding of the poetic word promoted by the romantics and reinforced by later dire historical circumstances has spurred intense verbal skepticism. The higher the claims made by verbal idealists, the easier it is to challenge these claims. If, on the other hand, poetry is "only poetry," why blame it for not accomplishing more?

Precisely because logocentrism, unlike its counterpart, has been amply analyzed, I choose more strongly antiverbal poems at the expense of logocentric works and works that contain both logocentric and logophobic polarities. Like any critical perspective, mine does not aspire to a comprehensiveness of analysis. Rather, I undertake this approach as legitimate and useful here and now because it allows me to direct a focused light at meanings that have more often than not been left in the shadows. Since word exaltation and word devaluation reinforce each other, a strain between the degrading and laudatory views of language that marks many a poet's protean thought constitutes not a contradiction but a productive dynamic. Tensions between exaltation and critique are often present throughout not just the oeuvre of the same poet but within poems of the same period or, indeed, within the same poem. I point out cases of such "poetic schizophrenia" in my analyses, but, for the sake of heuristic value, my own argument focuses on the latter. A close examination of logocentric lyrics falls beyond the scope of this work, but I acknowledge the existence and importance of logocentric and more ambivalent poems, and refer to relevant scholarship on the subject.[3]

If you grant my claim that Russian verbal skepticism exists, has been little studied, and deserves a more thorough examination, what else makes it an important subject of study? Put another way, what prompts a writer to degrade language, the medium of literary craft, and consequently the craft itself? Another central argument of this study is that attitudes toward language are closely linked to crucial existential concerns.

In his critique of the linguistic turn in twentieth-century Western philosophy, *Language Alone: The Critical Fetish of Modernity* (2002), Geoffrey Harpham claims that language has functioned as a modernist fetish—a way of addressing problems that cannot be addressed directly in a post-humanist climate. Thomas Seifrid's *The Word Made Self: Russian Writings on Language, 1860–1930* (2005), in its turn, posits that Russian linguists, philosophers, and theologians have developed a paradigm in which the notion of the self is bound to language. What I see in common in these two studies is the assumption that the idea of language serves as a proxy for something else (problems of modernity and the self, respectively).

To build upon and refine this insight, I argue that the articulation of verbal skepticism implies an ontological discussion. In other words, each narrative of verbal inadequacy is simultaneously an existential argument, one that raises a variety of issues: the meaning or meaninglessness of the universe; the existence and nature of the divine; good and evil; eternal life or annihilation; human vs. nature; human vs. other humans; communicability and incommunicability. By observing the existential queries that accompany, underscore, and explicate the subject, and by investigating why and how diverse aspects of verbal inadequacy come through in specific works and specific historical settings, this study aims to enrich our understanding of "silence" (word views) in its interplay with "the rest" (worldviews).

The guiding notion of this work, then, is that the poet's relationship to the word is grounded in his relationship to the cosmic order. History, I argue further, has shaped verbal skepticism. What may seem like a uniform discourse of word devaluation is nourished by diverse and frequently antithetical views of the world. The antiverbal paradigm evolves from the largely idealistic earlier notion of inexpressibility to the predominantly nihilist verbal skepticism of the twentieth century. If earlier articulations coexisted with, and contributed to, the poet's perception of some metaphysical ideal, over the past century antiverbal sentiment became a corollary of a more general ontological skepticism. Rather than stressing language's incommensurability with the ineffable plenitude of being, modern authors extend the existential sense of alienation to the verbal and the literary sphere. This view combines the motif of inexpressibility with that of incommunicability. Silence is seen not as a path to the transcendental but as a revelation of the inhuman.

Thus at one extreme we encounter the idealistic inexpressible, the Dantean "as it were a shadow of the true constellation";[4] at the other—the dark inexpressible of the inhuman and the absurd, beings "destroyed with the radioactive wind of your speech."[5] The older discourse of inexpressibility reflects a sanguine view of the world, while in modern absurdist discourse devaluation of the word functions as an analogy for an existential predicament. The argument that one cannot locate meaning in the text operates concurrently as an argument that the world is meaningless; conversely, the revelation of nothingness entails an exploration of verbal negativity. Death, as the furthermost case of inexpressibility and incommunicability, comes inevitably to the foreground.

Since there exist disparate approaches to the problem of the word, which are historically and culturally conditioned, and which emphasize divergent aspects of verbal failure, the term "verbal skepticism" will of necessity be multifaceted. Inasmuch as language is used to articulate all aspects of being, it may potentially be deemed deficient in articulating any of them. Word-devaluers develop along a number of branching paths, positing diverse forms and reasons for the limitations of language. Is language unable to convey just the greater reality of the divine or being in general? Are words unable to convey inner or external reality? Does language standardize the articulation of feelings in a way that cannot do justice to the uniqueness of inner experience? Does the failure of the word lie with inexpressibility (its inadequacy in conveying reality) or incommunicability (the impossibility of sharing a personal experience)? How does language deface the subject? How does it stand vis-à-vis silence, the other pole of sound? How does it express the silence of death?

Verbal skepticism, employed here as an umbrella term to subsume the gamut of antiverbal thinking (theological ineffability, romantic inexpressibility, absurdist logophobia), manifests itself in a variety of ways, and a monolithic definition is neither desirable nor possible. The boundaries of the idea are inevitably fluid. Yet while different types of verbal skepticism have different emphases and sources, a single belief—that language provides an inadequate means of expressing being—underlies all of them. I keep in mind this common thread as well as the diversity of antiverbal thought as I explore the ways in which the critique of language has been encoded in Russian poetry.

Most of the poems I examine are classics that possess a rich history of interpretation. My primary intention is to analyze them for their verbal skepticism and thus illuminate important aspects of thought and expression that have gone unnoticed. These texts not only define the Russian antiverbal paradigm, they are also of prime importance in the oeuvre of their authors, encapsulating their artistic and philosophical problematics. While bringing the presence of verbal skepticism into sharper focus, I also offer close readings that reconsider and build upon previous analyses.

In my readings I consider individual antiverbal lyrics in light of the larger topos, pursue similarities and divergences of antiverbal thought, reconstruct axiological and rhetorical links that connect various writers, and balance broader conceptual linkages with details of imagery and lexicon. In some cases this means revising traditional views such as Mandelstam trusting language unequivocally in the acmeist tradition, or Brodsky puncturing the hollowed out absolute of apophaticism and problematizing the classical paradigm of the poet overcoming mortality through his verse. In other cases (Kibirov) this entails grounding a poet's logophobic thrust in the context of the evolution of verbal skepticism I trace here; the conceptualist/postmodern critique of language has been much discussed, but not in the light of the larger antiverbal paradigm.

This study explores numerous phenomena in Russian poetry that gravitate toward the antiverbal pole—but, of course, not to the same degree. Beliefs in the absolute capacity and the absolute inadequacy of the word occupy two schematic poles between which lay many subtle gradations. Inasmuch as skepticism means doubt, not necessarily denial, many texts analyzed here will question, rather than negate, the adequacy of the word. Some of them will be primarily concerned with verbal skepticism; some will suggest verbal skepticism to a greater or lesser extent in the context of other themes such as nature and the sublime, the frustrations of reaching the divine, or a general pessimism that results from the personal psyche or social conditions. While there are few statements of verbal skepticism as direct as Tiutchev's "Silentium!" many Russian poems interrogate the problem of language.

A forceful poem's assertion of verbal inadequacy is, of course, deeply paradoxical, and the text itself may be taken as testimony to the power, not impotence, of the word. Just as poetry is an experience of language at its most intense, poetry proclaiming the inadequacy of words by means of words—eloquent words in poetic forms—sharpens the operative contradiction that marks the antiverbal move at large. The fact that verbal critics undermine their central thesis in the very process of expressing it is the fundamental paradox of their procedure. The problem has to do with the self-referentiality of the claim that all verbal claims are false, a contradiction that parallels Epimenides's or the Liar's Paradox. This operative paradox marks the entire history of verbal skepticism, from Neoplatonists verbalizing profusely on the ineffable nature of the absolute, down to post-structuralists asserting the failure of communicating meaning in absolute language. The standard deconstructive gesture of exposing contradictions inherent in the text is perhaps too easy in the case of poems of verbal skepticism. Given the high degree of self-reflexiveness expressed by the poets under consideration, I view these poems not as falling prey to, but rather dramatizing the aporia of, language turning upon itself. Simultaneously, since it transcends discursive reasoning, poetry offers a fitting arena for exploring this phenomenon. It both exposes the paradox and overrides it—thus further advancing an anti-discursive critique.

This book undertakes an in-depth study of verbal skepticism, but it does not aspire to the impossible task of giving a survey of Russian antiverbal poetry. The topos of verbal skepticism is vast, and I am interested less in breadth and more in depth of analysis. Out of a multitude of lyrics expressing verbal skepticism, I focus on the more significant examples that are characteristic of a specific author, trend, and period.[6] By providing a conceptual model that addresses these lyrics as existential arguments and offering case studies of antiverbal poetry, I hope to offer a framework within which more works can be profitably reconsidered. This project has meant that I am highly selective in my choice of poets and poems.

This study may benefit studies of Russian poetry generally by opening a space in which the history of a poetic topos is not organized around Pushkin. I do not consider Pushkin's poems to be prime examples of verbal skepticism, a decision that may prompt questions. Although Pushkin does now and then touch upon the Shakespearean issue of "these are, you see, all words, words, words" (*vse eto, vidite l', slova, slova, slova*), his oeuvre is in part indebted to a neoclassicist reliance on reason and language and does not prominently feature skepticism.[7]

I take some time to establish the tradition in detail in chapter 1 (the romantic period), but my greater focus overall is on the twentieth century. My most sustained readings come in the single-author chapters (on Mandelstam, Brodsky, and Kibirov), all drawn from the twentieth century, in part to show that even within this century there were a variety of approaches to verbal skepticism. This topos becomes more central to the tradition in the twentieth century, for all the historical and philosophical reasons I will lay out. The important turn toward absurdist verbal skepticism also takes its most urgent form in the twentieth century.

With respect to the Silver Age, I choose to concentrate on Mandelstam's poetry rather than, say, symbolism and *zaum*. The task I have set myself is to explore poetry's critique of language, not its efforts to transcend this critique. Although some of the poets I analyze fall literally silent at one or another point in their lives (Batiushkov, Mandelstam, Brodsky), the critique of the word often prompts them to try to transform language into a more effective means of self-expression and communication. Symbolist and futurist poets alike reveal an ambivalent reaction to language, first criticizing it and then undermining that antiverbal gesture. A rejection of normal language is their first step in developing a unique kind of poetic tongue capable of vanquishing the deficiencies of ordinary speech. Mandelstam's poetry, in contrast, is more fundamentally antiverbal, richly tapping into the "whats," "hows," and "whys" of verbal inadequacy.

Likewise, I am purposefully selective as far as specific works by a poet are concerned—an approach that Mandelstam's and Brodsky's sizeable, challenging, and richly analyzed corpuses especially necessitate. Given that, in my argument, verbal skepticism permeates Mandelstam's and Brodsky's oeuvres in their entirety, I focus on those lyrics that capture, in a kind of microcosm, these poets' linguistic and existential concerns. Thus I devote the core of the Brodsky chapter to "Conversation with a Celestial Being" and lyrics of the cycle "A Part of Speech" as works that convey most vividly how he approaches the antiverbal topos in general. My primary focus in the Mandelstam chapter is his antiverbal verse in *Stone* in the context of Silver Age verbal skepticism. It was during this period that a significant revival of the topos took place, and Mandelstam's *Stone* lyrics render verbal inadequacy in ways at once more imaginative and more profound than those of his Silver Age contemporaries. I give somewhat less attention to Mandelstam's later poetry for two reasons. First, his later silence takes a political turn—as forced muteness or an act of resistance, it diverges from verbal skepticism proper as a philosophical problem. Second, his later antiverbal verse links the ontological absurd and the loss of meaning in language in a manner that reaches its apogee in Brodsky—and which, accordingly, I focus on in the Brodsky chapter.

The topos of verbal skepticism permeates theory as well as poetry. Since my project surveys essentially the whole period of modern Russian poetry, in relation to Western treatments (theological, philosophical, literary theoretical) of verbal skepticism, my tendency to paraphrase in a compressed way much of the thought processes (my own and others) stems from the objective to cover this expansive terrain as concisely as possible. I approach the poems through the history of ideas as well as literary criticism, combining a broad intellectual framework with close textual and intertextual analyses of individual lyrics. This foregrounds the vast philosophical, religious, and aesthetic heritage of verbal skepticism and at the same time treats individual instances of it with attention to a given historical, cultural, and personal moment.

The philosophers in question were widely read by the educated public, and the poets I focus on were reacting to them as well as to one another. But this book is not a study of influences. I note connections between philosophers and poets whenever they are pertinent, but my primary focus is a conceptual and rhetorical rapprochement (as well as divergence) between theorists and poets, whether or not these are supported by chains of influence. A set of principles, very much like those that inform the philosophical tradition of verbal skepticism in Russia and in Europe, also informs important elements of the poetic tradition. While these principles are common to theory and poetry, they develop slightly differently in the latter, and I present an account of both the similarities and the divergences. I explore the common patterns and various pathways of antiverbal thought and place lyrics of verbal skepticism within a general cultural framework.

While poetic-philosophical give-and-take is important, the linkages between poets themselves are even more critical. Even though Russian verbal skepticism is transmitted through both poetry and philosophy, its intrapoetic transmission predominates. As this study shows, Tiutchev's "Silentium!," an early critique of language, acquired the status of Ur-text. "Silentium!" commands exceptional status and has fathered many children in modernist poetry. A dialogic engagement with Tiutchev's poem later operates as an explicit marker that a poet is engaging the problem of verbal skepticism.

VERBAL SKEPTICISM AND EXISTENTIAL ARGUMENTS

In the remainder of the introduction, I consider classic Western and Russian theories of verbal skepticism to illustrate the ways these two kinds of discourse—antiverbal and existential—intersect. I concentrate on some of the most influential explorations of the antiverbal paradigm and highlight those views that are most relevant to the Russian tradition.[8] I briefly examine theology, German idealism (Kant, Schopenhauer), Nietzsche, and post-structuralism ("death of the author" doctrine) in relation to their assessments of language. Setting up categories that will be used in the poetry chapters (theological ineffability, romantic inexpressibility, and absurdist verbal skepticism), I trace Western antiverbal thought spanning a spectrum from "language cannot render the transcendental" to "there is nothing to render," with Nietzsche engineering that paradigm shift. Subsequently I examine Russian contributions to verbal skepticism and suggest differences between Western and Russian approaches. To close I move from philosophy to poetry and provide chapter outlines.

Theological Ineffability

From Plato to the post-structuralists, some of the most renowned thinkers were preoccupied with the problem of whether words provide an adequate means of comprehending and conveying being. Out of these debates two trends have emerged. One view, an exalted stance, lauds the power of the word in its capacity to convey truth. The other, the skeptical position, devalues language, seeing it as forever deficient at conceptualizing and expressing reality.

A prominent feature of (anti)verbal thought is its close embedding in theological discourse. The opening lines of the Gospel of John articulate the notion of divine Logos: "In the beginning was the Word, and the Word was with God, and the Word was God."[9] This combination of semantic ambiguity and formal magnificence impresses one as a fitting portrayal of matters beyond man's understanding, and reveals the powers of a verbal art that at the same time may be conceived in terms of its foibles. According to another biblical claim, after the world and man are created, Adam is assigned the task of naming the beasts. This act defines man as superior to the animal kingdom and locates this superiority in his possession of language.[10] The coexistence of two disparate notions of language in the Bible, as Logos and as human speech, complicates matters. Do there exist both the ineffably powerful Word "without which was not anything made that was made" and words that merely "name"? Is human language divinely sanctioned? The story of Babel further expresses ambivalence toward the gift of language for, in this instance, language itself becomes the means of divine punishment. The story betrays a dissatisfaction with the medium that is as prone to separate humans as to unite them.[11]

Language and writing, furthermore, may not have been bestowed on man but stolen in defiance of the divine will. Aeschylus's *Prometheus Bound* portrays Prometheus as the creator of humans. Among the gifts Prometheus gives to mankind is an ability to reason, along with letters and their combination, an art that fosters memory.[12] The possession of verbal arts makes humans into the gods' rivals. For that both humankind and Prometheus are punished. In the Prometheus myth enlightenment is linked to pain and retribution, and speech, the medium of thought, is judged to be an outrage no less than a blessing. Other classical myths relate the birth of verbal art as stories of cruelty, deception, and suffering. Whether the myths underscore verbal art's transgressive quality (the stories of Apollo and Marsyas, Apollo and Pan, Prometheus), expose poetry's and music's connection to pain and loss (the tales of Orpheus, and Athena and the Gorgons), posit their dark origin (the Medusa and Pegasus myth), or emphasize madness, compulsion, or deceit (the stories of Pythia, Apollo's prophetess, of Dionysian orgies), they reveal an anxiety humans experience regarding the gift of poetic word.[13]

Given the theological preoccupation with the word, it comes as no surprise that ineffability is a religious concept. The ineffability topos, engaged by Christian mystics, has antecedents in Plato and Neoplatonism.[14] According to Plato, the knowledge of the absolute cannot be put into words. The ultimate reality is a "colorless, formless, intangible essence, visible only to the mind."[15] In the Neoplatonic argument, language may portray things of the physical world in their differentiation, yet it fails to capture "the One" because linguistic structures reflect a realm of differences and particularities while "the One" is absolutely unitary. It is the source of all things in which the mystic loses himself. Grasping the limitations of language may move one toward a higher form of insight.[16]

The notion of the religious ineffable posits a gulf between divinity and the human ability to conceptualize and articulate the divine. Insofar as human language does not provide an adequate means of conceptualizing God, one cannot say anything about Him, and must instead strive for an awareness of Him beyond words, through silence and contemplation. The tautological statement about Yahweh, "I am that I am," and the prohibition against uttering His name are expressions of religious ineffability. The Mosaic law against the making of images fits into the same context. As Schoenberg's *Moses and Aaron* (1930–32) puts it, "An image asks for names . . . [But] thou shalt believe in the spirit."[17]

If relatively modern works like *Moses and Aaron* tend to regard God's transcendence of human speech and reason in a pessimistic light, earlier works glorify divine ineffability. Saint Augustine contemplates the operative paradox: God is not to be called ineffable because to say this is to speak of Him. Thus there arises "a curious contradiction of words, because if the unspeakable is what cannot be spoken of, it is not unspeakable if it can be called unspeakable."[18] Though one cannot say anything about God, formidable verbal skills are employed to intimate Him. The ineffability topos is a rhetorical technique that privileges the principle of divine authority and inspires awe before God's ineffable essence. Dante's *Paradiso* (*Divine Comedy*, 1308–21) depicts the encounter with the divine in a dazzling language, and yet asserts that this poetic achievement is but "the stuttering of a mute."[19] The same rhetorical strategy dominates Plotinus's and other Neoplatonists' writings on ineffability, as well as Spenser's *The Faerie Queene* (1590; 1596), Milton's *Paradise Lost* (1667), and other works.[20] Divine transcendence does not entail silence. Instead, language is carried to its limits, only to be undercut by an admission of impotence. In contrast to a more modern tendency to dramatize silence ("what we cannot speak about we must consign to silence"; Wittgenstein, *Tractatus Logico-Philosophicus*, 1921), these older texts do speak about that which is unspeakable.[21] Often this topos degenerates into a device that is employed for the sake of convention, or as a roundabout method to raise one's creative credentials.[22]

(Pre-)romantic Inexpressibility

Theological ineffability and secular inexpressibility constitute two divergent strains of antiverbal thought. Although most premodern articulations of verbal skepticism concentrate on ineffability, inexpressibility arises as well.[23] In the opening scene of *King Lear* (1603–06) Shakespeare exposes the disparity between the ineffability device and genuine inexpressibility of love. Goneril, loquacious on her devotion, claims that her love "makes speech unable." In opposition, Cordelia's love is truly "more ponderous than her tongue." She finds speech devalued through her sisters' deceitful employment of words, and elects "to love, and be silent."[24] It is the profundity of her devotion that forces Lear's youngest daughter not to speak.[25]

In this episode, it is emotion toward another human being, rather than one's conceptualization of the divine, that cannot be adequately expressed. Secular inexpressibility is brought to fruition during the age of (pre-)romanticism. The period introduces essential new aspects of the antiverbal argument. For the romantics, language fails to convey not only transcendent realms but also ordinary physical and psychic reality. Theological ineffability had asserted the limits of human reason and language with respect to the divine; romantic inexpressibility makes these limits ubiquitous.

Kant's *Critique of Pure Reason* (1781) claims that human perception of the world is mediated because sense perceptions are the only data we have about the world and because cognition enters the process of perception itself. Kant links sensibility and understanding, arguing that they stand in connection to each other through the synthesis of imagination; otherwise sensibility would supply no objects of knowledge and, consequently, no experience.[26] The connection between perception and cognition is an illustration of Kant's thesis that we have no immediate access to the world. External reality is inexpressible insofar as language, the instrument of cognition, fails one just as cognition does. The life of the heart and the mind is inexpressible both by virtue of its singularity and because cognition is incapable of attending to itself.

By postulating the incommensurability between sensory perception and speech and cognitive processes, post-Kantians conceptualize inexpressibility as a fact of everyday life rather than a characteristic of mystical experiences. Kant's emphasis on the subject elicits the belief that an individual human experience is unique. The romantics reimagine art as an expression of the inimitable self, not a faithful mimesis of external reality, and so extol the values of authenticity and individuality in artistic production. A problem arises of how to convey unique experiences when the word binds one to express feelings in a conventional way that cannot do justice to the singularity of inner being. Insofar as the romantics underscore the inexpressibility of the subject's emotional life as he intuits the transcendental, romantic inexpressibility reveals an affinity with religious ineffability.[27] Likewise, the analogues of Neoplatonists' and other mystics' loss of a singular identity in an exalted fusion with the "essence of things" become components of romantic treatments of inexpressibility. At the same time any human experience becomes, by virtue of its singularity, inexpressible.

The notion that each individual human experience is distinctive and nontransferable in language is an important one for the romantics. The privileging of reality over logos and of perception over cognition and articulation shifts the emphasis from divine ineffability to human inexpressibility. Although the two types of inexpressibility, that of the inner being and that of the external world, go together (inner and outer realities cannot be easily separated), the romantics privilege the ineffability of the subject over the ineffability of the object as exemplified by Kant's exploration of the sublime. *The Critique of Judgment* (1790) envisions the sublime as referring to a human encounter with an entity so vast and magnificent that it challenges one's ability to comprehend it. While natural beauty "conveys a finality in its form making the object appear, as it were, pre-adopted to our power of judgment, the feeling of the sublime, may appear, indeed, in point of form to contravene the ends of our power of judgment, to be ill adopted to our faculty of imagination."[28] The sublime experience, like mystical visions, contains an element of ineffability, impressing one with grandeur and defying one's capacities to contain it. In the case of the mathematical sublime, human beings have no standard to estimate the magnitude of nature but recognize the superiority of their cognitive powers and admire their ability to conceptualize infinity. The dynamic sublime makes humans recognize their physical impotence but reveals their ability to judge themselves independent of nature. Sublimity is contained in the mind: the subject becomes conscious of superiority over nature within itself and thereby also over external nature. Commencing with the idea of nature's ineffable infinity and might, Kant concludes that the feeling of the sublime in nature is a measure of respect for our own vocation. Typical for romantic treatments of the theme, the analysis of the mathematical and the dynamic sublime shifts the focus from nature's ineffability per se to the subject's intimation of nature's ineffability and uses this sentiment to honor the subject.

Kant posits that perception is superior to conceptualization. Essential properties of creativity are inexpressible. The genius exhibits aesthetic ideas that cannot be conveyed conceptually, that is, a presentation of the imagination that prompts thought, but to which no concept can be adequate, "so that no language can express it completely and allow us to grasp it."[29] He produces works that do not merely reveal ideas for given concepts but communicate the feeling that those ideas arouse. Kant terms the latter "mental attunement" or "spirit." Conceptual language is deficient, and it is only the ineffable spiritual component of the work of genius that makes language come alive.

Like Kant, Schopenhauer prefers perception to concepts. Concepts, though useful tools of cognition, offer knowledge in its most impoverished form, whereas perception is rich, immediate, and profound:

> The concept . . . is something completely determinable, hence something to be exhausted, something distinctly thought, which can be, according to its whole content, communicated coldly and dispassionately by words . . . The ideas . . . are essentially something of perception, and therefore, in its fuller determinations, something inexhaustible.[30]

The artist ratiocinates when creating his work, but only the idea that was perceived before it was thought has stimulating value when communicated. There is, however, the problem of retaining and communicating perception, for it is unique and fleeting. We are entirely satisfied with an artistic work only when it leaves behind something that, in spite of our reasoning powers, we cannot formulate as a distinct concept. The very best in art, its ineffable *geist,* is too spiritual to be given directly to the senses. It must be born in the beholder's imagination, though it must be begotten by the work of art.

Schopenhauer privileges the richness of human perception over the "abstract, transparent universality of concepts."[31] Language fails when engaging allegory, for allegory links symbols and concepts in an orthodox way that constrains perception. It is even worse to employ symbolism, a degenerate kind of allegory, with no connection between what is depicted and the concept indicated, with the sign and the thing signified connected only conventionally and arbitrarily.

Verbal art, moreover, cannot compare with music. Music lacks the problem of the conventionality of the sign. It expresses the innermost nature of existence, speaking "in a language intelligible with absolute directness, yet not capable of translation into that of our faculty of reason."[32] Unlike language, music can be understood by anyone, is trans-rational, and expresses emotion in the most powerful way. If the word focuses on specific incidents and motives that give rise to emotion, music gives emotion as such, revealing the inner significance of the incidents depicted in language. Language and music are as particular is to universal, or example is to rule—the most indirect and the most direct modes of knowledge.

Romantic inexpressibility is to a large extent affirmative in the same sense that theological ineffability is affirmative. Both devalue speech in order to elevate the subject of speech, be it the divine, external reality or, most prominently, emotional life. Analogously, when the romantics suggest that human feelings cannot be fully recovered verbally, they aim not so much to devalue language as to privilege a raw experience of emotion. At the same time, the belief that experiences are at best partially shared offers a darker vision of inexpressibility that, instead of exalting one's uniqueness, laments the impossibility of communication. Although it is arguable when exactly modern verbal skepticism begins to prevail over the older idealistic inexpressibility, I take the boundary between Kant and Schopenhauer as symptomatic of a larger paradigm shift. If Schopenhauer's critique of concepts and privileging of music over poetry fall in line with the idealistic strain of the romantic antiverbal imagination, his observation that music and word deceive by artificially assuaging desires that can never be satisfied in real life opens up a more skeptical line of thought. Rhythm and rhyme prompt one to follow the reading more willingly and stimulate an automatic agreement with what is read prior to judgment. Like rhyme, harmonious melody satisfies our yearning for the reconciliation of discordant elements "as if by accident," providing "the copy of the meeting of our desires with the favorable external circumstances independent of them, and is thus the picture of happiness."[33]

Schopenhauer's consideration of the void in *The World as Will and Representation* (1819) departs from the notions of idealistic inexpressibility. He adopts the Kantian idea that the world of experience is the result of a cognitive process and sets up a dichotomy between the world as we see it (representation), and the world's inner essence (cosmic will), which manifests itself both externally in nature and internally in man. One may not perceive the world-in-itself conceptually, from without, but may prepare oneself for living from within, where all knowledge ceases. As with Plotinus and other mystics, the goal is to attain the unity of one's inner being with the source of existence. To achieve this state, one must renounce willing and to accept life as suffering. In humans, the will to live becomes self-conscious for the first time when standing face to face with death. Only the state of will-less artistic contemplation can bring tranquility—an appearance of ineffable "nothingness."[34] Schopenhauer's nothingness departs from the religious ineffable, however. The merger with the kernel of the world brings will-less knowledge, which is not the discernment of a benign transcendental cause but knowledge of the will that is the principle of the struggle for survival. The union with the void may be a liberating experience, but it is precisely a union with the void, not a Dantean or Augustinian fusion with the divine.

Absurdist Logophobia

If Schopenhauer's notion of the inexpressible is dark insofar as it is embedded in a tragic view of life, it was Friedrich Nietzsche who went furthest in the direction of absurdist logophobia. Just as he undermined all the fundamental doctrines of Western civilization, he carried on an assault against the medium that articulates these doctrines.[35]

Archetypal romantic notions are rendered darker existential underpinnings. *The Will to Power* (1883–88) picks up the idea that music is superior to language: "Compared with music . . . words dilute and brutalize; words depersonalize; words make the uncommon common."[36] Nietzsche's assertion that art transfigures human suffering also follows Schopenhauer, but, while for Schopenhauer poetry and music assuage pain, for Nietzsche art makes one embrace it.

Nietzsche emphasizes incommunicability, the impossibility of reaching to the other, which is linked to, but not equal to inexpressibility (verbal deficiency). Language is suitable for communicating only trivial, moderate feelings. With it the speaker vulgarizes himself. *Thus Spake Zarathustra* (1885) distinguishes between public and private language. It is only private language, spoken in happy solitude, that is truthful. Public language, language in its communicative capacity, is a dissemblance before "the mean other." Zarathustra chooses to separate himself from other people, speaking only to himself and to his animals. Furthermore, language is a comforting delusion that covers up the cleft between subject and object. For Zarathustra words are illusionary bridges between things that are eternally separated. Words deceive us into thinking that we have right of entry into the world: "How lovely . . . that there are words and sounds! Are not words and sounds rainbows and illusive bridges between things which are eternally apart? . . . For me—how should there be any outside-myself? There is no outside. But all sounds make us forget this."[37]

Like Kant and Schopenhauer, Nietzsche prefers perception to concepts: the latter are "rattling bones" that remain after perceptions have been drained of blood (*The Joyful Wisdom,* 1882).[38] *On Truth and Lying in an Extra-Moral Sense* (1873) intensifies the critique of concepts by arguing that they ensnare humans in a false picture of the world. A concept begins in an image that gets designated by a sound. The sensation, evoked through a nerve impulse, is presented externally through a sound image. The sound, once it is fixed to this particular image, metaphorically designates all the images that are more or less similar to the original one. Concepts are arbitrary artificial phenomena since the sound is invented and randomly fixed to the image. The invented sound, converted to the concept, induces one to think that, by knowing it, one knows the thing itself. But the consciousness that forms language grasps not things but the manner in which one stands toward them. Therefore language conveys an attitude and a partial view rather than a genuine knowledge of the thing. This perspectival language structures human thought and experience.

While Plato distinguished two ways of speaking, the truthful and unadorned way, and deceptive poetic rhetoric, for Nietzsche all language is the result of rhetorical arts. Language can never be natural or connected to the essence of objects:

> The power to discover and to make operative that which works and impresses, with respect to each thing, a power which Aristotle calls rhetoric, is,

> at the same time, the essence of language; the latter is based just as little as rhetoric is upon that which is true, upon the essence of things.[39]

Moreover, language gives a flawed perspective on the world since all words are tropes. As tropes, words present not what truly takes place but a sound image fading away with time. Tropes are partial, transferable, and reversible; they do not express things completely but display only prominent traits; they can be assigned new meanings metaphorically and thus involve a transferability that is not true of the objects represented; and they reverse the nature of things since they can metonymically substitute cause and effect.

"On the Origin of Language" (1870) bonds verbal and theological critiques. Nietzsche rejects the view that language is conditioned by conceptual content and claims that it came into being by arbitrary formation. He refers to the Bible as the authority that posits words' necessary relation to things, a view that, he claims, has been refuted by comparative linguistics. Language is the depository of human truths about which it has been forgotten that they are illusions. Interpretations of things and, consequently, language are shaped by our desire to make the world resemble ourselves. Words limit thought so successfully that we scarcely perceive them as constraints: "We cease to think when we refuse to do so under the constraint of language; we barely reach the doubt that sees this limitation as a limitation."[40]

Nietzsche's condemnation of poetry, no less pervasive than his censure of language, is as explicitly implicated in an anti-theological thrust. Insofar as language constitutes the medium of literary art, all the problems of verbal inadequacy apply to literature as well. Besides, an antiliterary move introduces a number of additional concerns, such as those of the aporia between art and life, and art's falsehoods, escapism, and impotence against evil. It is poetry that deludes man by transfiguring everything into the beautiful. "The Song of Melancholy" mocks Zarathustra's pretensions at truth:

> This, the suitor of truth?
> No! Only fool! Only poet!
> Only speaking colorfully out of fools' masks,
> Climbing around on mendacious word bridges.[41]

Poetry is taken to reveal "higher truth" because people are tired of reality. Though poetry makes things seem more valuable, and hence more "true and real," the view that what is valuable to us is real is false. Both the poet and the public delude themselves into believing that poetry brings something new and exceptional to life. This effect is simulated by poetic artifices and the accompanying quasi-religious excitement: "The magic in rhythm consists in a quite elementary symbolism by which the regular and the orderly imposes itself on our understanding as a higher realm, a life above and beyond this irregular life." It becomes an adhesive for our attention, "since we follow the reading more willingly, and partly gives rise to a blind agreement with what is read."[42] The fascination of art is correlated with pain and death—poetry provides a simulacrum of the harmony absent in real life. Thus the very existence of art proves that existence is an evil and serious phenomenon.

Poets are the greatest liars on earth, and their most important lie is about the divine, for "all gods are poets' prevarications."[43] Besides, their creations are not genuine since they experience no real passion when they write; they are shameless in the sense that they exploit their emotions artistically; and their talent begrudges them any squandering of energy in emotion.[44] According to *Twilight of the Idols* (1888), Nietzsche's own works refer to things he had outlived: "Our true experiences . . . could not communicate themselves even if they tried . . . Whatever we have words for, that we have already got behind."[45] So long as one experiences an emotion one does not examine or paint it because examination requires a secret antagonism involved in comparison. Art permits one to rest from the self by observing life from a distance, for life is endurable only as an aesthetic phenomenon, but reflection signifies a dwindling of vitality. Genuine feelings are expressed only in action, and in times of suffering man embraces silence, not Zarathustra's haughty alienation from the "mean other," but a humble silence of a sufferer ashamed of betraying his pain.

Nietzsche's verbal skepticism supports his ontological nihilism. The lie of the transcendental, just like the lie of the subject, are quintessentially verbal delusions. The subject itself is our interpretation, something projected behind what there is. The idea that, when there is thinking, someone must be there who thinks, stems from the grammatical habit that posits a doer for what is done: "Language everywhere sees a doer and a doing; it believes in will as the cause; it believes in the ego as being, in the ego as substance, and it projects this faith in the ego-substance upon all things—only thereby does it first create the concept of 'thing.'"[46] The illusion of the unified subject is importantly misleading since the ideas of unity and of the transcendental are traditionally connected (e.g., by Neoplatonists).

Nietzsche's linguistic perspectivism assists him in questioning human morals, knowledge, and beliefs, while his assault on poetic art is simultaneously an assault on religion, since art is a substitute religion of modernity. Hence the observations that "we are not rid of God because we still have faith in grammar"; and, in *Beyond Good and Evil* (1886), "one believed in 'the soul' as one believed in grammar and the grammatical subject."[47] The principle of individuality is an illusion created by language that, paradoxically, depersonalizes. Just as linguistic habits create the illusion of the subject and its will, they create the illusion of the ultimate Will. Like Kant and Schopenhauer, Nietzsche stresses that we have no access to facts but only to our interpretations; but, while neither Kant nor Schopenhauer question the validity of ethical principles, Nietzsche reasons that there are no moral phenomena at all, only a moral interpretation of phenomena. Man is not a free agent capable of taking responsibility for his actions; it is language that deceives us into believing in the existence of the free subject.

Nietzsche's focus on the metaphysical falsehoods of the word, on rhetoric's construction of knowledge, and on the function of power in discourse anticipates developments of antiverbal thought in the twentieth century. He lays the basis for deconstruction's reconceptualization of events as quasi-linguistic constructs. His shift of focus on discourse and his analysis of the role of power in language anticipates Foucault just as his critique of tropes does de Man. The antagonism that is involved in thinking and articulation predates Derrida's analysis of the doubling that attends any examination and exposure of the self. Most importantly, his linkage of antiverbal and antireligious thought, and his grounding of the assault on the traditional notion of the subject in an attack on language, anticipate deconstruction's key moves. The chaining of verbal and ontological critiques lays the groundwork for a correlation of verbal and ontological skepticism in post-structuralist thought.

Deconstruction updates Nietzsche's "death of God" as a critique of the "metaphysics of presence" and a subversion of notions of a unifying center to reality. The deconstructive version of the ineffable, the wholly negative non-presence of the transcendental, indeed, of any kind of reality, beyond a self-enclosed dance of signifiers, is the reverse of religious experience, including apophatic experience with its faith in, and a silent intuition of, an unknowable but all-positive, transcendent being. Derrida in "How to Avoid Speaking: Denials" (1986) posits how his discourse diverges from negative theology: "'Negative theology' seems to reserve, beyond all positive predication, beyond all negation, even beyond Being, some hyperessentiality, a being beyond Being."[48] What he objects to is that, for Christian apophatic (negative) theologians, following Plato and Neoplatonists, the "beyond Being" is "not a non-being" but a hyperbolism that "obeys the logic of the sur, of the hyper, over and beyond, which heralds all the hyperessentialisms of Christian apophases."[49] While apophatic theology sees language as a deficient medium to be transcended as one strives toward a higher truth, deconstruction subverts ontology and insists on the impossibility of escaping language—"There is nothing outside the text."[50]

Like Nietzsche's views of language, post-structuralism's antiverbal thrust ministers to, and is subsumed by, ontological skepticism. Derrida repeats Nietzsche's twofold assault on language and theology as truth-generating discourses: "The sign and divinity have the same place and time of birth. The age of the sign is essentially theological."[51] For him ("How to Avoid Speaking") "language has started without us, in us and before us. This is what theology calls God."[52] For Paul de Man ("Intentional Structure of the Romantic Image," 1960), words fail "to originate as an incarnation of a transcendental principle" and "designate a desire to be an epiphany but necessarily fail to be an epiphany." Thus "the existence of the poetic image is itself sign of the divine absence, and the conscious use of this imagery an admission of this absence."[53]

Post-structuralism's "death of the author" doctrine that proclaims the text's impersonal and autonomous nature is simultaneously an anti-theological commentary. In Derrida's depiction ("Limited Inc abc. . . ," 1976), once an utterance leaves the author, it is detached from authorial intention, may be repeated by someone else, and takes on a life of its own in other contexts. This repeatability is termed "iterability" since the repeated utterance becomes "other": "Iterability alters, contaminating parasitically what it identifies and enables to repeat 'itself.'"[54] Challenging the traditional understanding of writing as a means of communication, and proposing a view of the text as cut from consciousness and context, Derrida in "Signature Event Context" (1971) couches his analysis in theological terms:

> To write is to produce a mark that will constitute a kind of machine that is in turn productive, that my future disappearance in principle will not prevent from functioning and from yielding, and yielding itself to, reading and rewriting . . . This essential drifting, due to writing as an iterative structure cut off from all absolute responsibility, from consciousness as the authority of the last analysis, writing orphaned, and separated at birth from the assistance of his father, is indeed what Plato condemned in *The Phaedrus.*[55]

Barthes in "Death of the Author" (1967) and Foucault in "What Is an Author?" (1969) are even more explicit. For Barthes the text is an oblique space where all identity is lost, "not a line of words releasing a single theological meaning (the message of the 'Author-God')," and "to refuse to fix meaning is, in the end, to refuse God and his hypostases—reason, science, law."[56] For Foucault "the author has disappeared. God and man died a common death."[57]

With the banishment of the author (a proxy for the banishment of the divine), all the writer can do is to produce an accumulation of quotations separated from his consciousness. Just as the despiritualized, and therefore dehumanized, vision of language promotes a dehumanized vision of being, the argument that meaning is non-locatable in the text serves to assert the meaninglessness of the world. So, in "Shelley Disfigured" (1979), de Man warns that "nothing, whether deed, word, thought, or text, ever happens in relation, positive or negative, to anything that precedes, follows, or exists elsewhere, but only as a random event whose power, like the power of death, is due to the randomness of its occurrence."[58]

Deconstruction continues to censure concepts that incarcerate man in a falsely polarized and static view of life, and disparages the word by drawing attention to Saussure's notions that signifiers and signifieds are connected arbitrarily and that the value of elements in a linguistic system is generated by their difference from other elements (*Cours de linguistique générale / Course in General Linguistics,* 1906–11), as exemplified in Derrida's concept of *différance* ("The Difference," 1968). Like Nietzsche, Derrida denies the possibility of metaphysical revelation through language. In his view, the desanctified view of the word must not be lamented but, on the contrary, welcomed: one must embrace existence "outside of the myth of a purely maternal or paternal language, a lost native country of thought."[59]

Likewise, deconstruction takes on Nietzsche's critique of the rhetorical nature of language. De Man's *Allegories of Reading* (1979) envisions figuration as a mode of pseudo-analysis that divulges a Nietzschean self-split within the narrator (rhetorical distancing from lived experience). Building on Nietzsche's notes for a course on rhetoric at the University of Basel (1872–73) and "On Truth and Lying in an Extra-Moral Sense," de Man stresses in "Nietzsche's Theory of Rhetoric" (1974) that tropes, not at all an aberrant form of language, constitute the very core of the linguistic paradigm. Language, always rhetorical, generates opinions and not truths. This way Nietzsche subverts the status of language vis-à-vis extralinguistic meanings and establishes his critique of metaphysics.

De Man's "Autobiography as De-Facement" (1979) in *The Rhetoric of Romanticism* (1956–83) deals with figure, figuration, and disfiguration in language. Any book with a readable title page is for him in a sense autobiographical, but, rather than life producing the autobiography as an act produces its consequences, the writer is constrained by the demands of self-portraiture and resources of the verbal medium. De Man highlights the defacing power of language through prosopopeia, the trope of autobiography,

> the fiction of an apostrophe to an absent, deceased, or voiceless entity, which posits the possibility of the latter's reply and confers upon it the power of speech. Voice assumes mouth, eye, and finally face, a chain that is manifest in the etymology of the trope's name, *prosopon poein,* to confer a mask (*prosopon*). Prosopopeia is the trope of bibliography, by which one's name . . . is made as intelligible and memorable as a face.[60]

Disputing Wordsworth's claim for restoration in the face of death in *Essays upon Epitaphs* (1810–12), de Man posits that, as figuration, language is always privative, and is not the subject itself but the mute representation of the subject. Therefore death "is a displaced name for a linguistic predicament."[61]

De Man depicts language as out of human control, in terms that characterize a negative absolute, an utterly dehumanized power. The text as a unified system in which unrelated mechanical parts are meaningfully integrated is a mirage of cognition. The "madness of words" ("Shelley Disfigured") is the illusion language confers that the author is within our reach. No degree of knowledge can stop this madness for it is verbal madness, and it would be naive "to believe that this strategy [verbal], which is not our strategy as subjects, since we are its product rather than its agent, can be a source of value and has to be celebrated or denounced accordingly."[62] His analysis of Walter Benjamin's "Task of the Translator" (1923) rejects the traditional notion that language defines humanity. Benjamin's language of historical, messianic, and exilic pathos describes linguistic events that are by no means human. "The inhuman is: linguistic structures, the play of linguistic tensions, linguistic events that occur, possibilities which are inherent in language—independently of any intent or any drive or any wish or any desire we intend or any drive or any wish or any desire we might have."[63]

While de Man, Derrida, Foucault, and other post-structuralists adopt Nietzsche's view of language as a power that shapes and constrains thought, they have gone further to conceptualize language as a sort of inexorable authority that, rather than being manipulated by humans, manipulates them instead.[64] This authority defies human intentions and desires, speaking through humans, disembodying them, and simultaneously generating the illusion of an autonomous subject. Language is something of a Big Brother that imprisons men in a perfect totalitarian society. Alternatively, given deconstruction's predilection for (anti)religious metaphors, language can be seen as an omniscient evil deity that has seized possession of humans to play its inscrutable games with them.

RUSSIAN CONTRIBUTIONS TO VERBAL SKEPTICISM

Idealistic and negative strains of antiverbal thought tend to coexist, but the latter have attained more prominence in modernity. Russian antiverbal thought is a part of this history. However, Russian verbal skepticism both plays an especially important role in the culture and possesses distinctive features.

The antiverbal paradigm has been a consistent element of Russian thought. An antiverbal thrust marks Russian Orthodoxy, placing it in opposition to Western scholasticism. As early as eleventh-century Kiev, in the vita of princes Boris and Gleb there emerged the ideal of kenosis, a way to salvation through the imitation of Christ's humility and voluntary sacrifice. From then onward, Orthodox spirituality has privileged the emulation of

Christ's deeds over theological argumentation. It insists on the unconditional acceptance of divine mysteries versus the rationalization of faith and reveals mistrust of language as a means of carrying out arguments on matters that transcend logic.

If cataphatic (positive) theology prevails in the West, apophatic theology is essential to Orthodoxy. The former conveys what the divine is; the latter denies the possibility of verbally conveying the divine. The introduction of hesychasm in the fourteenth to fifteenth centuries further bolstered the importance of ineffability in Orthodoxy. Hesychasm ("quietness"), a variety of apophaticism, claims that the external ritual side of Christianity fails to connect man with God and instead concentrates on inner religious experience. In the argument of Pseudo-Dionysius the Areopagite (late 5th–early 6th century), religious action must lead away from any dependence on words or reason. His advice is to leave behind everything perceived and understood and strive toward union with the divine, which is beyond knowledge: "The higher we ascend in prayer, the more our language becomes restricted by the more synoptic view of what is intelligible. Now, however, that we are to enter the darkness beyond intellect, you will not find a brief discourse but a complete absence of discourse and intelligibility."[65] The mystic surrenders to the unnamable by renouncing himself and his perceptions. This leads to the ineffable condition of *gnosos,* the direct experience of a source not mediated by the senses. Pseudo-Dionysius considers the notions of cataphatic theology (God as good, wise, powerful) and then negates them in order of decreasing incongruity, from the obviously false attributes up to those that seem more and more abstract and plausible. He then moves beyond all conceptual attributes of divinity including negations, abandoning language and thought altogether.[66]

For the Russian hesychasts prayer is not an articulation of words but an inward action, spiritual prayer. In the words of Nil Sorsky, a proponent of ascetic monasticism and hesychastic prayer, "If prayers are only on the lips, but the spirit is not involved, it is as though prayer is being offered to the air."[67] A special technique of praying, beginning with the invocations of Jesus and ending in prayer without words, aims at the perception of the light that language does not possess. Even if the visions of the mystic are not believed to be deceptive, one tries to push beyond them, to achieve a higher awareness of divinity beyond words and images. However, in Sorsky's admission of the operative paradox, he cannot bear to hold spiritual secrets in silence, and shows himself unwisely eager to teach others.[68]

The transformation of Old Russian literature by the Second South Slav Influence (new developments emerging in East Slavic writing toward the end of the fourteenth century, borrowed from Bulgarian and Serbian cultures) leads to the paradoxical situation observed in works of medieval Western inexpressibility. Instead of imposing voluntary silence upon themselves, the writers develop a highly ornate "weaving of words" (*pletenie sloves*) style full of complicated compounds, tautologies, hyperbole, paronomasia, and other rhetorical adornments. Epiphanius the Wise's "Panegyric to St. Stephen of Perm" ("Panegirik Stefanu permskomu," early 15th century) suggests a long list of attributes, all posed as questions: "Shall I call you a prophet? . . . an Apostle? . . . a lawgiver?"[69] Just as all the notions of cataphatic theology fail to capture the essence of the divine, all the writer's epithets fail to capture the essence of sainthood. Ironically, the purpose of these techniques, which give rise to excessive wordiness, is to transcend the word.

The influence of hesychasm informs the entire history of Russian Orthodoxy.[70] As indigenous philosophical thought emerged in Russia in the nineteenth century, its religiously oriented aspect preoccupied itself with apophaticism. The early Slavophile thinkers urged the development of a native philosophical tradition that would harmonize with Orthodox spirituality and offer an alternative to European, concept-driven philosophy.[71] In "On the Necessity and Possibility of New Principles for Philosophy" ("O neobkhodimosti i vozmozhnosti novykh nachal dlia filosofii," 1856), Ivan Kireevsky censures Western thought, from Aristotle onward, for its over-reliance on concepts. For Kireevsky, abstract reasoning performed through the medium of language is not sufficient to apprehend the truth of being. Western Christianity's privileging of reason over divine mysteries undermines faith. Reason, having attained equal status with revelation, first serves as the foundation of religion and then replaces it. By keeping firm the boundaries between reason and faith, and by insisting on the ineffability of the divine, Orthodoxy preserves its faith intact.[72]

In terms of Kireevsky's theory of integral knowledge, philosophizing as a Russian means a critique of conceptual thinking:

> Having grown used to abstract–logical thinking, whereas all knowledge depends upon the formal development of the subject of thinking, and all the meaning is absorbed by the expressible aspect of thought, they [Westerners] pay no attention to that inner force of the mind, which performs the movement of thinking in the objects of living knowledge, superseding the formality of logical cohesion, accompanies it constantly, hovers, so to speak, over expressed thought and gives it meaning that is not contained in an external definition, and results that do not depend on external form.[73]

The right way to harmonize belief and reason is not to subordinate conceptual knowledge to church dogma but to strive to elevate the mind to a sympathetic agreement with belief, uniting all psychic forces into one whole. Such an integration of man's faculties yields richer insights about life—insights not reducible to verbal expression.

Russian philosophical thought in its emerging stage defined its originality by problematizing Western philosophy's investment in the capabilities of the word; the heyday of Russian idealist philosophy displayed the same tendency. A focus on inexpressibility and the critique of concepts are key elements in the works of Solovyev, Frank, Lossky, Shestov, and others.[74]

Like Kireevsky, Vladimir Solovyev argues in "The Meaning of Art" ("Obshchii smysl iskusstva," 1890) that conceptual knowledge fails to grasp the whole of reality. The world is reflected in reason by means of abstract notions that do not express the inner being of things but only their superficial logical schemata. Therefore rational knowledge does not capture the presence of the universal idea in the knower and the known. Solovyev advocates a synthesis of diverse approaches—rational, empirical, and mystical—that permits one to discern the total unity of mankind, nature, and God. There are two ways of knowing: "externally, from the side of our phenomenal separateness," and "interiorly, from the side of our absolute being, internally linked with the being of what is known."[75] One must strive to unite with the ineffable essence of things, and art must convey the idea of total unity by intensifying its pallid expressions in nature.

Nikolai Lossky's *The World as an Organic Whole* (*Mir kak organicheskoe tseloe,* 1928) describes the absolute as a principle that is the source of the world's plurality and its unification, a principle that does not contain plurality in itself. No collection of positive definitions can express its nature, for that would imply an impossible unity of the manifold. A single positive definition is likewise inadequate, since a definite characteristic is found only in relation to other things, that is, within a system, whereas the absolute transcends systems. Therefore one can speak about the absolute only in terms of negations. These negations "should be understood as a demand to rise to the higher sphere of the super-personal—not of the impersonal, of the super-rational—not of the irrational, and so on."[76] These are not negations in an ordinary sense; that is, they do not reduce the absolute to nothing but only refer to the characteristics that fall short of the fullness of being. The assertion that the absolute has no reason does not mean that it is senseless, and the assertion that it has no personality does not mean that it is a thing.

In Lossky, religious ineffability loses its idealistic features, gravitating toward absurdist verbal skepticism, even as his verbal skepticism remains theological. As opposed to the divine of affirmative theology (God as truth, beauty, grace), the absolute of apophaticism stands in danger of being dehumanized. One may strive to perceive it as super-personal and super-rational rather than impersonal or irrational, but that is neither personhood nor reason in human terms.[77] As much as apophatic theologians may insist that their negations are "negations of all negativity," the ineffable absolute easily presents itself as hollowed out. Insisting on God's goodness in relation to the world, Lossky is hard pressed to explain the problem of theodicy:

> Such an attitude [of the Absolute's hostility toward the world], were it possible, would be a stain of evil upon the Absolute, but fortunately it is impossible; mutual hostility requires that two entities should stand to one another in the relation of conflicting opposition, and this can only happen when both entities belong to the sphere of finite, limited being, which is incompatible with the idea of the Absolute.[78]

As opposed to a more clear-cut cataphatic doctrine, apophaticism supplies better grounds for, if not vindicating, then at least manipulating the issue of theodicy. Incapable of justifying evil, as a last resort one falls back on the idea that divine essence and workings transcend human understanding.

As seen in Lossky, Russian antiverbal thought in the twentieth century both partakes of the West's move toward ontological skepticism and retains a stronger religious basis. In contrast to Lossky, who strives to build a rational argument hinging on super-rational notions, Semyon Frank in *The Unknowable: An Ontological Introduction to the Philosophy of Religion* (*Nepostizhimoe: Ontologicheskoe vvedenie v filosofiiu religii,* 1939) admits that the problem of theodicy is unsolvable in a rational way: "The only legitimate attitude toward evil is to reject it, to cast it off, but not to explain and thus to legitimize and justify it."[79] Like Solovyev and Lossky, Frank seeks to penetrate the spheres of reality that transcend conceptual analysis. The idea of inexpressibility pertains to phenomenal reality and to human psychic life as well. The depths of personality and our most intense experiences defy articulation: a tendency to conceal "characterizes us not only in relation to what is bad in us but also in relation to what is best in us, in relation to everything we cannot express in ordinary words or generally acceptable, rational, habitual concepts. And if we are intellectually honest, we must admit that what is unknowable and incomprehensible in us . . . makes up our genuine essence." Like Nietzsche, Frank views conceptual knowledge as subsuming "everything that is fluid and diverse in the world under 'concepts', i.e., finding in the world identical 'essences' . . . on the basis of which we can apprehend the new and altered as a repetition of the familiar."[80] For Frank, a religious thinker, such a practical orientation pervades not only life experience but also metaphysics. God (unknowable and inexpressible) cannot be discerned through analogies with the realm of phenomenal reality (knowable and expressible).

Lev Shestov's religious inexpressibility veers further in the direction of the absurd. Shestov stresses the limits of conceptual knowledge, disputes the validity of logic as the necessary criteria of truth, denies the principle of noncontradiction, and maintains that profound truths can be expressed in a paradox. In the spirit of Nietzsche, he lashes out at the "human, all too human" predilection for comforting illusions and assaults language as a vehicle for perpetuating these illusions. According to *In Job's Balances* (*Na vesakh Iova,* 1929), language makes human life pleasant, or at least bearable:

> The word was discovered for life; to hide from man the secret of the eternal and to divert his attention to that which passes here on earth . . . Under such conditions man cannot, of course, so much as dream of "knowing," and what passes with us for knowledge is only a sort of mimicry by which our temporal, common existence is made as easy and pleasant as possible, or is actually made possible for us at all.[81]

The verbal medium possesses an ability to allow only agreeable notions to filter in. It expresses our relations to things rather than things themselves. Through the word, humans domesticate the world, veiling its unfathomable and alien nature.

Shestov's verbal skepticism is characterized by a paradoxical combination of theological inexpressibility and absurdist logophobia, a combination that stems from the dehumanization of the ineffable divinity observed in Lossky and carried to the limit by Shestov. The "great truths" that language hides fall into two fundamentally opposed categories: the ideal of the divine, and inhuman horror and suffering; Shestov's inexpressible subsumes both. What lies beyond language is the horror of non-being, which may be conveyed by those who behold it only by cries that denote death, but at the same time these cries strive toward the One:

> Even as man comes into the world wailing, or awakes with a cry from a tortured fever dream, so too the transition from life to death must clearly be accompanied by a senseless, desperate cry or a wild sob. . . . There is perhaps someone who can apprehend more easily tears and groans, even silence, than the word, who perceives more sense in the unspoken than in clear and plain, well-grounded and proved assertions. Philosophy, however . . . does she listen to . . . that which strives toward the last "One," toward the being which knows no needs and therefore does not understand human needs?[82]

If Lossky attempts a compromise between the ineffable absolute-as-such, which transcends human notions of goodness and grace, and a loving, personal God-for-the-world, Shestov rejects all the traditional attributes of God. The God of cataphatic theology is an illusion arising out of human needs and weaknesses. In attributing to the perfect being this or that quality, men think of their own interests; for example, to deliver themselves into His hands, it is necessary for them that the being be omniscient.[83] The God of the Bible is not fraternal love or justice or grace, nor is he good or conscious. He has no need to distinguish between good and evil, since for Him everything is good. It is because men need order that they attribute to God the same love and respect for order. Of all these attributes, it is only that of omnipotence that Shestov deems valid. Being all-powerful, God does not obey any principle. In His dealings with the world He is completely arbitrary or outright unjust. He will raise from the dead only those who should expect the worst fate, and the first on earth will remain the first in afterlife, while not even a memory will remain of the lowest.

The radical nature of Shestov's inexpressibility sets him apart from the other Russian religious philosophers. His ineffable absolute is a Nietzschean principle "beyond good and evil," but one that is nonetheless construed by Shestov in religious terms. He mocks all attempts at theodicy and disdains metaphysical demagoguery, seeking to explain evil and death, the most unnatural and enigmatic occurrences. *All Things Are Possible* (*Apofeoz bespochvennosti,* 1920) sees metaphysicians as "invested in a purple veil of fine words," and *Penultimate Words* (*Nachala i kontsy,* 1908) exposes the lies of conventional deism: "The religion of almost all nations has always thought of forms outwardly beautiful without stopping even before . . . a golden cross studded with diamonds"; it "overlooks great truths for the sake of sumptuous words and golden crosses."[84]

Apophaticism also informs Mikhail Bakhtin's work. *Notes* (1970–71) posits that the author surpasses his work in the sense that his essence cannot be deduced from it: "The primary author cannot be an image. When we try to imagine the primary author figuratively, we ourselves are creating his image, that is, we ourselves become the primary author of the image."[85] The author's creativity is animated by his loving grace toward the protagonist. The former idea parallels one of God's ineffability in His relation to the world; the latter is analogous to God's loving attitude toward man.

Concurrently, Bakhtin criticizes verbal art on secular terms. The author's word cannot be his own because it is always grounded in the impersonal (science, data, authority). The author expresses himself through silence, which manifests itself covertly in a dialogized style (irony, parody). Bakhtin envisions the evolution of the self as occurring through response to its representation by others, by encountering novel images and reacting to them, and so on. However, just as the primary author transcends the text, the self may not be reduced to images made by others. Not infrequently, verbal images do not possess the requisite "loving grace," and thus endanger the self.

The theory of dialogism points out that languages do not permit a virginal perception of objects. Between the subject and the object there lie other, alien words about the same object, which are hard to penetrate; only the mystical Adam could access the world directly with his first words. "Discourse in the Novel" ("Slovo v romane," 1934–35) explores the connection between languages and ideology, viewing language not as a system of abstract grammatical categories but as ideologically saturated. One's language determines one's worldview, and all languages (hence all worldviews) are bounded historically and socially. Sensitive to this linguistic relativism and wary of the constraints of each and every language, the writer of prose does not express himself in it but exhibits it as something reified:

> [The writer] does not speak in a given language (from which he distances himself to a greater or lesser degree), but he speaks, as it were through language, a language that has somehow more or less materialized, become objectified, that he merely ventriloquates.[86]

Bakhtin praises prose writers for sensing the limitations of languages, their historical, social, and ideological determination, and thereby developing a critical relationship to them. The very concepts of a linguistic system and a speaking individual are not absolute truths but are conditioned by ideological discourse. Bakhtin pays attention to parody, the ironic, and the polemical mode as the sharpest manifestations of dialogism, and he praises parodic literature of the Middle Ages for its appreciation of linguistic relativism:

> On the lower levels . . . the heteroglossia of the clown sounded forth, ridiculing all languages and dialects; there developed the literature . . . where there was no language-center at all, where there was to be found a lively play with the "languages" of poets, scholars, monks, knights and others, where all "languages" were masks and where no language could claim to be an authentic, incontestable face.[87]

Like Bakhtin's ideas, Roman Jakobson's and Yuri Lotman's theories of the word involve religious and existential queries. Relying on Saussure's view of language as a system of arbitrarily connected signifiers and signifieds, Jakobson's "The Statue in Pushkin's Poetic Mythology" (1937) notes that the statue foregrounds the opposition between dead stone (signifier) and human being (signified). The essay links linguistic and theological concerns: it was the semiotic antinomy between the sign and the object signified that led to the fights around Byzantine iconoclasm.[88] "What Is Poetry?" (1933–34) likewise notes that awareness of the non-identity between signs and objects is essential, for otherwise reality would be shielded with the veil of words:

> Why is it necessary to make a special point of the fact that sign does not fall together with object? Because, besides the direct awareness of the identity between sign and object (A is A1), there is a necessity for the direct awareness of the inadequacy of that identity (A is not A1). The reason this antinomy is essential is that without contradiction there is no mobility of concepts,

> no mobility of signs, and the relationship between concept and sign becomes automatized. Activity comes to a halt, and the awareness of reality dies out.[89]

"Linguistics and Poetics" (1960) offers a model of language in operation in which the phatic function in a speech act takes on the issue of (in)communicability. There are messages which serve to establish, prolong, or discontinue communication. The set for contact "may be displayed by a profuse exchange of ritualized formulas, by entire dialogues with the mere purport of prolonging communication."[90]

Lotman's *Culture and Explosion* (*Kul'tura i vzryv*, 1992) claims that a degree of incommunicability is innate to the speech act. If Jakobson's model of language in operation assumes the usage of the same code as well as the same amount of memory for the addresser and the addressee, Lotman posits that human communication is based on the speaker's and the listener's non-identity. Verbal spaces intersect only in part, and, paradoxically, one is interested in communication precisely when it is made difficult and, at its limit, impossible. The more challenging the translation of one part of verbal space into the language of another part, the more valuable the act of communication. Incommunicability at its maximum makes a verbal exchange most potent but impossible, while zero incommunicability devalues the act of communication.

Culture and Explosion points out the paradox of attempting to critique language from within the system and suggests that we project onto the word what are essentially human flaws and predicaments:

> We are immersed in verbal space. Even in our most basic abstractions we cannot tear ourselves out of it: it envelops us, but we are a part of it, and it is simultaneously our part. And at the same time our relationship to language is far from idyllic. We expend gigantic efforts to transcend its boundaries; we accuse it of lies, deviations from the natural, the larger share of our own vices and transgressions. The attempts to fight language are as ancient as language itself. History convinces us of their hopelessness, on the one hand, and their inexhaustibility, on the other.[91]

Lotman bonds ontological and semiotic issues by transposing Kant's opposition between phenomenal and noumenal reality as the dichotomy between the cultural–semiotic layer and the realm "fatally beyond culture." Rejecting the content–expression dichotomy, Lotman posits that it is nonsensical to speak about unexpressed content, although, as with the inexpressibility topos, expression may be present as absence. Instead, he contrasts the field of language with its content and expression and the nonverbal realm. A problem is the extent to which the world created by language is adequate to the world lying outside, and unconnected to, the verbal sphere. No single language is capable of encompassing the external world, necessitating a series of diverse tongues mutually untranslatable or translatable with limitations only. A system of cultural symbols may become a language only through the loss of its immediate reality and its transfer into a purely formal sphere, empty and thus ready for any content.

Lotman's "'Agreement' and 'Self-Giving' as Archetypal Models of Culture" ("Dogovor i vruchenie sebia kak arkhetipicheskie modeli kul'tury," 1981) posits the relationship between the signifier and the signified as a theological problem. The essay offers a dichotomy between an ethics of contract characteristic of the West and an ethics of unconditional self-giving characteristic of Russia. Self-giving pertains to one's relation with the divine. By contrast, one can enter into a contract with powers of light and darkness alike, and the transactional outcome is obtained through a production of arbitrary signs:

> It is in dealing with such forces [the powers of darkness] that the fact that communication through verbal signs is based on convention and that this enables words to be used for deception, is made apparent. The possibility of variously interpreting a word (casuistry) was likewise understood as the wish to deceive rather than an attempt to explain its true meaning.[92]

The means of communication between man and God are symbols that preclude the possibility of expression being alienated from content and consequently of deception, whereas the conventionality of signification offers opportunities for cheating. The attitude of self-giving is oriented toward the symbol and practical action; the psychology of contract cultivates the sign and formalized ritual.[93] Lotman couches the problem of symbol and iconicity versus sign and conventionality, one as old as Plato's *Phaedrus,* in divine versus demonic terms.

Like Lotman, Mikhail Epstein, a spokesman for Russian postmodernism, concentrates on the Saussurean non-motivated nature of signs. Postmodern writing sets language against itself, laying bare the limitations of existing monolanguages and exposing the conventionality and arbitrariness of all sign systems. Conceptualists, the foremost representatives of Russian postmodernism, point to the dangers of language that bypasses consciousness. Conceptualism is a system of linguistic gestures that reveals the split between signifier and signified, aiming at anti-art and the subversion of language. The twentieth century produced such an abundance of words that it destroyed the psychological foundations underlying language. All that we have been left with are "dead words," which are swept away by conceptualist poetry.

These notions largely coincide with Western postmodernist and poststructuralist views. Yet Epstein's characterization of conceptualist verbal mockery is colored by apophaticism. "Like a Corpse in the Desert: Dehumanization in the New Moscow Poetry" (1987) sees Russian postmodernism as not stopping with the deconstruction of concepts and values, but taking aim also at the perception of the ineffable:

> If conceptualist poetry is not met with sheer laughter, taken as a parody of stereotypes of mass consciousness, then it is possible to perceive something else through it: the authentic lyricism of the silent super-Subjectivity standing behind the speaking No One. For it is only in relation to Its super-abundant silence that all words ring hollow, flat, trivial, and disharmonious—just as they are made to ring, deliberately, in conceptualist poetry.[94]

This play with clichés conceals an undercurrent of alienation and incommunicability. At the same time, it betrays a striving toward the negative absolute. Concepts—artistic trifles—point at emptiness but emptiness in place of something significant. For Epstein, conceptualism, pop art, and sots art stress the humiliation of speech and vulgarization of sense to indicate another, silent reality for which there are no words. That's why nonfigurativeness and dehumanization, principles of the avant-garde, are supplemented in late twentieth-century art "by the third principle—apophasis or negative theology."[95]

WESTERN PHILOSOPHY VERSUS RUSSIAN PHILOSOPHY VERSUS RUSSIAN POETRY

Clearly, verbal skepticism has long been crucial to Russian culture. Not only is antiverbal thought integral to the culture, but the very issue of Russian national distinctiveness is bound to the problem of the word. So, for example, Lotman merges linguistic, theological, and national issues. The ethics of contract involves the conventionality of the signifier; it is linked to the demonic; and it is characteristic of the West. The ethics of self-giving depends on the word's symbolic qualities; it pertains to one's relationship to the divine; and it is peculiarly Russian.

While the progression from a more idealistic to a darker verbal skepticism is characteristic of Western and Russian paradigms alike, the Russian version possesses significant sui generis features. As Western antiverbal thought moves to modern skepticism based on dwindling religious sensibilities and a view of the world as meaningless vis-à-vis human values, Russian verbal skepticism both participates in this movement and maintains its theological nexus. Lossky's ineffability approximates the absurdist inexpressible while remaining theological. Frank's criticism of language is akin to Nietzsche's critique of concepts, which reflect a human relationship to the object, not the object as such; but, in contrast to Nietzsche, Frank insists that the noumenal is beyond language. Shestov's ineffable absolute takes on absurdist qualities, but his antiverbal thought remains circumscribed within the apophatic context. Epstein's absolute, like that of Lossky and Shestov, merges with the unspeakable of the absurd, and what distinguishes him from many modern Western thinkers is his linkage of postmodernism and negative theology. Apophaticism and the absurd coexist in a tenacious, if uneasy, union.

Russian thought holds onto its theological antecedents, and is reluctant to draw post-humanist inferences from its critique of the word. The same applies to the secular strain of Russian verbal skepticism. In post-Nietzschean views, the absolute is an illusion of semiotic practices, and the principle of individuality is an illusory effect of verbal mechanisms acting on man. The subject is both a victim and a chimera of the word: "A figure occurring between two modes of language . . . [man] is erased, like a face drawn in sand at the edge of the sea."[96] The Russian version does not recast the subject as a quasi-linguistic construct but, on the contrary, privileges the subject, viewing it as non-encompassable by the word.

Let me provide some illustrations. In Bakhtin the primary author transcends the text, and the self is not reducible to its verbal representations. Jakobson (an alumnus of the formalist school with its implications against biography and a vision of impersonal innovation as an engine of verbal art) takes on the Saussurean principle of language as a closed system that plays off itself not to subvert traditional ontology (selfhood, being, presence), but to emphasize the necessity of distinguishing between linguistic constructs and being. Lotman envisions the essential instability of language and the existence of different systems in the minds of addressors and addressees not as sheer negativity (the impossibility of fixed terms and systems) but as an issue of (in)communicability contingent on, and made essential by, the singularity of the parties involved in the communicative process.

Analogously, if in post-Nietzschean terms ethics is a mirage of language, the Russian version disputes the ability of language to function as an ethical agent, but not ethical principles per se. To give another Bakhtinian example, his problematization of the concept of a unitary language that directly expresses authorial individuality, his emphasis on the ideological underpinnings of languages, and his interest in a dialogic orientation of the word resonate with major Western post-structuralist notions, for example, Foucault's discursive practices. However, his interest in linguistic relativism does not lead him to question moral norms. Indeed, his work displays strong ethical concerns.

From the standpoint of this study, the divergence of Russian and Western antiverbal paradigms can be conceptualized as the opposition of post-romantic verbal skepticism (lyrical subjectivity exceeds language) to post-Nietzschean and post-structuralist critiques of logocentrism (selfhood is an illusion of language). Several factors contribute to the enduring vitality of the romantic antiverbal paradigm. German idealism had a formative influence on nineteenth-century Russian thought, and that impact extended into the Silver Age and the school of Russian idealist philosophy. The romantic period, coinciding with the Golden Age of Russian poetry, introduced the antiverbal topos into Russian literature. Poets of the period produced antiverbal lyrics that became some of the cornerstones of the Russian poetic tradition. That same period advanced the vision of the bard's exalted status that would later blossom into a key mythologeme of Russian culture. As a result, verbal disfiguration becomes a singularly fraught issue.

Russian and Western antiverbal paradigms begin to diverge around the age of modernism. As Saussure outlines his view of language as a self-enclosed system of relations, Eliot emphasizes the impersonality of poetry ("Tradition and the Individual Talent," 1919), and Mallarmé and the Parnassians, among others, usher in the "death of the author" in the West, this turn does not take root in Russia. For Russian philosophy and poetry alike, language is deemed fallible as an incarnation of personal agency as well as an ethical agent, but neither personal agency nor ethics themselves are judged to be illusions based in linguistic practices.

How do Russian poets specifically conceptualize the word? Of the numerous disparities in Russian thought, a tension between laudatory and degrading views of language is especially prominent. Pushkin's celebrated "The Prophet" ("Prorok," 1826), a cornerstone of Russian logocentrism, describes the hero tortured by a spiritual thirst. Wandering in the desert, he meets a six-winged seraph who transforms him into a prophet:

И он к устам моим приник,	And he leaned to my lips
И вырвал грешный мой язык,	And tore out my sinful tongue,
И празднословный и лукавый,	Empty-worded and cunning,
И жало мудрыя змеи	And placed the wise serpent's tongue
В уста замершие мои	Into my lips that went numb
Вложил десницею кровавой.	With his bloody hand.
И он мне грудь рассек мечом,	And he split my chest open with his sword
И сердце трепетное вынул,	And took out my trembling heart,
И угль, пылающий огнем,	And put a piece of coil flaming with fire
Во грудь отверстую водвинул.[97]	Into my open chest.

The angel then bids the poet to go into the world to "burn people's hearts with the word" (*glagolom zhgi serdtsa liudei*).[98]

In Valentin Nepomniashchii's analysis of "The Prophet,"

> Pushkin talks about the word addressed to a secular consciousness—the word of art, the word that is artistic in its deepest essence; as regards the word that is straightforward, prophetic, in the sphere of art . . . it is unavoidably threatened with the erasure of the stamp of the divine, i.e., with being lowered to "moralization." And precisely with the help of "the word that is artistic in its deepest essence" he produces such a powerful effect. This is no "thought" or "idea" but experience which does not find enough room, either in its content or in its force, in conceptual or even habitual "poetic" forms, but is expressible only through the language of myth which exceeds the capabilities of reason . . . "The Prophet" presents the world, precisely through immediate experience, as spiritual cosmos, as logos (which means word, and deed, and reason, and law, and sense); and it is no accident that the word "glagol" sounds in the last line—the word that means act and action and is derived from the root common with the Greek "logos."[99]

This traditional logocentric interpretation of "The Prophet" reveals an intriguing interplay of verbal idealism and verbal skepticism. The word *glagol* in the last line of the poem invokes the Greek Logos in its Johannine conception as the word through which all things are made. The word of the poet aspires to the function of divine Logos just as it is threatened with losing the touch of the divine. For the word to achieve potency, it must "exceed the capabilities of reason," overcome language in its conceptual and rationalistic limitations—a Schopenhauerian antiverbal notion.

"The Prophet," a work analyzed too exhaustively to be reexamined here, does make one wonder if the hero's transformation by the brutal tearing out of his heart and his tongue unequivocally represents the ideal of phatic bardhood. Is a text contrasting the deficient human tongue—"sinful," "empty-worded and cunning" (*greshnyi, prazdnoslovnyi i lukavyi*)—epithets typical of hesychasm and the weaving of words—to the miracle of the transcendental word such a clear-cut statement of word exaltation?

These remarks do not aim to challenge Pushkin's stance as verbal idealist.[100] Rather, they suggest that verbal idealism and verbal skepticism function in Russian culture as parts of a key antinomy. Even such a famous example of logocentrism as "The Prophet" contains its opposite, a more skeptical impulse. What are the differences between the poetic word and Logos? What does it take for the poet to become a prophet? What are the reasons behind the human tongue being sinful, empty-worded, and cunning?

Issues like these have been explored by philosophers, and the very same issues are addressed by poets. The domains of philosophy and poetry can interpenetrate in surprising ways, and the presence of a poetry of verbal skepticism in Russia is itself a valuable contribution to the arguments the philosophers have made. Philosophy may be articulated in poetic form, but the opposite is just as important since rhetorical features of poetry inform philosophy. A common perception that poetic thinking may be too impressionistic elicits resistance to reading poetry on a par with theory and leads to disregarding poetry's contributions to philosophical problems. The polyvalence and density of poetry, however, make its approach to philosophical problems more rather than less illuminating, an observation especially pertinent in the case of verbal skepticism, organized as it is around the critique of conceptual and logical discourse.

It is not only poets' now and again unique take on the problem, but the manner in which they articulate verbal skepticism that is noteworthy. Philosophical ideas are conveyed by the way a poem is put together, and poetic language presents meaning in a more complex manner. Even poets seemingly in tune with a specific philosophical trend compose lyrics in which intricate imagery suggests multiple lines of interpretation, and verbal inadequacy is articulated in subtler ways than a conceptual system would ever be able to accommodate. The presentation of antiverbal motifs partakes of semantic polyvalence and overloading characteristic of poetic discourse, advancing a lyrical antiverbal stance that is richer than the kinds of philosophical canon it can be juxtaposed to. Poets may anticipate later theoretical developments or challenge established theoretical notions.

What existential queries characterize Russian lyrics of verbal skepticism? How does this poetry evolve from its early articulations to contemporaneity? Which theoretical views, Russian or Western, are most relevant to the Russian tradition, and how do poets react to theorists and to one another? Which unique insights does Russian antiverbal poetry contain, and how does it enrich the philosophical picture? And finally, what techniques does Russian verse employ to articulate the limits of the word? I pursue these and related questions in the chapters to follow.

Each of the four chapters offers a case study in Russian antiverbal poetry. Chapter 1 examines the inauguration of the Russian antiverbal paradigm in romantic lyrics of the inexpressible. It traces the development of this topos from the time of its inception in sentimentalism and pre-romanticism (Batiushkov) through its exploration in high romanticism (Zhukovsky, Venevitinov, Tiutchev) to the "tamed" romantic renditions (Baratynsky, Lermontov). I analyze one lyric by each of these romantic poets, focusing on the more important statements that illustrate antiverbal developments during the period. I ground these poems in the context of others on the subject by the same authors to show that their antiverbal poetry is not confined to the examples considered in this chapter. It was during the romantic period that most major facets of the argument were introduced in literature and in literary theory and philosophy. It was also during this period that Russian poetry produced influential articulations of inexpressibility that supply the point of reference for the later Russian poetry of verbal skepticism.

Chapters 2 through 4 focus on individual poets. Chapter 2 looks at the revival of the antiverbal paradigm during the Silver Age, in Osip Mandelstam's musings on verbal inadequacy. Preceding the analysis of Mandelstam's poems is a survey of modernist movements which aims only to contextualize Mandelstam's works. Next I explore *Stone,* showing that it contains a high concentration of lyrics of verbal skepticism. I conclude the chapter with a brief look at Mandelstam's later work. His numerous returns to this topos engage the capacious heritage of verbal skepticism to an extent that no other modernist poet's writings on the subject can match.

Chapter 3 focuses on Mandelstam's Petersburg heir, Joseph Brodsky, who further intensifies, expands upon, and reworks the Russian antiverbal legacy. I contend that the majority of his poems as well as many of his essays are expressions of skepticism rather than verbal exaltation. In particular, I examine Brodsky's "Conversation with a Celestial Being" and the cycle "A Part of Speech," which summarize his metalinguistic and existential concerns. Simultaneously, I consider how Brodsky's texts reflect critically on postmodern theory.

Chapter 4 concentrates on the reappearance of verbal skepticism as a crucial motif and strategy in conceptualism and post-conceptualism, with Timur Kibirov's dramatization of verbal aversion as representative of the larger trend. With the loftiness of Russian letters challenged as never before during the post-Soviet period, skepticism becomes ubiquitous in poetic practice. Kibirov demonstrates verbal aversion in a more light-hearted way than the poets previously discussed. At the same time, I show that his mockery is all-pervasive.

The conclusion returns to the uniqueness of Russian verbal skepticism. The Russian approach is distinct, with a great part of it elaborated in poetic form. Russian poetic philosophy makes a powerful contribution to verbal skepticism by approaching this fundamental philosophical question in original and complex ways.

Chapter One

Initiating the Paradigm: The Inexpressible in Russian Romanticism

IT WAS DURING the romantic period that the topos of verbal skepticism was inaugurated in Russian literature, and poetry in particular. Romantic poetry engages the ineffability device as much more than mere rhetorical technique; it probes manifestations of, and reasons for, the failure of the word. Romanticism makes inexpressibility an attribute of human life in general. Precisely because inexpressibility becomes ubiquitous—no longer an exclusive property of the divine, or of human encounters with the divine—the poems considered here highlight divergent aspects of being as incommensurate with language and suggest diverse grounds for verbal inadequacy; but there is always unity behind the diversity, a shared belief that language is deficient for articulating extra-linguistic reality.

This chapter examines Russian romantic lyrics of verbal skepticism from early explorations by Batiushkov and Zhukovsky, through Venevitinov's work of the 1820s, to Tiutchev's celebrated metaphysical statement, the hero text of this study, and finally Baratynsky's and Lermontov's late romantic renditions. I consider the conventional notion—the inexpressibility of the lyrical subject's emotional life as he intuits the infinite—and show that romantic skepticism cannot be reduced to the uniform idea of a "chosen one's" inexpressible transcendental experiences. Russian romantic verbal skepticism ranges from the ineffable ideality of the absolute, nature, and emotional life, to incommunicability vis-à-vis the other, to the inexpressibility of pain and death.

My analysis commences with Batiushkov and Zhukovsky, whose poems treat language as incapable of expressing the sublime, and proceeds to a discussion of Venevitinov where the nuance of incommunicability is added to inexpressibility. Following consideration of Tiutchev's view of "otherness" as an ontological position that cannot be overcome, I explore Baratynsky's presentation of a world in which the agony of annihilation renders any kind of verbalization meaningless, and finally Lermontov's rejection of the notion of the poetic word as divinely inspired. These developments show how a darker strain of existential anxiety to a large extent superseded the earlier idealistic vision. In addition, later romantic poems ironize the discourse of inexpressibility, bringing the paradox of versification on silence into the limelight and thus enacting a more compelling critique of language.

Russian romantic articulations of verbal skepticism describe a complex field of action that entailed rich possibilities for the development of modern antiverbal poetry. Seminal romantic works (especially Tiutchev's "Silentium!") become reference points for later Russian poetry. While they partake of the Western romantic conceptual critique of language, Russian lyrics of the period introduce their own distinct metaphors and imagery which formed the basis of a subsequent poetry of verbal skepticism.

ROMANTIC INEXPRESSIBILITY

It was during the romantic period that verbal inadequacy became a central idea in philosophy, literature, and literary criticism. In Germany, Herder asserted that, since the meanings of words "are arbitrary and thus not so closely attached to the nature of feelings," speech would enfeeble emotion; Wackenroder claimed that "the invisible force which hovers over us is not drawn down into our hearts by words"; and Humboldt argued that "the word, after all, is a constraint upon the soul's ever more capacious inner sensitivity."[1] Among the English romantics, Coleridge emphasized the value of silence vis-à-vis the paltry restrictions of language, and Wordsworth was pessimistic regarding poetic language's ability to function as "the emanation of reality and truth."[2] But Batiushkov went farther, noting that those "who possess a refined taste and genuine feeling hardly respect the vain sounds of words," and Venevitinov suggested a total cessation of poetic composition so that Russian poets could "think more and create less."[3]

A traditional critical approach to romantic inexpressibility focuses on the lyrical subject's intuition of the infinite, along the lines of Wackenroder's "invisible force that hovers over us." Viktor Zhirmunsky offers an example:

> The struggle with the word . . . is characteristic of the Romantics. This is seen primarily . . . in the inexpressibility of the boundless experience of the soul . . . Romantic style presents an attempt to express the inexpressible, to create . . . the mood of the positive sentiment of the infinite.[4]

However, romantic verbal skepticism was not limited to transcendental experiences. The post-Kantian emphasis on subjectivity prompted the romantics to underscore the inimitability of the self and its sentiments and simultaneously to question the power of language as a conventional means of expression to convey singular experiences (Herder, Humboldt, Batiushkov). Even with regard to the experience of the absolute, the romantics accentuated the ineffability of their experience of the transcendental more than that of the transcendental per se (Kantian sublimity as contained in the mind; Wackenroder's force which "is not drawn into our hearts"). Insofar as the romantics championed human uniqueness and valorized the values of authenticity and individuality, their inexpressible encompassed all aspects of life, not only mystical experiences.

Mme de Staël's *On Germany* (1813) articulates a typical romantic vision of the inexpressibility of the subject:

> The gift of revealing through language what one feels in the depth of one's heart is very rare . . . But the poet can disengage the sentiment imprisoned in the depth of the soul . . . Less civilized nations always commence with poetry, and as soon as a strong passion agitates the soul, the most earthy men . . . appeal for help to external nature to express the inexpressible which takes place within them . . . To conceive the true grandeur of lyric poetry, one must wander in reverie into the ethereal regions . . . and consider the entire universe as a symbol of the emotions of the soul . . . The poet conceives his whole poem at once in his soul; were it not for the difficulties of language, he would, like the Sybil and the prophets, improvise the sacred hymns of genius.[5]

This passage brings into play several familiar notions: first, the linguistic medium's constraining function in terms of emotional expression; second, the paradoxical character of the situation in which the poet, aware of the futility of his endeavor, nevertheless struggles "to express the inexpressible"; third, the linkage of romantic inexpressible to the post-Kantian conceptualization of relations between the subject and the object which prompts the romantics to view nature as an emanation of the poet's inner being.[6] Steeped in German idealism, Russian poets of the period engage all of these issues.[7]

BATIUSHKOV, ZHUKOVSKY, VENEVITINOV: INEXPRESSIBLE IDEALITY AND INCOMMUNICABILITY

Ineffability topoi appeared in Russian poetry earlier than the romantic period, for example, in eighteenth-century poetry by Mikhail Lomonosov and Gavriil Derzhavin.[8] As the romantics reconsidered the role of the subject and rejected normative classicist poetics in favor of an individualized poetic vision, verbal inadequacy became an especially fraught issue, one not limited to theological ineffability.

Batiushkov

Konstantin Batiushkov produced some of the first lyrics to dwell on the theme of inexpressibility. "An Epistle to I. M. Murav'ev-Apostol" ("Poslanie I. M. Murav'evu-Apostolu," 1814–15), for instance, characterizes the hero as one who "will be a poet in his very silence" (*V samom molchanii on budet vse piit*).[9] Batiushkov's last elegy, "There is enjoyment in a wilderness of forests" ("Est' naslazhdenie i v dikosti lesov," 1819–20), offers the poet's most explicit statement of inexpressibility:

Есть наслаждение и в дикости лесов,	There is delight also in a wilderness of forests,
Есть радость на приморском бреге,	Joy by the seashore,
И есть гармония в сем говоре валов,	And there is harmony in a talk of billows,
Дробящихся в пустынном беге.	Breaking up in lonely flight.
Я ближнего люблю, но ты, природа-мать,	I love my neighbor, but you, mother nature,
Для сердца ты всего дороже!	Within my heart are dearest of all!
С тобой, владычица, привык я забывать	With you, O sovereign one, I grew used to forgetting
И то, чем был, как был моложе,	Both what I was when I was younger,
И то, чем ныне стал под холодом годов.	And what I have become beneath the chill of time.
Тобою в чувствах оживаю:	Through you my feelings are awakened:
Их выразить душа не знает стройных слов,	My soul knows no harmonious words to express them,
И как молчать об них—не знаю.[10]	Yet I do not know how to be silent about them.

This poem is a translation of canto 4, stanza 178, of Byron's *Childe Harold's Pilgrimage* (1812–1818), but the issue of language is more pointedly raised in the Russian version: "a talk of billows," as opposed to Byron's noncommunicative "roar" (of the sea).[11] The inexpressibility statement comes in the coda. Although it is not explicitly stated that poetic speech is inferior to nature's language, the movement of the lyric from the celebration of nature's "harmony" to the expression of poetic frustration suggests precisely this. The theme of music, as with Schopenhauer and later Nietzsche, often accompanies romantic inexpressibility: Byron's "music" becomes Batiushkov's universal "harmony."[12] Batiushkov's hero is more passive than Byron's (notice "interviews" and "stealing" into nature).[13] In the Russian version an active benign nature first empties the passive poet of memories ("Forgetting both what I was when I was younger, / And what I have become beneath the chill of time"), and then revives his emotions ("Through you my feelings are awakened," absent in Byron). In addition, Batiushkov's antiverbal thrust is specifically anti-poetic. He does not say that he cannot express his feelings verbally at all, only that he cannot express them in "harmonious words," as opposed to Byron's "what I can ne'er express."[14]

Batiushkov's inexpressibility originates in a joyful pantheistic experience of his communion with nature—one resembling yet not identical to experiences of theological ineffability—and is bereft of dark or problematic aspects. The Russian version's merger with nature (saturation of poetic consciousness by nature, the hero's passivity) recalls the mystical union with the "essence of things" to a greater extent than Byron's. Religious hints are conveyed via Batiushkov's uses of the biblical "neighbor" (*blizhnego*) and "sovereign one" (*vladychitsa*) absent in Byron.[15] The apostrophes "you, mother nature," and "O sovereign one," absent in the original, establish a more immediate relationship with the addressee. However, Batiushkov emphasizes the inexpressibility of his emotions ("My soul does not know how to express them [feelings]") rather than the ineffability of the noumenal. Batiushkov highlights concord in nature ("a talk of billows"), mentions the human component of external reality with appreciation ("I love my neighbor"), and eliminates Byron's expression of the desire to escape into nature where "none intrudes."[16] He also leaves out Byron's depiction of nature's destructive fury that follows his Schellingesque portrayal of mingling with the universe. The context in which this inexpressibility is articulated is altogether benign.

Zhukovsky

Like Batiushkov, Vasily Zhukovsky conceptualized inexpressibility in positive terms, in the sense that it coexists with, and contributes to, an exaltation of nature and human in their harmonious relationship.[17] Zhukovsky is generally known for one lyric of verbal skepticism—"The Inexpressible" (A Fragment) ("Nevyrazimoe" [Fragment], 1819), but in fact his oeuvre makes liberal usage of the inexpressibility topos. "I ought to praise your eyes!" ("Tvoi glaza khvalit' mne dolzhno," 1802–03) already contains the germ of "The Inexpressible," a heart whose "silence speaks all the more lucidly" (*Ego molchanie iasnee govorit*).[18] "A Detailed Account About the Moon" ("Podrobnyi otchet o lune," 1820) decries the poet's ability to capture the beauty of this heavenly body "with his pale etchings" (*blednymi chertami*), and "To Empress Grand Duchess Aleksandra Fedorovna" ("Gosudaryne velikoi kniagine Aleksandre Fedorovne," 1818) doubts the ability of an earthly tongue to portray the heroine's sublime experience (*kakoi iazyk zemnoi / Izobrazit sie ocharovan'e*).[19]

Some of these lyrics, for example, "A Detailed Account About the Moon," employ the topos as a conventional device, opening with a humility statement and plunging into a grandiloquent depiction of the phenomenon in question. Others, for example, "To Empress Grand Duchess Aleksandra Fedorovna" and "The Inexpressible," present a more meticulous analysis of inexpressibility per se. The latter poem is Zhukovsky's most sustained articulation of verbal inadequacy:[20]

Что наш язык земной пред дивною природой?	What is our earthly tongue before delightful nature?
С какой небрежною и легкою свободой	With what a nonchalant and easy freedom
Она рассыпала повсюду красоту	It poured out beauty everywhere
И разновидное с единством согласила!	And harmonized variety and unity!
Но где, какая кисть ее изобразила?	But where, what brush painted it?
Едва-едва одну ее черту	Hardly a single one of her features
С усилием поймать удастся вдохновенью . . .	Can with effort be caught by imagination . . .
Но льзя ли в мертвое живое передать?	But can what is alive be conveyed in the lifeless?
Кто мог создание в словах пересоздать?	Who could re-create creation in words?
Невыразимое подвластно ль выраженью?. .	Is the inexpressible subject to expression?. .
Святые таинства, лишь сердце знает вас.	O holy sacraments, only the heart knows you.
Не часто ли в величественный час	Does it not often happen that, during the sublime hour
Вечернего земли преображенья—	Of the earth's evening transfiguration—

Когда душа смятенная полна
Пророчеством великого виденья
И в беспредельное унесена, —
Спирается в груди болезненное чувство,
Хотим прекрасное в полете удержать,
Ненареченному хотим названье дать —
И обессиленно безмолвствует искусство?
Что видимо очам—сей пламень облаков,
По небу тихому летящих,
Сие дрожанье вод блестящих,
Сии картины берегов
В пожаре пышного заката—
Сии столь *яркие черты*—
Легко их ловит мысль крылата,
И есть *слова* для их *блестящей* красоты.
Но то, что слито с сей блестящей красотою,—
Сие столь смутное, волнующее нас,
Сей внемлемый одной душою
Обворожающего глас,
Сие к далекому стремленье,
Сей миновавшего привет
(Как прилетевшее незапно дуновенье
От луга родины, где был когда-то цвет,
Святая молодость, где жило упованье),
Сие шепнувшее душе воспоминанье
О милом радостном и скорбном старины,
Сия сходящая святыня с вышины,

When the perturbed soul is full
Of prophecy's grand vision
And carried into the infinite —
A painful feeling tightens in the chest,
We want to capture the beautiful in flight,
We want to give a name to what is unspoken—
And drained of power, art keeps silent!
What is visible to the eyes—the blaze of clouds,
Quietly flying across the sky,
The flutter of shining waters,
The pictures of the banks
In the conflagration of the magnificent sunset—
The *features* that are so *bright*—
Winged thought catches them easily,
And there are words for their *radiant* beauty.
But what is merged with this radiant beauty—
This hazy something that agitates us,
This voice of charm
To which only the soul hearkens,
This yearning for the distant,
These greetings of the past
(Like a breeze that suddenly came flying
From a native meadow, once in bloom,
Sacred youth, where hope once lived),
This recollection, whispering to the soul
About what was sweet joyous and doleful long ago
This sacred object, descending from the heights,

Сие присутствие создателя в созданье—	This presence of the Creator in creation—
Какой для них язык?. . Горе душа летит,	What tongue could there be for these? The soul flies up,
Все необъятное в единый вздох теснится,	All the infinite is crowded into one sigh,
И лишь молчание понятно говорит.[21]	And only silence speaks understandably.

Like Batiushkov, Zhukovsky combines antiverbal and anti-poetic critiques. That our "earthly tongue" is inferior to nature's language suggests that his skepticism is directed at language at large, but "drained of power, art keeps silent" makes his critique specifically anti-literary. Both poets identify the outer world with nature; indeed, the human realm is totally ignored in "The Inexpressible." However, if Batiushkov's lyric occupies itself with nature's emotional transformation of the subject, "The Inexpressible" takes as a given the externalized amalgamation of the organic ("the blaze of clouds," "the pictures of the banks") and the emotional ("this yearning for the distant," "these greetings of the past"), and focuses on the latter. Zhukovsky strives to convey inner sentiments through his portrayal of natural scenery, as emotion permeates nature.

The poem consists of three sections.[22] First comes the idea that art's possibilities are meager in comparison with nature's great means of expression; second, a portrayal is given of the external features of the sunset; finally, there is an attempt to register the picture's spiritual content. The first part laments art's failure to re-create natural beauty: "But where, what brush painted it?" Poetry and painting are linked as mere arts of the surface, capable of conveying the body ("what is visible to the eyes"), but not the spirit of the object. Nature, by contrast, is portrayed as a romantic artist par excellence, carefree, diverse and yet harmonious in its creations.[23]

There is a discrepancy between the initial declaration and the way the poem unfolds. Notwithstanding the earlier lamentation that art cannot recreate nature's splendor, a dichotomy is built between the objective world of natural beauty, which can be captured in poetry, and the poet's sentiments, which cannot: "But what is merged with this radiant beauty . . . What tongue could there be for these?" The latter part of Zhukovsky's poem identifies the inexpressible with feelings "entangled" in the landscape, and not with the landscape per se.[24] There is a way of resolving this discrepancy—by allowing for the lyrical subject's awareness of the perceived domain as partially formed by his consciousness. If the poem is informed by Kantian ideas about the mind making external reality, the boundary between the objective and the subjective becomes blurred, and the beauties of the sunset become inexpressible insofar as they are interwoven with inexpressible sentiments.[25] The task of expressing the inexpressible, then, means disengaging and verbalizing the emotional component of the landscape. Zhukovsky, like Batiushkov, stresses the inexpressibility of emotion over the inexpressibility of natural beauty. The passage offering a tangible portrayal of nature (lines 21–28) is significantly shorter than the passage depicting the poet's feelings (lines 29–42).

Zhukovsky's inexpressibility stems from the transitory and complex nature of both reality and emotion. The poet strives to capture and communicate nuances of experience that vanish as quickly as they appear, but his perceptions and sentiments may be too intricate and evanescent ("the beautiful in flight") to be fully recoverable. Both observation and articulation are unable to arrest what is "holy, delicate, fleeting, airy, fragrant and imponderable."[26] The natural phenomena portrayed in the poem illuminate the romantic conceptualization of the subject-nature relationship. The image of the sunset functions as an external representation of the perpetual external and inner transformation so important to the romantics.[27]

Another important aspect of the poem's inexpressibility has to do with the issue of unity versus fragmentariness. As Friedrich Schlegel contemplated the relationship between parts and the whole, he posited that expression fragments (and therefore impoverishes and distorts) what is experienced as a richer unity:

> Who could dissect himself and, like the subject of an anatomical lecture, tear the individual limb out of the context that alone makes it beautiful and intelligible, and, as it were, squirt out with words whatever is most subtle and delicate in it, so that the whole is distorted into a monstrosity?[28]

Subtitled "fragment," Zhukovsky's poem makes fragmentation one of its major themes. The poem presents a dichotomy between inspiration's ability to capture an isolated feature of nature, and nature's gift "to harmonize variety and unity." Observation and expression are always partial and incomplete, hence Zhukovsky's struggle to capture "but a single one of her features."

In addition to implying that verbalization fragments what is felt as a denser, more integrated experience, the dichotomy between isolated features and unity is metaphysically suggestive. August Schlegel drew on the traditional link between the notions of unity and of the transcendental, indicating that "the whole must be conceived before the parts," and concluded that no living entity can be understood solely in terms of its material components, that is, that there exists something besides matter.[29] To "re-create creation in words" means, as Zhukovsky phrases it, to represent "what is alive in something lifeless," that is, to represent matter devoid of spirit infused in it by a supra-human agency.

In light of the link between the ideas of unity and the transcendental, Zhukovsky's inexpressible is related to the poet's inability to convey his intuition of the absolute as a spirit that harmonizes discordant parts in one whole, an idea that occurs frequently in romantic poetry. For example, as the narrator crosses the Alps in Wordsworth's *The Prelude* (1805; 1850), he perceives all the diverse sites of nature "like workings of one mind, the features of the same face, blossoms upon one tree."[30] Similarly, "Lines Composed a Few Miles Above Tintern Abbey" (1798) depicts

> a sense sublime
> Of something far more deeply interfused. . .
> A motion and a spirit, that impels
> All thinking things, all objects of all thought,
> And rolls through all things.[31]

Zhukovsky's poet wants to capture this sublime sense of unity, to compress "all the infinite into one sigh."

Zhukovsky's verbal skepticism, tinged as it is with nostalgia for the ineffable past (lines 34–39), depends on his perception of metaphysical ideality. An emphasis on reflecting surfaces (clouds, the sky, water) and on the blaze of the setting sun, mirrored in and illuminating those surfaces, enacts a romantic analogy between poetic consciousness and a source of light (a lamp in Hazlitt's, Wordsworth's, and Coleridge's writings, the sun in Zhukovsky's).[32] The sun, the lyrical subject, reproduces itself in the natural scenery. The phrase "this presence of the Creator in creation" can yield two interpretations: as a Schellingian pantheist statement but also a more solipsistic sense of the subject producing external reality. The poem's religious hints ("who could re-create creation in words," "O holy sacraments," "transfiguration," "prophecy's grand vision," "carried in the infinite," "sacred youth," "sacred object descending from the height") make it more likely that Zhukovsky's inexpressible signifies the Schellingian absolute that infuses both poetic consciousness and the physical world.[33] The critique of language comes in the service of reverence for the beauty of being.

Zhukovsky takes on the issue of inexpressibility formally as well as semantically. The lyric rhymes unpredictably and is written in free iambs, thus conveying subtle fluctuations of emotion. It has three ellipses (lines 7, 10, and 42), and abounds in question marks (lines 1, 5, 8, 9, 10, and 20) and dashes (lines 13, 16, 19, 21, 25, 26, 29, and 41).[34] Multiple dashes accelerate the flow of the poem, pushing it forward in a breathless charge to give the intimation of an all-powerful sentiment. Questions, like negations, are more fitting than assertions in matters of inexpressibility, suggesting ideas and feelings without clearly delineating them. Punctuation-wise, ellipsis is the most apt marker of the topos. It indicates an urge to convey a feeling and an attendant inability and unwillingness to do so, which opens up a multitude of co-creative possibilities for the reader. The first two ellipses occur in the beginning, where Zhukovsky muses on art's impotence to portray nature; the third occurs toward the conclusion of the poem. Of these syntactically marked gaps, the latter is especially noteworthy, coming at the end of a prolonged statement on the inexpressible and gesturing in the direction of the realm beyond what has been articulated on the page.

The language of the heart cannot be conveyed adequately in precise terms, therefore the syntactical links between the clauses loosen. The statement on the inexpressible ending on the ellipsis is a single, winding sentence, the longest in the lyric, sprawling all the way from line 29 to line 42. It rushes forward in a flood of clauses connected by commas or, in a few instances, by commas and dashes. The relations between "greetings," "sigh," "bloom," "sacred youth," "meadow," and "hope" are not self-evident.[35] Syntactical slackening is made manifest in the missing punctuation between "bloom" and "sacred" (end of line 36), as well in the somewhat arbitrarily placed parentheses (the beginning of line 35—the end of line 37), which could equally close at the end of lines 36, 38, or 39. The loosened syntax better renders the flux of feeling. Besides, in the benign realm where everything is connected to everything else, it does not really matter what precise relations obtain between "greetings," "sigh," "bloom," and so on, for everything is "crowded into one sigh."

Zhukovsky piles up one appellation of the inexpressible after another, each commencing with an elevated "this" (*sie, sei, siia*), struggling to probe the subject. As in "weaving of words," the sentence employs anaphora (lines 24, 30, 31, 33, 38, 39, 40), repetitions ("this"; "sacred"—"sacred object"; "Creator"—"creation"), oxymorons ("sweet joyous and doleful"), and alliterations (for example, *no to, chto slito s sei blestiashchei krasotoiu; sie prisutstvie sozdatelia v sozdan'i*), and culminates in the admission of an alleged defeat. The unrhymed "crowded into one sigh" sets off the penultimate line. The oxymoron "sweet joyous and doleful" captures the contradictory nature of the sentiment. The syntax is vague again (does "sweet" refer to "joyous" or to both "joyous" and "doleful"?), and the oxymoron has no noun following it.

By replacing substances with qualities, Zhukovsky makes his description more vague, shifting his emphasis from denotation to attributes and emotion. In several instances the inexpressibility passage has adjectives or participles but no nouns: "this hazy" (*sie stol' smutnoe*); "that agitate us" (*volnuiushchee nas*); "of charm" (*obvorozhaiushchego);* "for the distant" (*k dalekomu*); "of the past" (*minovavshego*). While the Russian language permits adjectives and participles to be used as nouns, their profusion in the passage, as well as the more idiosyncratic stringing together of three adjectives in a row in "sweet joyous and doleful," stands out.

As in the work of medieval artists employing the ineffability topos, this lyric falls prey to the inconsistency of expressing the inexpressible. It specifies various emotions (nostalgia, love, longing) in the very act of denying the possibility of adequately conveying them. Zhukovsky chose to underplay the incongruous aspects of "The Inexpressible," as shown by his decision to remove the original two final lines: "But inspiration speaks again, / And my passionate muse forgot its report" (*No vdokhnovenie opiat' zagovorilos', / I muza pylkaia zabyla svoi otchet*).[36] The charge of inconsistency may be reduced if one assumes that the lyric does not denote but rather hints at these emotions. In a traditional romantic manner, Zhukovsky here strives to achieve an awareness of the inexpressible by approximating those sensations of which one can speak to an inexpressible ideal.[37] As the ineffability topos aims to aggrandize both divine authority and one's own transcendental insight, Zhukovsky's poem exalts both the ideal of the beautiful and the lyrical subject that intimates this ideal. Inexpressibility endows Zhukovsky's poetry with added power: if such a compelling portrayal of sublime sentiment is inadequate, how lofty must the sentiment itself be?

Venevitinov

"The Inexpressible" concludes with advice to resort to silence, a theme taken up by Dmitry Venevitinov. Venevitinov's "The Poet" ("Poet," 1826–27) adds the nuance of the incommunicable to the inexpressible:

Тебе знаком ли сын богов,	Are you acquainted with the son of the gods,
Любимец муз и вдохновенья?	The favorite of muses and of inspiration?
Узнал ли б меж земных сынов	Would you recognize his speech and movements
Ты речь его, его движенья?	Among the sons of earth?
Не вспыльчив он, и строгий ум	He is not hot-tempered, and his strict mind
Не блещет в шумном разговоре,	Is not conspicuous in noisy chatter,
Но ясный луч высоких дум	But a clear ray of lofty thoughts
Невольно светит в ясном взоре.	Shines involuntarily in his clear gaze.
Пусть вкруг него, в чаду утех,	Let giddy youth, bemused by pleasure,
Бушует ветреная младость,	Rise up around him,
Безумный крик, нескромный смех	Mad shout, immodest laughter,
И необузданная радость:	And unruly joy:

Всё чуждо, дико для него,
На всё спокойно он взирает,
Лишь редко что-то с уст его
Улыбку беглую срывает.
Его богиня—простота,
И тихий гений размышленья
Ему поставил от рожденья
Печать молчанья на уста.
Его мечты, его желанья,
Его боязни, упованья—
Всё тайна в нем, всё в нем молчит:
В душе заботливо хранит
Он неразгаданные чувства . . .
Когда ж внезапно что-нибудь
Взволнует огненную грудь—
Душа, без страха, без искусства,
Готова вылиться в речах
И блещет в пламенных очах . . .
И снова тих он, и стыдливый
К земле он опускает взор,
Как будто слышит он укор
За невозвратные порывы.
О, если встретишь ты его
С раздумьем на челе суровом—
Пройди без шума близ него,
Не нарушай холодным словом
Его священных, тихих снов;
Взгляни с слезой благоговенья
И молви: это сын богов,
Любимец муз и вдохновенья.[38]

All is alien, strange to him.
He looks at everything calmly,
Only rarely does something
Pluck a quick smile from his lips.
His goddess is simplicity,
And a quiet genius of reflection
Placed at his birth
A seal of silence on his lips.
His dreams, his desires,
His fears and his expectations—
All are enigma in him, all is silent:
In his soul he carefully preserves
Unfathomed feelings . . .
But when suddenly something
Agitates his fiery breast—
His soul without fear, artlessly,
Is ready to pour out in speeches
And shines in his flaming eyes . . .
And he is quiet again, and
Lowers his bashful gaze toward the earth,
As if he heard a reproach
For his irrevocable outbursts.
Oh, if you meet him
With reflection on his stern brow—
Pass by him noiselessly,
Do not interrupt with a cold word
His sacred, quiet dreams;
Look at him with a tear of reverence,
And say: this is son of the gods,
Darling of muses and of inspiration.

"The Poet," like Batiushkov's and Zhukovsky's lyrics, focuses on mysteries of inner life which are difficult to convey in words: "All are enigma in him, all is silent." The poem veers between general verbal skepticism ("a seal of silence on his lips," "all is silent," "do not interrupt with a cold word") and specifically anti-poetic critique. Venevitinov emphasizes the artless outpouring of the poet's soul when he is agitated, his simplicity and restraint.

A change takes place in how the theme of silence is rendered. It is not clear whether or not the poet's "unfathomed feelings" are a riddle to him. What is obvious is that they are a mystery for the "rabble." The external reality against which the lyrical subject positions himself is no longer equated with nature but primarily with human society, with which Venevitinov's poet finds himself at odds: "All is alien, strange to him, / He looks at everything mutely." One observes a shift from the theme of inexpressibility to that of incommunicability.[39]

The stress in this treatment of the inexpressible is no longer linguistic deficiency but rather the emotional ineptitude of other humans among whom "the chosen one" finds himself. Unlike Batiushkov and Zhukovsky, who lamented their lyrical heroes' inability to adequately express their inner life, Venevitinov emphasizes his poet's alienation from the human community, the latter being incapable of appreciating "poetic sentiment." Venevitinov's hero largely refuses to communicate but makes it seem as if communication would be possible if he tried: "But when suddenly something agitates his fiery breast—/ His soul without fear, artlessly, / Is ready to pour out in speech / And shines in his flaming eyes." Still, incommunicability is also involuntary in the sense that the poet, even when willing to express himself, would likely be misunderstood.[40]

TIUTCHEV: ONTOLOGY OF OTHERNESS AND THE OPERATIVE PARADOX

Batiushkov's and Zhukovsky's poems both conclude with statements of verbal skepticism: "My soul does not know how to express them in well-composed words, / Yet I do not know how to be silent about them" (Batiushkov); "And only silence speaks understandably" (Zhukovsky). Batiushkov takes a stanza out of *Childe Harold's Pilgrimage* and turns it into an independent lyric, which ends with a declaration of verbal inadequacy but nonetheless exists as a poem, thus addressing both sides of the operative paradox. Zhukovsky, similarly, offers his strongest inexpressibility statement in the poem's finale. Moving the inexpressibility statement from the poem's opening where it would have been placed in older works transforms it from a rhetorical convention denied by the poem's progression into its main point. Zhukovsky goes further than Batiushkov—he does not merely decry the deficiency of his poetic word but states that silence is the highest form of poetry.

A more radical step will be taken by Fyodor Tiutchev in his celebrated "Silentium!" (1830), a poem which calls for silence. This poem, more than any other lyric, has come to epitomize the way Russian poetry articulates verbal inadequacy. Much analyzed and widely influential, the lyric is habitually treated outside the context of Tiutchev's oeuvre as if this antiverbal masterpiece were atypical for him. In fact, though "Silentium!" is unique in its form and address to humans, it is no stand-alone piece, but belongs to a cluster of Tiutchev's poems on language and silence.

Tiutchev discussed the problem of the word in his letters as well. In one missive to Prince Gagarin of July 7, 1836, he relates how, having set out to sort his papers, he destroyed a major portion of his verses. He notes that he was somewhat chagrined but quickly consoled himself, and remarks that "fate, or rather, providence dealt justly with them." He refers to them in a denigrating way as "rhymes" and "poetic verbiage" (Tiutchev 4:50–51).[41] In a letter to Gagarin of April 20–21, 1836, Tiutchev expresses hostility to writing in even starker terms:

> Writing is a terrible evil, it is like the second fall for the poor mind, like the doubling up of matter. I feel that, should I permit myself to do this, I'd write a very long letter to you with a single objective of proving the inadequacy, uselessness, and absurdity of letters . . . One should express only general notions in letters since only general notions can be perceived at a distance. But there are some minutes when life suddenly breaks upon these generalizations and begins to pick on you like a nasty bretteur. Precisely this constitutes the genuine tragedy of being. Under ordinary circumstances the horrible reality of life permits thought to hover around itself, but as soon as it feels safe and confident of its strength, all of a sudden reality comes alive and, with a single blow of its paw, breaks its spine. But this is also only a general consideration. (Tiutchev 4:39–40)

This passage is noteworthy in several respects. As Tiutchev insists that writing is evil, he envisions its evil nature in religious terms ("the second fall"). According to Richard Gregg, writing is evil because "it invokes and reenacts previous emotions or thoughts . . . which seem wrong" to Tiutchev.[42] However, Tiutchev does not specify what kinds of thoughts or emotions are reflected in words; rather, he makes a more totalizing claim that writing is evil.[43] He foregrounds the irony of denigrating writing in writing, and notes that the distance between speaker and addressee makes writing capable of conveying general notions only. Lastly, he couches the inadequacy of writing in existentially urgent terms. It is because "a horrible reality of life breaks its [thought's] spine" that writing fails. Tiutchev concludes the passage with another assertion of the operative paradox: "But this is also but a general consideration."

Tiutchev's transpositions of the problem of the word emerge in multiple lyrics, and are variegated, but he invariably conveys metaphysical notions (time, the sublime, chaos, death) via ideas of language and silence. Thus "A Vision" ("Videnie," 1829) describes a mystical experience taking place at night when the kernel of being is revealed to the poet. This revelation comes to him with the consciousness of the self suppressed and in the absence of sound—at a "certain hour, at night, of universal silence" (*nekii chas, v nochi, vsemirnogo molchan'ia*) (Tiutchev 1:70).[44] Like "A Vision," "Insomnia" ("Bessonnitsa," 1829) depicts a mystical experience that takes place in the dead of night and employs the phrase "of universal silence" (*vsemirnogo molchan'ia*). The monotonous striking of the clock intrudes upon the silence of the universe. The clock's uncanny language, "equally strange to everyone / And audible to everyone like a conscience" (*Iazyk dlia vsekh ravno chuzhoi / I vniatnyi kazhdomy, kak sovest'*) (Tiutchev 1:75) conveys the ruthlessness of time in a manner that is alien and yet somehow comprehensible. This speech bespeaks the horror of non-being while the muteness of life all around highlights the hero's loneliness.[45]

Like "A Vision" and "Insomnia," "I sit pensive, and alone" ("Sizhu zadumchiv i odin," 1836) and "Day and Night" ("Den' i noch'," 1839) portray mystical revelations described in terms of their ineffability as wordless and supra-rational experiences. What changes is the coloring of ineffability: the mystery of the sublime ("A Vision") versus the mystery of non-being ("Insomnia"), transience ("I sit pensive, and alone"), or chaos ("Day and Night"). "I sit pensive, and alone" finds human language deficient for articulating the hero's perception of transience: "And I find no words / In my melancholy" (*I slov, v unynii moem, / Ne nakhozhu*) (Tiutchev 1:165). "Day and Night" describes the dark core of being as a "nameless chasm / Covered by a gold-brocaded shroud" (*Nad etoi bezdnoi bezymiannoi, / Pokrov nabroshen zlatotkannyi*) (Tiutchev 1:185).

"And there is no feeling in your eyes" ("I chuvstva net v tvoikh ochakh," 1836), similarly, employs speech as a premise in an ontological argument. The poem links the falsity of the word, the soullessness of the addressee, and the absence of God. It draws a double analogy, first, between the absence of feeling in the addressee's eyes, the truthfulness in her words (*I chuvstva net v tvoikh ochakh, / I pravdy net v tvoikh rechakh*), and the absence of her soul, and subsequently, between the addressee's soullessness and the absence of the Creator in creation (*I net v tvorenii tvortsa*) (Tiutchev 1:172). This is the very opposite of Zhukovsky's "presence of the Creator in creation."

"Nature is not what you think it is" ("Ne to, chto mnite vy, priroda," 1836) is another ontological as verbal argument. The poem couches its rejection of the mechanistic view of nature as a statement on language. Contrary to views of nature as soulless matter, "It has a soul, freedom, / Love, and language" (*V nei est' dusha, v nei est' svoboda, / V nei est' liubov', v nei est' iazyk*) (Tiutchev 1:169). The lyric laments the incommunicability between the natural world and "deaf-mute" rationalistic humans who fail to understand nature's tongue. The "organ" in "understand, if able, / The life of the organ, deaf-mute" (*poimi, kol' mozhet, / Organa zhizn' glukhonemoi*) (Tiutchev 1:170) reinforces the poem's religious coloring. Nature is a cathedral but humans have no access to the voices speaking beneath its vaults.

Similar to "Nature is not what you think it is," "There is melodiousness in sea waves" ("Pevuchest' est' v morskikh volnakh," 1865) posits the presence of harmony in nature, and laments the incommunicability between nature and the human, whose voice, like the voice of the one crying in the wilderness, receives no response (*Vse bezotveten i ponyne / Glas vopiiushchego v pustyne*) (Tiutchev 2:131). Man, as an individualistic being asserting his freedom, exists in a state of separation from the whole.[46]

Like "Nature is not what you think it is," "The night sky is so grim" ("Nochnoe nebo tak ugriumo," 1865) again employs the epithet "deaf-mute" but, in contrast to the benign message of the earlier poem, transposes incommunicability onto nature. Here lightning, not humans oblivious to nature's harmony, is likened to "deaf-mute demons / Speaking among themselves" (*Kak demony glukhonemye, / Vedut besedu mezh soboi*) (Tiutchev 2:151). "Two Voices" ("Dva golosa," 1850), another statement in which silence epitomizes the meaninglessness of the world, also presents a grimmer vision—of humans caught between two silences, of the heavens above and of graves below.

Lastly, "When with a sympathy to our word" ("Kogda sochuvstvenno na nashe slovo," 1866) and "We cannot foresee" ("Nam ne dano predugadat'," 1869) hinge on the problem of (in)communicability. In the former, even a single soul's sympathetic response to one's words (*Kogda sochuvstvenno na nashe slovo / Odna dusha otozvalas'*) is a blessing (Tiutchev 2:156). The latter expresses hope that one's words will not be uttered in vain, and envisions communicability as divine grace: "And sympathy is given to us / As grace is given to us" (*I nam sochuvstvie daetsia, / Kak nam daetsia blagodat'*) (Tiutchev 2:197). Although the poems hope that one's words will find a sympathetic echo, the suggestion that even one soul's response is ample recompense to poetic speech ("When with a sympathy to our word"), and the notion that another's response is dispensed as divine grace ("We cannot foresee") are testimony to a skepticism that underlies these utterances just as they set out to polemicize with it.[47]

"Silentium!" goes farther than any of the poems above in its expression of verbal skepticism; it conceptualizes the problem of the word not in terms of the older religious or pantheist ineffability (as in "A Vision" or "There is melodiousness in sea waves") but as a modern problem of incommunicability and estrangement, with the self asserted rather than suppressed. At the same time Tiutchev's most forthright statement of verbal skepticism grows out of the same imagery, and responds to the same set of problems, as his other word-versus-silence poems.

"Silentium!" turns a call for silence into a refrain (each of its three stanzas ends with an imperative to keep silent), synthesizes the motifs of the inexpressibility and incommunicability of inner life, and foregrounds the irony of articulating silence:

Молчи, скрывайся и таи	Be silent, be secret and hide
И чувства и мечты свои—	Both your feelings and your dreams!
Пускай в душевной глубине	Let them rise and set
Встают и заходят оне	In the depths of your soul
Безмолвно, как звезды в ночи,	Mutely, like stars in the night,
Любуйся ими—и молчи.	Admire them—and be silent.
Как сердцу высказать себя?	How can the heart speak out?
Другому как понять тебя?	How can the other understand you?
Поймёт ли он, чем ты живёшь?	Will he understand what you live by?
Мысль изречённая есть ложь.	An uttered thought is a lie.
Взрывая, возмутишь ключи—	Burrowing, you will trouble the springs—
Питайся ими—и молчи.	Be nourished by them—and be silent.
Лишь жить в себе самом умей—	Know how to live only in yourself—
Есть целый мир в душе твоей	There is an entire world in your soul
Таинственно-волшебных дум;	Of mysteriously magical thoughts;
Их оглушит наружный шум,	External noise will stifle them,
Дневные разгонят лучи, —	Daytime rays will drive them away,—
Внимай их пенью—и молчи! . .	Attend to their singing—and be silent! . .

(Tiutchev 1:123)[48]

Written in archaic iambic couplets that accentuate the lyric's artifice, this poem brings into relief the quandary of the word and verbal art as a conventional means of expressing unique sentiments. With all the couplets ending on the same masculine rhyme (*nochi–molchi–kliuchi–molchi–luchi–molchi*), with an unexpected switch in meter in the first and the third stanzas, and with the relentless repetition of "be silent!," the poem has both a hammering and a stumbling quality, formally communicating the tensions inherent in its theme.[49] The rhythm is broken in lines 4, 5, and 17. The amphibrachical deviations from the iambic tetrameter occur when rising and setting feelings and dreams are mentioned, and when the poem refers to daytime rays that will drive away magical thoughts. The switches in meter underscore the peculiar (which is difficult, if not impossible, to convey) order of inner life, and dramatize how even attempted exposure of the inner being infringes upon this order.[50]

"Silentium!" ends with an ellipsis, the marker of inexpressibility, and so enacts its theme on the structural level. The lyric proceeds in a circular arrangement that reflects its solipsistic philosophy of "living only in yourself." It starts and ends with the imperative "be silent!," and its first and last stanzas focus on the depiction of inner life, zealously guarded against intrusion from the outside; the middle stanza states reasons for shunning contact with outer reality. The inner world is portrayed in cosmological terms: "Let them rise and set / In the depths of your soul / Mutely, like stars in the night." Such a portrayal drives home the idea of "an entire world in your soul" and locates the sublime within the confines of the self. If in Zhukovsky's case the self is externalized, in Tiutchev's the universe lies within the soul's stronghold. According to the traditional romantic model, the self expands on the universe.[51] Tiutchev depicts the self as estranged from the totality of the outer world and advocates complete discreteness.

The theme of music, interpreted by Batiushkov as nature's melody, gets recast in "Silentium!" as the motif of the singing soul.[52] The sound structure of "Silentium!" suggests inner unity: "m," "l," and "ch" have high frequency in the poem, a sound repetition that may relate to the privileging of music (in this case, inner singing). Since the theme of music tends to accompany the idealistic variety of word devaluation when silence is conceptualized as a path to the transcendental (for example, in Keats's "Ode on a Grecian Urn" [1819], and Shelley's "To a Sky-lark" [1820]), Tiutchev's allusion to interior singing seems to connect "Silentium!" to the exploration of transcendental inexpressibility. But Tiutchev's lyric is concerned with the idea of incommunicability, the impossibility of reaching the Other. A suggestion of interior singing does not alleviate the double difficulty of linguistic inadequacy and alienation that makes "Silentium!" a bleak existential reflection. "Silentium!" does not pursue the common romantic ambition to present external reality in rapport with the poet's soul. Instead, it portrays the mind's absolute withdrawal into itself, with heavens and earth located within the soul rather than reflective or symbolic of the soul's emotions.

The second, explicatory stanza of "Silentium!" unites the theme of the inexpressible ("How can the heart speak out?") with the motif of alienation ("How can the other understand you?"). Fraize and Zailer's view that the poem progresses from delight to nourishment to a genuine appeal to the Other by moving from "admire them" (stanza 1) to "be nourished by them" (stanza 2) to "attend to their singing" (stanza 3) is not supported by the poem, since by its closure the poet's attention is still focused on the self (his "inner springs").[53] Nor do I share Kirill Pigarev's contention that the poem primarily "develops one of Romantic poetry's common motifs, juxtaposing a strongly and subtly feeling person to cold and indifferent society."[54] The motif of alienation is not an instance of conventional romantic posturing. While Venevitinov obviously depicts the lyrical subject as a superior being whose lofty experiences placed him at a distance from the common folk, in "Silentium!" the emphasis lies elsewhere. Here it is no longer primarily important whether "the Other" is inferior to the lyrical subject; what matters is that one encounters "the Other." "Otherness" is seen as an ontological position that precludes any possibility of true understanding among human beings.

From Batiushkov to Tiutchev, then, we can observe a gradual intensification of the hero's estrangement from the world. Batiushkov's poet is fond of both men and nature; Zhukovsky's hero does not discuss his relationship to people but dotes on nature; in Venevitinov only the human component of external reality is considered alien. As opposed to Venevitinov's voluntary non-communication, Tiutchev's lyric insists on the impossibility of communication. The unavoidability of mediation by inadequate linguistic means contributes to this existential plight but does not take up the whole picture. Verbal deficiency and alienation together make "Silentium!" assert that genuine comprehension among humans is unattainable.

The operative paradox of versification on silence at the crux of "Silentium!" also distinguishes Tiutchev's lyric from the preceding ones. Zhukovsky's decision to remove the initial closure to his poem suggests that he was sensitive to its irony but did not want to emphasize it. "The Inexpressible" does not deconstruct itself the way "Silentium!" does, for never does it actually urge the need for silence nor does it explicitly claim to "express the inexpressible," but denies its capability to accomplish this task. According to Yuri Mann, Tiutchev's poem, like Zhukovsky's, simultaneously "argues for silence and depicts diverse spiritual conditions."[55] However, in contrast to Zhukovsky, who hinted at ineffable sentiments in the very act of denying his ability to do this, Tiutchev does not specify the lyrical subject's thoughts and feelings. In this sense Tiutchev's lyric is more consistent than Zhukovsky's. But a poem calling for silence is, of course, an instance of supreme irony.

"Silentium!" belies its basic argument by the mere fact of its existence. It is a tour de force of romantic irony, in which an "alternation between self-creation and self-destruction" is carried on the macroscale of the whole poem.[56] Tiutchev's introduction of the poem's famous aphorism, a rhythmically marked "an uttered thought is a lie," adds a more radically ironic layer, a variation of the Cretan liar paradox. It is precisely this tension in the poem's rhetorical structure that constitutes its most dramatic aspect. The type of irony engendered by Tiutchev's introduction of the liar paradox is more extreme than traditional romantic irony, which is produced with the author switching between contradictory viewpoints throughout the text. Romantic ironists such as Byron and Pushkin "never give up their right not to coincide with themselves, to create a sincere new identity with every utterance—a series of 'stills' of a subjectivity in constant motion."[57] If the romantic crisis lyric emphasizes continual self-revision and a refusal to succumb to the temptation of closure, Tiutchev goes well beyond exercising his right "to freely relinquish first one and then another part of one's being," for "Silentium!" does not state contradictory viewpoints sequentially and explicitly, but deconstructs its main thesis in the very process of expressing it.[58]

The poem exposes the inconsistent nature of the discourse of inexpressibility, which up to that point had not been fully appreciated. "The forceful verb *est'* presents 'an uttered thought is a lie' as an existential assertion," an assertion that is rent by self-contradiction.[59] In a further ironic twist, "be silent!," as any imperative, intensifies the communicative immediacy with the reader. "Silentium!" is one of Tiutchev's oratorical poems, which "often show the presence of the addressee or the crowd to which he preaches," except that this time the paradoxical rhetor preaches non-communication.[60]

Was Tiutchev conscious of the problematic nature of his lyric? That is, does "Silentium!" fall prey to the operative paradox or does it deliberately dramatize it, exposing the theme of verbal deficiency? I believe the latter to be true, not least because the poem's Latin title positions it alongside medieval scholastic arguments in the tradition of Saint Augustine and other Western theologians, just as the formulaic *est'* in "an uttered thought is a lie" and the high stylistic register of the language (*izrechennaia, dum, one*) endows it with the quality of a metaphysical poem.[61] As a formal argument on inexpressibility, "Silentium!" exposes the indeterminacy inherent in the critique of language by means of language—the same problem that Tiutchev brings forth in his letter to Gagarin.

Through self-reference, the poem undermines its own validity and as such exposes verbal rupture. Philosophical poetry remains the site of thought or, more precisely, "the procedure of truth, or a generating procedure." Poets incorporate the maxims of thought, "key moments in the poem in which a thought (the poem) points at itself as a relation or a development of thought 'in general.' "[62] This characterization of twentieth-century poetry taking on the functions of philosophy applies equally to "Silentium!" The key moment of the poem, its maxim "an uttered thought is a lie," is a thought in general, a generating procedure of truth.

Yet one does not perceive the logical contradiction as the lyric's only meaningful aspect. Assuming that readers appreciate the liar paradox, its recognition does not lead them to dismiss Tiutchev's maxim "an uttered thought is a lie." This statement presents itself as logically problematic but intuitively true. This is evidently how Tiutchev means us to perceive it, for, were he to deny his maxim any positive meaning, he would be reduced to silence. Tiutchev (like Kireevsky or Shestov later) intimates that what is logically flawed may be valid nonetheless. This is another aspect of the lyric's verbal critique, performed by, first, exposing the logical problem of conceptualizing inexpressibility in language and, second, defying logic altogether. As with any paradox, Tiutchev's highlights the limits of logic attending the use of language.[63]

The poem acts out the theme of verbal deficiency in one more way. The famous aphorism is by no means self-explanatory; it offers an enigma that suggests a variety of possible meanings. Evidently Tiutchev calls for silence since we cannot adequately convey our innermost thoughts and feelings. Does this happen because language conveys only general notions or because it is "fallen" in its materiality (the letter to Gagarin)? According to the lyric, thoughts precede language. If words are not equivalent to thoughts, then how do they relate? Is an uttered thought a lie because language cannot effectively express inner being (a traditional romantic notion), or does a spoken utterance make a thought a lie by destroying its authenticity in the process of verbalization? The difference is not merely a matter of degree. Does an utterance fall short of satisfactorily conveying inner reality while the reality remains intact, or does an articulation of inner reality injure that reality? In other words, does speech merely present inner being in a distorted way (the classical problem of inexpressibility), or does it actually distort it (inexpressibility plus the problem of the word's destructiveness)?

If speech cannot effectively articulate thought, does this happen because, keeping in mind the romantic stress on individualism, language binds one to express one's perceptions in a standardized way that cannot do justice to the uniqueness of inner reality? Are personal conditions too complex, and do they change too fast, for one to be able to capture and convey them? Is the rupture between the inner and the external caused by the loss of the emotional component of thought as it is articulated? If speech actively deforms thought, is this a problem of language per se? Does this happen because, for example, we replace the vague outline of a sentiment with its conceptually determined, limiting version? Or is this a problem not of language as such but of self-exposure through language, that is, of rejecting sentiment as unworthy after exposure? Or is it an issue of self-exposure in verbal art, of poetry's immodesty? This hermeneutic openness carries through the problem of verbal inadequacy that is the metaliterary theme of the poem. In a sense, "Silentium!" remains closed to the reader, itself constituting a vivid example of communicative difficulties, an enactment of the inexpressible.[64]

The word's active destructiveness is suggested by the imagery of the second and third stanzas emphasizing the damage done to spiritual reality: "Burrowing, you will trouble the springs"; "External noise will stifle them, / Daytime rays will drive them away." That the word is not merely inadequate as a means of communicating one's inner being, but may be detrimental to one's feelings, is the poem's most arresting insight. Nothing like that had been intuited in the poems discussed earlier. Tiutchev's puzzling attitude to his writings, ranging from indifference to revulsion, acquires a new significance. One may assume that, in the poet's opinion, writing is "a terrible evil" not only (and not so much) because it records sinful thoughts and emotions but because the act of writing damages these thoughts and emotions.

How does the act of writing damage the inner being? Either a richer pre-articulation sentiment may be replaced by its conceptually expressible variant or the sentiment may become false because of its exposure. Within Tiutchev's discourse of total self-enclosure, the externalization of inner being would be read as a loss. Given the standard romantic interpretation of poetic art as an uttering forth of internal reality, one would next be moved to question the validity of poetry's existence. Since the poet resists revealing his private self and desires to safeguard the sanctity of his feeling, his inner realities, once verbalized, may become lies also because he (consciously or unconsciously) rejects them as worthless after revealing them.[65]

"Silentium!" offers a skeptical view of the poetic vocation that challenges the idealist romantic faith in poetic art's unlimited power.[66] It deplores the double predicament of verbal inadequacy and human incommunicability. It envisions the word as inherently flawed, inferior to the poet's internal reality. The poem both reflects typical traits of Tiutchev's poetics (such as the opposition between a revelatory night and a deceiving day—inner thoughts that arise "mutely, like stars in the night," and daytime rays that "will drive them away"), and encapsulates key problems of his philosophy (man's uniqueness and individualism that alienate him from the harmony of the whole). In a larger sense, the poem exhibits a pessimistic outlook on the human condition, anticipating the twentieth century's explorations of the existential predicament, a disillusioned vision quite different from Batiushkov's and Zhukovsky's strivings to convey their inexpressible intuition of the transcendental.

BARATYNSKY AND LERMONTOV: INCOMMUNICABILITY, SILENCE, NIHILISM

Baratynsky

Like the poets above, Evgeny Baratynsky explored a range of problems of the poetic word in his lyrics. "The Last Death" ("Posledniaia smert'," 1827), for instance, portrays a vision of the coming ages of mankind as revealed to the poet, yet the poet doubts his mystical powers. "My gift is poor, and my voice is not loud" ("Moi dar ubog, i golos moi negromok," 1828), akin to Tiutchev's "When with a sympathy to our word" and "We cannot foresee," displays concurrent currents of skepticism and hope for communicability, even if only with an addressee located in a distant future. Despite the smallness of the poet's voice, perhaps his soul will communicate with that of a future reader (*Kak znat', dusha moia / Okazhetsia s dushoi ego v snoshen'i*).[67] Like "My gift is poor, and my voice is not loud," "The Last Poet" ("Poslednii poet," 1835) reveals an ambivalence toward the poetic word. It laments the degradation of poetry under the "iron age" of mankind when materialism, industrialization, and avarice reign. When a poet emerges in this sterile world, singing of love and beauty, people laugh at him. Claims of poetry and reason are presented oppositionally, and from the latter perspective poetry is "childish dreams" (*rebiacheskie sny*), and the poet is "simple-hearted" (*prostodushnyi*).[68] Ultimately the poet buries his "useless gift" in the sea. "Rhyme" ("Rifma," 1836–37) similarly laments the denigration of poetry in the modern age. In an ancient past, the poet-seer, possessing a divinely inspired wisdom, ruled over fellow members of his society. The modern age has unseated him from his position. "Rhyme" wonders whether poetry is "a laughable sickness or the highest gift" (*smeshnoi nedug il' vysshii dar*).[69] "When your voice, o poet" ("Kogda tvoi golos, o poet," 1843), a poem written during the last year of Baratynsky's life, directly asserts incommunicability.[70]

Baratynsky's long lyric "Autumn" ("Osen'," 1836–37) contains, among a number of themes, an articulation of inexpressibility and incommunicability that I will concentrate on here.[71]

Like Zhukovsky, Baratynsky starts with a depiction of natural scenery, and then considers its emotional and metaphysical implications. In contrast to "The Inexpressible," which synchronizes man and nature, "Autumn" opposes natural and human conditions. Nature eternally renews itself, oblivious to the destruction wrought upon individual beings. It is the opulence of the harvest that brings into relief the tragedy of the hero. The stanzas that hail the fruit of autumnal fields (4–5) are followed by ones portraying the grim autumn of the protagonist's life (6 onward), and this structure emphasizes the disparity between autumnal and life's harvest. As opposed to nature's bounty, human life's outcome is disastrous—shame, deceptions, and injuries of the soul. The hero is disappointed after his youthful aspirations. He who once reigned over radiant dreams now contemplates barren mazes.

Like "Silentium!," "Autumn" embeds inexpressibility within the broader context of man's existential plight. The poem raises the problems of human communication.[72] Indeed, these problems are the crux of the poem and are most explicitly articulated in stanzas 11–13:

Какое же потом в груди твоей
  Ни водворится озаренье,
Чем дум и чувств ни разрешится
    в ней
  Последнее
    вихревращенье—
Пусть в торжестве насмешливом
    своем
  Ум бесполезный сердца трепет
Угомонит и тщетных жалоб в нем
  Удушит запоздалый лепет,
	Whatever illumination will settle
	  Then in your breast,
	In whatever way the last
	    whirlwind
	  Of thoughts and feelings will
	    resolve itself in it—
	Let the mind, in its mocking
	    triumph,
	  Quell the heart's useless shudder,
	And choke the belated babble
	  Of vain complaints in it,

И примешь ты, как лучший жизни клад,	And you will accept, as the best hidden treasure of life,
Дар опыта, мертвящий душу хлад.	The gift of experience, the cold, deadening the soul.
Иль, отряхнув видения земли	Or, having shaken off earthly visions
Порывом скорби животворной,	With a burst of vivifying grief,
Ее предел завидя невдали,	Seeing its limit not far away,
Цветущий брег за мглою черной,	A blooming shore beyond black mist,
Возмездий край, благовестящим снам	A land of retributions, to dreams of annunciation
Доверясь чувством обновленным,	Entrusting the self with renewed feeling,
И бытия мятежным голосам,	And to the rebellious voices of being,
В великом гимне примиренным,	Reconciled in a great hymn,
Внимающий, как арфам, коих строй	Hearkening as to harps whose elevated harmony
Превыспренний не понят был тобой, —	Was not understood by you, —
Пред промыслом оправданным ты ниц	Before justified providence you prostrate
Падешь с признательным смиреньем,	Yourself with thankful humility,
С надеждою, не видящей границ,	With hope that knows no bounds
И утоленным разуменьем, —	And with quenched understanding, —
Знай, внутренней своей вовеки ты	Know, you will never transmit
Не передашь земному звуку	Your interior one to earthly sound
И легких чад житейской суеты	And you will not initiate the carefree children
Не посвятишь в свою науку;	Of life's vanity into your knowledge;
Знай, горняя иль дольная, она	Know, whether it is of highlands or of lowlands,
Нам на земле не для земли дана.	It is not given us on earth for the earthly.[73]

Baratynsky is generally known for his difficult syntax but the passage in question is especially complex. A single, sprawling sentence, longer than

Zhukovsky's inexpressibility statement, runs from the beginning of stanza 12, preceding the expression of verbal skepticism, all the way to the conclusion of stanza 13. These stanzas stand out against preceding ones, which are composed of several shorter sentences. The last two lines of a stanza normally contain a coda, but at the end of stanza 12, a comma and a hyphen fling the sentence over into the next stanza, speeding up the narrative as it approaches the articulation of inexpressibility.

Syntactic twists and ambiguities highlight the tumultuous quality of the sentiment. Syntax and meter collide, inversions come aplenty, and participial and gerundive clauses pile one upon another. "A land of retributions" (*vozmezdii krai*), an inversion, modifies "seeing" (*zavidia*) but comes together with "dreams of annunciation" (*blagovestiashchim snam*). "Entrusting the self with renewed feeling" (*Doverias' chuvstvom obnovlennym*), another inversion, governs both "dreams of annunciation" and "And to the rebellious voices of being" (*I bytiia miatezhnym golosam*), an inversion again, but, inserted between these two phrases, makes the "and" (*i*) of "And to the rebellious voices of being" puzzling. "Your interior one" (*vnutrennei svoei*) is another idiosyncratic construction which may refer to "hope" (*nadezhdoiu*), but which is removed from the noun by several lines as well as put in a different case (genitive vs. instrumental). The appearance of "hearkening" (*vnimaiushchii*) at the end of stanza 12 is especially marked, for one does not immediately realize that the participle modifies "you" (*ty*), which occurs nine lines above, in the preceding stanza 11. The coiled clauses of the passage enact the "whirlwind" (*vikhrevrashchen'e*) of thoughts and feelings indicated in stanza 11.

Like Tiutchev, Baratynsky presents a metaphysical argument on inexpressibility, albeit filled with a later-day angst. The poem, written in 10-line iambic stanzas and employing a high style, an antiquated syntax, and a blend of scientific and philosophical lexicon, summons the rhetorical tradition of the eighteenth century.[74] The argument itself is more modern. Like "Silentium!," "Autumn" laments the double quandary of inexpressibility and incommunicability, both the inadequacy of earthly sound to capture inner feeling ("your interior one") and the hero's inability to convey his knowledge to others ("carefree children of life's vanity"). The poet is alienated from people as well as from nature. The source of inexpressibility is internal (the hero is himself unclear; his mind and his heart are in conflict) as well as existential, though the latter is more prominent.

The theme of music, "harps whose elevated harmony was not understood by you," is modified to convey Baratynsky's darker vision. That it is not possible to convey mystical experience, for this knowledge "is not given us on earth for the earthly," corresponds to traditional idealistic inexpressibility. Baratynsky's hymn of the elements invokes the ancient music of the spheres, the notion that the whole universe is filled with harmony, living and breathing in unison.[75] The hymn reminds one of Batiushkov's "harmony in a talk of billows," and the lines introduce the idea of the transcendental, total unity that binds discordant aspects of being, analogous to Zhukovsky's "harmonization of variety and unity." However, in distinction to those scenarios in which the romantics perceive a hidden organic unity, Baratynsky's hero discerns universal harmony only in the proximity of death. In everyday existence the sounds of being appear chaotic.[76]

The belated revelation of universal harmony, as well as of the afterlife, cannot appease the hero. In order to have such an insight, he, like religious mystics, must submit himself to the order of things ("Before justified providence you prostrate / Yourself with thankful humility") and transcend "the passionate earthly" state of being (*strastnoe zemnoe*), another construction lacking a noun, leaving behind all the world's desires and regrets, including the very desire to live. Existence in "Autumn" means never satisfied desire and pain, a demolition of "gilded dreams" (*sny pozlashchennye*) replaced by "mordant shame" (*iazvitel'nyi styd*).[77] One may reconcile oneself to being only by "having shaken off earthly visions / With a burst of vivifying grief." This grief permits one to reject this world and leads to a discernment of noumenal harmony, but the act of self-renunciation proves impossible.

At the finale of the poem, rather than adhering to the traditional notion of the afterlife, the hero again concentrates on himself, agonizing over his impending exclusion from the world. As Nietzsche and Shestov would do later, Baratynsky suggests that intense suffering does not unite man with fellow men but separates him from the others.[78] An expression of the hero's pain, a wail of anguish, would not find a sympathetic response in fellow humans but would kill the man in man: a baby at play would drop his toy, and "man would die alive in him" (*i zazhivo b v nem umer chelovek*).[79]

Throughout the poem Baratynsky switches between two notions of inexpressibility—the divine and suffering, which equally defy the power of the word. An anguish which can be conveyed only in screams also suggests the ineffable absolute. In anticipation of Shestov, Baratynsky refers to inarticulate expressions of torment: "moan" (*ston*), "cry" (*krik*), "scream" (*vopl'*), "wail" (*voi*). The agony of impending death may not be conveyed in language but only in inarticulate shrieks, yet these shrieks strive toward an absolute beyond man's powers of understanding. The poem vacillates between idealism and negativity, expressing despair (stanzas 6–11), the hope of the beyond (stanzas 12–14), and despair again (stanzas 15–16).

Only three stanzas are devoted to the metaphysical ideal. The passages that precede and the last two stanzas overshadow the intimation of metaphysical hope. Just as men are indifferent to the death of a solitary star, the cosmos pays no heed to its destruction. The music of the spheres (stanza 12) is offset by the imagery of cosmic indifference attending the fall of the star (stanza 15): "The ear of the world is not stricken / With the distant wail of its fall" (*Ne porazhaet ucho mira / Padeniia ee dalekii voi*).[80] The star's inarticulate wail echoes the cries, moans, and wails of the hero. The fall of the star, an allusion to Pushkin's death, also engages the topos of the music of the spheres.[81] The wrong path the star has taken disrupts the harmonious ordering of elements in the universe. Wanton destruction, not harmony, permeates the world. Stanza 14 presents an arch-romantic description of untamed nature: forests, oceans, and tempests. These lines build a triad of nature–people–language (*govor–glas–glagol*), the last in parallel to Pushkin's "The Prophet." Baratynsky equates nature's "language" (*govor,* also used by Batiushkov) with the rabble's vulgar voice. The natural features in Batiushkov's poem are reimagined in a negative light.

The concluding stanza presents a wasteland of death. Under the circumstances, the protagonist's last resort is a stoic, silent acceptance of fate, "with anguish whose deathly moan / Is hardly muffled by your pride" (*s toskoi, kotoroi smertnyi ston / Edva tvoei gordynei zadushen*).[82] The redeeming visions of an afterlife are but one possibility, the other being experience deadening the soul. The conjunction "or" (*ili*) that connects stanzas 11 and 12 presents the acceptance of cold that stifles the soul and sublime visions as either/or alternatives, but stanza 11 itself, "Whatever illumination will settle / Then in your breast" sees the acceptance of deadening experience as the ultimate conclusion, superseding whatever last "whirlwind" of thoughts and feelings may occur. And even if ultimate illumination comes to him, in the end the hero faces "the rest that is silence" alone.

Lermontov

Like Tiutchev and Baratynsky, Mikhail Lermontov explores incommunicability, but adds to the impasse of verbal corruption and the plight of human alienation the problem of squandering the self in the word. Though Tiutchev is concerned with the trivialization of inner being in poetry, it is Lermontov who inaugurates a powerful portrayal of the shamefulness of poetic self-exposure.

The problem of language and verbal art is one of the central themes of Lermontov's oeuvre. "June 11, 1831" ("1831–go iiunia 11 dnia," 1831) already raises the problem of inexpressibility: "I feel / The heat of exalted passions but / Do not find words" (*Pyl strastei / Vozvyshennykh ia chuvstvuiu, no slov / Ne nakhozhu*).[83]

"The Angel" ("Angel," 1831) builds an opposition between an ineffable heavenly sound, "without words but alive" (*bez slov, no zhivoi*), and "wearisome earthly songs" (*skuchnye pesni zemli*).[84] Lermontov again links the subject of the ineffable to the motif of music. Devoid of words (trans-rational), the angel's song remains alive and forcefully expressive, incommensurate with the songs of the earth. Like Shelley in "To a Sky-Lark," Lermontov describes a cleft between the heavenly realm in which the singer is located, and sad earthly existence. And, like Shelley, Lermontov predicates the perfection of the spirit's ineffable song on its artlessness: the angel's praise to God is "unfeigned" (*nepritvorna*); the sky-lark "from heaven or near it / Pourest [its] full heart / In profuse strains of unpremeditated art."[85]

"There are speeches—meaning" ("Est' rechi—znachen'e," 1840), like "The Angel," creates a dichotomy between mundane earthly language and the unique sounds the poet hears. The referential value of these speeches is suppressed while their affective value is at its peak: their meaning is "dark or petty" (*temno il' nichtozhno*), "But one cannot hear them / Without emotion" (*No im bez volnen'ia / Vnimat' nevozmozhno*).[86] These sounds are like music in its Schopenhauerian understanding—the most direct and the most powerful expression of emotion—full of desire, "tears of parting, and trembling of meeting" (*V nikh slezy razluki, / V nikh trepet svidan'ia*).[87] Shot through with feeling, these are active, living words that prompt the poet to follow their call. The speeches, or, more properly, music since they have no referential value, are antithetical to the world; only the poet will respond to them.

If "The Angel" and "There are speeches—meaning" assert the supremacy of music over words and emotion over reference in the manner of idealistic romantic ineffability, poems such as "The Poet" ("Poet," 1838), "Do not trust yourself" ("Ne ver' sebe," 1839), and "Journalist, Reader, and Writer" ("Zhurnalist, chitatel' i pisatel'," 1840) put a more skeptical spin on the issue of the poetic word. "The Poet" explores the degradation of verbal art through a simile likening poetry to an old dagger. The weapon, having faithfully served its owner in battles of yore, now just hangs on the wall, a pretty but useless decoration. Like the dagger, poetry has lost its heroic function and been degraded to a pretty plaything. Whereas "The Poet" focuses on the insignificance of poetry, "Journalist, Reader, and Writer" both criticizes the current state of poetry and stresses the failure of the poetic word. From the reader's perspective, poetry is inane, lacking thought or emotion: "Words without sense, no feeling" (*Slova bez smysla, chuvstva netu*).[88] In the writer's monologue that follows he talks about his inspiration but states that he does not write lest the mob turn its malice upon him.[89]

"Do not trust yourself," Lermontov's poetic manifesto, like "The Poet" and "Journalist, Reader, and Writer," highlights incommunicability and paints poetry in denigrating terms. It goes further than these other works in denigrating the value of the poetic word:

Que nous font après tout les vulgaires abois
De tous ces charlatans qui donnent de la voix,
Les marchands de pathos et les faiseurs d'emphase
Et tous les baladins qui dansent sur la phrase?
(A. Barbier)

Не верь, не верь себе, мечтатель молодой,
Как язвы, бойся вдохновенья . . .
Оно—тяжелый бред души твоей больной
Иль пленной мысли раздраженье.
В нем признака небес напрасно не ищи:
—То кровь кипит, то сил избыток!
Скорее жизнь свою в заботах истощи,
Разлей отравленный напиток!

Do not, do not trust yourself, young dreamer,
Fear as an ulcer your inspiration . . .
It is a heavy delirium of your sick soul
Or an irritation of your captive thought.
Do not seek in vain a sign of the heavens in it:
That is blood seething, a surplus of strength!
Drain your life sooner in concerns,
Spill the poisoned potion!

Случится ли тебе в заветный, чудный миг
Отрыть в душе, давно безмолвной,
Еще неведомый и девственный родник,
Простых и сладких звуков полный,
Не вслушивайся в них, не предавайся им,
Набрось на них покров забвенья:
Стихом размеренным и словом ледяным
Не передашь ты их значенья.

If, by chance, upon some cherished, magic hour,
You unearth in your soul, long mute,
An unknown and pristine spring,
Full of simple and sweet sounds,
Do not hearken to them, do not give yourself up to them,
Throw a cover of oblivion over them:
With your measured verse and icy word
You will not convey their meaning.

Закрадется ль печаль в тайник души твоей,
Зайдет ли страсть с грозой и вьюгой

If sadness sneaks in the inmost recesses of your soul,
If passion enters, with thunderstorm and blizzard

Не выходи тогда на шумный пир людей
С своею бешеной подругой;
Не унижай себя. Стыдися торговать
То гневом, то тоской послушной
И гной душевных ран надменно выставлять
На диво черни простодушной.

Do not come out to the people's noisy feast
With your furious friend;
Do not abase yourself. Be ashamed of trading
In wrath or in obedient grief
And of haughtily exhibiting the pus of soul's wounds
To the wonder of the simple-minded rabble!

Какое дело нам, страдал ты или нет?
На что нам знать твои волненья,
Надежды глупые первоначальных лет,
Рассудка злые сожаленья?
Взгляни: перед тобой играючи идет
Толпа дорогою привычной,
На лицах праздничных чуть виден след забот,
Слезы не встретишь неприличной.

What concern is it of ours whether you suffered or not?
Why should we know your worries,
The silly hopes of your earliest years,
Your reason's angry regrets?
Behold: in front of you the playing crowd moves
Along its customary path,
On festive faces there is hardly a trace of cares,
You will not encounter an indecorous tear.

А между тем из них едва ли есть один,
Тяжелой пыткой не измятый,
До преждевременных добравшийся морщин
Без преступленья иль утраты! . .
Поверь: для них смешон твой плач и твой укор,
С своим напевом заученным,
Как разрумяненный трагический актер,
Махающий мечом картонным . . .

And yet there is hardly a single man,
Not ravaged by a heavy torture,
Having reached premature wrinkles
Without crime or loss! . .
Believe: they are amused by your weeping
And reproach with its studied tune,
As by a rouged tragic actor
Waving a sword of cardboard . . .

Lermontov's contemporaries such as Shevyrev and Belinsky saw in this lyric an attack on "elegiac poetry of feigned sadness," a critique of the false inspiration of romantic epigones.[91] In my reading, more global issues than poetic mastery or lack of it are at stake. In the high romantic paradigm, poetic art is a divinely inspired apprehension of "the true and the beautiful," as voiced, for example, in Shelley's "A Defense of Poetry" (1821). Lermontov is the first of the poets considered here who challenges the power of the poetic word by refusing to see it as a mark of the transcendental.

The poem's epigraph, taken from Auguste Barbier's "Prologue" to *Iambs* (1832), introduces the theme of squandering the self in verbal art: "What concern is it of ours— / All the vulgar barking of all those shouting charlatans, / Merchants of pathos and makers of bombast, / And all the clowns who dance on the phrase?"

The opening of the poem subverts the theme of poetic ecstasy. Like nihilists lashing at "romantic nonsense" decades later, Lermontov explicates "sublime" sentiment in down-to-earth physical terms, denying it to be proof of the divine. Although the young dreamer is deluded into thinking he is divinely inspired, it is physiology that explains his exaltation, not "a sign of the heavens," but "blood seething, a surplus of strength."[92] Stanza 1 puts a heavy emphasis on physicality: inspiration is likened to an ulcer, it is a "heavy delirium of your sick soul," and a "poisoned potion." Not only do these lines reduce sublime sentiments to physiology, they also advance a strong claim that inspiration is a dangerous physical affliction.

There remains the traditional idea of inexpressibility, but the injunction not to hearken to inner singing (stanza 2) is new. "Do not trust yourself," like "Silentium!," mentions inner springs that sing and urges one to keep silent, but whereas Tiutchev's poem bids the reader to subsist on the soul's singing, Lermontov's work insists on ignoring "the spring, full of simple and sweet sounds." Lermontov's advice to ignore the sounds of the soul comes in direct opposition to Tiutchev's summons to keep silent but attend to the soul's melody, and makes Lermontov's critique of poetic vocation harsher than those of his predecessors.[93]

The last two lines of stanza 2 explain the call to ignore sweet sounds by necessity of deficient linguistic mediation: "With your measured verse and icy word / You will not convey their meaning." "Measured verse and icy word" recalls Batiushkov's "well-composed words" and Venevitinov's "cold word." As previously, Lermontov's attack on the word is an attack on poetry. It is not a question of poetic mastery, certainly not of the failure of elegiac effusions, which could hardly be characterized as "measured verse and icy word." Verbal mediation per se is found deficient, with icy words freezing the spring of poetry. In light of the first stanza, however, it is not only, and not so much, the impossibility of conveying these sounds, but the delusion of metaphysical ideality, promoted by the sentiments, that prompts the lyric to reject attending to inner music.

Stanza 3 presents the poetic vocation not as a sublime calling but as a denigrating experience, with all the attending dangers posed to the lyrical subject by exposing his most precious feelings for petty purposes.[94] The chief question is no longer whether or not one's experiences are communicable; the stress here falls on the call not to communicate them. It is degrading to reveal the naked self before the world, and it is doubly degrading to prostitute the self in art, trading in "wrath or obedient grief." As physically graphic as the expressions of stanza 1, the "pus of soul's wounds" highlights the indecency of bargaining one's pain. The phrase likens the poet to the pauper who exposes his mutilations to elicit sympathy. Besides, the poet does not merely violate the sanctity of his heart. More odiously, he manipulates his pliant passions to entertain his audience. "Obedient grief" suggests that the poet is not entirely authentic in his outbursts. Instead he engages in vulgar histrionics, coercing himself, as it were, to the wonder of the rabble.[95]

Stanza 4 appears to advance the notion of incommunicability in its traditional romantic guise, with the young poet's turbulent emotional life contrasted to the crowd's coldness, only to upset the reader's expectations. These lines convey the crowd's indifference toward the poet: "What concern is it of ours whether you suffered or not?" One awaits the traditional assertion that the lyrical hero's passions are so far above the rabble as to be incomprehensible to it. In a reversal of the romantic paradigm, common man is rendered, through the depth of his mute suffering, superior to the lyrical hero. The fact that he does not express his anguish does not mean that he does not experience it. Rather, he suffers no less, and perhaps more, than the poet: "And yet there is hardly a single one, / Not ravaged by a heavy torture." But, in distinction to the poet with his vociferous laments, he is silently stoic.

Although stanza 4 hints that the crowd's silence may be motivated by mere propriety, not permitting "an indecorous tear," the remaining lines of the poem emphasize its genuine suffering, challenging the earlier explication that the crowd's reticence was due to its shallowness. Lest one assume that, as opposed to the acutely feeling poet, the rabble is less sensitive to the injuries life delivers, it is described as "ravaged by a heavy torture." The rabble disregards the poet's laments not so much because it is shallow or heartless (although it may very likely be both), but chiefly because its own transgressions and losses make the poet's rhymed moans seem ridiculous. In the words of Wordsworth, "however exalted a notion we would wish to cherish of the character of a Poet, it is obvious, that, while he describes and imitates passions, his situation is altogether slavish and mechanical, compared with the freedom and power of real and substantial action and suffering."[96] The artist's "weeping and reproach, with its studied tune" pales before the real tragedy of life.

Even if the poet's grief is genuine and unexaggerated (which may not always be the case), the artifice of poetry makes it appear pretentious and fraudulent. The all-too-mellifluous sufferer looks as histrionic as "a rouged tragic actor waving a sword of cardboard." Ironically, poetic expression of pain reduces the chance of eliciting compassion from the others because its authenticity is suspect, and the poet's lack of self-restraint is easy to despise. Were the poet's grief to be fully genuine, and were articulation possible in this case, its dismissal would be unjustified.

"Do not trust yourself" does not so much reveal "Lermontov's growing tendency to identify with the crowd" as show us, like "Autumn," the mutual rupture brought about by life's hardships.[97] The crowd is not idealized, since not only are its grievances mentioned, but also its crimes.[98] The rabble remains callous and self-absorbed just as the poet is childishly naive in his hope of eliciting sympathy from the others. The rabble's only redeeming feature is its silent suffering.

The conclusion of the poem, like "Silentium!," universalizes the theme of inexpressibility and incommunicability. It liberates the theme from its attachment to the romantic lyrical subject and transfers it to the person from the crowd, thus turning the motif of a chosen being's angst into that of common human situation. Lermontov's incommunicability, like that of Baratynsky, is chiefly one of suffering. Stanza 2 may mention sweet sounds, but the rest of the poem focuses on pain. The poet promotes stoic silence as the most dignified state.

The paradox of promoting stoic silence comes to the fore again. The phrase "measured verse and icy word" aptly characterizes the lyric itself, which is written in six-foot masculine iambs alternating with four-foot feminine ones, Lermontov's signature "iron verse." As a dialogic poem, "Do not trust yourself" problematizes its message. It addresses the young poet from the point of view of a person who alternately identifies himself with the crowd (stanza 4) and disengages himself from it (stanzas 3, 5). The change in the epigraph from Barbier's *que me font* to *que nous font* is also telling. The possibility that the speaker may be one of the rabble puts into question the authority of the argument, ironizing the poem. The suspicion may arise that such a person would discourage the poet out of spite. The speaker's volatile affinities destabilize "Do not trust yourself."[99] The poem's self-destabilization is not, however, an instance of Biedermeier irony, "almost a reinforcement of the Romantic paradigm, which is now plausible to a hard-headed, realistic audience only when accompanied by a thin, deprecatory smile" or an instance of high romantic irony of consciousness free to change its scale of values.[100] As in "Silentium!," it is an act of operative irony that subverts the lyric from within. "Do not trust yourself" opens on an ellipsis, a space beyond the written lines, an alluring continuation of the argument.

Lermontov's critique of the word and of verbal art is the most radical of all those discussed so far. It anticipates Nietzsche's writings in the degree of harshness with which it calls out poetic falsehoods. The lyric is contemptuous of poetry in the face of real experience, censures it for its shameless exploitation of spiritual being and its disingenuousness, and negates its metaphysical implications. Like Zarathustra who "speaks colorfully out of fools' masks, climbs around on mendacious word bridges," Lermontov's poet is a buffoon waving his cardboard sword.

Russian romantic poetry made verbal skepticism a subject of sustained reflection. As the many varieties of inexpressibility, including but not limited to theological ineffability, eroded the authority that the ineffable once commanded, the romantic skeptical outlook toward language presented an increasingly variegated picture. Beginning with Batiushkov's and Zhukovsky's versions of idealistic inexpressibility, the topos was later enriched by the subject of the incommunicable (Venevitinov, Tiutchev), adding to the impasse of linguistic impotence the plight of human alienation. This in turn would be further complicated and reinforced through the employment of irony (Tiutchev, Lermontov). Most importantly, criticism of language and the poetic art became increasingly penetrating in correlation with an ever more skeptical view of the existential condition expressed (Tiutchev, Baratynsky, Lermontov). As the lyrical subject became more alienated (first from people, then from nature), his relationship to the poetic word became progressively more uncomfortable. It comes as no surprise, therefore, that the twentieth century would produce, in parallel with a darkening existential outlook, an even more scathing critique of language, and that death, in a catchy figuration by a critic keen on deconstructing figuration, would be termed "a displaced name for a linguistic predicament."

Chapter Two

Osip Mandelstam's Many-Voiced Silentiums

AN IMPORTANT REVIVAL of verbal skepticism came during the Silver Age of Russian poetry, and Osip Mandelstam must be singled out among other poets of the age for his explorations of this topos. The traditional view of Mandelstam trusting language in the acmeist tradition invites a polemical corrective—an analysis of his antiverbal thrust as the other side of the coin. His lyrics give play to verbal inadequacy in more attenuated variations than those of any of his peers and provide a unique treatment of the ancient motif that "pronounces another's song as one's own" (Mandel'shtam 1:103).[1]

I begin by considering how Fet and various early twentieth-century movements shaped verbal skepticism as a way to contextualize Mandelstam's work. These ambivalent examples (both criticizing language and undercutting their critique) will lead us to Mandelstam's more fundamental verbal skepticism. I examine its expression in *Stone,* a collection that contains a multitude of antiverbal lyrics. In this work verbal skepticism is manifested through the motif of word versus silence, the latter being the other pole of sound or language. Commencing with Mandelstam's "Silentium," I reconsider the lyric not merely as a reply to Tiutchev but in the larger context of the antiverbal topos. I explore the ways in which "Silentium" is embedded in *Stone*'s expansive antiverbal cluster and show that the dominant temper of the collection is represented not by the widely known idealistic "Silentium" but by the "silence-as-emptiness" poems, which are prominent and numerous in ways not usually acknowledged. I conclude the chapter with a comment on Mandelstam's later works. Mandelstam's youthful studies yielded to concrete, immediate, and harsh expressions of the world and the word that disintegrate, but the continuity of the antiverbal concern throughout his oeuvre is conspicuous.

(PRE)-MODERNIST VERBAL SKEPTICISM: FET, SYMBOLISM, AND POST-SYMBOLISM

While many key aspects of the antiverbal argument were defined in the romantic period, they have continued to concern Russian poets.[2] Afanasy Fet's "How poor our language is!—I want and I cannot—" ("Kak beden nash iazyk!—Khochu i ne mogu—," 1887), for example, takes on the problematic nature of Tiutchev's rhetorical structure. The hero yearns to convey his feelings to the other, but is unable to do this, and "The man of wisdom bends his venerable head / Before this fatal lie" (*I klonit golovu mastituiu mudrets / Pred etoi lozh'iu rokovoiu*).[3] The expression "fatal lie" echoes Tiutchev's "an uttered thought is a lie," raising the idea of verbal inadequacy and simultaneously referring to the notion that our language is poor. One must submit to an insoluble contradiction.[4] Logically, "I want and I cannot" (*Khochu i ne mogu*) (line 1) and "not to pass on to either friend or foe" (*Ne peredat' togo ni drugu, ne vragu*) (line 2) both belong in one sentence. The abrupt stop after "cannot" suggests the difficulty of articulation. The "transparent wave that storms [in the poet's] chest" (*Chto buistvuet v grudi prozrachnoiu volnoiu*) points to the turbulent yet pure character of his emotion. When pushing toward music, "the winged sound of the word" (*krylatyi slova zvuk*) becomes capable of capturing indefinable sensations. The metaphor for the poetic word—bird in flight—transforms itself into the image of "Jupiter's eagle" (*Iupitera orel*) tearing away from the mundane. Poetry "catches in flight" (*khvataet na letu*) and "fastens" (*zakrepliaet*) something ephemeral and obscure, be it a private experience or a sensory perception.

If earlier lyrics voice why language fails to adequately convey being (though Tiutchev also enacts antiverbal critique), Fet's poems dramatize his disparagement of concepts by watering down the discursive content and intensifying poetry's musical effects.[5] "Like midges at twilight" ("Kak moshki zareiu," 1844), for instance, wishes "If only without a word / The soul could speak!" (*O, esli b bez slova / Skazat'sia dushoi bylo mozhno*), and strives to enunciate fleeting fragmentary emotions through elliptical, impressionistic phrase-strokes: "Like midges at twilight, / Winged sounds crowd around" (*Kak moshki zareiu, / Krylatye zvuki tolpiatsia*). Short melodious lines (in this unusual pattern, even-numbered lines are longer than odd ones) quickly follow one another, crowding around like "winged sounds." The stanzas conjoined by "but" (*no*) emphasize the contradictory nature of the feelings as well as the poet's anxiety and the spontaneity of his output: one does not want to part with a beloved dream (stanza 1); but bygone inspiration is sad (stanza 2); but memory of the past does not go away (stanza 3). Neither beloved dream nor bygone aspiration are defined. Memory of the past is hazy and distant. The words' emotional coloring dominates over their denotative value, as is the case with "everyday thorns" (*budnichnykh ternii*) and "evening reflection" (*otblesk vechernii*). The first lines portray the subject enveloped by chaotic musical sounds; the rest of the lyric communicates this vague musicality. As Fet puts it in "Share your living dreams" ("Podelis' zhivymi snami," 1847), poetry "casts over the soul by the sound / That which you cannot express in words" (*Chto ne vyskazhesh' slovami / Zvukom na dushu navei*).[6] In Schopenhauer's terms, "Like midges at twilight" conveys feeling rather than distinct thought, an aesthetic idea that is not reducible to abstractions. The expression of intricate emotions is privileged over plot development, corresponding to Schopenhauer's notion of music, which gives not a particularized instance of emotion but emotion as such.[7]

Fet's coordination of content and form and his striving toward music prefigured the poetics of the Silver Age, and of symbolist inexpressibility especially.[8] The topos of verbal skepticism was reinvigorated at the end of the nineteenth century when symbolism established itself as the dominant poetic movement. Like romanticism, symbolism embraced the tension generated by simultaneously exalting and demeaning views of language. Both the notion of the poetic word's special powers and the opposing view of verbal impotence reemerged in a more strident key. The former reappeared as poetry's theurgist capacity to divulge the very soul of phenomena. The latter came back via the symbolists' persistent invoking of Tiutchev's famed aphorism with which they "fell in love so much during [their] Neo-Romantic epoch."[9]

In its heyday symbolism produced ardent reinterpretations of Tiutchev's "Silentium!" Vladimir Solovyev praised Tiutchev's metaphysical musings in "F. I. Tiutchev's Poetry" ("Poeziia F. I. Tiutcheva," 1895). Dmitry Merezhkovsky appealed to "Silentium!" in "On the Reasons for the Decline of, and on New Trends in, Contemporary Russian Literature" ("O prichinakh upadka i o novykh techeniiakh sovremennoi russkoi literatury," 1893) to argue for the value of silence and symbols. Viacheslav Ivanov discussed "Silentium!" in his theoretical statements, "The Poet and the Mob" ("Poet i chern'," 1904) and "The Testaments of Symbolism" ("Zavety simvolizma," 1910). According to Ivanov, the word was no longer equal to the task of expressing lyrical subjectivity because the self had grown more intricate. "The Poet and the Mob" characterizes Tiutchev as the foremost poet of silence:

> "Be silent, be secret, and hide. . ." is the new banner he raised. Moreover, Tiutchev's main feat is the feat of poetic silence. That's why we have so few of his verses, and that's why his few words are weighty and enigmatic like some mysterious portents of a spirit's great and untold music. The time has come when "an uttered thought" has become a lie.[10]

In his "Testaments of Symbolism" Ivanov asserts that Tiutchev revealed the symbolic nature of his poetry through this aphorism. Ivanov's symbolist manifesto "The Alpine Horn" ("Al'piiskii rog," 1902) echoes "an uttered thought is a lie" with its "unutteredly sweet consonance" (*neizrechenno-sladostnym sozvuch'em*).[11]

The symbolists, like the romantics, reacted against the rationalist spirit of the preceding epoch by criticizing conceptual knowledge; they underscored the uniqueness of individual feeling and questioned the power of language to capture it, and exalted music over language and lived experience over poetic artifice. Idealistic inexpressibility dominated high symbolism of the first decade of the twentieth century. Ivanov's "Silence" ("Molchanie," 1904–07) is an example of this kind of inexpressibility. This lyric portrays a mystical communion with the world's soul in Neoplatonic terms with erotic overtones. The poet and his beloved are initiated into the workings of the universe. To experience this revelation they must leave behind worldly passions, go away from "cries and clangs" (*ot etikh klikov i briatsanii*) and enter "the hiding place of rich silence" (*tainik bogatoi tishiny*). In a hesychast fashion, they achieve a state of pure contemplation, turning their "will-less impulse" (*poryv bezvol'nyi*) to the heavens. The silence that envelops them is pregnant with religious meaning, surrounding them like the walls of a cathedral: "Let us descend under the vaults of silence" (*Soidem pod svody tishiny*).[12] Like Zhukovsky's silence that "alone speaks understandably," this silence, too, has voices: "Let us open our souls to the voices / Of unuttered silence!" (*Otkroem dushi golosam / Neizrechennogo molchan'ia*).[13]

Ivanov's transcendental experience is here couched in terms of the myth of Sibyl, Apollo's prophetess at Delphi. Like Sibyl, the heroes acquire knowledge about the fates of the world, recalling Mme de Staël's assertion that "were it not for the difficulties of language, he [the poet] would, like the Sybil and the prophets, improvise the sacred hymns of genius." The cosmic imagery of "Clinging to the divine scales / At their hour of universal swinging" (*Pril'nuv k bozhestvennym vesam / V ikh chas vsemirnogo kachan'ia*) is in the tradition of the medieval inexpressibility topos. The scales, echoing the title of the most important symbolist journal (1904–09), allude both to the zodiacal sign Libra (realia) and to the fate of the world in the hands of the divine (realiora). Formally, Ivanov's lyric resembles Zhukovsky and the Old Russian weaving of words. There is the oxymoron ("voices of silence" [*golosam molchan'ia*]), the tautology ("unuttered silence" [*neizrechennogo molchan'ia*]), repetitions of "silence" (*tishiny*), "souls" (*dushi*), "heavens" (*nebesa*), and "let us commit" (*predadim*), and alliterations ("in a ray of the moon" [*v luche luny*], "Sybil with a resin candle" [*Sivilla so svechoiu smol'noi*], "let us commit our impulse" [*predadim poryv*]), and so on. Ivanov weaves an intricate verbal pattern, intertwining words, swaying back and forth, seeking to "cast over," in Fet's phraseology, what cannot be conveyed discursively.[14]

In Ivanov's view, a poem arises out of "an initial, purely sonic infection of the singer" ("On Pushkin's 'The Gypsies'" ["O 'Tsyganakh' Pushkina," 1908]) and verbal inadequacy may be overcome by drawing on music, a means that discursive reasoning cannot employ.[15] His "On the Borders of Art" ("O granitsakh iskusstva," 1912) describes how a poem emerges from a special spiritual (and musical) experience:

> Out of erotic ecstasy there emerges a mystical epiphany; out of this epiphany, a spiritual conception accompanied by a clear calm of an enriched, gladdened soul; out of this calm, a new musical stirring . . . out of this musical stirring, a poetic dream in which memories serve only as material for the contemplation of the Apollonian image that is to reflect itself in the word as a harmonious body of rhythmic creation; until finally, out of the desire, inflamed by the contemplation of this Apollonian image, there emerges the verbal flesh of a sonnet.[16]

Like the romantics, Schopenhauer, and Nietzsche, the symbolists privileged music over verbal art, developing a new poetics that aimed to turn poetry into "music." Paul Verlaine's symbolist manifesto "Poetic Art" ("L'Art Poétique," 1884) elevates the musical aspects of poetry over logos and urges other poets not to worry about the exact choice of words, but to convey the mood by hints; it extols nuance over bold strokes and scorns wit, eloquence, and rhyme. Such is real poetry, while all the rest is "merely literature." In Andrey Bely's "The Magic of Words" ("Magiia slov," 1908) poetry is "the music of the inexpressible." It creates a new world—"a world of musical meaning by means of which both enigmas of the world lying outside of oneself and the enigmas of the world one contains within the self are illuminated."[17]

As music communicates itself to everyone, the symbol is capable of transmitting what cannot be rendered conceptually. Ivanov claims in "Thoughts about Symbolism" ("Mysli o simvolizme," 1912) that a true symbolist must "betroth his silence to his [the reader's] silence" and "arouse in the heart of the listener a subtle hint or influence . . . incommunicable sensations."[18] Bely similarly posits in "The Magic of Words" that Tiutchev's aphorism applies to ordinary concept-driven speech but not to poetry. For Balmont symbolist poetry is that "in which two contents are fused organically, not forcibly: a hidden abstraction and visible beauty flow together as easily and naturally as the waters of a river are harmoniously suffused with sunlight on a summer morning."[19]

Directly related to verbal skepticism is the relation of the word to the higher symbolist realm. Ivanov's "Two Elements in Contemporary Symbolism" ("Dve stikhii v sovremennom simvolizme," 1908) states that the "right" kind of symbol is able to transmute mystical insight into an organ of collective thought on account of its suprapersonal nature:

> For idealistic symbolism, the symbol, being only a means of artistic portrayal, is but a signal that must establish communication between divided individual consciousnesses. In realistic symbolism, the symbol is of course also a beginning point linking separate consciousnesses, but their ecumenical unity is achieved through a common mystical contemplation of the objective essence that is one for all. In idealistic symbolism, the symbol is a conventional sign exchanged by the conspirators of individualism, a secret sign that expresses the solidarity of their personal self-consciousness, their subjective self-definition.[20]

For Ivanov the criterion of differentiation is present in the very notion of the symbol. Idealistic symbolism employs conventional signs which are the means of poetry to transfer subjective sentiments. Realistic symbolism involves symbols that are organic, suprapersonal, and able to capture things "the way they are." By realistic symbolism the poet conveys not subjective perceptions of objects but their essences. Clairvoyance is assumed on the part of the poet and the reader alike.

Other symbolist variations on the theme of inexpressibility have a darker coloration. Bely's deification of the living word in "The Magic of Words" takes a turn toward skepticism: "Any kind of cognition is an illusion following the word . . . If speech were not to be put in the forms of metaphor, metonymy, synecdoche, Kant's doctrine on the schematic nature of the notion of pure reason would not exist because it is neither teaching nor cognition but a verbal representation, nothing more."[21] His "Symbolism and Contemporary Russian Art" ("Simvolizm i sovremennoe russkoe iskusstvo," 1908) further states that art is incapable of transmitting the fullness of reality; it claims that verbal creation is a mere illusion of cognition, and suggests that it is possible to create arbitrary symbols that lead away from reality. Ivanov for his part in "Testaments of Symbolism" concludes that symbolism had not achieved its theurgist goals. His *Matters Native and Universal* (*Rodnoe i vselenskoe*, 1917) presents silence as "constituting the mathematical limit of gravitation toward the inner pole of the tragic."[22]

Blok's valorization of mystical ineffability gives way to a problematization of the belief in the power of symbolist poetry, and demonization of mystic visions.[23] "On the Present Status of Russian Symbolism" ("O sovremennom sostoianii russkogo simvolizma," 1910) is an illustration of Ivanov's confession in "Testaments of Symbolism" that symbolism did not succeed as theurgy. The essay commences with a mystical vision of a "radiant sword" and "Someone's radiant gaze." At this point the poet is celebrated as a possessor of secret knowledge, but the tone changes as he continues:

> The worlds that appear in the light of the radiant sword become more and more appealing; melancholic musical sounds, appeals, whispers, almost words,

already float from their depths . . . The storm has already touched the Radiant image, it is almost incarnate, i.e.—the Name has almost been guessed. Everything has been foreseen except for one thing: the dead point of triumph . . . In the violet twilight of an immense world a huge white catafalque sways, and on it lies a dead doll with a face that is vaguely reminiscent of the one that appeared through the heavenly roses . . . The person who experiences this is no longer alone; he is full of many demons . . . Their master throws them into the crucible of his artistic creativity and finally, with the help of incantations, he obtains what he is seeking—a pretty doll for his wonder and amusement.[24]

Blok may "note the steps Symbolists had followed as theurgists, from the freedom of the magical world to transformation by the real world to the creation of art," yet this passage outlines the failure of verbal creativity.[25] The "radiant sword" stands for the noumenal. The stage of communion with the divine is pre-linguistic. At this moment the "Radiant image" has nearly revealed itself, "the Name has almost been guessed." From thence onward the poet loses his touch with the higher realm. Inasmuch as it is ineffable, the divine disappears on the verge of acquiring a definite form and a name. It does not merely elude poetic expression but turns into its negation—"the devil's alloy of many worlds." Poetic creation is demonic, and "art is hell."[26] At the conclusion of his article, Blok contrasts prophecy and poetry, and, in a hesychast fashion, demands an apprenticeship, a persevering gaze, and a spiritual diet.

Post-symbolist movements betray, in a variety of ways, an analogous suspicion that ordinary language cannot fully convey life's realities, and produce numerous offspring of Tiutchev's antiverbal classic.[27] As futurist poets reject conventional language, they refer back to "Silentium!" Aleksey Kruchenykh's "New Ways of the Word" ("Novye puti slova," 1913) offers a futurist spin on Tiutchev:

"Oh, if one could express one's soul without words" (Fet). "A thought put into words is a lie" (Tiutchev). Three times true!
Why not get away from rational thought, and write not by means of word concepts, but of words freely formed?[28]

Tiutchev is here reinterpreted to promote a new poetics, the formation of arbitrary words and trans-rational language (*zaum*) as a way to overcome verbal inadequacy. "Declaration of the Word as Such" ("Deklaratsiia slova kak takovogo," 1913) elaborates on this idea. Since language ("frozen words," "word-tortures") cannot keep up with the emotion of someone in a state of inspiration, poets strive for a free language. Thus the flower lily is beautiful but the word "lily," overused and raped, is ugly. Therefore Kruchenykh proposes to call the lily "euy" to restore its primordial purity. At its limit, the rejection of existing language produces literal silence (blank space).[29]

Velimir Khlebnikov's poetic experiments search for a new kind of language in which phonetic and graphic properties of the word incarnate meaning. Khlebnikov's "Bobeobi sang the lips" ("Bobeobi pelis' guby," 1908–09), an early example of his sound writing (*zvukopis'*), tries to eliminate the conventionality of the sign by linking colors and sounds. For Khlebnikov the letter "B" corresponds to the color red, so "bobeobi sang the lips" (*bobeobi pelis' guby*), the letter "V" corresponds to the color blue, so "veeomi sang the eyes" (*veeomi pelis' vzory*), and so on.[30] His "Incantation by Laughter" ("Zakliatie smekhom," 1910) also focuses on the signifier, challenging traditional poetry with its focus on the message. The poem consists of multiple neologisms coined from the single root for "laughter" (*smekh*). Words are created arbitrarily by men, but roots are given by God; if one goes back to these roots, one is able not only to open up new meanings in language but also to influence reality. This language cannot be paraphrased; rather, it is more like a folk sorcery spell, or, as Khlebnikov himself calls it, an incantation.[31]

In accordance with the belief that, once semantics are suppressed, a language of feelings will emerge, *zaum* poetry exhibits a heightened consciousness of the signifier in its phonic and graphic properties. This may mean linguistic fragmentation all the way to phonemes, as in the following experiment by Kruchenykh: "thingbreaker / mindbreaker / speech- / breaker / let- / terbreake / r" (*veshchelom / umolom / rech- / elom / bu / kvolo / m*).[32] The poem enacts verbal breakup on multiple levels: of things, of consciousness, of words, of letters. Typically for trans-sense poetry, this lyric does not advance an antiverbal argument (as one would need to be more conceptual to argue against concepts) but plays with the word as such.

Like the symbolists and the futurists, the acmeists interrogate the capabilities of the word. Mikhail Kuzmin, who anticipates acmeism with his essay "On Beautiful Clarity" ("O prekrasnoi iasnosti," 1910), finds verbal generalities at variance with the fullness and variety of being. His "Where do I find a language to describe a walk" ("Gde slog naidu, chtob opisat' progulku," 1906), for instance, suggests that delicate particulars, "a spirit of small things, lovely and airy" (*dukh melochei, prelestnykh i vozdushnykh*) are hard to capture in words.[33]

The failure of verbal art is also the leitmotif in the oeuvre and letters of Innokenty Annensky—another precursor of the Poets' Guild (Tsekh Poetov). In a letter of May 19, 1906, Annensky notes the predicament of entrapment in the generalities of the word:

> Boredom is the consciousness that you can't escape from the squares of the verbal set, from the links of logical chains, from the insistent embraces of this

> "like everyone". . . Lord, if only to have a moment of freedom, fiery freedom, madness . . . But these squares, this ruled paper, and this terrible clock-face, marking nothing, but also forgiving nothing and no one.[34]

The prison house of language is castigated in a letter of June 25, 1906, where poetry, "with its comparative adjectives and the fetters of syllogisms as consolation," is contrasted to the passion of music. In the same letter Annensky locates the poetic in a feeling of unity between self and the world, a feeling outside verbal embodiment: "The minutes of the soul's complete identification with the external world—minutes that have no way out and fall joylessly into oblivion."[35]

Annensky's "On Contemporary Lyricism" ("O sovremennom lirizme," 1909), an article in which he discusses symbolist poetry, cautions against equating words and images:

> In poetry there is only relativity, only proximity—because it has never been other than symbolic, and cannot be otherwise. Everything rests with how imposing the image lying within us, but always outside of poetry, is. There are several forces that prevent words from breaking into superficial symbolism. The first is contained in a cult legend. Aphrodite forgets the mystical distance of her symbol Ashtoreth, and the Greek boatmen force her to rise from the Aegean foam as an already formed Greek girl, Kupris (Cyprus), the daughter of Zeus or Chronos, which one is not important. Here is an image that replaces a symbol.[36]

The essay explores the relationship between image as a concrete representation of an object and symbol as a representation of an entity by association that cannot be made clear or precise. Poetry can only be symbolic because words are its medium. Words invoke images, but the connection between the word and the image is equivocal; there is only a "glimmering" possibility of an image in words. A poem is composed of word-symbols while images lie "within us" and "outside poetry." "Superficial symbolism" then means an unproblematic equation of symbol and image.

Annensky questions the word on multiple grounds—as imprisoning man in the fetters of logic, as evading particularities, and by the image-symbol dichotomy. The word is also unable to preserve beauty or memories of the past. The epigraph to *Quiet Songs* (*Tikhie pesni,* 1904) encapsulates the impossibility of capturing beauty in poetry: "Alas! Not beauty. / Only the torment of the ideal" (*No uvy! Ne krasota. / Tol'ko muka ideala*) is spilled into songs.[37] In "The Anguish of Recollection" ("Toska pripominaniia") (from the collection *The Cypress Chest / Kiparisovyi larets* [1910]), language loses all meaning, burying one in pitch darkness: "And the forgotten lines have merged / Until dawn into murky-black spots" (*I slilis' pozabytye stroki / Do zari v mutno-chernye piatna.*)[38] In "To the Portrait" ("K portretu," 1910) Annensky formulates the defeat of a fallacious and worn-out word: "But woe to those who hear how in words / Worn-out keys sing out of tune" (*No gore tem, kto slyshit, kak v slovakh / Zaigrannye klavishi fal'shiviat*).[39]

That Tsekh Poetov goes against symbolism's preoccupation with the mystical is a staple of criticism.[40] Yet as Nikolai Gumilev criticizes symbolist mysticism in his manifesto "The Heritage of Symbolism and Acmeism" ("Nasledie simvolizma i akmeizm," 1913), he does this not because the acmeists reject the mystical but because the mystical is ineffable: "To remember always the ineffable but not to insult one's thought with more or less probable guesses—this is the principle of Acmeism."[41] Just as Gumilev's observation emphasizes epistemological limitations of language, the well-known acmeist objective to recover the primordial force of image and word (Adamism) stems from the perception that language has ossified.

Gumilev's "The Word" ("Slovo," 1921) views language as having lost its magic powers. Gumilev quotes the beginning of the Gospel of John, with its conception of Logos: "And in the Gospel of John / It is said that this word is God" (*I v Evangelii ot Ioanna / Skazano, chto Slovo eto—Bog*). The magic word of the poet-prophet used to resemble the omnipotent Word uttered at the creation of the world. It has now grown lifeless, unable, like a dead bee, to gather the honey of poetry: "And like bees in a deserted hive / Dead words smell bad" (*I kak pchely v ul'e opustelom / Durno pakhnut mertvye slova*).[42]

Like the symbolists and the futurists, the acmeists veered between an exaltation and a repudiation of the word. For the symbolists ordinary language could not convey mystical insight but symbols could. The avant-garde, by rejecting ordinary language, both represented verbal skepticism and strove to establish communication with a higher order through the development of trans-sense language (a return to logocentrism). Gumilev expressed the ancient Platonic and Christian dichotomy between the Word as divine Logos and the fallen human word. It would ultimately be Gumilev's fellow acmeist, Osip Mandelstam, who would offer a critique at once more forceful and richer than those of other Silver Age poets.[43]

SILENTIUM OF "SILENTIUM"

Mandelstam's logocentrism, in both his verses and essays, has been extensively commented upon.[44] And yet, for a certified verbal idealist Mandelstam doth protest too much. Some of his archetypal word-exalting theoretical statements turn problematic on closer examination. Thus "On the Addressee" ("O sobesednike," 1913), an essay about the providential future interlocutor, considers the problem of communication with the reader in posterity through the metaphor of a bottle tossed by a seafarer to the mercy of the waves. What makes this metaphor so charged is the seafarer's (poet's) precarious situation: the bottle-poem contains an SOS in the face of imminent shipwreck.[45] Even "On the Nature of the Word" ("O prirode slova," 1922), a celebrated eulogy of Russian nominalism, is informed by a post-Saussurean consciousness of the split between signifier and signified, though reimagined in a positive vein and peculiarly combined with Potebnia's ideas on the inner form of the word.[46] This same essay echoes "On the Addressee," featuring the passage about "the fragile barque of the human word, carried into the open sea of the future which lacks sympathetic understanding and where tedious commentary replaces the fresh breeze of contemporary hostility and sympathy" (Mandel'shtam 1:230). As late as his "Conversation About Dante" ("Razgovor o Dante," 1933), Mandelstam restates a dichotomy that emerges in his early poetry, between a poetic utterance and the "absolutely mute" pre-verbal poetic impulse without which the former would be amenable to paraphrase, a sure sign of the absence of poetry.

Nor are his logocentric poems, aesthetic gems shot through with conceptual contradictions, exempt from skepticism. Some of his better-known works, such as "The Slate Ode" ("Grifel'naia oda," 1923) or "January 1st, 1924" ("1 ianvaria 1924"), present an attenuated interplay of logocentrism and logophobia.[47] To provide another example, "And still on Mount Athos" ("I ponyne na Afone," 1915) convincingly reads as an endorsement of the name-worshipping (*imiaslavie*) movement since it embraces the "beautiful heresy" of *imiaslavie* but also posits that, together with the name, we kill unnamed love.[48] These instances suggest that even, and perhaps especially, the most logocentric positions cannot but call up their opposites. Mandelstam's work represents the competing tugs of word exaltation and verbal critique, and I argue that verbal skepticism is a more fundamental aspect of his poetics than is usually assumed.[49]

The centrality of the word-and-silence theme in Mandelstam is evident from his early work to the lyrics of the 1930s. The theme of silence is prominent in Mandelstam's early poetry, and in the collection *Stone* (*Kamen'*, 1913) in particular.[50] "Silentium" (1910), the second poem in the first edition of *Stone* (1913), is traditionally regarded as Mandelstam's key rendition of verbal skepticism:

Она еще не родилась,	She has not yet been born,
Она и музыка и слово,	She is both music and the word,
И потому всего	And therefore the indestructible
живого	connection
Ненарушаемая связь.	Of everything living.

Спокойно дышат моря груди,
Но, как безумный, светел день,
И пены бледная сирень
В черно-лазоревом сосуде.

The sea's breasts breathe calmly,
But, like a madman, the day is bright.
And pale lilac foam
Is in the black-azure vessel.

Да обретут мои уста
Первоначальную немоту,
Как кристаллическую ноту,
Что от рождения чиста!

May my lips find
Primary muteness,
Like a crystalline note
That is pure from birth!

Останься пеной, Афродита,
И слово в музыку вернись,
И сердце сердца устыдись,
С первоосновой жизни слито!

Remain foam, Aphrodite,
And word, return to music,
And heart grow ashamed of heart,
Merged with the fundamental principle
of life!

(Mandel'shtam 1:50–51)

Easily the most renowned Silver Age continuation of the Russian romantics' exploration of verbal inadequacy, this lyric proclaims Tiutchev's "Silentium!" as its principal subtext. Mandelstam's poem has been habitually linked to Tiutchev's, either as a restatement of Tiutchev's themes or as a polemic. According to Dmitry Segal, both Tiutchev and Mandelstam assert the value of silence, but Mandelstam "actually talks not about silence but about the soul's return to the world before its birth."[51] For Victor Terras Mandelstam's poem "does not challenge Tiutchev's position," though it "suggests that the acoustic—or musical form of the word is valuable and meaningful."[52] Mikhail Gasparov reads "Silentium" as a Verlaine-like response to Tiutchev—a denial of words, a return to pre-linguistic music.[53] Kirill Taranovsky sees the poem as a polemic with Tiutchev that emphasizes the uselessness of poetry as opposed to its impossibility.[54] Clare Cavanagh argues that Mandelstam exceeds both Tiutchev and the symbolists in his appeal: "word, return to music."[55] According to Mikhail Epstein, "for Tiutchev, as later for Mandelstam, silence is a break through a verbal, cultural shroud that envelops the speaking animal, a birth into a higher, mysterious world where the human meets the divine and falls silent."[56] In Lada Panova's view, Mandelstam's silence responds to Tiutchev's, but is different as a programmatic poem about pre-time.[57] John Malmstad, on the other hand, observes that "the exclusive concern with Tiutchev has . . . obscured the no less profound influence of Ivanov" and provides an analysis of Mandelstam-Ivanov connections.[58]

To do justice to Mandelstam's poem, one needs to consider it not merely as a Tiutchevian venture, whether straightforward or polemical, but in the broader context of the antiverbal topos. Mandelstam "rarely gave titles to his poems, and 'Silentium' was the first to which he did so."[59] Mandelstam clearly wished to highlight his Tiutchevian subtext, yet his poem departs from Tiutchev's to a considerable extent. "Silentium!" is employed as a generic marker of verbal inadequacy, its renown contextualizing Mandelstam's own rendition of the topos. Aspects of the poem that have been regarded as Mandelstam's polemic with Tiutchev in fact draw on other conceptions of verbal inadequacy within the tradition.

The ambiguities of "Silentium" are noteworthy. An attempt to disentangle Mandelstam's imagery in a precise pattern is not always entirely productive. For instance, the "she" (*ona*) of the first quatrain is not identified until stanza 4.[60] This "she," referring, in my view, to Aphrodite, has been taken to refer to "silence."[61] As much ambivalence pertains to other words and images in the poem ("like a madman, the day is bright"; "black-azure vessel," etc.). While any serious literary text generates multiple, often contradictory, interpretations, this poem reaches toward semantic multiplicity to a greater extent than most of the works previously discussed. Not every "word as such" could constitute the "monstrously condensed reality" Mandelstam envisions (Mandel'shtam 1:177), but his own creations certainly do. This happens not only because Mandelstam, as Yuri Levin suggests, is "more overbookish and over-cultured than any other poet of the twentieth century" but also because he picks bits and pieces of philosophical notions and literary allusions and interweaves them with his own sensory perceptions, feelings, and memories through idiosyncratic associative leaps.[62] The semantic line that elaborates on global themes "closely merges with the semantic lines that interpret a concrete-sensory condition of the world . . . and a concrete-sensory condition of man."[63] The conceptual line and the concrete-sensory line interweave. Besides, both are modified by "the word as such," which Mandelstam taps to the fullest, and which to a large degree directs him in creation. The result is a kaleidoscope of imagery ("the sea's breasts," "pale lilac foam," "the black-azure vessel," "a crystalline note"), peculiar associations ("like a madman, the day is bright"), overflowing subtext, and phonic play, all of which produces a different pattern every time it is shaken.[64]

The poem's debt to symbolist poetics is apparent enough.[65] Like the romantics and the symbolists, Mandelstam links the theme of inexpressibility to that of music: "She has not yet been born, / She is both music and the word." He distrusts the verbal medium and venerates singing nature: "And word, return to music."[66] The third stanza urges one to go mute, and equates music and silence in the traditional inexpressibility paradox: "May my lips find / Primary muteness, / Like a crystalline note / That is pure from birth!" As in Zhukovsky's poem, Mandelstam's silence "speaks understandably." Like Shelley in "To a Sky-lark" ("Or how could thy notes flow in such a crystal stream?"), Mandelstam emphasizes the purity of the ineffable: his sounding silence is "crystalline" (*kristallicheskaia*), that is, crystal clear.[67] This paradoxical sounding silence is the necessary condition for intimating the transcendental. The fourth stanza links silence to modesty, and the word—in a Lermontovian or Tiutchevian way—to shamelessness: "And heart grow ashamed of heart." It is advisable to keep chaste, that is, silent.

"Silentium" stands apart from numerous twentieth-century works, including Mandelstam's own, in which an antiverbal sentiment becomes a corollary of ontological skepticism. The urge to merge with the kernel of being goes against Tiutchev's striving for total self-enclosure, and instead replicates the idealistic ineffability of losing the self in the absolute observed in Batiushkov, Zhukovsky, and Ivanov, as well as in a host of philosophers and theologians from Neoplatonists onward. The poem's setting (the sea) reminds one of Batiushkov's "harmony in a talk of billows." "Merged" (*slito*) evokes Zhukovsky's "but what is merged with this radiant beauty." Like Ivanov's "Silence" and other symbolist poems, "Silentium" returns to Batiushkov and Zhukovsky's initial sanguine conception of inexpressibility. However, where those two poets try to convey their discernment of transcendental ineffability, Mandelstam expresses longing for the primeval state in which such discernment is possible: "May my lips find primary muteness"; "word, return to music."

Mandelstam's mythological referent is Aphrodite's birth from sea foam. In Hesiod's description of Aphrodite's birth in *Theogony,* the goddess is born following Uranus's castration by his son Chronos. Uranus, Heaven, refuses to allow his children to emerge into the light, as he perpetually embraces the Earth, his wife Gaia. Chronos castrates him, throws his genitals into the sea, and a maiden emerges from the foam spreading around Uranus's genitals. Aphrodite's birth marks the creation of the world and the beginning of time. She is born of an act that separated Heaven and Earth.

Botticelli's *Birth of Venus* (1482), the image of Aphrodite being wafted over the sea on a seashell, is Mandelstam's painterly subtext.[68] Ecstatic mystical experience is often likened to the ecstasy of love. Botticelli's pictures of Venus, as well as paintings of her by other Renaissance artists, for example, Titian's *Sacred and Profane Love* (1513–14), are interpreted as Neoplatonic statements on the noumenal, as well as ideal versus sensual love.[69] This is likely why Mandelstam relates mystical experience as the myth of Aphrodite's birth. Botticelli's painting, a visualization of Homer's *Hymn to Venus,* has the goddess blown to the shore on a seashell and showered with roses. On reaching shore she will be clothed by the Hours—a significant detail given Mandelstam's portrayal of entrance into time when one is "formed" and the magical feeling of suspended temporality prior to creation.

It is this same myth of Aphrodite's birth that Annensky alludes to in "On Contemporary Lyricism" published in *Apollo* (*Apollon*) not long before "Silentium" was composed. Cyprus, "an already-formed Greek girl," relates to Ashtoreth as an image outside poetry to the word-symbol within it. The legend "prevents words from breaking into superficial symbolism" (the equation of symbol and image) by highlighting the difference between Ashtoreth and Cyprus or Aphrodite. Mandelstam must have been acquainted with the article and kept in mind Annensky's distinction between Aphrodite and Ashtoreth. Both poets work from the myth of Aphrodite's emergence, but where Annensky explores the link between words and the imagery they invoke, Mandelstam imagines the link between pre-creation and the poem. In "Silentium" the rising of Aphrodite from foam marks the transformation of symbol into image, pronoun into noun, the ineffable conception in the poet's soul into the body of the poem. So long as Aphrodite remains a "symbol" (Greek "to join together"), she represents "the indestructible connection / Of everything living."

The sea conveys nature's (and poetry's) musical element. As Ivanov reexamines the symbolist privileging of music in "On the Problem of the Sound-Image in Pushkin" ("K probleme zvukoobraza u Pushkina," 1930), he couches his musings in terms of seaside imagery:

> The romantics and early symbolists loved this stage of flowing and unstable [*tekuchikh i zyblemykh*] images glimmering indefinitely in the surf of sounds [*priboe zvukov*] because it captured something of the initial unconscious impulse in which they saw the sign of genuine "inspiration."[70]

The sea is an old figure of the poetic self, and a metaphor of language and inspiration, as, for instance, in T. S. Eliot's "Choruses from the Rock" (1934), a poem that resonates with Mandelstam:

> Out of the sea of sound the life of music,
> Out of the slimy mud of words, out of the sleet and hail of
> verbal imprecisions,
> Approximate thoughts and feelings, words that have taken
> the place of thoughts and feelings,
> There spring the perfect order of speech, and the beauty
> of incantation.[71]

This is a place where the first living forms arose, therefore it is the "fundamental principle of life" and mother of all living whose "breasts breathe calmly." In Wallace Stevens's "The Idea of Order at Key West" (1934), the words of the sea are "words of the fragrant portals, dimly starred, and of ourselves and of our origins."[72] The sea also embodies chaos, which in Stevens's poem tempts the singer to order it "in ghostlier demarcations, keener sounds" or conversely, as in Batiushkov, an interplay between chaos and cosmos.

In Vladimir Solovyev's "Beauty in Nature" ("Krasota v prirode," 1889) the sea represents a dialectic of chaos and cosmos that reveals unity at the heart of things:

> Life in its most general sense is the free play or movement of particular forces and positions united in an individual whole . . . The aesthetic significance of this living movement is enhanced by its boundlessness, which seems as it were to express the insatiable longing of finite beings separated from the absolute all-inclusive unity. And the boundless sea itself acquires a new beauty in its stormy motion as the symbol of . . . the gigantic struggle of elemental forces which cannot break the universal connectedness of the cosmos or destroy its unity, and only fill it with movement, brilliance and thunder.[73]

As in "The Meaning of Art" and elsewhere, Solovyev argues for the total unity of mankind, nature, and God. Beauty, as the material embodiment of the idea of total unity, is seen best in those aspects of nature that highlight the movement of discordant elements and simultaneously stress their concord. That is what one beholds in the sea, full of rebellious motion but unable to destroy the cosmic whole, and tempting one to lose the self in this "all-inclusive unity." Therefore it is in the "calmly breathing" sea that Mandelstam observes the "indestructible connection / Of everything living" and dreams of his heart "merged with the fundamental principle of life." Solovyev also views chaos as the necessary background of earthly beauty and contrasts it to the architectonic principle of the universe, which "kindles the flame of life in matter from within."[74] This opposition resembles the opposition between Chaos and Eros informing "Silentium." Aphrodite as Eros is an architectonic principle of the universe, which moves the sea in Mandelstam, just as it moves the sun and the other stars in Dante.[75]

For Mandelstam, Aphrodite, more than the goddess of love, designates an ineffable all-unity and a non-material principle of origination. "Silentium" focuses on the moment before Aphrodite has emerged from the foam of the Aegean. She must remain foam because, as Eros—that is, as the ineffable Absolute—she cannot be incarnated in the finite form of the goddess lest its intangible essence be misrepresented. Like Shelley's invisible bird, the emblem of pure spirit, Aphrodite as Eros must remain "unbodied." As an incorporeal spirit it exists out of time and space and can be anything, whereas Aphrodite the divinity of the Greek pantheon is more of a "finite" being. Eros, the all-inclusive unity beyond words and images, must not arise as the anthropomorphic goddess.

Aphrodite means "born of sea-foam." Several poems of the same period, like "Silentium," are set by the sea and have "foam" (*pena*) as their key image.[76] "I see a stony sky" ("Ia vizhu kamennoe nebo," 1910) links the absence of foam (Aphrodite as sheer potentiality) and the absence of meaning in the world, thus presenting Aphrodite-Eros as the key spiritual principle of the universe: "I understand this horror / And comprehend this connection: / And the sky falls without collapsing, / And the sea splashes without foam" (*Ia ponimaiu etot uzhas / I postigaiu etu sviaz': / I nebo padaet, ne rushas', / I more pleshchet, ne penias'*) (Mandel'shtam 1:55). The "connection" is between petrifaction in nature ("a stony sky over a dim web of waters" [*kamennoe nebo nad tuskloi pautinoi vod*]) and death as represented by "the clutches of the odious Erebus" (*v tiskakh postylogo Ereba*) associated with Hades. Erebus, the son of Chaos, opposes Aphrodite as Eros. That the sea "splashes without foam" means that there can be no Aphrodite arising. As in Stevens's "The Idea of Order at Key West" ("the meaningless plungings of water and the wind"), nature is devoid of meaning.[77] The horror perceived by the lyrical persona is that of metaphysical emptiness.

Foam is also the salient image in "Where glass breaks away from captivity" ("Gde vyryvaetsia iz plena," 1910), a poem placed right after "Silentium" in *Stone.* Again it represents a concord of elements but also transience.[78] The lyric likens foam to a bird's wing: "Curling foam sets / Like a swan's wing" (*Klubiashchaiasia stynet pena, / Kak lebedinoe krylo*) (Mandel'shtam 1:50). Like the foam in "Silentium" that hides Aphrodite, the foam in "Where glass breaks away from captivity" contains the potential of form and is presented in the process of acquiring it. The lyric appeals to time, asking "not to torture with envy / One who has congealed at the right moment," whom "chance has raised up like foam / And joined like lace" (*O, vremia, zavist'iu ne muchai / Togo, kto vovremia zastyl / Nas penoiu vozdvignul sluchai / I kruzhevom soedinil*) (Mandel'shtam 1:50). The appeal to time reverberates with "Silentium"s' yearning for Aphrodite's preexistence as a supratemporal boundless potential. When one arises as foam from eternity, one becomes a finite being subject to time—and therefore one must envy it.

Foam and sea recur in "The Seashell" ("Rakovina," 1911), a poem that, juxtaposed to "Silentium," reinforces a reading of the latter as an allegory of poetic creation.[79] It likens the author to a seashell being filled with "the whispers of foam, / Mist, wind, and rain" (*shepotami peny, / Tumanom, vetrom i dozhdem* [Mandel'shtam 1:68]). As in Fet's "How poor our language is!" inspiration storms with a transparent wave within the poet. Aphrodite—the poem will arise from the seashell, which is filled with foam, and which is the poet's soul.

The moment before the birth of a poem is the most precious.[80] As Mandelstam makes explicit in "There are orioles in the woods and the length of vowels" (*Est' ivolgi v lesakh i glasnykh dolgota*) ("The Equinox" [Ravnodenstvie"], 1914), this is when the poet overflows with life and feels the bonds of time fall away, when the day "yawns like a caesura" (*kak by tsezuroiu ziiaet*), and there is "golden idleness / To extract the richness of a whole note from a reed" (*zolotaia len' / Iz trostnika izvlech' bogatstvo tseloi noty*) (Mandel'shtam 1:103). The state in which one attends to the music of nature but had not yet translated it into the realized actuality of a poem is one of stopped time.[81] A sense of magical unity with the world accompanies this pre-verbal state. These are Annensky's "minutes of the soul's complete identification with the external world—minutes that have no way out and fall joylessly into oblivion."

The moment prior to creation is one when the poem is already alive, though no words have as yet been put together, as in the following passage from Victor Shklovsky's "Poetics" ("Poetika," 1919):

> There is no word that designates inner sound-speech, and when one wants to talk about it, the word "music" offers itself as a designation of certain sounds that are not words; in this case there are still no words since they in the end flow out wordlike. Among contemporary poets O. Mandelstam wrote about this: "Remain foam, Aphrodite, and word, return to music."[82]

Mandelstam's own "Word and Culture" ("Slovo i kul'tura," 1921) describes the same phenomenon:

> Write image-less poems, if you can, if you manage . . . A poem is alive because of its inner image, because of that sounding mold of form that anticipates the written work. There is not a single word yet, but the poem already sounds. What sounds is its inner image, which is perceived by the poet's ear. (Mandel'shtam 1:215)

This passage has been read as inspired by Potebnia's notion of the word as distinguished by its outer form (sound), its content, and its inner form (the means by which the content is expressed).[83] For Potebnia the essence of language is not speech but the mental activity preceding it. In this instance, Potebnia discusses the inner form of the word (its etymological meaning) as the basis of poetry, while Mandelstam talks about the inner image, the sounding mold of form that exists prior to the writing down of a single word. Another way to read the passage, I would concur with Mikhail Gasparov, is that it presents the word in which "the sound speaks to consciousness," "carrying out an old appeal, 'word, return to music.'"[84] This echoes Mme de Staël's observation that a true poet "conceives his whole poem at once in his soul." "Silentium" then celebrates the state before a single word has been written but the poem already sounds. The poem is imageless in the sense that Aphrodite is not yet incarnated. The moment prior to verbalization is sheer music, or spirit ("unbodied" Aphrodite), while the actual poem is language, or form ("embodied" Aphrodite).

Nadezhda Mandelstam's recollection of the way her husband composed verse conveys this notion of poetry's preexistence, and its emergence from music:

> At some moment words suddenly showed through the musical phrase, and then the lips started moving . . . I had an impression that all the process of creation consists of a strained capture and manifestation of the harmonic and semantic unity that is already existing, and is being transmitted from an unknown place, which is gradually being embodied in words.[85]

Transition from a pre-creative state to a state of verbalization is explored elsewhere in the literature of the age, as, for example, in Ivanov's "On the Borders of Art" and Blok's "On the Present Status of Russian Symbolism." If Ivanov's portrayal of the emergence of a poem is optimistic (erotic passion transforms itself into a spiritual conception; spiritual conception gives rise to music; out of music materializes the poem), Blok contrasts the ecstatic condition bordering on creation and the fallen state of actual verbalization. The emergence of language marks the point when the sublime vision starts to disintegrate. In "Silentium" love gives rise to music, and the intimation of all-inclusive unity is to be materialized in verbal flesh, that is, an incorporeal principle of love comes to light as the embodied Aphrodite—the poem. Mandelstam wants to prolong the moment when the poem is intimated but its music has not yet been transcribed. Like Ivanov, Mandelstam describes the birth of a poem in erotic terms, but like Blok he states the impossibility of translating such mystical experience into language.

According to Schopenhauer, music relates to the word as spirit (Mandelstam's unbodied Eros) to form (Aphrodite after her birth), and the ideas are apprehended through pure perception, which demands a loss of the self.[86] If one needs silence to merge "with the fundamental principle of life," the acquisition of consciousness, the separation from the cosmos, and the emergence of speech are concurrent and codependent states. In "Silentium" Aphrodite as a poem-in-waiting is music and language, a harmony preexisting in nature that awaits its articulation in the poem. The condition prior to creation is the primordial state where music equals words. But the first stanza of "Silentium" does not merely say that the goddess is "music and the word, / And the indestructible connection of everything living," but says that Aphrodite is "both music and the word, / And therefore the indestructible connection of everything living." If signifier, music as the word's euphonic properties, and signified, the word as logos, are organically connected (a problem which also preoccupied Ivanov) or if the means of communication are, in Lotman's terms, symbolic, the divine is present in the world.

Water (*voda*) contains the affirmation of harmony—"yes" (*da*), a pun that surfaces in Mandelstam's late poem "The blue island is great by its potters" ("Goncharami velik ostrov sinii," 1937). This poem develops the ideas of "Silentium" by imagining a primordial Cretan culture in which existence is musical, and language bears no evidence of humans' separation from the all-inclusive unity: "This was and was sung" (*Eto bylo i pelos'*); "Before food and drink / Were called 'mine'" (*Do togo, kak edu i pit'e / Nazyvali 'moia' i 'moe'*) (Mandel'shtam 3:133). Water, Solovyev's paradigmatic embodiment of discord versus unity, here says "yes" (*I voda, govoriashchaia 'da'*), a part of its signifier (music), and this "yes" (its logos) is a testimony of concord, though nostalgically tinged, between humans and nature. For Mandelstam the punning line is a manifestation of linguistic non-arbitrariness, and therefore of harmony in the world. The verbal argument again functions as an ontological argument.

Verbal iconicity means one's connection to others and to the cosmos. Restated in terms of Potebnia's theory of language (*Thought and Language* [*Mysl' i iazyk*, 1862]), Mandelstam's poetic etymology envisions the inner form of *voda* as containing *da*. Some years after "Silentium" was composed, Pavel Florensky also employed etymological disquisitions to demonstrate the iconic embodiment of signified in signifier. His "The Term" ("Termin," 1917) engages Potebnia (and Humboldt), claiming the word's organic connection to the referent and, therefore, its ability to merge the individual self with the collective: "Through the word I leave the boundaries of my limitedness and fuse with the historically expressed will of the people that has collectively manifested itself by forming this particular sememe of the word."[87] This replicates "water saying 'yes,'" but in Mandelstam verbal iconicity and, consequently, all-unity is a utopia of the past.

"Silentium" presents the rapport of external reality and the self as more of a wish than an actual state but nevertheless departs from its Tiutchevian near-namesake in that it is more akin to idealistic treatments of inexpressibility. "Remain foam, Aphrodite" asks that the bond between sound and logos as secured in the unborn Aphrodite be preserved; "And word, return to music" calls for the submersion of logos in sound. Mandelstam pushes to the limit Verlaine's preference for "music above all else," not merely striving to set music above all arts or longing for verbal iconicity but dreaming of recovering a time when the word, with its unity of logos and sound, did not yet exist, when there was nothing but music.

The poem also departs from Tiutchev's by dispensing with the exclamation mark in the title. Even though Mandelstam's lyric does include imperatives, where Tiutchev's poem is primarily prescriptive, Mandelstam's is primarily descriptive. Tiutchev gives a didactically formulated order to the hypothetical "you"; Mandelstam directs the order at himself and tries to convey the feelings and perceptions that arise around "silentium." Like Fet and the symbolists, Mandelstam does not explicitly articulate a doctrine of inexpressibility but tries to "cast over" what cannot be formulated overtly. By rejecting the construction of a narrative or an argument, this poetics of hint enacts an anti-conceptual critique.

"Silentium" suggests a great deal but asserts very little. This highly polysemic little lyric manages to hint at, rather than explicitly articulate, a host of verbal inadequacy motifs. Yet one manages, to use Lossky's distinction, to "apprehend without cognizing" what the poet says. The poem is elastic in the sense that it can be interpreted in light of divergent philosophical and literary views, but the "feeling" it conveys (Schopenhauer's "aesthetic idea") is stable.

OTHER SHADES OF SILENCE

Like romantic and symbolist poems, "Silentium" desires that the word return to music because language cannot be equal either to the melodiousness of the soul or to universal harmony. The verbal reduction the poem represents, in comparison with its pre-created state, is balanced by a sense of cosmic harmony between nature and man even though this harmony is a utopia of the past. This is, however, only one version of the verbal skepticism present in *Stone.* The collection's inexpressibility ranges from divine to deathly—and everything in between. The young Mandelstam seems to have treated the topos as something of a poetic exercise, and his practicing transpositions on a single theme appears akin to a singer's warm-up, a means of developing artistic virtuosity. Yet the poems are not solely improvisation. Though Mandelstam turns out to be no less a devotee of romantic irony than Tiutchev, his work makes it clear that if romantic irony is to mean anything, it must be more than an exercise in contradiction for contradiction's sake —an acknowledgment that some contradictions cannot be resolved. Mandelstam's "silentiums" cover a wide spectrum of ontological underpinnings, but the more negative poems are prominent. The "bond" with the world Mandelstam often portrays is not a Solovyev-like unity-of-all-living-things but an all-encompassing tie of meaninglessness.

"A sound cautious and muted" ("Zvuk ostorozhnyi i glukhoi," 1908), the poem that opens the second edition of *Stone: The First Book of Poems* (*Kamen': pervaia kniga stikhov,* 1916), imagines the interaction between the poet and the world as an utterance in the face of universal silence:

Звук осторожный и глухой	A sound cautious and muted
Плода, сорвавшегося с древа,	Of a fruit broken loose from a tree
Среди немолчного напева	Amidst the never-ceasing tune
Глубокой тишины лесной . . .	Of the forest's deep silence. . .
(Mandel'shtam 1:34)	

This poem, like "Silentium," assumes the emergence of self and speech to be concurrent. As Marina Tsvetaeva has noted, it enacts its contents:

the stanza is the fruit broken loose from the tree.[88] Before it breaks loose, its condition is pre-linguistic and preconscious. Next it acquires identity and voice, and produces a brief, timid sound that dissolves into silence. The sound-stanza is "cautious," for it hesitates to interrupt nature's eternal silent music. The sound's cautiousness and muteness, as well as its transitoriness (hence the lyric's tiny size), are contrasted to nature's powerful singing quiet. The very brevity of the poem that ends on an ellipsis, "an unfinished sentence without a predicate," makes palpable the silence that surrounds it.[89]

This lyric evokes the old romantic and symbolist juxtaposition of human speech and nature's silent music. More precisely, it is like Baratynsky's music of the spheres, for Mandelstam's singing quiet bears no positive connotation. Silence is metaphysically neutral, or even slightly negative in the sense that it is opposed to the sound of the falling fruit. The modifier "mute(d)" (*glukhoi*) is Mandelstam's word-signal for existential alienation and incommunicability. It occurs again and again in his oeuvre, likely having captured his imagination for its onomatopoeic quality.[90] The muted sound of the fruit works allegorically as a result of the interaction between the self and its poetic expression and the world; it is a feeble echo that responds to the poet's speech. Since a fruit falls to the ground at the highest point of ripeness, and, if not picked up, rots or withers afterward, its mute fall signifies something like the movement of Baratynsky's star that does not strike "the ear of the world." This is not merely a poem that may decompose unheard. This is the self that may disappear unnoticed, "vanish like a nameless stone" (*bezymiannym kamnem kanut'*), as Mandelstam puts it in another early poem (Mandel'shtam 1:54).

"There are chaste charms" ("Est' tselomudrennye chary," 1909) elaborates on the opposition between the muted self and the silent world, substituting the forest's transcendental quiet with the silence of words of the past. The art of the past, moreover, is miniaturized and fragmented:

Есть целомудренные чары— Высокий лад, глубокий мир, Далеко от эфирных лир Мной установленные лары.	There are chaste charms— High concord, deep peace, Far from ethereal lyres Are the Lares placed by me.
У тщательно обмытых ниш В часы внимательных закатов Я слушаю моих пенатов Всегда восторженную тишь.	By carefully washed niches At the hours of attentive sunsets I listen to my Penates' Always rapturous quiet.
Какой игрушечный удел, Какие робкие законы	What a toy lot, What timid laws

Приказывает торс точеный	Are commanded by the chiseled torso
И холод этих хрупких тел!	And the cold of these frail bodies!
Иных богов не надо славить:	There is no need to praise some gods:
Они как равные с тобой,	They are like equals to you,
И, осторожною рукой,	And, with a cautious hand,
Позволено их переставить.	It is permitted to rearrange them.
(Mandel'shtam 1:35–36)	

The poem contrasts grand universal music, ethereal lyres, and art's diminutiveness, the hero's "Lares." The hero purposefully separates himself from the music of the spheres, creating a miniature realm of his own. The poet's mediation is always demure: the "cautious" rearrangement of domestic gods echoes "A sound cautious and muted." Here art is a miniaturization of life, and turning life into an aesthetic phenomenon provides shelter from the larger world (Penates), but it also means assuming self-conscious artificiality. As opposed to the relentless laws of reality, the laws of this artificial realm are "timid."[91] These tentative laws are summoned forth by poetic gods of the past. "Mandelstam's gods are silent," and, as the "chiseled torso" suggests, are preserved only in parts.[92]

The theme of one's relation to precursors (Penates stand for Mandelstam's poetic ancestors) becomes a facet of the antiverbal topos when prior articulations silence the poet.[93] Victor Terras, evidently keeping in mind Mandelstam's later ideal of domesticity, and of philology as family, interpreted the poem as expressing "an early acmeist theme, that of the individuality, value and sanctity of things—even domestic utensils."[94] For Dmitry Segal, likewise, the poet's creative power is "tender, quiet, attentive," hence he compares poetic images to household gods.[95] Yet the "chiseled torso," the "cold of these frail bodies," and their careful arrangement all have a museum-like quality. "Niches" refer to the places for Penates, but they also evoke a museum display. The worship of art as an assembly of little domestic idols is colored by a consciousness of the idols' precariousness. The word of the past is mute, cold, and fragmented. Not exactly a graveyard of art, Mandelstam's minuscule principality is art's *nature morte,* betraying an inert quality, if in a less ominous form. Like Keats's "Ode on a Grecian Urn," "There are chaste charms" conveys a cold and immobile beauty that is inscrutable and "dost tease us out of thought." Art is a "still unravish'd bride of quietness" but also a plaything.[96]

While "There are chaste charms" preserves a tension between the poetic word's beauty and safety, and its miniaturization and fragmentation, "Why is the soul so melodious" ("Otchego dusha tak pevucha," 1911), in a thread of increasing ontological skepticism and increasing doubt about the word, shows it to be artificial, ephemeral, and illusory. Poetry fails to convey inner music and gives a mere illusion of fusion with the universe:

Отчего душа так певуча
И так мало милых имен,
И мгновенный ритм—только случай,
Нсожиданный Аквилон?

Он подымет облако пыли,
зашумит бумажной листвой
И совсем не вернется—или
Он вернется совсем другой.

О, широкий ветер Орфея,
Ты уйдешь в морские края, —
И несозданный мир лелея,
Я забыл ненужное "я."

Я блуждал в игрушечной чаще
И открыл лазоревый грот . . .
Неужели я настоящий
И действительно смерть придет?
(Mandel'shtam 1:68)

Why is the soul so melodious
And why are there so few sweet names,
And why is a momentary rhythm but an accident,
Unexpected Aquilon?

It will raise a cloud of dust,
Will rustle with paper leaves,
And will never return—or
It will return completely different.

Oh, wide wind of Orpheus,
You will depart for the seashore—
And, cherishing the uncreated world,
I forgot the unnecessary "I."

I wandered in a toy thicket
And discovered an azure grotto . . .
Can it be that I am real
And death will really come?

The first quatrain recalls Tiutchev's, Lermontov's, and Fet's singing of the soul, as well as Stephane Mallarmé's soul as a melody from "Crisis of Verse ("Crise de vers," 1896). As in "Silentium," this inner music cannot be conveyed in language: There are "so few sweet names." Poetry is contingent and transitory: rhythm is "but an accident," a gust of wind from the north. As "paper leaves" show, this is one of *Stone*'s numerous poems of reverse mimesis, perception of nature as artifice.[97] Mandelstam's "Aquilon" invokes Pushkin's "Aquilon" ("Akvilon," 1824), in which the wind breaks a majestic oak tree, but in Mandelstam, Orpheus's wind, the wind of poetry, does not reveal the mysteries of the universe, nor does it wrench trees out of the ground but merely raises a cloud of dust. Inspiration may leave one at any moment, or else "return completely different," that is, in the form that betrays the poet's initial conception.[98] The hero again relishes his "uncreated world." Engrossed in it, he forgets himself ("the unnecessary 'I' ").

This poem has been read as contrasting the symbolists' individualism with the acmeists' love of existence, reflecting "the Acmeists' belief that human existence precedes the 'I.' "[99] It has also been interpreted as asserting the hero's power to suppress the self and thus to intimate the mysteries of the cosmos, "the Orphic idea of the 'I' being a hindrance to the attainment of a true reality."[100] However, given the lyric's manifest skepticism as to the potency of poetic creativity, I see stanza 3 as conceptualizing creativity as a Schopenhauerian retreat from reality and respite from the will. The dissolution of the self in artistic reverie minimizes the pain of living and the horror of death.[101] The concluding stanza makes this notion explicit. It recasts the "toy lot" of "There are chaste charms" as a "toy thicket," confusing, untamed, but still a plaything. Mesmerized by his doll-like existence, the hero feels himself immune to the laws of being. Hence the wonder and the fear at the finale: "Can it be that I am real / And death will really come?" If "Silentium" imagines a possibility of mystical fusion with the cosmos, "Why is the soul so melodious" suggests that this fusion is an illusion of creative ardor.

"The Seashell," another homage to Tiutchev, takes the next step in the shrinkage of the power of the word by asserting the falsehood of poetry. Stanza 2 reads:

Ты равнодушно волны пенишь	You froth waves indifferently
И несговорчиво поешь;	And sing intractably;
Но ты полюбишь, ты оценишь	But you will learn to love and value
Ненужной раковины ложь.	The useless shell's lie.
(Mandel'shtam 1:68)	

The image of the seashell is employed to raise the issue of (in)communicability. The cosmos is presently indifferent to the poet, and unmanageable: "Perhaps you do not need me" (*Byt' mozhet, ia tebe ne nuzhen*). However, the hero imagines that its life-giving spirit will animate him. As a seashell is being filled with seawater, "the house of [his] uninhabited heart" (*nezhilogo serdtsa dom*) will be filled with the music of the universe. He acknowledges the falsehood of his art but expresses a hope that the cosmos will learn to love his lies.[102]

Several other poems meditate on theological ineffability. These poems both engage the conventional ineffability topos and put a twist on it in line with a growing verbal and ontological skepticism. One such lyric is "Murdered by evening copper" ("Ubity med'iu vechernei," 1910), a poem in which the hero yearns for silence and kenosis. The first four lines read:

Убиты медью вечерней	Murdered by evening copper
И сломаны венчики слов.	And broken are corollas of words.
И тело требует терний,	And the body requires thorns,
И вера—безумных цветов.	And faith requires insane flowers.
(Mandel'shtam 1:55)	

"Evening copper" refers to the color of the sunset but also evokes the sound of evening church bells, particularly since the last stanza mentions a "cathedral" (*khram*). *Venchik* is the flower's corolla, a small wreath, a saint's nimbus, and a band placed around the head of a dead Orthodox person. The corollas of words are killed by evening copper, that is, words are overpowered by the sunset (death) and the sound of church bells (Christian faith). The lines also mean that Christ as God's "Word" is dying, as suggested by the crown of thorns and *venchik*.[103] The lyric likens Christ on the cross to a flower: "Like a corolla, the head hung / On a thin and strange stem" (*Kak venchik, golova visela / Na steble tonkom i chuzhom*). Inspired by Christ's passion, the hero is silenced, and wants to suffer in kenosis and to have faith. In the ecstasy of prayer "all feelings / Are merged in one grace" (*molitvoi slity / Vse chuvstva v odnu blagodat'*), as in Zhukovsky's "but what is merged . . . " and "all the infinite is crowded into one sigh."

If "Murdered by evening copper" is a dream of religious self-abandon, "The Serpent" ("Zmei," 1910) outlines the inexpressibility of skepticism. The lyrical persona is incapable of articulating his doubt, not wanting "his soul's curves, / Reason, or the muse" (*I ne khochu dushi svoei izluchin, / I razuma, i muzy ne khochu*) (Mandel'shtam 1:58). *Izluchiny* summons Blok's "The Stranger," "all the curves of my soul" (*vse dushi moei izluchiny*).[104] The poet rejects the Blokian muse who penetrated his soul-curves with tart wine. He feels the serpent of Eden within his soul. The serpent conjures up Eden's Satan, as well as Christ's temptation in the wilderness. Exhausted by a painful self-split, the hero rejects his reason and his art. The rejection of reason suggests the concepts of the holy fool and kenosis, yet he fails in his attempt at faith. He feels himself a cunning trickster (the issue of lies is thus raised again) bereft of an appropriate language to depict his depressing and superficial lot:

Нет стройных слов для жалоб и признаний И кубок мой тяжел и неглубок. (Mandel'shtam 1:58)	There are no well-composed words for complaints and confessions And my cup is heavy and shallow.

"No well-composed words" echoes Batiushkov, but the hero of "The Serpent" lacks words to express not his communion with nature but his pedestrian misery. "Why breathe?" (*K chemu dyshat'?*) (Mandel'shtam 1:58) conveys his desire to die. In the last stanza the hero is a prisoner awaiting his execution without fear but in vain shaken by his vision and music.[105]

"Your image, tormenting and elusive" ("Obraz tvoi, muchitel'nyi i zybkii," 1912) is an ingenious conceit of ineffability:

Образ твой, мучительный и зыбкий, Я не мог в тумане осязать. "Господи!" сказал я по ошибке, Сам того не думая сказать.	Your image, tormenting and elusive, I could not feel in the fog. "Lord!" I said by mistake, Myself not intending to say this.
Божье имя, как большая птица, Вылетело из моей груди! Впереди густой туман клубится, И пустая клетка позади . . . (Mandel'shtam 1:73)	God's name, like a large bird, Flew out of my breast! Ahead a dense fog swirls, And an empty cage behind . . .

It has been suggested that this poem reveals "Mandelstam's peculiar Johannine conception of the word which he shared with Gumilev."[106] In my view, the poem should be read in the context of apophaticism. It develops around the conceit of God's name as His spirit, represented by a bird. God is unknowable and unnamable. Although the hero strives to perceive Him, His image eludes him. The poem replays the hesychast Jesus prayer returned to in the *imiaslavie* debate. God's name, the living force for *imiaslavie* advocates, cannot be articulated without dire consequences.[107] At the same time, the lyric resonates with the Judaic prohibition to utter the name of the divine. The elusiveness of the image of the divine, in turn, recalls the Mosaic law against the making of images, which underscores human inability to represent God's nature or His workings.[108]

The poem both evokes and challenges traditional ineffability topoi. The lines call to mind a hesychast injunction to move beyond images and names into wordless prayer. This same observation is pertinent if the image that swirls in the fog belongs to a human being (*tvoi* is not capitalized), "quite likely a woman though this is not important."[109] In this case the hero wastes the name of the divine on an earthly being, a being as elusive as the divine itself. As soon as the name is uttered, the apparition, "like a large bird" (Shelley's metaphor for an intangible spirit), vanishes in the mist. Still Mandelstam struggles against divine ineffability. Though uttering the name is forbidden, the poet yearns to sense One and to pronounce One's name. The last lines, then, convey loss as well as liberation, with the bird-spirit breaking away from his prison.

Stone's silentiums imaginatively intertwine strands of mythological, Neoplatonic, Judeo-Christian, and absurdist inexpressibilities. A number of these poems play with the opposition between a speechless and unconscious fusion with the world, and an awakening into consciousness and language similar to "A sound cautious and muted."[110] Both conditions are found alternately tempting and diminishing and are often conceptualized in conflicting terms. The former condition may entail an intensification of vitality, but more often it permits a Schopenhauerian respite from the will. The self, thus dissolved in cosmos, is not conscious of pain and desire: its very thinness proves to be its saving grace.

Mandelstam's wordless dissolution in the world transforms a romantic or symbolist mystical union with the universe (e.g., as in Batiushkov and Ivanov) to portray the self going blank not in a benign act of apophasis but as a meeting of two voids—inner and external. Thus in "In the spaces of a twilight hall" ("V prostorakh sumerechnoi zaly," 1909) the self betrays a hypnotized or drugged aspect, with silence being sweet but also somnolent, while in "Enough of cunning: I know" ("Dovol'no lukavit': ia znaiu," 1911) the hero "wisely keeps silent" (*mudro bezmolstvuet*), lulling himself into a semiconscious condition (Mandel'shtam 1:61). Silence connotes the soul's coldness and drowsiness. Fusion with the universe becomes an emptying out of the self and a refusal or inability to communicate with other humans, as in "In the frosty air a light smoke has melted" ("V moroznom vozdukhe rastaial legkii dym," 1909) where the hero wants to disappear, feels estranged from the whole world, and rejects communication: "Do not speak to me—what can I answer you?" (*Ne govori so mnoi—chto ia tebe otvechu?*) (Mandel'shtam 1:47).

Symmetrical to this inner emptiness and silence are external emptiness and silence (meaninglessness). "In the calm of my gardens" ("V bezvetrii moikh sadov," 1909) reimagines Tiutchev's and Ivanov's inexpressibility in a darker light:

В безветрии моих садов	In the calm of my gardens
Искуственная никнет роза;	An artificial rose droops;
Над ней не тяготит угроза	A threat of unutterable hours
Неизрекаемых часов.	Does not hang over it.
В юдоли дольней бытия	In the vale of life
Она участвует невольно;	It participates involuntarily;
Над нею небо безглагольно	Over it the sky is wordless
И ясно . . .	And clear . . .
(Mandel'shtam 1:39)	

Mandelstam recognizes a synthetic, glass-house quality in the world of art. Precisely because the flower is artificial, the laws of being do not apply to it. "Unutterable hours" echoes Tiutchev's "Silentium!" ("an uttered thought is a lie") and Ivanov's "Silence" ("unuttered silence"), but in contrast to Ivanov Mandelstam's unutterability is malevolent. Likewise, this poem's "sky is wordless" recalls Ivanov's "let us commit a wordless impulse" (*poryv doverim bezglagol'nyi*) but designates existential emptiness rather than mystical ineffability.

In "The keen ear strains a sail" ("Slukh chutkii parus napriagaet," 1910) the universe itself has gone voiceless:

Слух чуткий парус напрягает, Расширенный пустеет взор, И тишину переплывает Полночных птиц незвучный хор.	The keen ear strains a sail, Dilated, the gaze is being emptied, And across silence swims A chorus without sound of midnight birds.
Я так же беден, как природа, И так же прост, как небеса, И призрачна моя свобода, Как птиц полночных голоса.	I am as poor as nature, And as simple as the skies, And my freedom is spectral Like the voices of midnight birds.
Я вижу месяц бездыханный И небо мертвенней холста; Твой мир, болезненный и странный, Я принимаю, пустота! (Mandel'shtam 1:51)	I see a moon that does not breathe And the sky more deathly than a canvas; Your world, sickly and strange, I accept, emptiness!

The hero struggles to hear the world. Like religious mystics, he suppresses the self in order to take in the cosmos, but his gaze is being emptied not because he becomes the recipient of mystical insight but because all that he encounters is nature's silence and emptiness. Nature's music becomes its muteness, a "chorus without sound of midnight birds."

The shift of silence to the universe is distinctive, not a common device of poetic fallacy. Like Batiushkov and Zhukovsky, Mandelstam synchronizes inner and external reality, which are for him equally "poor" and "simple." One's freedom is spectral, and in a harsh reverse mimesis, nature is completely lifeless: the "moon does not breathe," the sky "is more deathly than a canvas." Silence is made material: the birds swim across it as across a body of water. Emptiness becomes palpable, nothing has presence: "Your world, sickly and strange, / I accept, emptiness!" Like Baratynsky, Mandelstam contemplates barren space. All the hero can do is resign himself to the void or, rather, to alleviate the pain by voiding the self.

Many other poems in *Stone* present silence as metaphysical emptiness. "In the meekly wise heights" ("V smirennomudrykh vysotakh," 1909) describes a void that invites the self to go blank, a union of external and inner silences. This poem transforms the ancient motif of the music of the spheres into an expression of metaphysical bareness. "Does not nature embody / The harmony of lofty numbers?" (*Ne voploshchaet li priroda / Garmoniiu vysokikh chisel?*) reimagines Pythagoras's elemental music as an icy numerical ordering of the universe (Mandel'shtam 1:43). The cosmos in all its astronomical vastness is devoid of emotion and meaning: "And there is neither comfort / Nor bitterness in the worlds" (*I netu nikakoi otrady, / I netu gorechi v mirakh*) (Mandel'shtam 1:43). "With vaguely-breathing leaves" ("Smutno-dyshashchimi list'iami," 1911) notes the abundance of silence and the scarcity of music in the world: "Why is there so little music / And such silence?" (*Otchego tak malo muzyki / I takaia tishina?*) (Mandel'shtam 1:62).

Other poems like "A meager ray with a cold measure" ("Skudnyi luch kholodnoi meroiu," 1911) equate silence and death, a poetic convention the persistence of which in Mandelstam is worth considering: "The firmament fell silent, died" (*Tverd' umolkla, umerla*) (Mandel'shtam 1:61). "Under thunderclouds" ("Pod grozovymi oblakami," 1910) not only links silence and death but recasts the romantic inexpressibility of the unique subject as the inexpressibility of existence under the shadow of extinction: "And every creature, with its soul, / Like a swallow before a thunderstorm, / Performed an indescribable flight" (*I kazhdyi sovershil dushoiu, / Kak lastochka pered grozoiu, / Neopisuemyi polet*) (Mandel'shtam 1:53). Finally, "We cannot bear an intense silence" ("My napriazhennogo molchan'ia ne vynosim," 1912) intimates a Nietzschean and Shestovian notion that the word camouflages the more painful truths of being. Imperfect humans require that "in confusion a reader turned up" (*I v zameshatel'stve uzh ob'iavilsia chtets*) (Mandel'shtam 1:80) lest silence as meaninglessness become all too apparent.

FROM SILVER SILENTIUM TO IRON SILENCE

Mandelstam's silentiums in *Stone* span a range of ontological underpinnings, from the word unable to express the ideal to the word unable to express death, yet poems about silence as emptiness dominate. One might imagine that, around 1912, as Mandelstam becomes a fully fledged acmeist, for whom "the sound of a chisel is a metaphysical proof" (Mandel'shtam 1:178), the topos of verbal skepticism would disappear from his poetry: "The youthful Mandelstam wrote about the loveliness of silence. The mature Mandelstam knows that an incarnated thought is the poet's necessity, his highest duty."[111] In reality, however, the theme of verbal inadequacy remains Mandelstam's preoccupation throughout his work, an observation that goes against the belief that his life experiences in the Stalin period were the major sources of despondency in his later poetry. Even the bright acmeist morning witnessed some poems on the topos, though they were not as numerous as those of the preceding period.[112] The dawn of the "real twentieth century," commencing, according to Akhmatova, on the eve of World War I, produced a multiplicity of poems on verbal skepticism that are expressions of existential horror.

I will look briefly at two poems that exemplify Mandelstam's later treatment of verbal skepticism, "The Horseshoe Finder (A Pindaric Fragment)" ("Nashedshii podkovu" [Pindaricheskii otryvok"], 1923) and "Earphones, my earphones"("Naushniki, naushnichki moi," 1935). These poems reveal major developments in the poetry of verbal skepticism that appear later in the twentieth century. They show the dialogue of literary and literal silences, and they connect the ontological absurd and verbal inflation.

"The Horseshoe Finder" has been interpreted as promoting the notion of poetry's timelessness in a transient world:

> Mandelstam and Pindar share an essentially similar view toward poetry's ability to remain timeless in a transitory, often disorderly world. It is the poem which is uniquely able to remain intact while all else changes, and hence to contact an unknown future recipient of an unexpected gift in which is preserved also a part of the poet. In Olympian X, for example, Pindar likens his ode to a child born to an old father who thus carries on his father's name . . . It is precisely in "Nashedshii podkovu" that Mandelstam gives one of the fullest poetic expressions to this concept.[113]

While one can certainly see the possibility of this interpretation, I side with the view that the poem "exhibits a crisis in language, more specifically in poetic language."[114] I would further argue that "The Horseshoe Finder" joins a harsh critique of the word with a dark modern existential vision.

Mandelstam writes in an austere style that goes against his earlier poetics, abandoning rhyme and resorting to free-verse rhythm. This gives the work the odic meter and style of antiquity.[115] At the same time, where Nietzsche explicated the effect of rhythm in religious terms, as the perception of the regular and the orderly as a higher realm, rejecting meter, rhyme, and conventional poetic harmony as here permits one to represent a chaotic and meaningless world, a world bereft of cosmic harmony that also emerges in "Concert at the Railway Station" ("Kontsert na vokzale," 1921) and "The Age" ("Vek," 1922).[116]

From the poem's opening stanzas to its finale, "The Horseshoe Finder" moves through a series of disjointed images, exposing the disintegration of the poet's word, his past, and his very self:

С чего начать?	With what to begin?
Все трещит и качается.	Everything cracks and sways.
Воздух дрожит от сравнений.	The air shakes from similes.

Ни одно слово не лучше другого,	Not a single word is better than another,
Земля гудит метафорой,	The earth buzzes with metaphor,
И легкие двуколки	And light-weight carts
В броской упряжи густых от натуги птичьих стай	In a flamboyant harness of flocks of birds
Разрываются на части,	Dense with strain, burst to pieces
Соперничая с храпящими любимцами ристалищ.	Competing with the snorting favorites of the races.
То, что я сейчас говорю, говорю не я,	What I am saying now is not said by me,
А вырыто из земли, подобно зернам окаменелой пшеницы.	But is dug from the ground like grains of petrified wheat
Одни	Some
на монетах изображают льва,	portray a lion on their coins,
Другие—	Others—
голову.	A head.
Разнообразные медные, золотые и бронзовые лепешки	Assorted copper, gold, and bronze cakes
С одинаковой почестью лежат в земле,	Lie with equal honor in the ground,
Век, пробуя их перегрызть, оттиснул на них свои зубы.	The age, trying to gnaw them through, has imprinted its teeth on them.
Время срезает меня, как монету,	Time cuts me like a coin
И мне уж не хватает меня самого . . .	And there is no longer enough of me for me . . .

(Mandel'shtam 2:42–45, stanzas 3 and 9)[117]

Like Zhukovsky's "The Inexpressible," Mandelstam's poem is subtitled "fragment," and ends on an ellipsis.[118] In Mandelstam's case, fragmentariness acquires a destructive character. All that remains of the racehorse portrayed in the ode—that is, of the language of the past, as well as of the poet himself—is a petrified fragment, a horseshoe. "These fragments I have shored against my ruins," writes Eliot toward the conclusion of *The Wasteland* (1922).[119] In the manner of this Anglophone rendition of the collapse of the old culture, Mandelstam conveys skepticism of a violent, absurdist kind—one only too fitting for the new age.

The new order of the era dismisses the poet with his arcane humanistic values as a devalued currency.[120] The figure of currency appears in Tynianov's appraisal of Mandelstam's language in "The Interval" ("Promezhutok," 1924):

> His meanings are seeming, indirect . . . that become obligatory only through verse. He has no words, only shadows of words . . . And that's why Mandelstam is a pure lyricist, a poet of the small form. His chemical experiments are possible only within limited space . . . His shades are unthinkable in the space of the epos. Mandelstam has no word—resonant coin. He has shades, promissory notes transferred from line to line. So far this is his strength. So far—because during an interval a resonant coin is most often fake.[121]

In this reading, the main thrust of Mandelstam's poetry is creation of special meanings, semantic shades peculiar to his poetic system. If Pasternak's word becomes a palpable "word-thing," in Mandelstam, by contrast, things turn into poetic abstractions. That's why the theme of the forgotten word is characteristic of him and that's why he loves names, mere shadows of words. For Tynianov Mandelstam is a poet's poet par excellence, both in the positive sense of his fine craftsmanship and concentration on meaning-generating properties of the poetic system promoted by the formalists (his meanings "become obligatory only through verse") and in the negative sense critical of his bookishness ("shades of words"), artificiality ("chemical experiments"), and limited scope (his technique "is unthinkable in the space of the epos"). Tynianov's concluding language-money metaphor captures this ambivalence: Mandelstam has only "promissory notes," but so far this has been to his advantage since this period's "resonant coins" (a nod to Sergei Esenin) most frequently turn out to be fake.

Mandelstam's self-appraisal in "The Horseshoe Finder" is more straightforwardly negative. The obsolete lyricist fails to perform on a par with revolutionary odists. His precarious carts of poetry, "dense with strain, burst to pieces / Competing with the snorting favorites of the races"—a much less hopeful echo of "We have bound swallows / Into battle regions" (*My v legion boevye / sviazali lastochek*) (Mandel'shtam 1:135) of "The Twilight of Freedom."[122] He is culturally bankrupt, "has fluffed, botched his reckoning" (*sbilsia, zaputalsia v schete*) (Mandel'shtam 2:44). He lives in accordance with an outdated calendar: "The frail chronology of our era comes to a close" (*Khrupkoe letoischislenie nashei ery podkhodit k kontsu*) (Mandel'shtam 2:44). Time is "out of joint" for him: "Children play knucklebones with the vertebrae of dead animals" (*deti igraiut v babki pozvonkami umershikh zhivotnykh*) (Mandel'shtam 2:44) evokes Heraclitus's "eternity is a child playing dice—a child's kingdom" as well as Mandelstam's own image of a broken spine which appears in "The Age."[123]

The third stanza, preceded by an introductory odic meditation on poetry and time, presents the poet as no longer knowing how to write, for all words have lost their value: "The air shakes from similes. / Not a single word is better than another, / The earth buzzes with metaphor." The departing Christian era used to give brief and honest replies: "At every touch it responded 'yes' and 'no.'" (*Na vsiakoe prikosnovenie otvechala 'da' i 'net'*) (Mandel'shtam 2:44). In the present, by contrast, everything swings to and fro in an overpowering verbal nausea. Language is inflated. Nature chokes with words.[124]

Like Mandelstam, Nietzsche in "On Truth and Lying in an Extra-Moral Sense" discusses language, and metaphors specifically, in terms of money. His objective is to subvert the epistemological value of words:

> What is truth? a mobile army of metaphors, metonymies and anthropomorphisms, in short, a sum of human relations which were poetically and rhetorically heightened, transferred, and adorned, and after long use seem solid, canonical, and binding to a nation. Truths are illusions about which it has been forgotten that they are illusions, worn-out metaphors without sensory impact, coins which have lost their image and now can be used only as metal, and no longer as coins.[125]

What humans take for truths are anthropomorphizing tropes congealed into concepts, so-called knowledge.[126] In Nietzsche's thoroughly self-subverting rhetoric, these worn-out metaphors are compared to coins turned into metal since their markings have been erased—an image akin to Mandelstam's "assorted copper, gold, and bronze cakes [that] lie with equal honor in the ground."

In "The Horseshoe Finder" the same operative paradox comes to the fore: rhetoric (figurative language) subverts the idea (rejection of figuration). Multiple metaphors of the poem's first section are oriented toward the ancient tradition, yet are especially striking in light of the poem's wariness of tropes. The lines renounce figurative language, yet almost immediately (the fifth stanza) the author employs one simile after another: "The air can be dark as water" (*Vozdukh byvaet temnym, kak voda*); it is like "A crystal in which wheels move and horses dash aside" (*Khrustal', v kotorom dvizhutsia kolesa i sharakhaiutsia loshadi*); it is like "The moist black earth of Neaira" (*Vlazhnyi chernozem Neery*); "The air is mixed as densely as earth" (*Vozdukh zameshen tak zhe gusto, kak zemlia*) (Mandel'shtam 2:44). A particularly ironic disjointedness occurs when Mandelstam, like Nietzsche, uses "metaphor" as his term of comparison. As was the case with "Silentium!," "The Horseshoe Finder" does not unconsciously fall prey to the disjointedness between language and argument. Rather, the poem deliberately undermines itself, a move in which Mandelstam does not give the reader even the "rotten fish" of words from *The Noise of Time* (*Shum vremeni,* 1925).

The operative paradox is also the focus of Florensky's attention in "Second Letter: Doubt" ("Pis'mo vtoroe: Somnenie") in *The Pillar and the*

Ground of the Truth (*Stolp i utverzhdenie istiny*, 1914), the work that contains a passage which Mandelstam's "With what to begin . . ." "follows virtually word for word":[127]

> I do not affirm anything. But having just stated what I have stated, I must remove this proposition as well, for it too is unproved . . . Absolute doubt has now begun. This is doubt as the total impossibility of affirming anything, even its own nonaffirmation. Progressing stage by stage, manifesting the idea that inheres in it *in nuce*, skepticism reaches its own negation but cannot leap across this negation . . . I enter the last circle of the skeptical hell—that part where the very meaning of words is lost. Words cease to be fixed and fall from their nests. Everything transforms into everything else, every word combination is totally equivalent to every other, and any word can exchange places with any other. Here the mind loses itself, gets lost in an invisible and disorderly abyss.[128]

In a way familiar from the discussion of ineffability in Russian idealist philosophy (Solovyev, Lossky, Frank), Florensky promotes Orthodoxy as a living religious experience which is the only legitimate way of beholding truth that is non-accessible empirically or conceptually. The first letter, "Two Worlds" ("Dva mira"), like Shestov's works, challenges conventional logical axioms, such as the law of identity and non-contradiction, on the grounds that they betray humanity's alienation from the world and itself. The second letter envisions truth as non-encompassable by its signifier—something complete, containing everything (akin to the Neoplatonic idea of the Absolute) and, therefore, only conditionally expressed by its name. Since neither "objective" evidence of the senses nor "subjective" reason can provide definite proof of truth, one falls into doubt and despair that express themselves as language losing all meaning.

If for Florensky rationality cannot progress past doubt and results in nihilistic despair and loss of the value of words but can be transcended by faith, less theologically confident treatments of the language crisis have no such certitude with which to counter skepticism. "Abstract concepts at the end of a historical epoch stink like rotten fish" (Mandel'shtam 2:388). Hugo von Hofmannsthal's testament to the modern language crisis, "Lord Chandos' Letter" (1902), offers a similar account: "The abstract terms of which the tongue must avail itself as a matter of course in order to voice a judgment—these terms crumbled in my mouth like moldy fungi."[129] "Lord Chandos' Letter" and "The Horseshoe Finder" both highlight destructive fragmentariness: "For me everything disintegrated into parts, those parts again into parts; no longer would anything let itself be encompassed by one idea";[130] the horseshoe and "grains of petrified wheat" imagery (Mandelstam). Likewise, both works convey a verbal nausea and the disintegration of meaning: "Single words floated round me; they congealed into eyes which stared at me and into which I was forced to stare back—whirlpools which gave me vertigo and, reeling incessantly, led into the void";[131] "Everything cracks and sways . . . Not a single word is better than another" (Mandelstam). And finally, both authors link the disintegration of language and the dissolution of selfhood, claiming that there is "no longer enough of me for me."

The breakup of language in "The Horseshoe Finder" corresponds to, and embodies, the breakup of the poet's world. Social disruption is outweighed by a more sweeping physical collapse of the universe that is portrayed through a kind of dizzying seismographic imagery Florensky and Hofmannsthal also make use of: "the air shakes," it "can be dark as water," it is "mixed as densely as the earth" (Mandelstam); "fiery yearning melts with fire-damp," "the mind gets lost in an invisible and disorderly abyss" (Florensky); "whirlpools gave me vertigo and, reeling incessantly, led into the void" (Hofmannsthal). As the facts of language acquire physicality, they disrupt the earth: "the air shakes from comparisons," "the earth buzzes with metaphor." Everything falls apart. The confusion of elements in the fifth stanza (air like water, like crystal, like earth) is essentially eschatological.

Verbal apocalypse is an analogy, an enactment, and a cause of a cosmic apocalypse. A necessary connection of signifier to signified is testimony to ontological harmony, including man's harmonious connection to others and to the cosmos, as in "Silentium" and "The blue island is great by its potters." The obverse is the unmotivated, deceitful sign, at its furthest reach—an utter disruption of the connection between the referee and the referent, the hypertrophy of an empty signifier. In popular consciousness unmotivated signs are regarded as coming from the devil, and in "The Horseshoe Finder" the earth is furrowed by "pitchforks, tridents" (*vilami, trezubtsami*) (Mandel'shtam 2:44).[132] The pitchfork, related to working on the land, is paired with Poseidon's trident, belonging to the water realm, indicating the confusion of elements. Tools are erroneously linked through their formal similarity—their multiple prongs. Like language, these implements have lost their semantic value. The world has grown demonic (tools no longer obey man), just as language has grown devilish through the proliferation of meaningless verbiage ("Not a single word is better than another").[133]

The motif of money raises the Lermontovian (and Pushkinian, as in "Conversation between Bookseller and Poet" ["Razgovor knigoprodavtsa s poetom," 1824]) theme of selling the self in art: "Do not abase yourself. Be ashamed of trading / In wrath or in obedient grief" (Lermontov); "Blest is he who was a poet silently . . . But the manuscript can be sold" (*Blazhen, kto molcha byl poet . . . No mozhno rukopis' prodat'*) (Pushkin).[134] At the close of the nineteenth century Mallarmé will characterize everyday speech as "no more than a commercial approach to reality" that operates in a social world defined by economic laws and is produced with a view toward monetary gain.[135] Like Pindar, Mandelstam's poet is for hire. Unfortunately he is not valued and finds himself insolvent.[136]

The motif of money points to the collapse of meaning in another sense. Currency is an apt metaphor for an arbitrarily fixed signification. For Mallarmé "a commercial approach to reality" in language obtains not only because language is subject to economic laws but also because in everyday usage words communicate by acting as a medium of exchange, that is, they are like money used to buy things (objects, ideas) in the marketplace. "Crisis of Verse" draws attention to the challenge the arbitrary nature of the relation between the signifier and the signified poses to poetry by likening the ordinary use of language to the exchange of money in the marketplace: "Narrate, teach, even describe, that's fine . . . in order to exchange human thought, to take from or place in the hand of someone else a coin in silence."[137] The problem for poets is that words casually represent their referents with no inherent connection between signifier and signified (Saussure's arbitrariness of signs).[138] Saussure himself in *Course in General Linguistics* uses the analogy between linguistic and monetary forms of exchange to elucidate his claim of the arbitrariness of the sign along with the notion that each sign in the system that makes up a language gets its meaning only because of its difference with other signs:

> To determine the value of a five-franc coin, for instance, what must be known is: (1) that the coin can be exchanged for a certain quantity of something different, e.g., bread, and (2) that its value can be compared with another value in the same system, e.g., a one-franc coin, or of a coin belonging to another system (e.g., a dollar). Similarly, a word can be substituted for something dissimilar: an idea. At the same time, it can be compared to something of like nature: another word. Its value is therefore not determined merely by that concept or meaning for which it is a token. It must also be assessed against comparable values, by contrast with other words. The content of a word is determined in the final analysis not by what it contains but by what exists outside of it.[139]

Like money, signs are constituted by something different which is liable to be exchanged with the thing whose value is determined (signification) as well as by similar things that can be compared with the thing whose value is in question (other signs).

The notion of value in currency, as in language, is based on trust. Money, like the sign, can be iconic if coin is worth its weight in precious metal or arbitrary if its value is conventionally assigned. A cheat might have "cut slivers from the coin while pawning off the coin at its face value, which no longer corresponded to its weight."[140] A cut coin is a deceptive, demonic sign since the signifier (the appearance of the slivered coin—the text) misleads one with respect to the signified (monetary value—poetic interiority). If figurative language is rejected ("the earth buzzes with metaphor"), "time cuts me like a coin" is doubly vacuous as a figuration of figuration.

Not only is figuration suspect—the problem of the word also expresses itself as the dangers of amnesia. "The Horseshoe Finder" abounds in tropes yet has few proper names; therefore, on its own terms, it is not "singled out among its friends with a headband / Curing unconsciousness/loss of memory" (*otmechena sredi podrug poviazkoi na lbu, / Istseliaiushchei ot bespamiatstva*) (Mandel'shtam 2:43). As in the Lethean poems as well as in "January 1st, 1924" Mandelstam points out the threat of memory loss.[141] Like *The Pillar and the Ground of the Truth* in which "words cease to be fixed and fall from their nests" and "The Swallow" ("Lastochka," 1920) in which the blind swallow stands for the forgotten word, "The Horseshoe Finder" employs the bird-word simile to convey the loss of poetic power. The light-weight cart of poetry, harnessed to birds, bursts into pieces.

Memory and Mnemosyne-poetry that embody the past are strategies to compensate for loss but this kind of compensation can hardly be adequate. As Florensky traces the etymology of *ἀλήθεια* ("truth" in Greek) in the second letter of *The Pillar and the Ground of the Truth,* he notes that the word consists of the negative particle *a* and *lethos* (I lose for memory, i.e., for consciousness in general, I forget). The ancient idea of death "as a transition to an illusory experience, almost to self-forgetting and unconsciousness, and, in any case, to the forgetting of everything earthly, finds its symbol in the image of the shades' drinking of water from the underground river of forgetfulness, 'Lethe.' . . . This power of forgetting is the power of all-devouring time."[142] "The Swallow" closely follows this scenario; "The Horseshoe Finder," in turn, takes on the problem of the "unconscious" (*bespamiatstvuiushchee*) word. Language does not preserve the poet's living essence but only represents lifeless fragments, "grains of petrified wheat."[143]

As "The Horseshoe Finder" unfolds, it captures the transformation of a vibrant reality of the past into archaeological residua. The dynamic world (ships, horses, wheels) of the poem's first half, Pompeii-like, is fossilized in the latter section. Movement is arrested into *nature morte*—"vertebrae of dead animals," "the sharp turn of [a horse's] neck / Still keeps the memory of racing" (*krutoi povorot ego shei / Eshche sokhraniaet vospominanie o bege*), a horseshoe "will no more strike sparks from flint" (*I bol'she uzh ei ne pridetsia vysekat' iskry iz kremnia*) (Mandel'shtam 2:45). As in another Lethean poem, "Take for joy from my palms" ("Voz'mi na radost' iz moikh ladonei," 1920), many relics of the past are reductive remnants of poetic selfhood, specifically: the horseshoe (Mandelstam's version of Lermontov's formerly powerful dagger of poetry now just hanging on the wall), the poet's lips stiffened into the shape of their final utterance, words as grains of petrified wheat, devalued coins.[144]

Mandelstam's poem contests verbal immortality. Previous poetic utterances, like coins, lie in the earth. Seemingly able to resist the assault of time, they are in fact disfigured by it, bearing imprints of the age's teeth over their original patterns. More precisely, the coins are newly minted through disfiguration; defacement itself becomes their identity. Poetic interiority is compromised in the case of older poets, and yet more extremely so in the case of the poem's protagonist—"cut like a coin by time."

An answer to the question "why is such a personal poem by Mandelstam placed under the impersonal genre of the ode?" is that the poem focuses on the depersonalization of poetic interiority.[145] The poet will speak no more: "Human lips, / which have nothing more to say, / Preserve the shape of the last word spoken" (*Chelovecheskie guby, / kotorym bol'she nechego skazat', / Sokhraniaiut formu poslednego skazannogo slova*) (Mandel'shtam 2:45).

The text that has been produced is no longer under the poet's control; it has become an iterative structure cut from his consciousness and existence: "What I am saying now is not said by me." Personal pronouns "vanish entirely in stanzas 3 through 5: there is already apparently 'not enough of me for me,' and the past passive form of 'dug up' (*vyryto*) shows that it is not the poet himself performing exhumation."[146] Like a distant star shining in the skies though it died out long ago, the author "sounds" after he is gone: "The sound still rings, though its reason is gone" (*Zvuk eshche zvenit, khotia prichina zvuka ischezla*) (Mandel'shtam 2:44). The text is not a museum of the past, as in "There are chaste charms," not even a funereal urn of the poetic self; it is a geological stratum in which a frail fossil of the poet is buried. The trace—the horseshoe—may not be totally valueless but it is a reductive remnant of a living and breathing lyrical subjectivity.

Shortly after the composition of "The Horseshoe Finder" poem, Mandelstam's poetic silence became literal. For some five years (1925–30) he composed no verse. "Earphones, my earphones" ("Naushniki, naushnichki moi," 1935), like "The Horseshoe Finder," exemplifies Mandelstam's later harsh rendition of verbal skepticism:

Наушники, наушнички мои!	Earphones, my earphones!
Попомню я воронежские ночки:	I will mark Voronezh nights:
Недопитого голоса Аи	The voices of unfinished Ai
И в полночь с Красной площади гудочки . . .	And at midnight honks from the Red Square. . .
Ну как метро? Молчи, в себе таи,	So how is the metro? Be silent, hide in the self,

Не спрашивай, как набухают почки,	Do not ask how buds swell,
И вы, часов кремлевские бои, —	And you, the chimes of the Kremlin clock—
Язык пространства, сжатого до точки . . .	The language of space, compressed to a dot . . .
(Mandel'shtam 3:90)	

Voronezh nights point to the poet's exile. He listens for the chimes of the Kremlin, the seat of totalitarian power. *Naushniki* refer to the earphones of old radio sets and "earflaps," as well as to a "slanderer" or "informer."[147] Cut off from the outside world, the poet tries to imagine Moscow and his past but abruptly catches himself. Under the control of the Kremlin, with "language of space, compressed to a dot," it is better not to utter a word, not even to remember but to simply shut the self off from everyone and everything.

A passage from Mandelstam's novella *The Egyptian Stamp* (*Egipetskaia marka,* 1927) shows that *naushniki,* just like *glukhoi,* are his personal markers of existential alienation and incommunicability:

> The boys were used to being equipped for outside as knights for tournament: warm gaiters, quilted trousers, hoods, earflaps [*naushniki*]. There was a noise in the head from earflaps, and deafness rolled on. To respond to someone, one had to untie sharp braids at the chin. He turned round and round in the heavy winter armor like a little deaf knight, not hearing his voice. The first disconnection with people and with the self . . . were embodied in the earflaps; and the six-year-old quilted Beethoven in gaiters, armed with deafness, was pushed out on the stairs. (Mandel'shtam 2:487)

In the poem, silence and incommunicability as existential notions (*naushniki* as "earflaps") interplay with silence and incommunicability in the political context (*naushniki* as the earphones through which Mandelstam listens to the voice of Moscow and *naushnik* as a colloquialism for an "informer"). The lyric's diminutives and melodic outline have a distinct prison cant, reinforcing the poem's political connotations. Mandelstam conveys the feel of the times, with everyone surrounded by spies and living under the threat of imprisonment.

The end of the first line of the second stanza quotes the opening of Tiutchev's "Silentium!" "Earphones, my earphones" grounds Tiutchev's classic in the context of literal, rather than literary, estrangement and incommunicability. The interplay of the romantic exaltation of silence and the more prosaic implications of the silenced writer, in effect making figurative silence literal, is twofold. Mandelstam is able to covertly criticize the stifling political climate of the time as well as to poke fun at the notion of inexpressibility, which had by that time become a romantic cliché. The inexpressibility topos is exposed as a mere rhetorical device, but the interaction of literary and literal silence is contextually ominous. One does not read in a vacuum, and Mandelstam's approaching annihilation under Stalin's terror looms over the poem.[148]

Not only does "Earphones, my earphones" defamiliarize Tiutchev's bookish formula by its political connotations, it also handles Tiutchev's paradigm not in a dreamy re-creation typical of the youthful Mandelstam but in a dry, matter-of-fact, even grammatically uncouth way. Unembellished everyday language emphasizes the graveness of the subject. The poem truncates Tiutchev's first line: "Be silent, be secret, and hide" (Tiutchev); "Be silent, hide in the self" (Mandelstam). "In the self," taken from the third stanza of Tiutchev's poem, intensifies the feeling of alienation. The absence of a direct object after "hide" stresses how tongue-tied or unable to speak clearly the poetic subject is. As it also happens in "Do not say to anyone" ("Ne govori nikomu," 1930), which omits a noun, and in "Turn silent! About nothing, never, to none" ("Zamolchi! ni o chem, nikogda, nikomu," 1931) where there is no verb after "none," broken syntax and elliptical style highlight the poet's stifled state.

Like "Earphones, my earphones," numerous poems of the 1930s involve formulations such as "to be silent" (*molchat'*), "muteness" (*nemota*), "do not speak" (*ne govori*), and other manifestations of a compulsory creative silence, something "of which Tiutchev could not have even dreamed."[149] Russian silence "has two types, two degrees, which then appear in political and mystical spheres."[150] The former emerges in Mandelstam as early as "January 1st, 1924": "I know, with each day life's exhale weakens, / A little longer—they will cut / This simple song about clay offenses / And lay lead over the lips" (*Ia znaiu, s kazhdym dnem slabeet zhizni vydokh, / Eshche nemnogo,—oborvut / Prostuiu pesenku o glinianykh obidakh / I guby olovom zal'iut*) (Mandel'shtam 2:50).

This theme persists to the poet's death. Speech is dangerous, and so is memory: "I will mark [*popomniu*] Voronezh nights" ("Earphones"); "Forget all that you saw" (*Vse, chto uvidel, zabud'*) ("Do not say to anyone") (Mandel'shtam 3:40). Silence can be a sign of fear as well as defiance: "hide in the self" ("Earphones"); "Not to ask, not to complain! Hush! Not to whine! Have the raznochintsy / Treaded in their cracked boots for me to betray them?" (*Chur! Ne prosit', ne zhalovat'sia! Tsyts! Ne khnykat'! Dlia togo li raznochintsy / Rassokhlye toptali sapogi, chtob ia teper' ikh predal?*) ("Midnight in Moscow" ["Polnoch' v Moskve," 1931]) (Mandel'shtam 3:52). Existential alienation is simultaneously verbal: "Be silent, hide in the self" ("Earphones"); "I want to depart from our speech / For everything that I forever owe it" (*Mne khochetsia uiti iz nashei rechi / Za vse, chem ia obiazan ei bessrochno*) ("To German Speech" ["K nemetskoi rechi," 1932]) (Mandel'shtam 3:69).

All communicative links are severed: the imperatives of "Earphones" address, Tiutchev-like, the author himself; "Where shall I go this January?" ("Kuda mne det'sia v etom ianvare?" 1937) is an apogee of incommunicability, loneliness, and pain: "A reader! An advisor! A doctor! / A conversation on a prickly staircase" (*Chitatelia! Sovetchika! Vracha! / Na lestnitse koliuchei—razgovora b*) (Mandel'shtam 3:119). Lastly, "The Theta and Iota of a Greek Flute" ("Fleity grecheskoi theta i iota," 1937) resurrects "Silentium"'s early dream of a primordial, pre-verbal, sea-inspired music that "cannot be pushed into words by the tongue / Or kneaded by the lips" (*I v slova iazykom ne prodvinut', / I gubami ee ne razmiat'*) (Mandel'shtam 3:135). In a paranomastic play of "the sea" (*more*), "pestilence" (*mor*), and "measure" (*mera*), creativity on this occasion is nothing less than deadly.[151]

Contrary to a widespread perception of Mandelstam, many of his works call into question the fine capacity of the poetic word. Not only are there many more silences than has been appreciated in the early collection *Stone,* beyond the well-known "Silentium," but verbal skepticism remains salient throughout Mandelstam's oeuvre, from his juvenile to his late work. What is different is the tenor of Mandelstam's later poems. His early "silentiums," even the darker ones, are genteel studies of the topos, as unmistakably part and parcel of the prewar world as his later works would be of the Stalinist age. Pessimistic though they may be, the early poems exhibit an old-fashioned, abstract, Tiutchevian quality. They are precisely silentiums, not silences. The works of the 1920s and the 1930s, by contrast, contain harsh expressions of the crumbling word and world. The motifs of incommunicability, discontinuity, and the absurd are now embodied rhetorically. Formal polish, euphony, mythopoeism, and an atmospheric recasting of subtext yield to stridency and prosiness. Literary inexpressibility turns literal. Most prominently, ontological and verbal skepticism escalate in parallel. Mandelstam's silence, both thematically and formally, becomes the iron silence of the twentieth century. Endangered but sustaining some remaining value even as poetic residue in Mandelstam, lyrical interiority will prove beyond recall for Joseph Brodsky.

Chapter Three

A Figure That Leaves You Speechless: Joseph Brodsky on Death and Language

TO FALL BACK ON Isaiah Berlin's well-known dichotomy between the hedgehog and the fox, Mandelstam's latter-day heir, the Nobel-winning poet Joseph Brodsky, is a hedgehog par excellence. The key theme of his poetry and essays, an obsessive focus of his philosophizing, his primary interlocutor, arch-nemesis, and arch-protagonist, the alpha and omega of his art—death—is as conspicuous as Brodskyan idiosyncrasies of syntax, rhyming, or tenor. Time, memory, exile, empire, love, art, language—all familiar Brodskyan subjects—are only death's subsidiaries, their conceptualization and treatment conditioned by his gaze into the void. Of these subjects, it is language that is death's most frequent companion, strange or otherwise.

Commentators on Brodsky have often noted that ruminations on language are prominent throughout his oeuvre. The traditional and most frequently expressed view holds that Brodsky was a verbal idealist of a specifically Russian, post-acmeist kind, his engaging anachronism at odds with the late twentieth-century Western deconstructionist and anti-poetic climate. George Kline expresses the critical consensus when he states: "Through his poetry the poet can overcome the destructive power of time and death. What the poet leaves behind is his 'chast' rechi,' his 'part of speech' or 'language part.'"[1]

My objective here is to revise this established view of Brodsky as an unequivocal verbal idealist. As with Mandelstam, Brodsky's verbal musings reveal the warring of word idealization and word devaluation. His much-advertised and excellently analyzed idealization of the word has, as its dialectical counterpoint, a darker vision of poetic language unable to withstand the forces of destruction. Focusing on works of the 1970s, specifically, "Conversation with a Celestial Being" and lyrics of the cycle "A Part of Speech," poems that encapsulate Brodsky's meta-linguistic and existential preoccupations, I show the prominence of the antiverbal topos among Brodsky's concerns. In Brodsky, verbal critique prevails even more markedly than in

Mandelstam. This critique, moreover, augments absurdist qualities present in Mandelstam's later oeuvre. Brodsky forcefully links the ontological absurd and the devaluation of language.

Besides the manifestations of verbal skepticism explored in the preceding chapters, Brodsky's oeuvre features two more corollaries of verbal inadequacy: the failure of memory and the failure of the literary endeavor, which ensues with a work's separation from the creative subjectivity of the author. In the former, memories are ineffable inasmuch as the past can be neither remembered with accuracy nor recuperated in the poetic text. The activities of recollection and articulation are carried out in unison by the poet, and the treacherous nature of memory is interwoven with the inadequacy of the word. In the case of the "death of the author," familiar from post-structuralist theory, language defaces the subject through its impersonal and autonomous nature. As an iterative structure cut from consciousness and context, the text offers an assembly of unrelated mechanical parts that disfigures no less than restores its originator.

For Brodsky, this "death of the author" issue is especially troubling, but he takes it in a direction distinct from those of its various post-structuralist treatments. Accordingly, I do not apply post-structuralist concepts to Brodsky's texts, but juxtapose his views on language with relevant post-structuralist ideas and observe their points of contact as well as divergences. Rather than pushing an earnest understanding of Brodsky toward postmodernism based on forms of verbal skepticism in his work, I examine how Brodsky's texts comment on post-structuralist theory to reflect critically on notions taken for granted in theoretical discourse. Instead of celebrating poetic self-effacement, Brodsky remains nostalgic for the reign of the poet as human being and as creator in life and art alike.

RESIDENCE PERMIT FOR HEAVEN: DIVINE INEFFABILITY AND ITS DISCONTENTS

Brodsky "is a bundle of contradictions. This statement might be problematic if he were a philosopher, but his consistent inconsistency makes perfect sense to those studying his primary status—that of poet."[2] It was Brodsky who was so much taken with "time . . . worships language and forgives / Everyone by whom it lives" as to casually dismiss the poem's subsequent segment, "pardons cowardice, conceit, / Lays its honors at their feet . . . " as well as "poetry makes nothing happen" in Auden's "In Memory of W. B. Yeats" (1939).[3] It was this same Brodsky who came up with the striking imagery of words devouring living beings, and tersely and grimly restated the ancient, benevolent "Exegi Monumentum" motif in his Audenesque "Verses on the

Death of T. S. Eliot" ("Stikhi na smert' T. S. Eliota," 1965): death invariably chooses to murder the author, not his parts of speech.[4]

Brodsky's seemingly staunch logocentric pronouncements betray, upon closer scrutiny, curious rhetorical qualifications. Such is the case in the following claim from "The Condition We Call Exile, or Acorns Aweigh" (1988): "Yet talk we must; and not only because literature, like poverty, is known for taking care of its own kind, but mainly because of the ancient and perhaps as yet unfounded belief that, were the masters of this world better read, the mismanagement and grief that make millions hit the road could be somewhat reduced" (*On Grief and Reason* 23).[5] Similarly, "Merely a word is / repeatable: by another word" (*Povtorimo vsego lish' / slovo: slovom drugim*) in "Strophes" ("Strofy," 1978) (Brodsky, *Collected Poems in English* 152; Brodskii 3:183), interpreted as "it is the poetic word that, in Brodsky's world, is capable of overcoming separation, ruins, and unrepeatability of the moment," draws attention with its "merely" just as "perhaps as yet unfounded" is noteworthy in the passage from "The Condition We Call Exile."[6]

Key tenets of Brodsky's celebrated *lingvoditseia*—through poetry, time and matter articulate themselves; the voice of the muse is the dictate of language; aesthetics is the mother of ethics—harbor some unexamined twists. That language is inhuman in the sense of being extratemporal as well as the voice of inanimate matter, legitimately interpreted as the words' power to access realities outside the realm of ordinary comprehension, also suggests verbal inhumaneness—affinity not with eternity but infinity, dullness, indifference of inanimate matter to breathing sentient beings.[7]

Likewise, Brodsky's insistence that language has its own intentionality, to which it subjects the writer, has been read as evidence of his verbal idealization, a post-acmeist glorification of the all-powerful logos.[8] Such an interpretation is by no means unfounded, for the notion that language determines thought is not necessarily a facet of verbal skepticism; it is when the power of language is construed to be in conflict with human agency that the notion of the word's primacy becomes an antiverbal argument. Yet even a canonical "verbal idealist" statement such as Brodsky's Nobel speech (1987) exhibits rhetoric akin to that of verbal skeptics:

> The consequence of starting to write is a perception of an immediate falling into the state of dependence on language . . . A poet always knows that what in the vernacular is called the voice of the Muse is, in reality, the dictate of the language; that it's not that the language happens to be his instrument, but that he is the means of language toward the continuation of its existence. Language, however, even if one imagines it as a certain animate creature (which would only be just), is not capable of ethical choice . . . The immediate consequence of this enterprise is the sensation of coming into direct contact with

> language or, more precisely, the sensation of immediately falling into dependence on it, on everything that has already been uttered, written, and accomplished in it. This dependence is absolute, despotic; but it unshackles as well . . . One who writes a poem writes it because the language prompts, or simply dictates, the next line . . . One falls into dependency on this process, the way others fall into dependence on drugs or on alcohol.[9]

As the muse becomes "the dictate of the language," the writer does not possess language but is possessed by it. He is beset by the "burden of influence" and develops such dependence that the agency of writing becomes blurred as language "prompts, or simply dictates, the next line." The author acquires a physiological dependency on the process "the way others fall into dependence on drugs or on alcohol." Thus, Brodsky's notion of the poet's relationship to language has less to do with a Mandelstamian idealization of logos (itself not entirely unproblematic) than with later skeptical views in which the word assumes a manipulative character.[10]

Even Brodsky's oft-cited maxim that "aesthetics is the mother of ethics," nonchalantly followed by "language . . . not capable of ethical choice," is contingent upon the romantic notion of poetry as the sphere of ineffable subjectivity.[11] Brodsky's belief that each human is "an independent essence that can be touched and understood only superficially" underlies his key notion that art fosters human autonomy: "The surest defense [of aesthetics/poetry] against Evil is extreme individualism, originality of thinking, whimsicality . . . Something, in other words, that can't be shared, like your own skin" (*Less Than One* 385).[12] The same notion, equally, points at poetry's Tiutchevian limitations as an expression of the incommunicable self.

While some of Brodsky's word-exalting postulates reveal an edge of uncertainty, his other statements display a clear critical force. Thus in the essay "In the Shadow of Dante" (1977) Brodsky articulates a time-honored romantic antiverbal view:

> Poetry after all in itself is a translation; or, to put it another way, poetry is one of the aspects of the psyche rendered in language . . . Essentially poetry is the articulation of perception, the translation of that perception into the heritage of language—language is, after all, the best available tool. But for all the value of this tool in ramifying and deepening perceptions—revealing sometimes more than was originally intended, which, in the happiest cases, merges with the perceptions—every more or less experienced poet knows how much is left out or has suffered because of it. This suggests that poetry is somehow also alien or resistant to language, be it Italian, English, or Swahili, and that the human psyche because of its synthesizing nature is infinitely superior to any language we are bound to use (having somewhat better chances with inflected ones). (*Less Than One* 104–5)

The "psyche rendered in language" subscribes to the expressive view of poetry. Poetry as an articulation of perception follows Schopenhauer. The "synthesizing nature of the psyche" raises the issue of unity versus fragmentariness. "One of the aspects," along with "left out or has suffered," indicates the reductionism of the verbal medium.[13]

"Conversation with a Celestial Being" ("Razgovor s nebozhitelem"), a long work of twenty-eight stanzas composed in 1970, has a romantic, in a Lermontovian mode, cast to it, but goes beyond romantic antiverbalism.This poem has been insightfully analyzed by a number of commentators, several of whom considered it in the context of existentialist thought.[14] Valentina Polukhina argues that, in contrast to Kierkegaard and Shestov, for Brodsky language contains an ultimate resolution to the enigma of being, and that the poem represents "the surmounting of alienation through memory, faith, and language."[15] Andrei Ranchin posits that Brodsky is reiterating a traditional argument on religious ineffability by presenting language as fallible on account of it "cutting one off from higher reality," and at the same time departs from Kierkegaard and Shestov by depicting God "not as a person but as a suprapersonal source, free from suffering."[16] In Lev Loseff's view, Brodsky gives a Christian interpretation of suffering.[17] Jane Knox interprets the poem as a testament to Brodsky's affinities with religious existentialists like Kierkegaard or Shestov, who contrast a leap of faith to rational knowledge. Like Shestov, Brodsky "demonstrates a connection with the God of the Old Testament, a judge indifferent to suffering" and relies on Shestov's polemic juxtaposition of faith and knowledge according to which "man must take his fate on faith, in the spirit of Abraham and Job."[18] Alexander Zholkovsky reads the poem as "an earnest 'Prophet' à la Brodsky," in which death is overcome through poetry. The poet does not die but "'having closed his lips and having descended from the cross,' embarks 'on things in the second circle,' i.e., the lips [Mandelstam's poetic lips] participate in an easier manner of resurrection."[19] According to Irina Sluzhevskaia, Brodsky subscribes to Shestov's notion of the inhumanity of the divine, yet at the same time he reverses the traditional power relationship between the poet and the angel: "Only one character has the power of the word," so "force, power, and resoluteness are on the side of the inhabitant of earth." Brodsky "completely overturns their inequality: not 'i and Him,' but 'I and him.'"[20] Ekaterina Ozherel'eva, in turn, argues that the poem engages four incompatible conceptions of the divine: loving father, incomprehensible force, hostile despotic force, and an illusion.[21]

One can see the possibility of these interpretations, but there is another way of looking at the poem—as a critique of theological ineffability as well as a challenge to Pushkin's canonical logocentric lyric. In Brodsky's poem the violence of the Pushkinian transformation is emphasized and proven futile, divine inexpressibility pushes in the direction of the absurd, the loophole in apophaticism is brought to the fore, and a leap of faith is shown to be impossible. The disparate conceptions of the absolute do not coexist independently in the poem but are synthesized to produce a vision of the divine as suprapersonal—and therefore a largely hostile force—with humanized divinity exposed as an illusion and the idea of the saving powers of language dismissed. Since Shestov envisioned the divine precisely as a suprapersonal entity, what, in my view, separates Brodsky's "Conversation with a Celestial Being" from Lossky, Frank, Shestov, and other religious existentialists is his problematization of the hollowed-out absolute of apophaticism. The suffering the hero undergoes is not rewarded by God's response, as in Kierkegaard. Unlike Lossky, Brodsky sees through the apophatic manipulation of theodicy. Finally, unlike Shestov, he resists accepting the void as the secret of the transcendental. In light of Brodsky's poem, Shestov's ontology comes perilously closely to gnosticism with its notion of an evil demiurge, or even to atheism, which acknowledges only a blind and arbitrary nature. Brodsky rejects the Shestovian ineffable absolute, which "knows no needs and therefore does not understand human needs," in favor of the small humane idol of memory. But memories cannot be recovered in words, and language fails to provide a sanctuary against death.

The rupture between the abodes and perspectives of the celestial being and the poet constitutes a key motif of the poem. Brodsky's designation of his addressee is worth noting: he converses not with God or an angel (though he does call his interlocutor an "angel" once) but with a *nebozhitel'*, "an inhabitant of heaven." He highlights the two parts in the name, *nebo* and *zhitel'*, in the first line, where "Here, on earth" (*Zdes', na zemle*) (Brodskii 2:361) pointedly contrasts the positions of the addressee and the hero. This same phrase, "here, on earth," will be reiterated three more times in the poem—in stanzas 9, 10, and 11. Similarly, we see repeated juxtaposition of "here" and "there, above" "these" (uncertainties, fears, passions, memories, losses, words) and "those" (silences, gardens, cupolas, windows).

Poetic structure reflects the philosophical problematic. In the eight-line stanzas, short two-foot lines are interspersed with five-foot iambs. The difficulty of this pseudo-conversation (the hero never obtains a response from his heavenly addressee) is seen in the uneven layout of the lines, all of them of a fluctuating length.This layout, along with a broken syntax that collides with meter, a Brodskian trait generally, create an effect of awkwardness appropriate to addressing a transcendental silent entity. The opening line of each stanza, running significantly shorter than the subsequent line, conveys the abruptness of the hero's speech.[22] In the first stanza specifically, the curt "here, on earth," followed by "where I would lapse first into fervency, then into heresy" (*gde ia vpadal to v istovost', to v eres'*) (Brodskii 2:361) creates an effect of beginning in medias res, as if something important unsaid has preceded the poem.

The interspersing of high Slavonicisms with contemporary, vulgar colloquialisms rhetorically challenges the discourse of ineffability. Brodsky mixes elevated biblical language such as "hence" (*poeliku*), "visage" (*liku*), "naked and orphaned" (*nag i sir*) with contemporary jargon—"to speak coarsely" (*zhloblius'*), "shit on the thought of camouflage" (*kladu na mysl' o kamufliazhe*). The lower discourse functions as a mode of poetic deconstruction, as does a tongue-in-cheek recourse to Russianist clichés of the "accursed questions" kind. The frequent conjoining of clauses by "but" ("But this is a confirmation and a sign"; "But either his or its [pain's] limit / is unknown to him") (*No eto podtverzhdenie i znak; No to li svoi emu nevedom, to li / ee predel*) (Brodskii 2:361–62) forges a chain of contradictions (similar to Fet's "Like midges at twilight"), one clause to the next, which convey the problematic nature of this conversation.

Brodsky's poem evokes Tiutchev's "Cicero" ("Tsitseron," 1830) with its epigrammatic conclusion, but subverts the notion of a conversation with heaven:

Блажен, кто посетил сей мир	Blessed is he who visited this world
В его минуты роковые!	In its fateful minutes!
Его призвали всеблагие	He was summoned by the all-holy
Как собеседника на пир.	As an interlocutor to their feast.
Он их высоких зрелищ зритель,	He is a viewer of their lofty spectacles,
Он в их совет допущен был—	He was permitted into their council—
И заживо, как небожитель,	And he, alive, as a celestial being,
Из чаши их бессмертье пил!	Drank immortality from their cup!
(Tiutchev 1:122)	

Like Tiutchev's lyrical persona, Brodsky's hero is initially presented as an interlocutor of the divine. Where Tiutchev singles out the world's "fateful minutes" and deems the witnesses of these lofty moments blessed, Brodsky emphasizes the mundane nature of the lethal in earthly existence. Fateful moments, of which Christ's Crucifixion is archetypal, for Brodsky signal only life's bad infinity: "you embark on things in the second circle, / having descended from the cross" (*idesh' na veshchi po vtoromu krugu, / soidia s kresta*) (Brodskii 2:363). Tiutchev's witness of lofty moments drinks immortality from the cup of celestial dwellers; Brodsky's hero has drunk his fill of "the broth of minutes" (*vareva minut*) (Brodskii 2:363), the very opposite of Tiutchev's brew of the gods. Satiated with mortality, he loses touch with life. As he no longer perceives the sounds of life surrounding him, his celestial addressee is deaf to his supplications.

The hero's earthly language is alien to the celestial being. From the onset of the poem the verbal gift is presented in a diminished light, the poet "warming himself in somebody else's memories, / like a mouse in the ashes, /

where worse than a mouse [he] gnawed on the brevier type of his native dictionary" (*v chuzhikh vospominan'iakh greias', / kak mysh' v zole, / gde khuzhe myshi / glodal petit rodnogo slovaria*) (Brodskii 2:361). Memories, the staff of poetry, do not belong to him, and he can only furtively try to warm himself in them. Just as the comparison to a mouse makes the hero seem small and insignificant, the "brevier type" emphasizes the pettiness of his language when juxtaposed to the divine.

In the second stanza Brodsky, like Lermontov, severs the customary link between the poetic gift and the divine, and claims that inspiration is akin to illness. His poetic gift is not the transcendental Logos but a sickly compulsion: "no master of his throat" (*ne vladeia gorlom*), he exists "choking / with a nod of resonant carrion, / sprinkling his lips with saliva instead of Castalian water" (*davias' kivkom / zvonkogolosoi padali, sliunoi / kropia usta vzamen kastal'skoi vlagi*) (Brodskii 2:361), an evocation of the celestial poetic spring. In an argument with Pushkin's "The Prophet" Brodsky states that he lives "no longer seeing a place in anyone which he could touch with his word" (*ne vidia mesta, koego glagolom / kosnut'sia mog by*) (Brodskii 2:361).[23] Assaulted by metaphysical darkness, he clings to writing, "listing over paper like the tower of Pisa" (*krenias' Pizanskoi bashneiu k bumage*) (Brodskii 2:361), a simile conveying the precarious conditions "here, on earth." The act of writing is done out of desperation.

The protagonist declares that he returns his poetic gift to the celestial being (*tebe tvoi dar ia vozvrashchaiu*) (stanza 3) (Brodskii 2:361). His soul, which is "but a mold of his sad gift" (*vsego lish' slepok s gorestnogo dara*) (Brodskii 2:361), evokes Mandelstam's imagery of poetic voice petrifying into molds in "The Horseshoe Finder." The returning of the gift runs in the spirit of Fyodor Dostoevsky's Ivan Karamazov (*The Brothers Karamazov,* 1880), who returns his ticket to heaven because of worldly injustices. In a gesture of defiance and an exercise of freedom, Brodsky's hero chooses to part with his most precious possession. The proposition that the mortal hero is more merciful than his divine addressee, for he will not "be burning / him with word, confession, or request" (*Ne stanu zhech' / tebia glagolom, ispoved'iu, pros'boi*) (Brodskii 2:361), again alludes to Pushkin's prophet burning words into human hearts, though here the purported object of burning is the unresponsive divine.

As in Mandelstam's *The Egyptian Stamp,* the word carries the danger of contagion.[24] For Brodsky, accursed questions, another Dostoevskian allusion, are like smallpox "with which speech / is infected almost / from the cradle" (*kotoroi rech' / pochti s pelen / zarazhena*) (stanza 4) (Brodskii 2:361). Language carries the bacilli of accursed questions—the issues of theodicy and the silence of the divine with which Dostoevsky's and Brodsky's heroes struggle. The hero suggests that the celestial being itself may have infected human speech with these burning questions to torture humans, thus denying them the mercy shown by the mortal interlocutor. The conclusion of the fourth stanza, "so that you are removed from pain / in a reliable manner" (*nadezhnym to est' obrazom ot boli / ty udalen*) (Brodskii 2:361) expresses the idea that the omnipotent divinity never suffers. It also reiterates the notion that divinity does not suffer because its humble interlocutor will spare it the pain that is thrust on humankind.

Next the poem takes on theological ineffability in its harsher Shestovian version. Rather than subscribing to the idea, Brodsky strikes at its core problem in the fifth and sixth stanzas:

Не стану ждать
твоих ответов, ангел, поелику
столь плохо представляемому лику,
как твой, под стать,
должно быть, лишь
молчанье—столь просторное, что эха
в нем не сподобятся ни всплески смеха,
ни вопль: "Услышь!"

Вот это мне
и блазнит слух, привыкший к разнобою,
и облегчает разговор с тобою
наедине.
В ковчег птенец
не возвратившись, доказует то, что
вся вера есть не более, чем почта
в один конец.

I will not wait
for your answers, Angel, since
to such a badly conceived image
as yours, only silence
is most likely fitting—
so spacious that with an echo
it will honor neither splashes of laughter,
nor a scream: "Hear!"

And this is what
my ear, used to discord, fancies,
and makes easier my talk with you
in private.
To the Ark a nestling,

not returning, proves that
all faith is but
one-way mail.
(Brodskii 2:362)

These lines expose the circular logic of apophaticism that characterizes conventional musings on ineffability. According to Brodsky, the divinity will remain unresponsive to his supplications because as "a badly conceived image," that is, as something ineffable, it must remain silent. The issue of theodicy, the "accursed questions" that infect human speech, is not resolved but shown only to have been circumvented. The sixth stanza offers an epigrammatic definition of "all faith as one-way mail."

A tension between self-denigration and pride—the poet is "a mouse" but he is also capable of greater generosity than the divine—informs the subsequent lines. The seventh stanza revises the Sermon on the Mount: "You poor . . . You that hunger . . . You that weep."[25] The beginning of the stanza is an exercise in religious humility: "So look at me, naked / and orphaned, speaking coarsely about God" (*Smotri zh, kak nag / i sir, zhloblius' o gospode*) (Brodskii 2:362). The inference that—insofar as the poet is naked and orphaned—the divinity is spared the need to respond is, however, the opposite of Jesus's beatitudes, which promise special grace to the lowest of the world. The hero takes pride in his anguish not because he is one of the poor in spirit beloved by God, but because the divine is silent.[26] He prefers the clear knowledge of being on his own and "shits on the thought of camouflage" (*kladu na mys' o kamufliazhe*) (Brodskii 2:362) or a saving illusion of being under the deity's wing. Understanding that suffering is not a violation of rules but a law of being, when put on the cross, he will not cry out to God for deliverance. The definition of man as "a tester of pain" (*ispytatel' boli*) (stanza 8) (Brodskii 2:362) suggests that in the laboratory of life man is not just a helpless victim. Rather, he is the guinea pig (or mouse) of the divine and also an experimenter in his own right. Although it is not in his power to elude pain, that he can endure it without crying out to the divine testifies to his dignity. The concluding lines of the stanza present another contradiction: if man is "a tester of pain," he knows neither his own limits nor the limits of suffering.

The ninth stanza reenvisions Christ's Crucifixion as an ordinary occurrence of earthly existence. Stanzas 9, 10, and 11 reiterate the dichotomy between terrestrial ("here, on earth") and heavenly dwellings. The tenth stanza suggests that the poet's thoughts of the divine are a comforting fiction: "all forms of life are accommodation. / Including / a gaze at the ceiling / and the craving to merge with God as with the landscape / in which one shot, let's say, / searches for us" (*vse formy zhizni est' prisposoblen'e. / I v tom chisle / vzgliad v potolok / i zhazhda slit'sia s Bogom, kak s peizhazhem, /*

v kotorom nas razyskivaet, skazhem, / odin strelok) (Brodskii 2:363). "Accommodation" degrades the notion of the divine to an instinct for self-preservation. Man yearns to merge with God because his situation is that of hunted game. These lines ridicule the romantic fondness for deifying nature, for spreading oneself all over the landscape, as it were; they also resonate with the "camouflage" figure of the seventh stanza.[27] Poetry and faith are Darwinian accommodations that make existence bearable by providing a subterfuge.

The assault on romanticism, poetry, and religion continues in the eleventh stanza: "As on a bit of snot, / everything hangs on the hooks of its questions, / like a tram thief, a bard, or a philosopher" (*Kak na sople, / vse visnet na kriukakh svoikh voprosov, / kak vor tramvainyi, bard ili filosof*) (Brodskii 3:363). "Everything hangs on the hooks of its questions" is built through visual association—the question mark iconically suggests hooks. Tram thieves, poets, and philosophers hanging by their questions nods in the direction of Kant, with his glorification of the human subject for its ability to conceptualize infinity. By this concrete physical embodiment of an abstract concept, poets and philosophers literally clutch at the skies by asking about God's existence. It is language that crowns the list of "foul-smelling" illusions: "from all corners / everything stinks like fish, from right and left, / of merging with nature or a maiden, / and with the tower of words!" (*iz vsekh uglov / neset, kak ryboi, s odesnoi i s levoi / sliianiem s prirodoi ili s devoi / i bashnei slov!*) (Brodskii 2:363). As in Mandelstam, "abstract concepts at the end of a historical epoch stink like rotten fish." Just so, thinkers are caught by the hooks of their questions about the transcendental. Further, Brodsky takes a poke at the erotic implications of the romantic fusion with nature, which are exposed in his mocking juxtaposition of "nature or a maiden."

Stanzas 12 and 13 develop the theme of imprisonment in the temporal. The appellation "spirit-healer" (*dukh-istselitel'*) in the beginning of the twelfth stanza is clearly sarcastic for the celestial being cannot heal the hero, who is poisoned by time. Other colloquialisms point to the idea of life as prison. "Broth" (*varevo*) suggests prison food. Likewise, the metaphor "From Moser's bottomless dishes / I gobbled up so much of the broth of minutes" (*Ia iz bezdonnykh mozerovskikh bliud / tak nakhlebalsia vareva minut*) (Brodskii 2:363) grows from a play on *kotly* as "cauldrons" but also "timepiece" in prison jargon, reinforcing the idea that temporal existence is prisonlike. Choking on mortality, the hero can find no consolation in the sounds of nature.

The thirteenth stanza extends the clock imagery: Johann Heinrich Moser's watches, the hands of the clock, alarm clocks. The speaker again stresses his resolution not to appeal to the celestial dweller, for separation from loved ones is a law of life: "There are no embraces that would not part / like hands of a clock at midnight" (*Tekh net ob'iatii, chtob ne razoshlis' / kak strelki v polnoch'*) (Brodskii 2:363). The parting hands of the clock evoke

John Donne's conceit of comparing a drawing compass and parting lovers in "A Valediction: Forbidding Mourning" (1633): "If they be two, they are two so / As stiff twin compasses are two."[28] Crucified by time, the hero wraps his stigmata in sackcloth (stanza 9). Alarm clocks are wrapped in dresses in an attempt to stifle through love the shrill sounding of time, yet this attempt proves futile since alarm clocks still ring out at night "opening iron embraces" (*razzhav zheleznye ob'iat'ia*) (Brodskii 2:363).The clock functions as a single vehicle for two tenors, time and love, suggesting that they may not only oppose but also complement each other. A new designation for the divine, "the aforesaid height" (*oznachennaia vys'*) (Brodskii 2:3623), a scholarly and bureaucratic idiom, highlights the speaker's ironic intent.

The fourteenth stanza contains the poem's key statement on verbal inadequacy:

И в этой башне,
в правнучке вавилонской, в башне слов,
все время недостроенной, ты кров
найти не дашь мне!
Такая тишь
там, наверху, встречает златоротца,
что, на чердак карабкаясь, летишь
на дно колодца.

And in this tower,
Babylonian great-granddaughter, the tower of words,
all the time unfinished, you will not
let me have shelter!
Such a quiet
There, above, meets the golden-mouthed one,
that, clambering up the garret, you plunge
to the bottom of a well.
(Brodskii 2:364)

These lines have been interpreted as a testament to verbal power: "Severed from his linguistic milieu, Brodsky seems to survive thanks to language alone."[29] I would argue that they insist on verbal impotence. The poet does not find refuge in language. Likewise, Brodsky is not engaging conventional apophatic topoi but advancing a notion in a Nietzschean or Shestovian vein—that man employs language as an illusion to shield himself (hence "shelter") from the terror of being.[30]

In the poem's reimagining of the story of Babel, man erects his "tower of words," a further development of the clock conceit as in a "tower clock," to reach the divine, but he encounters silence. He is thrown down not in punishment for his presumption, as in the biblical tale, but because there is simply nothing to hear. The stanza echoes the earlier lines on Christ and the law of mortality: "all mountains—but in a narrow sense—/ end not with peaks but with descent / into pitch darkness" (*vse gory—no v znachenii ikh uzkom—/ konchaiutsia ne pikami, no spuskom / v kromeshnoi mgle*) (Brodskii 2:363). The tower of words turns into Golgotha for the "golden-mouthed one" (*zlatorotets*), as Brodsky sardonically refers to himself. This conjurer of words' image plays on John Chrysostom (Ioann Zlatoust), the apophatic theologian of the fourth to fifth centuries who preached divine ineffability yet indulged in mellifluous speeches. The hero uses language as a "hook" with which to climb to heaven (stanza 11), but his discovery of the void above, the "secret of the eternal" turned inside out, plunges him into the abyss.

The tower of Babel is like the leaning tower of Pisa, to which the hero is compared at the beginning of the poem. Both communicate the idea of the word's precariousness and, therefore, the flimsiness of the hero's project to seek verbal sanctuary. His "gratitude to heaven for his talent" must be read as sardonic since it is addressed to the void.[31] He thanks the "aforesaid height" for disposing of all that he had owned, the "product of his labor" (*produkt truda*) (stanza 15) (Brodskii 2:364), in a mockingly Marxian idiom that is incongruous in a discourse on ineffability. Just as earlier Brodsky turned man's victimization on its head by making it testimony to his grandeur, here he demonstrates his superiority by accepting suffering and refusing to utter anything but words of gratitude: "do not dare cry about betrayed hope" (*ne smei krichat' o predannoi nadezhde*) (stanza 16) (Brodskii 2:364). Though an element of earnest gratitude for existence may inform this utterance, it is predominantly the determination of a torture victim not to betray his pain, that is, to keep silent or, better, be grateful.[32]

His "gratitude" becomes an unambiguous expression of rebellion in the seventeenth stanza where the hero is grateful for his inability to attach himself to the placating make-believe that language perpetuates. He thanks the heavens for "not permitting him / to stick to those gardens, corpuses, and the dictionary" (*chto ne dal prilepit'sia / k tem kushcham, korpusam i slovariu*) (Brodskii 2:364). "Gardens" (*kushchi*) refers to the Garden of Eden (*raiskie kushchi*). "Corpuses" (*korpusa*) alludes to the Feast of Corpus Christi and the Eucharist. Together, "gardens, corpuses, and the dictionary" pertain to faith as expressed through language. Stanzas 17–18 also continue the theme of time ("watch case") and language ("primer"). The hero can neither struggle nor merge with time since he sees "behind every dial / in the wall—a tunnel" (*za kazhdym diskom / v stene—tunnel'*) (Brodskii 2:365).

The nineteenth stanza brings to the fore the violence of transformation as portrayed in Pushkin's "The Prophet." The twisted syntax of the lines contains another echo of "The Prophet," with the hero's "sinful tongue, empty-worded and cunning" torn out. Brodsky urges the divine to torture the protagonist more ruthlessly: "Dig deeper and, as torn out with flesh, sew fear to the heart of sad time, / of death hour"" (*Roi glubzhe i, kak vyrvannoe s miasom, / shei serdtsu strakh pred grustnoiu poroi, / pred smertnym chasom*) (Brodskii 2:365). Unlike Pushkin's violence, the torture here is useless, having nothing to do with the transformation of poet into prophet. The imperative "sew" in "sew fear. . ." and "sew an abyss of agony" (*shei bezdnu muk*) offers the imagery of needlework that recurs in Brodsky, a transcendental needlework that does not reconcile heaven and earth, but rather represents a torment by time.[33] The suggestion of a criminal prosecution, as in the slangy "to file a case" (*shit' delo*) reinforces an earlier mention of imprisonment in mortality (stanza 12) and ironizes the lofty discourse of ineffability. Analogously, this discourse is mocked by the "thought—how is it called!—of immortality" (*mysl'—o kak ego!—bessmert'i*) (Brodskii 2:365), which presents this notion as hackneyed and bookish.

The hero wishes to cry out to the heavens that "Even the thought of immortality / is a thought about loneliness" (*No dazhe mysl'—o kak ego!—bessmert'i / est' mysl' ob odinochestve*) (Brodskii 2:365). Like Baratynsky in "Autumn," he wonders whether heaven would respond to this cry or whether it would prove as unresponsive as the earth (stanza 20). The recurrence of "nighttime silence" in stanza 21 is the answer to this query. Inequality of the sides in the opposition "I and him" is indeed "determined by their relationship to the word"; but rather than demonstrating, as Irina Sluzhevskaia asserts, "the all-powerfulness of the inhabitant of earth and the powerfulness of heavens," this persistent refusal of the divine to engage in dialogue reinforces its power and the powerlessness of the human with his faith as "one-way mail."[34] In a move of reverse mimesis, a crowd of trees in the window is likened to "lungs in a school diagram" (*legkie na shkol'noi diagramme*) (Brodskii 2:365). It is not that, as Andrei Ranchin puts it, "in contrast to nature everything artificial, made up . . . is endowed with negative characteristics," but that nature itself appears lifeless and artificial.[35]

The twenty-second stanza dramatizes inexpressibility by opening with several short, broken clauses interspersed with ellipses: "Everything broke off. . . / Time. And fate. And about fate. . ." (*Vse otkololos' . . . / I vremia. I sud'ba. I o sud'be . . .*) (Brodskii 2:365). Fragmentariness becomes even more destructive in Brodsky than in Mandelstam. Language and memory are not like horseshoes, good luck charms, but merely preserve incoherent, lifeless bits of one's existence. The theme of memory echoes "somebody else's memories" of the poem's beginning. All that remains of one's recollections are "burned out dross, gravel, / on account of some letters, photos, / mirrors, a window" (*shlak peregorevshii, gravii, / za schet kakikh-to pisem, fotografii, / zerkal, okna*) (Brodskii 2:365).

The spirit of the past is extinguished in the word. The hero regrets that there is no god or even a small idol (*bozhok*) for memory in Christianity (stanza 23). Such an idol "with the visage of a junkman" (*s likom / star'evshchika*) (Brodskii 2:366) contrasts with "the badly conceived visage" of the ineffable celestial being. What endears the idol to the hero is precisely its humanness, its ability to help one "while away nights / that are too deaf" (*dlia korotan'ia slishkom / glukhikh nochei*) (Brodskii 2:366), as opposed to the impersonal divinity of apophaticism. Echoing "deaf nights," "nighttime silence" (*nochnaia tish'*) (stanza 24) is followed by the simile "crows' nests as cavities in the bronchial tubes" (*voron'i gnezda, kak kaverny v bronkhakh*) (Brodskii 2:366), which develops the reverse mimesis imagery of stanza 21. Crows—carrion eaters—represent carnage in nature, and their nests are likened to decaying lung tissue, the carnage of the human body. An epigrammatic statement on incommunicability follows, along with an admission of the operative paradox:

Любая речь
безадресна, увы, об эту пору—
чем я сумел, друг-небожитель, спору
нет, пренебречь.

Any speech
is without address, which, alas, this time—
I managed, it goes without saying, my celestial friend,
to ignore.
(Brodskii 2:366)

The twenty-sixth stanza recapitulates some of the poem's main themes, that is, it ironizes theological ineffability and exposes the mirage of the divine and infection inherent in speech. It also adds a new problem—the disintegration of the text into meaningless signs:

Не помню толком
о чем с тобой
витийствовал—верней, с одной из кукол,
пересекающих полночный купол.
Теперь отбой,
и невдомек,
зачем так много черного на белом?
Гортань исходит грифелем и мелом,
и в ней—комок

I do not recall quite
what it was that I orated about
to you—rather, to one of the dolls

who were crossing the midnight cupola.
Now sound off,
and I have no idea
why there is so much black on white?
The larynx dissolves into slate and chalk,
and in it—a clot
(Brodskii 2:366)

The hero no longer recalls (stanza 25) what it was that he orated about (stanza 26). The word "orated" (*vitiistvoval*), obsolete and bookish, expresses the poet's whimsical stance toward traditional ineffability.[36] The image of the doll crossing the midnight cupola, like the Blokian "pretty doll for man's wonder and amusement," develops the notion expressed previously that the divine, at least insofar as it is conceived of in human terms, is a comforting mirage. Furthermore, memories cannot be recuperated in language because all that remains on paper is a proliferation of signs devoid of meaning, "so much black on white." Just as the author feels estranged from the celestial, by the conclusion of the poem he is alienated from his own text as well, wondering with some distaste what made him pour out so many words.

There exists a gap in the lyrical person's consciousness—he cannot relate to his past, and he cannot comprehend what he has written. "So much black on white" resembles Annensky's lines of verse "merging into murky-black spots." The poet's larynx "dissolves" not in blood or tears, expressions of genuine suffering, but in the easily compromised media of verbal artifice, "slate and chalk," an echo of Mandelstam's "The Slate Ode" and, via Mandelstam, Derzhavin's "The river of time in its flowing" ("Reka vremen v svoem stremlen'i," 1816). The imagery of the dissolving larynx with its clot resonates with the theme of the dying old man with his failing lungs. As in Lermontov, not only does such imagery denigrate poetry, but more emphatically, it likens the poetry to illness, developing the motif of infected speech. A strange thought "about snow's victory" (*o pobede snega*) (stanza 27) (Brodskii 2:366) is the thought of death.[37] Given the overwhelming presence of death, the aftermath of prosodic flirting with eternity can only manifest as a hangover, "feeling bitter in the brain" (*v mozgu gorchit*) (Brodskii 2:366).

The conclusion of the poem (stanza 28), like the ending of Baratynsky's "Autumn," concentrates on transience. It is Holy Week, but there will be no resurrection. While a newborn baby "does not allow for the melting of snow" (*ne dopuskaet taian'ia snegov*) (Brodskii 2:366), the dying old man in the hospital knows for certain that he will not live to see the spring. The last lines of a poem, always marked, are especially so here since all the preceding stanzas contain eight rather than ten lines.[38] "He sees snow and knows that he will die / before it melts, before the ice breaks up" (*on vidit sneg i znaet, chto umret / do taian'ia ego, do ledokhoda*) (Brodskii 2:367)—these concluding extra lines provide a final verdict on the subject.

"Conversation with a Celestial Being" offers a critique of theological ineffability, shows the failure of language as man's sanctuary, and examines the problem of failing memory in its linkage to language. Like Baratynsky and Mandelstam, Brodsky brings forth death as the ultimate case of incommunicability and inexpressibility. Like Schopenhauer and Shestov, he stresses that pain is the law of the temporal world and strives to make his art an impersonal contemplation of the void. Finally, like Lermontov and Nietzsche, he advocates stoic silence as the last resort of mortals. The poem's disparate aspects, from stanzaic form to imagery, converge to convey the message that language cannot provide sanctuary against the assault of mortality. "Conversation with a Celestial Being" is exemplary of a darker, absurdist branch of verbal skepticism. These very qualities also characterize "A Part of Speech."

LINGUISTIC LUNACY

It is the sheer intensity and single-mindedness with which Brodsky dissects each and every aspect of absurdist inexpressibility that make his contributions to the topos unlike those of other twentieth-century poets. As was the case with Mandelstam's *Stone,* many poems in "A Part of Speech" ("Chast' rechi," 1974–76), a cycle included in a collection of the same name, are articulations of verbal skepticism.[39] Brodsky's cycle is composed of minimalist-style lyrics all placed on separate pages. "Silences" surround these short texts. The language is abrupt, dry, in a word (resembling Mandelstam's later verse) anti-poetic.[40]

I commence with "From nowhere with love the enth of Marchember" ("Niotkuda s liubov'iu, nadtsatogo martobria")—a poem that enacts mental and verbal disintegration, tapping into a pain that exceeds the word's capacity to express it:

Ниоткуда с любовью, надцатого
  мартобря,
	From nowhere with love the enth
	  of Marchember sir

дорогой уважаемый милая, но
  неважно
	sweetie respected darling but
	  in the end

даже кто, ибо черт лица,
  говоря
	it's irrelevant who for memory
	  won't restore

откровенно, не вспомнить уже, не
  ваш, но
	features not yours and no one's
	  devoted friend

и ничей верный друг вас
  приветствует с одного
	greets you from this fifth last part
	  of earth

из пяти континентов, держащегося
на ковбоях;
я любил тебя больше, чем ангелов
и самого,
и поэтому дальше теперь от тебя,
чем от них обоих;
поздно ночью, в уснувшей долине,
на самом дне
в городке, занесенном снегом по
ручку двери,
извиваясь ночью на простыне—
как не сказано ниже по крайней
мере—
я взбиваю подушку мычащим
"ты"
за морями, которым конца и
края,
в темноте всем телом твои
черты,
как безумное зеркало повторяя.
(Brodskii 3:120)

resting on whalelike backs of
cowherding boys
I loved you better than angels and
Him Himself
and am farther off due to that
from you than I am from both
of them now late at night in the
sleeping vale
in the little township up to its
doorknobs in
snow writhing upon the stale
sheets for the whole matter's
skin—
deep I'm howling "youuu" through
my pillow dike
many seas away that are milling
nearer
with my limbs in the dark playing
your double like
an insanity-stricken mirror.
(Brodsky, *Collected Poems in English* 103)[41]

Like "Conversation with a Celestial Being," this poem is preoccupied with incommunicability, loss, and the failure of memory. The addressee is not only absent but "badly conceived" as well. The hero hesitates in naming her, switching from the formal *vy* to informal *ty*, and even confuses genders: "dear respected darling" (*dorogoi uvazhaemyi milaia*). The author is disoriented in time and space—"from nowhere with love the enth of Marchember." Place, date, and the addressee are thrust together and scrambled. The lyric imitates an amnesiac condition: "since the features of the face, speaking / frankly, are not to be recalled." The author imagines himself as a nonbeing, his state depicted by a series of negations ("from nowhere," "not important," "not to be recalled," "not yours"), speaking from the void into the void. His sense of identity lost, he reflects his absent lover's features with his body.

The poem mimics the incoherent ravings of a madman in its alogical use of language. Gaps imitate impeded speech: "We have before us the sort of syntax which conveys stream of consciousness, and the kind of despair which no grammar can restrain: the sentence breaks off, picks up, and then is broken again."[42] The whole lyric is one twisting, long sentence composed of broken phrases, in which words like "God" (line 7), and "no" (line 14) are expected but omitted in the Russian original. "Bottom" [of what?] (line 9) is omitted as well, and the idiomatic "there is no end to it" (*kontsa i kraia net*) is truncated as *kontsa i kraia.* Broken syntax and a string of enjambments dramatize incommunicability and despair. Syntactic and grammatical rules are disrupted, as, for instance, in "I loved you more than angels and himself, / and that's why I am further from you than from both of them."[43] Punctuation marks are omitted, telegraph-style (as in *dorogoi uvazhaemyi milaia* in the Russian original). The collision of meter and syntax, a prominent feature of Brodsky's poetry, is here especially conspicuous. Of sixteen lines, five lines in the Russian original (2–3–4–5–6) are connected by enjambment, resulting in a highly fragmentary narrative. The English version, in which Brodsky pushes to the limit the incoherence of the Russian original, dispenses with punctuation altogether, and has nearly all of its lines connected by enjambment.

The deletion of logical links, the disruption of grammatical and syntactic rules, omissions, and interruptions all convey pain exceeding verbal expression. In his essay "The Keening Muse" (1982), a self-referential characterization of Anna Akhmatova's poetry, Brodsky states that "the elements of howl . . . would appear either in the form of idiosyncratic excessive rhyming or as a non sequitur line interjected in an otherwise coherent narrative" (*Less Than One* 50). "From nowhere with love" is such an approximation to a howl—one long rambling sentence with multiple non sequiturs like "writhing at night on the sheet—which is at least not said below" and compulsive repetitions ("at night" is said twice). This pseudo-howl culminates with the poet actually "bellowing 'you'" in the Russian original and, more emphatically, "howling 'youuu'" in the English version. This unpoetic wail, an elemental form of expression (the Shestovian "senseless, desperate cry or a wild sob") communicates pain more vividly than a coherent narrative.[44]

Incoherent speech, the disjunctures of the writer's amnesia, and the separation between the writer and the addressee all highlight communicative problems. The poem is a letter addressed to a real but unreachable interlocutor (Marina Basmanova). The author's body reflects her as his mind goes blank. As language proves inadequate to convey anguish, cries and bodily gestures take the place of speech: "in the darkness with all of my body your features / like an insane mirror repeating." Just as his physical self conjures the addressee's facial features, his emotion toward the addressee contrasts with the void from which his utterance emanates: "from nowhere" but "with love." To fall back on Jakobson's model of the functions of language, the utterance (a cry of pain) maximizes the emotive and weakens the referential functions; it orients itself toward the addressee with the vocative "dear respected darling" but problematizes the conative function through the addressee's obscurity; and it exposes phatic failure, for the hero's tongue-tied monologue is carried out in limbo. The Brodskian speech event presents itself as aborted communication.

This dramatic enactment of communicative problems is at the same time a tongue-in-cheek metaliterary play. The first line of the poem alludes both to Ian Fleming's James Bond novel and movie *From Russia with Love* (1957/1963), and to Nikolai Gogol's classic "Diary of a Madman" ("Zapiski sumasshedshego," 1835). Giving a foretaste of postmodern playfulness, the incongruous combination of pop (Fleming) and high culture (Gogol) in the opening line imparts a slightly humorous tinge. Brodsky's pretense of madness translates into a wry language game in which he turns verbal formulas on their heads. Such is the case with "not yours but no one else's faithful friend," which both expresses alienation and plays with trite writing formulas like "your devoted friend" or "devotedly, X." Similarly, "as it is not said below at least—" (*kak ne skazano nizhe po krainei mere*—) reverses the formulaic "as said below." This is a poem in progress, hence "dear respected darling" is a non sequitur but also a record of potential ways of approaching the addressee. The source of the poem, the individual's real pain, is transformed into a work of art.[45] In Brodsky's Nietzschean parlance, "the writer can suffer his grief in a genuine way, but the description of this grief is not genuine tears or gray hair. It is only an approximation of a genuine reaction, and the awareness of this detachment creates a truly insane situation."[46] In a doubling that attends the act of creativity, the poet splits into the experiencer of pain and its recorder, and therefore, to an extent, he also distances himself from it.

A bifurcation between the existential and metaliterary planes of this text, however, hardly dims its overall poignancy. Seemingly illogical utterances, upon closer inspection, reveal a reasoning based in despair. Thus "I loved you more than angels and himself, / and that's why I am further from you than from both of them" springs from the belief that one parts first from whatever is most precious. Similarly, "Not yours but / no one else's faithful friend" is a twist on Gogol's playfully noncommittal characterizations ("neither this nor that" [*ni to ni drugoe*]), but a twist imbued with grave import. The hero has lost touch with his former realities, but his new existence is defined only as a deficiency.

In "From nowhere with love" Brodsky reverses theological ineffability to intimate an anguish that eclipses the word. According to his essay "Less Than One" (1976), Brodsky always had difficulty grasping time's progression:

> A school is a factory is a poem is a prison is academia is boredom, with flashes of panic . . . Life never looked to me like a set of clearly marked transitions; rather, it snowballs, and the more it does, the more one place (or one time) looks like another. (*Less Than One* 17–18)

An estranged and damaged subjectivity locates itself in one lifelong moment outside space and time ("nowhere" and "Marchember the enth"), like an upside-down rendition of the experience of eternity in Orthodox worship. Brodsky's omission of punctuation further locates the utterance in the atemporal.[47] The poet's rejection of articulation and various forms of negation, common markers of apophaticism, reference not the divine with its surplus of being but a broken self. Instead of an unmentioned God, the hero yearns for his mortal and unreachable interlocutor. The author hardly falls silent, but the lyric's language goes as far as it can in challenging itself when tapping into pain beyond the word.

A SLICE OF THE MONOTONE OF INFINITY

Incommunicability, silence, amnesia, an estrangement from the outside world, and self-estrangement are persistent motifs of this cycle. "A list of some observations. In a corner, it's warm" ("Eto—riad nabliudenii. V uglu teplo") presents the silencing and petrifaction of the self. Man and his words turn into dead matter under the effect of time:

Это —ряд наблюдений. В углу— тепло. Взгляд оставляет на вещи след. Вода представляет собой стекло. Человек страшней, чем его скелет.	A list of some observations. In a corner, it's warm A glance leaves an imprint on anything it's dwelt on. Water is glass's most public form. Man is more frightening than his skeleton.
Зимний вечер с вином в нигде. Веранда под натиском ивняка. Тело покоется на локте, как морена вне ледника.	A nowhere winter evening with wine. A black porch resists an osier's stiff assaults Fixed on an elbow, the body bulks like a glacier's debris, a moraine of sorts.
Через тыщу лет из-за штор моллюск извлекут с проступившим сквозь бахрому оттиском "доброй ночи" уст не имевших сказать кому.	A millennium hence, they'll no doubt expose a fossil bivalve propped behind this gauze cloth, with the print of lips under the print of fringe, mumbling "Good night" to a window hinge.
(Brodskii 3:128)	(Brodsky, *Collected Poems in English* 104)

The first quatrain offers a series of terse statements, beginning with the most mundane remark, "in a corner it's warm." Less conventional asides follow, also disguised as axiomatic. These lines are pointedly nonpoetic "empirical observations," but even their matter-of-factness seems to be uttered with reluctance, as through clenched teeth. The "nowhere" of the second quatrain, as in "From nowhere with love," designates an existential vacuum. Nature is a mechanical principle that dully dislodges man and man-made objects. The porch is under the onslaught of a bare winter willow, and in Brodsky's auto-translation, the "stiff" assault on the porch emphasizes nature's mechanical force. Distant and disdainful observation of his body (like a moraine displaced by a glacier) conveys an intense self-estrangement. In English, the words "bulks," "fixed on an elbow," more strongly convey a sense of the living body as inanimate matter.

Impersonal physical laws, or rather Brodsky's idiosyncratic views masquerading as such, in the first quatrain combine with the deadening of the self in the second quatrain to articulate a total de-animation. The lines of the final quatrain are reminiscent of "human lips, / which have nothing more to say, / Preserve the shape of the last word spoken" in "The Horseshoe Finder." The fossil, a recurrent image in Brodsky, connotes the destructive power of time and usually functions in tandem with a post-apocalyptic temporality of the past-in-the-future or a distant future imagined as ancient past. In "A list of some observations," the fossil, a synecdochic reduction of the poet, conveys solitude in the present and impending silence and death. The utterance "good night" is addressed to the self since there is no one to talk to, and a petrified fragment will be all that remains of the hero.[48]

If "A list of some observations" portrays man and his language as dead matter under the effects of time, "I was born and grew up in the Baltic marshland" ("Ia rodilsia i vyros v baltiiskikh bolotakh") projects the stupefying effect of time on poetic language. Prosody is the twin of time in their shared inhumanness:

Я родился и вырос в балтийских болотах, подле
серых цинковых волн, всегда набегавших по две,
и отсюда—все рифмы, отсюда тот блеклый голос,
вьющийся между ними, как мокрый волос;
если вьется вообще. Облокотясь на локоть,
раковина ушная в них различит не рокот,

I was born and grew up in the Baltic marshland
by zinc-gray breakers that always marched on
in twos. Hence all rhymes, hence that wan flat voice
that ripples between them like hair still moist,
if it ripples at all. Propped on a pallid elbow,
the helix picks out of them no sea rumble

но хлопки полотна, ставень,
ладоней, чайник,
кипящий на керосинке, максимум—
крики чаек.
В этих плоских краях то и хранит
от фальши
сердце, что скрыться негде и видно
дальше.
Это только для звука пространство
всегда помеха:
глаз не посетует на недостаток эха.

(Brodskii 3:130)

but a clap of canvas, of shutters,
of hands, a kettle
on the burner, boiling—lastly, the
seagull's metal
cry. What keeps hearts from
falseness in this flat region
is that there is nowhere to hide
and plenty of room for vision.
Only sound needs echo and
dreads its lack.
A glance is accustomed to no
glance back.
(Brodsky, *Collected Poems in English* 101)

This poem has been read as a traditional deist statement, with the sea "the embodiment of cosmic and natural rhythm and 'harmony,' akin to rhyme."[49] I would suggest instead that the lyric engages deist conventions to take issue with the idealistic view of poetry. A subtext of "I was born and grew up in the Baltic marshland" is the deist maritime poetry of Batiushkov, Tiutchev, Mandelstam, and so on. Sea "rumble" recalls Batiushkov's "harmony in a talk of billows," and *rakovina* (meaning both "helix" and "seashell") brings to mind Mandelstam's "The Seashell," itself invoking Mandelstam's "Silentium," and Fet's "How poor our language is!" Batiushkov's and Mandelstam's poets are filled with the sea's music. For Mandelstam, even though the cosmos is indifferent to man, it will eventually embrace the poet's creation. If "The Seashell" is a pantheist conceit of poetic creation in which verbal harmonies, inferior to the harmony of the cosmos, still participate in the latter, Brodsky's poem describes poetic creativity inspired by the sea but partaking of the dullness of time, not the music of the spheres.[50] Just as water is formed into waves, language is arranged into lines and rhymes. The effect is not one of neutral organization but of torpor. The lyric's couplets march in droning twos. Couplets, stretched accentual lines with an unfixed caesura and feminine rhymes, many of them slant (*podle–po dve; chainik–chaek*), create a monotonous effect, an intonation as wan and flat as the marshscape. It is not that the poem as poem is dull (the variations in sound are often more interesting than exact rhymes and are among Brodsky's best-known poetic traits), but its tone is lackluster, also typical of Brodsky.[51]

Brodsky's poem, which is like water, which is like time, is infected with, and strives to imitate, cosmic emptiness. The poetic voice and the landscape in "I was born and grew up in the Baltic marshland" are equally lusterless: the latter deadens the former. There is a marshland instead of the sea, and an anatomical helix instead of the metaphorical seashell. "The helix will discern not a rumble in them," a negative dialogic reference, stresses a dismissal of deist poetic statements.

The hero's ear will hear only mundane sounds. In the auto-translation the seagulls' cry is "metal," as in "The Hawk's Cry in Autumn" ("Osennii krik iastreba," 1976) where the dying hawk emits a mechanical shriek, "mechanical for it's meant / for nobody, for no living ears" (*mechanicheskii, ibo ne / prednaznachennyi ni dlia ch'ikh ushei* (Brodsky, *Collected Poems in English* 261; Brodskii 3:105). In either case there is no comprehending ear. The hero learns his craft from sounds that are not merely devoid of cosmic concord but carry alienation and pain like the inarticulate shriek of the dying hawk. A tautological "leaning one's elbow on an elbow" (*oblokotias' na lokot'*) is an admission that no external support is present. "Gray zinc waves" evoke zinc-coated coffins. In "Conversation with a Celestial Being" the hero yearns to merge with God as with the landscape "in which one shot, let's say, searches for you." The flat region of "I was born and grew up in the Baltic marshland" offers no place for the hunted prey to hide.

Brodsky's poem correlates water, time, and poetry, all of them divulging a single truth—that of the inhuman. For Brodsky, as for Mandelstam, water, language, and time are metaphorically linked. As Brodsky notes in "The Sound of the Tide" (1983), Derek Walcott

> gives us a sense of infinity embodied in the language as well as in the ocean which is always present in his poems: as their background or foreground, as their subject, or as their meter. To put it differently, these poems represent a fusion of two versions of infinity: language and the ocean. The common parent of these two elements is, it must be remembered, time. (*Less Than One* 174)

Brodsky also said that he liked to spend New Year's eve by the sea because he could observe time coming out of the water—an image that recalls Aphrodite's emergence from foam in "Silentium," which marks the beginning of the temporal.[52] However, for Brodsky time has a stupefying effect: "The routine character of decay weakens the very sentiment of regret" (*Less Than One* 56). The sea is marked not by the rapturous pre-creative silence of Mandelstam's "Silentium" but by a prehistoric or post-historic silence of human absence.[53]

Prosody embodies the inhuman monotony of infinity. According to Valentina Polukhina, in Brodsky "the semantic class of language is very often found in thematic opposition to time."[54] In my view, though, poetry and time are more often represented as companions in arms, rather than as conflicting entities, as in the poem under consideration or in the following commentary on Akhmatova in "The Keening Muse":

> Her diction and, with it, the code, subsequently changed a great deal to make the monotone of the infinite more audible. In fact, it was already quite distinct in *Anno Domini MCMXXI* —her fifth and technically speaking last collection. In some of its poems, that monotone merges with the author's voice to the point that she has to sharpen the concreteness of detail or image in order to save them, and by the same token her own mind, from the inhuman neutrality of the meter. Their fusion, or rather the former's subordination to the latter, came later. In the meantime, she was trying to save her own notions of existence from being overtaken by those supplied to her by prosody: for prosody knows more about time than a human being would like to reckon with. (*Less Than One* 46)[55]

Exposure through prosody to the monotony of time has the effect of estranging one from life. To camouflage this estrangement, and, more importantly, to retain sanity, Akhmatova, a poet of strict meters, muffles her diction, but the more she does so, the more her voice merges with the depersonalized tenor of time.

In the manner of "The Keening Muse," Brodsky's essays on his favorite poets (Auden, Eugene Montale, Thomas Hardy) often comment on the inhuman neutrality of poetry.[56] Again, these commentaries pertain to Brodsky himself as much as to his poetic predecessors. The impersonal tonality of the temporal entails the faded voice of the lyric, and this effect is a staple of Brodsky's poetics. This bleak voice twists between gray waves like wet hair (an image born of the visual resemblance between hair and seaweed) "if it twists at all." For Brodsky, as for Mandelstam, the poet's voice is his living essence.[57] If prosody does not make present the author's spirit, it is indeed inhuman.

In a reversal of the formalist doctrine of estrangement, poetry in its prosodic hypostasis petrifies the self. Victor Shklovsky's programmatic "Art as Device" ("Iskusstvo kak priem," 1917), like "I was born and grew up in the Baltic marshland," employs maritime imagery to discuss automatization, the deadening pull of routine:

> People living at the seashore grow so accustomed to the murmur of the waves that they never hear it. By the same token, we scarcely ever hear the words we utter . . . We look at each other, but we do not see each other anymore. Our perception of the world has withered away, what has remained is mere recognition.[58]

For Shklovsky poetry restores the keenness of perception by presenting the habitual in a novel light and breaking the chain of automatic responses. For Brodsky poetry, in its prosodic neutrality, does exactly the opposite—it distances the self from the world.

Many of Brodsky's lyrics portray poetry as inhuman—inhuman not in the positive sense of verbal extratemporality but inhumane somewhat like Shestov's dehumanized absolute. Thus, "Verses on the Death of T. S. Eliot" conjoins poetry and time in their callous monotony, hence the droning triple rhymes of the elegy. The poem challenges the view that for Brodsky the poetic is capable of resisting the temporal: poetry "breeds within the glass of lonely days, / each echoing each, that swim to distance" (*Poeziia osnovana na skhodstve / begushchikh vdal' odnoobraznykh dnei* (Brodskii 2:115).[59] Similarly, "A Letter in a Bottle" ("Pis'mo v butylke," 1964) links temporal and prosodic indifference to the human hero: "What couplets may bring me I must pay back / in our days or in hours on my lonely track—/ for instance, these days in the snowy waste . . . / It's death alone, madam, that can't be repaid" (*Chto parnaia rifma nam dast, to ei / my vozvrashchaem pod vidom dnei. / Kak, skazhem, dannye dni v snegu . . . / Lish' smert' ostavliaet, madam, v dolgu*) (Brodskii 1:184).[60]

"I was born and grew up in the Baltic marshland," analogously, positions poetry as the twin of time, and fastens on the lack of response from the world. The concluding lines, "It is only for sound that space is an obstacle: / the eye will not regret the lack of an echo" bring to mind poems such as Pushkin's "The Echo" ("Echo," 1831) and Ivanov's "The Alpine Horn." In Pushkin the poet, like an echo, responds to everything in the world but receives no reply; in Ivanov the horn sounds to create an echo in the mountains, a parable of nature being echoed by God. The last line of Brodsky's poem, transposing the aural (an echo) onto the visual (the eye), offers a counter to Ivanov's idealist "echo" topoi. The ear of the hero may strain to catch a response but his vision, apparently more metaphysically sober, accepts emptiness as the truth of life.

"My quiet craft, my mute creation" ("Tikhotvorenie moe, moe nemoe") develops the facet of poetry's inhumanness, hinted at in "I was born and grew up in the Baltic marshland," that the text will be estranged from its author, and in addition points to the poet losing free agency, overpowered by the very operations of his language:

Тихотворение мое, мое немое,	My quiet craft, my mute creation,
однако, тяглое—на страх поводьям,	it is however, fraught—to each reign's trepidation,
куда пожалуемся на ярмо и	where to shall we complain about the yoke and
кому поведаем, как жизнь проводим?	to whom shall we confess the way our life is spent?
Как поздно заполночь ища глазунию	As, late past midnight, searching for the fried egg's eye

луны за шторами зажженной спичкою,	of moonlight past the drapes and with a flared-up match
вручную стряхиваешь пыль безумия	you take your hand and brush away the dust of madness
с осколков желтого оскала в писчую.	from off its yellow splintered grin onto the pages.
Как эту борзопись, что гуще патоки,	No matter how this scrambled script is spread—though denser
там ни размазывай, но с кем в колене и	it flows than honey, if you with your someone's knee
в локте хотя бы преломить, опять таки,	and her elbow, try to breach it in prostration, once again,
ломоть отрезанный, тихотворение?	you are a cut-off piece, serenely created?[61]

(Brodskii 3:136)

"My quiet craft" envisions a creative process where the power relationship between the author and language resembles that delineated in theoretical writings on the "death of the author." This self-referential poem depicts a process of creation in which the medium dominates creative consciousness. The first four lines position the protagonist vis-à-vis his production. The conceit of the "poem-horse," "fraught—to each rein's trepidation," highlights a notion of language that challenges authorial intention.[62] There is the problem of the addressee again: "where to shall we complain about the yoke?" Lines 1–4 employ feminine rhymes while the rest of the poem utilizes dactylic endings, slowing down the movement of the lyric and highlighting the strain inherent in poetic articulation.

Lines 5–8 outline the process of creation. The hero seeks "the fried egg's eye of moonlight past the drapes" and "brushes away the dust of madness / from off its yellow splintered grin onto the pages."[63] The moon acts as a double-edged metaphor of inspiration and lunacy. "Splinters" expresses the brokenness of the poetic universe, and the "yellow grin" of the moon stresses the predatory qualities of this hallowed symbol of poetic inspiration. The poet transmits on paper not the sublime voice of the muse but "the dust of madness." As "From nowhere with love," the lyric points at a precarious mental condition through its omission of "paper" (*bumagu*) after "writing" (*pishchuiu*).

The concluding lines highlight the work's separation from the author. A script that "flows denser than honey" suggests a poem written in a condensed private code, as well as cloying sweetness. No matter how hard the author may try to dilute it (to "spread"), this private code will be incomprehensible to the reader. There will be none to share his gift with. In the convoluted syntax of the last sentence, literally, "but with whom can you over the knee and / elbow at least, break, yet again, a cut-off slice, quiet craft?" The strained syntax, analogous to the twisted syntax of the conclusion to "A list of some observations," reflects the difficulty of transmitting the lyric to the world. *Borzopis'* degrades the hero's output (*borzopisets*—"hack writer") and extends the central conceit of the poem as a charging horse (*borzyi kon'*—"swift steed").

The hero's production is a "cut-off slice," the fragmentary quality of which is foreshadowed by "splinters." *Lomot' otrezannyi* designates, among other things, alienated offspring. "Over the knee and / elbow at least, break" (*v kolene i / v lokte khotia by prelomit'*) engages several idiomatic expressions: "to breach one's knees" (*prelomit' koleni*), "to break bread" (*prelomit' khleb*), and "sense of fellowship" (*chuvstvo loktia*), "to lean on the friend's elbow" (*operet'sia na lokot' druga*). Breaking bread suggests sharing but the poet has no one to share his words and grief. To breach one's knees is to bow in prayer. The breaking (*prelomlenie*) of the cut-off slice tallies with the breaking of bread at the Last Supper. The poem is Brodsky's "body" given to his readers in remembrance, but the poem's opening and closing questions make clear that no communion between author and reader will take place.

In the absence of external contact, all "My quiet craft" can do is address itself, which it does, starting and ending with the apostrophic *tikhotvorenie* (the analogue of "be silent" encircling "Silentium!"). The neologism *tikhotvorenie,* mute (*nemoe*), and "not mine" (*ne-moe*) dramatizes negativity, much like Paul Celan's "das Genicht" in "Etched Away" ("Weggebeizt," 1967):

Weggebeizt vom Strahlenwind deiner Sprache das bunte Gerede des An- erlebten—das hundert- zungige Mein- gedicht, das Genicht.[64]	Are destroyed with the radioactive wind of your speech motley rumors of what has been li- ved through—hundred- tongued mine- poem, no-em.

In Celan's poem the destructive wind of time leaves the negative form of the poet's word—"*das Genicht.*" In Brodsky, with the poem a fraction of a more complete whole ("cut-off slice"), and the author's agency undermined (*nemoe*), the creation of verse equals the production of silence.

THE CONDITION WE CALL EXILE AND THE DEATH OF THE AUTHOR

". . . and when 'the future' is uttered, swarms of mice" (". . . i pri slove 'griadushchee' iz russkogo iazyka") is the penultimate poem of the cycle "A Part of

Speech." The last line of the poem, "to a part. To his spoken part. To a part of speech" (*rechi. Chast' rechi voobshche. Chast' rechi*) makes it clear that this is a key piece in both the cycle and the collection.[65] This is Brodsky's programmatic articulation of verbal skepticism. The poem integrates the multiple facets of verbal inadequacy examined above: disintegration of the text into meaningless signs, language's failure to provide a sanctuary against death, the unrecoverable nature of memories ("Conversation with a Celestial Being"); disruption of communication ("From nowhere with love"); the silencing and petrification of the self ("A list of some observations"); the world's unresponsiveness and the inhumanness of prosody ("I was born and grew up in the Baltic marshland"); and authorial estrangement from the text and loss of free agency ("My quiet craft"). Cumulatively, Brodsky's lyric subverts the time-honored notion of the poet surviving this mortal coil by the word:

. . . и при слове "грядущее" из
  русского языка
	. . . and when "the future" is
	  uttered, swarms of mice

выбегают мыши и всей
  оравой
	rush out of the Russian language
	  and gnaw a piece

отгрызают от лакомого куска	of ripened memory which is twice
памяти, что твой сыр дырявой.	as hole-ridden as real cheese.

После стольких зим уже
  безразлично, что
	After all these years it hardly
	  matters who

или кто стоит в углу у окна за
  шторой,
	or what stands in the corner,
	  hidden by heavy drapes,

и в мозгу раздается не неземное
  "до,"
	and your mind resounds not with
	  a seraphic "doh,"

но ее шуршание. Жизнь,
  которой,
	only their rustle. Life, that no one
	  dares

как дареной вещи, не смотрят
  в пасть,
	to appraise, like that gift horse's
	  mouth,

обнажает зубы при каждой встрече.	bares its teeth in a grin at each

От всего человека вам остается
  часть
	Encounter. What gets left of a
	  man amounts

речи. Часть речи вообще. Часть речи.	to a part. To his spoken part. To a part of speech.
(Brodskii 3:143)	(Brodsky, *Collected Poems in* *English* 114)

This piece has been interpreted by Lev Loseff as proclaiming expansion through poetry, as inspired by Gavriil Derzhavin's rendition of Horace's "Exegi Monumentum," "Monument" ("Pamiatnik," 1795): "'Chast' menia bol'shaia' can be understood traditionally, as 'a great part of me,' but also as 'a part of me that is greater than I.' "[66] In Valentina Polukhina's reading, "language turned out to be the firm ground for the poet's groundlessness, while the technique of *pars pro toto* as a metonymical depiction of man has become a vehicle for his spiritual and poetic expansion."[67] Irina Sluzhevskaia and Irina Plekhanova offer similar interpretations: "Death is defeated by the only opponent that can withstand any enemy in Brodsky—speech . . . The cycle that started with torture and madness, unfolds as loneliness and despair, prepares and accomplishes a triumph"; "If the poet serves language, and language constitutes metaphysical unity that unites all and is realized in living speech . . . immortality is a partial continuation of the self in an ideal, but actual being."[68] These analyses are illuminating, but I see the poem as an expression of poetic reduction, with language shrinking one into "less than one." Brodsky positions his poem alongside Russian Horatian poems on overcoming death through the inscription of the self in poetry and rejects this traditional notion.

The image of mice rushing to gnaw at cheese already in some measure eaten away plays on the set phrase "holey memory" (*dyriavaia pamiat'*) and calls forth associations with decay, solitude, and empty dark spaces. Brodsky connects both absence and the loss of memory to language, with the mice "rushing out of the Russian language." Such vividly imagined desolation is characteristic of the poem, the cycle, and the collection, all composed in the 1970s, within a couple of years after Brodsky had left his homeland.

Brodsky's separation from his country, his reader, and his language, all literal rather than figurative, became the obsessive focus of his poetry. Exile subsumes a multiplicity of issues—physical, political, psychological, epistemological, and linguistic.[69] Of these, exile's linguistic consequences are at the forefront. Brodsky's exilic poetry interweaves physical and verbal deterioration, the loss of home, youthful vigor, and command of language as, for instance, in "1972" ("1972 god"), a poem preceded by eight months of silence:

чаши лишившись в пиру
  Отечества,
	Denied a chalice at the feast of the
	  fatherland,

нынче стою в незнакомой
  местности . . .
	now I stand in a strange place. The name
	  hardly matters . . .

здесь и скончаю я дни, теряя
волосы, зубы, глаголы,
  суффиксы.
	Here I'll live out my days, losing gradually
	hair, teeth, consonants, verbs, and
	  suffixes.

(Brodskii 3:16–18)	(Brodsky, *Collected Poems in English* 69)

Like Mandelstam in "Earphones, my earphones," Brodsky considers the actual silencing of the poet, interweaving the political, linguistic, and existential significations of silence.[70]

Like "1972," the essay "The Condition We Call Exile" connects existential, linguistic, and physical loss. First, Brodsky deromanticizes exile: "Displacement and misplacement are this century's commonplace" (*On Grief and Reason* 23). For him this predicament is not a special province of the intellectual elite but the plight of the common man. Second, he sees exile as a ubiquitous metaphysical condition: "At least, it has a very strong, very clear metaphysical dimension" (*On Grief and Reason* 25). It is hardly surprising that the image of the exiled man appears in Brodsky's work before his departure to the West and even prior to his northern exile, since for Brodsky exile is not a cruel twist of fate but a law of life on a par with suffering, which is, according to "Conversation with a Celestial Being," "an ability of bodies."[71] Third, exile is testimony to verbal inadequacy: "Exile covers, at best, the very moment of departure, expulsion; what follows is both too comfortable and too autonomous to be called by this name, which so strongly suggests a comprehensible grief" (*On Grief and Reason* 31). In this sense, exile is like death, which, as Brodsky states, for example, in "The Funeral of Bobo" ("Pokhorony Bobo," 1972), is inexpressible: emptiness "is like hell, but shittier" (*V nei kak v adu, no bolee kherovo*) (Brodsky, *Collected Poems in English* 57; Brodskii 3:35), so the poet strives to fill in with words the blank space on the page as Dante filled posthumous emptiness with words. Fourth, exile makes the dehumanizing tendency of time especially acute: "Famous for its pain, it should also be known for its pain-dulling infinity, for its forgetfulness, detachment, indifference, for its terrifying human and inhuman vistas for which we've got no yardstick except ourselves" (*On Grief and Reason* 33).

Most significantly, "The Condition We Call Exile" offers an ironically tinged critique of modern criticism's figurative destruction of the author's biography, and presents the exiled writer as psychologically the writer par excellence, who experiences more intensely than others the sense of disappearance in the text:[72]

> Of course a writer always takes himself posthumously: and an exiled writer especially so, inspired as he is not so much by the artificial oblivion to which he is subjected by his former state but by the way the critical profession in the free marketplace enthuses about his contemporaries . . . On the bookshelf your place will be occupied, not by you, but by your book. And long as they insist on making a distinction between art and life, it is better if they find your book good and your life foul than the other way around. Chances are, of course, that they won't care for either. Life in exile, abroad, in a foreign element, is essentially a premonition of your own book-form fate, of being lost on the shelf among those with whom all you have in common is the first letter of your surname. Here you are, in some gigantic library's reading room, still open . . . Your reader won't give a damn about how you got here . . . What

> binds us is our book-like fate, the same literal and symbolic lying open on the table or the floor of the gigantic library, at various ends, to be trampled on or picked up by a mildly curious reader or—worse—by a dutiful librarian. (*On Grief and Reason* 27–31)

Exile is a premonition of oblivion in the word. Physical banishment and literary fate alike, as the Borgesian infinite library, denote alienation. The exiled writer experiences in an intensified form what every writer does, that is, (self-)estrangement and the presentiment of extinction and disappearance in language and the reader.

". . . and when 'the future' is uttered" is Brodsky's poetic meditation on "the condition we call exile" in which the planes of physical and verbal absence intersect. Linguistic absence is fashioned through the imagery of language as a desolate space inhabited by mice. The lines dramatize decay and emptiness or, more precisely, desertion, and inaugurate the theme of losing control over language. This linguistic wasteland produces forces of destruction—mice gnawing on memory. Verbal mutilation is palpable in the mice's assault on the author's mind and his past.

Lines 5–8 further unfold this theme. "After so many winters" drops "summers" (*let*) from the idiomatic "it's been ages" (*skol'ko let, skol'ko zim*). After years of banishment, or years of solitude and pain, the hero no longer hears an angelic *do* but only the rustle of drapes. In its sense of "before" *do* reinforces the theme of disappearing memories of the past; as a musical note (the first note on the musical scale), it refers to the voice of the muse (music–muse–poetry) or the transcendental, which is no longer heard, or heard only in a degraded form.[73]

Since language destroys one's memories—and since poetry is like time in its inhuman monotony—exile, death, and the muse alike transform the author into a lifeless fragment. It is in this sense that "it no longer matters what / or who stands in the corner by the window behind the drape."[74] Drapes are mentioned two more times in the cycle: in "A list of some observations" and "My quiet craft." In light of these, the drapes in ". . . and when 'the future' is uttered" conceal the figure of death or a ghastly vision of the muse. The former interpretation does not contradict the latter but reinforces it since Brodsky repeatedly underscores the dehumanizing effect of time and time's kinship with poetry. Man becomes dead before he actually dies, so to speak, turning into a thing.

Brodsky's drapery should also be understood against the background of the more traditional image of the veil. The symbolist tradition poeticized the boundary between the everyday and the ideal. In Blok's "The Stranger," for instance, a veil symbolically marks off the physical from the spiritual world. The image of the veil also surfaces in Shestov's *All Things Are Pos-*

sible, Derrida's "How to Avoid Speaking: Denials," and de Man's "Autobiography As De-Facement": metaphysicians are "invested in a purple veil of fine words" (Shestov); in Meister Eckhart, Derrida says, there is "a certain signification of unveiling, of laying bare, of truth as what is beyond the covering of the garment"; the language of tropes, de Man comments on Wordsworth, "is indeed like the body, which is like its garments, the veil of the soul as the garment is the sheltering veil of the body."[75] Invariably these thinkers juxtapose appearances and essences, be they the noumenal hiding behind the phenomenal (Blok) or being obscured by language (Shestov, Derrida, de Man; for the latter two "being" requires quotation marks). Brodsky's poem is a darkly ironic comment on the poetic tradition of celebrating hidden vistas. What is concealed is not "an enchanted shore, and an enchanted distance" (Blok), but the ghost of extinction or a devastating muse. The "higher truth" hidden behind the drape is the truth of depersonalization.[76]

Brodsky's depersonalization is carried through on the level of grammar: "The most traditional component of lyric poetry, the 'I,' never appears."[77] The lyrical persona is a passive object that is acted upon, as underscored by reflexive verbs "is heard" (*razdaetsia*) and "remains" (*ostaetsia*). The adverb "doesn't matter" (*bezrazlichno*), the only descriptor of the subject's emotional reaction, denies feeling altogether. Dulled by the coldness of time ("after so many winters"), the hero is indifferent to the creature in the corner, be it muse, the ghost of death, or simply a rustling mouse.

The drape produces a meaningless rustle, which phonetically links it and the mice, and together they reinforce the ideas of the incomprehensibility of existence and life's transience. The past is disappearing, obliterated by mice, the hissing of language. These opening images are reminiscent of Pushkin's "Verses Composed at Night During Insomnia" ("Stikhi, sochinennye noch'iu vo vremia bessonnitsy," 1830).[78] Pushkin talks about the "mouse-like bustle of life" (*zhizni mysh'ia begotnia*), seeking to discern meaning in the indistinct murmur of daily existence.[79] In Brodsky no meaning is to be coaxed from that rustling.

Mandelstam's "After midnight the heart steals" ("Posle polunochi serdtse voruet," 1931) is another poem about a nocturnal vigil that uses the imagery of mice. Here the heart "steals forbidden quiet" (*voruet zapreshchennuiu tish'*) and "feasts, / Having bitten a silvery mouse" (*piruet, / Vziav na prikus serebristuiu mysh'*) (Mandel'shtam 3:44). This lyric speaks to the theme of time, with mice the traditional tokens of transience, and by its rhythm imitates the movement of the clock. The poem embodies the incoherent mouse-like scurrying of life that had been the subject of Pushkin's ruminations. Replete with the consonants "sh," even the poem's phonic texture resembles the sounds of mice running to and fro, and so does Brodsky's lyric in the multiple hushing sounds of its *griadushchee.*

Brodsky's poetry explores the disjunction between memory and language by casting an associative chain between the past, words, death, and mice. In "Conversation with a Celestial Being" the poet-mouse furtively composes his words from somebody else's memories.[80] Once completed, the poem's words are further estranged from memories, turning into meaningless hieroglyphics. ". . .and when 'the future' is uttered" takes the next step, with its mice coming out of the language to devour memories. The hushing sound "shch" in *griadushchee* and the alliterative interplay of *griadushchee* and *gryzun—gryzushchee* ("rodent"—"gnawing") phonically announce the mice's emergence from language. This image "refers in a way to the phonetics of the Russian word for 'future,' which phonetically resembles the word for 'rodents.' Therefore, I spin it off into the idea that the future, that is, the word itself, gnaws—or whatever it is, sinks its teeth—into the cheese of memory."[81] Semantically, mice, chthonic animals, are associated with Apollo, the muses, and Mnemosyne, and so mice cum the muse cum words destroy the past.[82]

Like Tiutchev's "Silentium!," which claims that the word is not only meager as a means of communication but actively detrimental to the inner being, Brodsky's lyric presents language as communicatively deficient and an actively destructive entity. This is "a strange, frightening idea. For any poet it is precisely language that opposes time, keeping memories."[83] Not so for Brodsky, whose idiosyncratic notion that language devours man and things alike is pervasive across his oeuvre. In Valentina Polukhina's analysis, Brodsky inserts the word as a fourth element of the triad "spirit-man-thing," and thus neutralizes this opposition. The word imitates and replaces any of these elements."[84] Related to this concept is Denis Akhapkin's notion of Brodsky's philological metaphor, namely, likening the world to language.[85] However, the word's replacement of "spirit-man-thing" and likening the world to the word frequently translate as reality consumed by language.

The image of words devouring matter occurs as early as "Gorbunov and Gorchakov" ("Gorbunov i Gorchakov," 1965–68):

"Вещь, имя получившая, тотчас	"The moment that we give a thing a name
становится немедля частью речи."	that thing's transformed into a part of speech."
"И части тела?" "Именно они."	"But what about the body?" "It obeys
"А место это?" "Названо же домом."	the rule. "And what about this place?" "It's called
"А дни?" "Поименованы же дни."	a madhouse." "And the days?" "Their names are days."
"О, все это становится Содомом	"Oh, everything's transformed again to old

слов алчущих! Откуда их права?"	Sodom, built of greedy words. But how
"Тут имя прозвучало бы зловеще."	do they come by their right?" "—a word that rings
"Как быстро разбухает голова	a nasty bell." "My head's already so
словами, пожирающими вещи!"	besotted with these words devouring things."
(Brodskii 2:276–77)	(Brodsky, *Collected Poems in English* 193)

A name "objectifies a signified with its unchanging signifier when it gobbles it."[86] Indeed, language's gobbling up of living matter implies a more assertive rhetoric of destruction than an objectification of the signified. Decades later Brodsky would employ the rhetoric of the word's predatory insatiability in his essay "On Dostoevsky" (1980): Dostoevsky exposes "the voracity [*prozhorlivost'*] of language which at some point becomes dissatisfied with man, reality, guilt, death, infinity and salvation and attacks itself" (Brodskii 4:183).[87]

In a sardonic reversal of acmeist logology, Brodsky portrays words consuming being. The words "to consume" (*pozhrat'*) and "thing" (*veshch'*) appear in Mandelstam's "The Word and Culture": "Time wants to devour the state. Do not demand thing-ness, concreteness, materiality from poetry. Why identify the word with the thing, the object which it designates?" (Mandel'shtam 1:214–15). "The Child of Civilization" (1977), Brodsky's take on Mandelstam, qualifies acmeist idealism by transforming Mandelstam's notion of the word-Psyche and characterizing poetry less optimistically as "a spirit seeking flesh but finding words" (*Less Than One* 123). His lyrics go further by advancing the notion that language devours animate and inanimate entities alike.

The word that "was flesh and dwelt among us" assaults flesh in Brodsky.[88] This idea recurs in works of the 1970s like "December in Florence" ("Dekabr' vo Florentsii," 1976), "Midday in a Room" ("Polden' v komnate," 1978), and "Strophes," to later poems like "The Fly" ("Mukha," 1985). In "December in Florence" "a man gets reduced to a pen's rustle on paper, / to wedges, ringlets of letters, and also, due / to the slippery surface, to commas and full stops" (*chelovek prevrashchaetsia v shorokh pera po bumage, v kol'tsa, / petli, klinyshki bukv i, potomu chto skol'zko, / v zapiatye i tochki*) (Brodsky, *Collected Poems in English* 131; Brodskii 3:112).[89] "Midday in a Room" notes the distortion and reduction of light and sound in language: "both are refracted, distorted, / reduced; first—/ until darkness, until silence; / turned into words" (*oba prelomleny, iskazheny, / sokrashcheny: sperva—/ do potemok, do tishiny; / prevrascheny v slova*) (Brodskii 3:173). In "Strophes" language victimizes a lost beloved: "you know, dear, all whom anguish / pleads for, those out of reach, / are prey of the laws of language—/ periods, commas, speech" (*znaesh', vse, kto daleche, / po kom golosit toska—/ zhertvy zakonov rechi, / zapiatykh, iazyka*) (Brodsky, *Collected Poems in English* 152; Brodskii 3:183). "The Fly" likens language to bacteria assaulting living matter: "Microbes and sentences respect no barriers, / Afflicting all that can inhale or hear" (*Mikroby, frazy / ravno sposobny porazhat' zhivoe*) (Brodsky, *Collected Poems in English* 323; Brodskii 3:284).

Memory in particular is damaged by verbalization.[90] As Brodsky confesses in "Less than One," "words fail reality as well. At least it's been my impression that any experience coming from the Russian realm, even when depicted with photographic precision, simply bounces off the English language, leaving no visible imprint on its surface" (*Less Than One* 30). Positing an organic connection between experience and language makes it important which language is used for recollection. Lest one assume, however, that only recollection in a foreign tongue is detrimental to memories, Brodsky's essay makes the more sweeping claim that any verbal performance fails memory:

> But even if a writer is fully equipped to imitate on paper the subtlest fluctuations of the mind, the effort to reproduce the tail [of memories] in all its spiral splendor is still doomed, for evolution was not for nothing. The perspective of years straightens things to the point of complete obliteration. Nothing brings them back, not even handwritten words with their coiled letters. Such an effort is doomed all the more if this tail happens to lag behind somewhere in Russia. (*Less Than One* 30)

The exilic situation intensifies the problem of memory, but, more importantly, language is unable to recuperate the past since memories are deformed through cognitive systematizing efforts. At issue here is not so much the specificity of Brodsky's émigré status (for Olga Glazunova, "when only remembrances occupy the poet's imagination, every new line moves him toward bankruptcy") but the fact that memories are pushed out in the process of recollection and verbalization.[91] Indeed, problems of disjunction between memory and words, silence, and verbal skepticism, while exacerbated by Brodsky's exile and bilingualism, are rooted in his metaphysical outlook and psychological makeup. They emerge in Brodsky prior to his exile to the West—something we can see from "Conversation with a Celestial Being" as well as such early poems as "A Letter in a Bottle" and "Gorbunov and Gorchakov."

For Brodsky "memory betrays everybody, especially those we know best. It is an ally of oblivion, it is an ally of death" (*Less Than One* 489). Generalization and distancing involved in the process of remembrance and verbalization are especially fraught when it concerns those who are closest. One issue is that logic- and concept-bound cognition deforms the convoluted mnemonic "tail."[92] Another problem is that memory and verbal art are fragmentary, showing "a taste for detail" (*Less Than One* 452). "As hole-ridden as real cheese," mnemonic representation cannot but fail to represent lived experience in its fullness.

More drastically, memories fixed in words are gobbled up. While Mandelstam's Lethean poems point out the threat of the oblivious word and in "The Horseshoe Finder" the past is reduced in the text, Brodsky shows language actively destroying memories. Life, like language, consumes man and his memories, but one dare not question this gift. Lines 9–10 of ". . . and when 'the future' is uttered" transform the proverb "one does not look a gift horse in the mouth" (*darenomu koniu v zuby ne smotriat*) into a leeringly predatory vision, that life "bares its teeth at each encounter," an image similar to the rapacious moon-muse of "My quiet craft." Rhyme words often "contain thematic as well as phonetic echoes" in Brodsky.[93] Developing the imagery of mice gnawing at memory, the rhyme *past'–chast'* links greedy deformation and language. Man is gnawed through until nothing remains of him.[94]

The dangers of a break between the text and its creator emerge in the metaliterary commentary in ". . .and when 'the future' is uttered." This idea culminates in the last two lines of the poem. The word "part" advertises the poem as a rejoinder in a long-running poetic dialogue on the relationship among the self, language, and death. The same word appears in "Gorbunov and Gorchakov," in "1972" where "the dearest part" (*luchshaia chast'*) of the poet is shorn off by approaching nonexistence (Brodsky, *Collected Poems in English* 70; Brodskii 3:18), and in "Elegy" ("Elegiia," 1982) where the lovers, "only parts of a big whole" (*tol'ko chasti krupnogo tselogo*) (Brodskii 3:252), become ossified in life. Severed from the authorial psyche, poetic utterance in "1972" is equated with silence:

Это —точней —первый крик
   молчания,
царствие чье представляю
   суммою
звуков, исторгнутых прежде
   мокрою,
затвердевающей ныне в
   мертвую
как бы натуру, гортанью твердою.
 	
(Brodskii 3:18)
	The first cry of
	   speechlessness
	whose domain could be thought
	   just as a total feat
	of sounds voiced by a once
	   scarlet and
	wet—now hardening into a
	   moribund
	more or less matter—strong
	   vocal vent.
	(Brodsky, *Collected Poems in*
	   English 70)

Analogously, ". . .and when 'the future' is uttered" stresses by several means the vacuity of the text severed from poetic interiority. A comparison of the original and Brodsky's auto-translation furthers our understanding of the finale:

От всего человека вам
  остается часть
речи. Часть речи вообще.
  Часть речи.
	What gets left of a man
	  amounts
	to a part. To his spoken part. To a part
	  of speech.

There are telling differences between the Russian and the English versions. First, the presence of "whole" (*vsego*) in the Russian text, absent in the translation, makes the opposition "whole" versus "part" more pronounced. As Brodsky puts it in "The Child of Civilization," "any poet, no matter how much he writes, expresses in his verse, physically or statistically speaking, at most one-tenth of his life's reality. The rest is normally shrouded in darkness" (*Less Than One* 135). In the Russian text, the juxtaposition of "part" and "whole" highlights the reductive aspect of the part.

Second, the translation also omits "to you" (*vam*). It is "you"—the reader, the critic, the addressee—who "gets" the remnants of the author. This reader, critic, addressee, at best "mildly curious," at worst "a dutiful librarian," will appropriate the text.[95] As Brodsky asserts the fact of incommunicability with the reader in "A Journey from Petersburg to Istanbul" (1985), "silence will fall not so much as a sign of assent but as a sign of indifference" (*Less Than One* 103). Or, as he puts it in "A Poet and Prose" (1979), for Marina Tsvetaeva (and equally himself) reading is a complicity in the creative process, a view in which "an alert ear can distinguish a note of despair . . . coming specifically from a poet sorely fatigued by the ever-widening rift—growing with each additional line—between author and audience" (*Less Than One* 179).

Third, although both the original and the translation have enjambment before the last line, the effect of the enjambment is lost in the translation. In English the enjambment occurs between "amounts" and "to a part," whereas in Russian it falls between "part" (*chast'*) and "speech" (*rechi*). Therefore

> if this sentence is pronounced correctly (with the requisite pause at the line ending), it initially reads: "From the whole person you are left with a part." Only after this pause does one realize what it really says: "From the whole person you are left with a part . . . of his speech."[96]

The enjambment highlights the semantic switch that occurs around the word "part."[97] Placed at the line break, "part" is first interpreted as an indication of reduction (the whole man versus a part of him), which is then semantically connected to "speech." Whereas a regular enjambment "sharpens the conflict between the unity and the fragmentariness of speech sequences," Brodsky's enjambment sharpens this conflict twofold—through the device itself, and semantically, through the division of "part" and "speech."[98] The division of "part" and "speech," eliminated in the translation, formally embodies the metaliterary issue explored in the text—the problematic relationship between "man" and "speech." The English version does not preserve the irony and hesitation present in the original. While retaining the technical device of the enjambment, Brodsky came up with a considerably weaker version of semantic reversal, with "amounts to" anticipating completeness but undercut by the reductive "part."[99]

Lyrical subjectivity here is contracted—shriveled really—into language. The enjambment in the original enacts the fragmentation of the author into parts, the theme of the lyric, and is anticipated by earlier ones such as ". . . piece / memory . . ." and ". . . what / or who. . ." (*chto / ili kto*). In the former case, the enjambment delivers the fragmentation of remembrances. In the latter case, *chto,* first taken to be a conjunction opening a subsidiary clause ("it does not matter that . . ."), is next scanned properly as an interrogative pronoun. As a conjunction, *chto* is a pure part of speech in its structural function, whereas as a pronoun it refers to an object. This interplay of relational versus substantive meanings engages the problematic of depersonalization expressed most forcibly as "part of speech."[100] While the Russian original moves from the inanimate to the animate, *chto ili kto,* the auto-translation makes depersonalization more palpable, reversing the movement "who or what," but loses the original play on *chto,* likely the reason Brodsky prefers the move from *chto* to *kto* in the original.

The final line of the poem engages the polysemy of the expression "part of speech," whose first, non-technical meaning is part of the author's speech, what he has managed to tell us; the second, its linguistic aspect, refers to a grammatical part of speech.[101] The poem comments on the relationship between poetic consciousness and text in the following sequence: part of man—part of man's speech—part of speech as a formal unit. The effect achieved is that of sequencing rather than simultaneity. "In general" as in "part of speech in general" stresses that this is "part of speech" as a grammatical category. By the time "part of speech" is uttered for the third time, the effect of multiple repetitions turns this phrase into a mechanical verbal unit, purged of semantics and perceived as words as such.[102] A similar effect is achieved earlier with "future" and "*doh*" enclosed in quotation marks, and thus to be read as words per se. In the poem's conclusion the mechanical meaning takes precedence over the first two (part of man, part of his art). Inimitable subjectivity is ousted by language as a general device. If the poet's self yields to the mechanical units and operations of the text, there can be no transcendence of time and death through language.

Brodsky's statement, hardly "a genuine apotheosis of the Word," subverts the lionization of verse in the classical Horatian topos in its Russian transpositions from Mikhail Lomonosov's "I have wrought a sign of immortality to myself" ("Ia znak bessmertiia sebe vozdvignul," 1747) and Derzhavin's "Monument" to Pushkin's "I have wrought a monument not made by hand."[103] Lomonosov's "great part of me" (*veliku chast' moiu*) and Derzhavin's "a big part of me" (*chast' menia bol'shaia*) are degraded to "parts of speech."[104] In the Russian text the last two words ("part" and "speech") align both horizontally and vertically.[105] These horizontal and vertical axes reinforce each other. If the acrostic in Derzhavin's "The river of time in its flowing," "respect the ruin" (*RUINA CHTI*), subverts the pessimistic "*vanitas vanitatum*" message of the poem, Brodsky's "acrostic" only bolsters the antiverbal thrust delivered by his poem.

Robert Browning's "A Grammarian's Funeral: Shortly After the Revival of Learning in Europe" (1855) provides a revealing contrast to the Russian Horatian tradition.[106] In Browning's poem parts of speech gain in vitality in reverse ratio to the protagonist's life's force:

> So, with the throttling hands of death at strife,
> Ground he at grammar;
> Still, thro the rattle, parts of speech were rife:
> While he could stammer
> He settled *Hoti's* business—let it be!—
> Properly based *Oun*—
> Gave us the doctrine of the enclitic *De*
> Dead from the waist down.[107]

The grammarian fails to truly live his life, preferring "not to Live but Know." He concentrates on books but gains his knowledge mechanically, "by heart." As he is aging, he is further removed from reality, exchanging second-order things ("crabbed text" of the book) for third-order things ("the comment"). The lyric promise is debased to grammar grinding and sickness. Born with the face and throat of Apollo, the hero has the potential to produce a song but instead, exhausted and falling ill with tussis, he utters only whooping coughs. Even as his formerly Apollonian throat is throttled by death, he continues his single-minded work. Alliterative pairs "rattle"–"rife," "De"–"dead" contrast parts of speech that gain in vigor as the grammarian loses his vitality. The protagonist dies without knowing life, leaving people parts of speech. It is only as a lifeless corpse on the shoulders of his students that he ascends to the heights he has aspired to reach.

In Brodsky, as in Browning, "parts of speech" indicate a mechanical reduction of the self. Fragmentation is important again. Browning's hero wants "to image the whole, then execute the parts," but his striving for wholeness is undercut by irony as he focuses on minuscule things like "the enclitic De." Like Zhukovsky's "The Inexpressible" and Mandelstam's "The Horseshoe Finder," Brodsky's ". . .and when 'the future' is uttered" is a fragment. That it is a fragment is clear from the title as well as from the poem's opening with an ellipsis. The title and the opening turn inexpressibility into a formal device. In the words of "In the Lake District" ("V ozernom kraiu," 1972), "Whatever I wrote then was incomplete: / my lines expired in strings of dots" (*Vse to, chto ia pisal v te vremena, / svodilos' neizbezhno k mnogotoch'iu*) (Brodsky, *Collected Poems in English* 71; Brodskii 3:25). The ellipsis, then, refers to the poet's reality preceding the poem. It is this reality from which the poem emanates, and to which the reader is not privy.[108]

Brodsky envisions death as a disintegration of the whole into parts. In "An Anatomy of the World" (1611), John Donne depicts another disintegration that attends the death of his patron's young daughter. The world is now all in pieces, "all coherence gone," for

> She that should all parts to reunion bow,
> She that had all magnetic force alone,
> To draw and fasten sundered parts in one . . .
> She, she is dead.[109]

For Donne, only this young girl kept the world from falling into disarray; for Brodsky, only poetic consciousness holds disparate parts united. The annihilation of consciousness, Ms. Drury's in Donne, the author's in Brodsky, may be compared to the banishment of the divine from the universe.

The cessation of the synthesizing activity of the subject (the poet) means the breakdown of a meaningful whole into meaningless constituents. Like Mandelstam's "The Horseshoe Finder," Brodsky's poem denies the possibility of a rewarding communication with the reader and suggests that verbal immortality is an illusion inasmuch as what language preserves are soulless mechanical units. The poem is not an example of failed communication; rather, the poem states that verbal art is failed communication. At the same time "part of speech," in a linguistic metaturn, dramatizes failed communication. The poem's coda denies resurrection in the word. Moreover, just as the deictic *eti* in "What I am saying now is not said by me" (*Eti slova govoriu ne ia*) of "The Horseshoe Finder" or Tiutchev's "an uttered thought is a lie" deconstruct themselves, so does "part of speech." This hermeneutic difficulty is further amplified by the title of the cycle and of the collection. How much can one derive from a "part of speech" about "parts" and "speeches"?

As in the critical discourse on "the death of the author," the writing in ". . . and when 'the future' is uttered" turns into an iterative structure drifting in a sea of alien significations. Writing, and this piece of writing in particular, will remain after the author is gone. It will continue to exist, cut off from the consciousness of its creator, and continue to perform and function however mechanically. This is a Derridian "future disappearance," which "in principle will not prevent [writing] from functioning and from yielding, and yielding itself to, reading and rewriting." Likewise, as in the "death of the author" theory, language in this poem mutilates the man, in this case by damaging his memory.

Brodsky's "A Part of Speech" cycle and other works reveal conceptual and rhetorical linkages with post-structuralist antiverbal notions. The "drift into isolation" ("The Condition we call exile") echoes Derrida's "essential drifting," which claims writing is a machine that will continue to function despite the author's disappearance. The imagery of mutilated bodies reverberates with post-structuralist metaphors of verbal disembodiment, and is conveyed by the hole-ridden memory (brain) in ". . . and when 'the future' is uttered." This imagery appears in numerous other poems of the period, for example, "The Torso" ("Tors," 1972), "Twenty Sonnets to Mary Queen of Scots" ("Dvadtsat' sonetov k Marii Stiuart," 1974), or "The Hawk's Cry in Autumn."[110] The "cut-off slice" of "My quiet craft" employs the metaphor of separation between father and child to characterize the relationship between the writer and the text as Derrida does with his "writing orphaned and separated at birth from the assistance of his father." Numerous lyrics present language as consuming bodies, turning men into inanimate objects and people and inanimate matter into parts of speech, and so resonate with de Man's and other post-structuralists' views of the disembodying powers of language.

Given these marked linkages, Brodsky departs from post-structuralist theory in key ways. His response to Akhmatova's "you cannot like my verse" is that "her influence was of a different kind—moral, ethical, as if it was an unprinted fragment of the text, precisely the one that was principal for him."[111] This statement captures Brodsky's conceptualization of ethics as extraverbal—but by no means a post-Nietzschean illusion of language. Equally important, as he points out in "The Keening Muse," "death, which she [Akhmatova] would previously evoke as a solution for this or that emotional tension, became too real for any emotion to matter. From a figure of speech it became a figure that leaves you speechless" (*Less Than One* 49). A simultaneous invocation of literal and literary exile cuts to the heart of the "death of the author" discourse, since the figurative linkage of writing and death is valid only insofar as it acknowledges itself as trope. In the case of the exiled writer, the "banishment of the author" is literal and as such may have a sobering effect on those prone to be swept away by seductive critical language. Brodsky's direct experience of banishment and his awareness of the real deaths of poets make him wary of the lower stakes of the criticism game.

What crucially differentiates Brodsky from Barthes, de Man, Derrida, and other post-structuralists is his negative, rather than laudatory, attitude toward the banishment of the author, and the subsequent dehumanization of the text. As Brodsky's essays (e.g., "Pendulum's Song," 1975) show, he was familiar with the tenets of author-dismissive criticism: "The uneventfulness of his [Cavafy's] life would have made the strictest of New Critics happy" (*Less Than One* 53). An accentuation of authorial will in the text, characteristic of Brodsky, shows his investment in the life of the author—and would, critical etiquette notwithstanding, make a posthumous "transformation into a closed and self-sufficient object of thought" hardly "a dream incarnate of this poet-metaphysician."[112] As "In the Shadow of Dante" observes, one reads "for the sake of analysis, the function of which is to return a poem to its stereoscopic origins—the way it existed in the poet's mind" (*Less Than One* 105). For all of Brodsky's contention that "it is better if they find your book good and your life foul than the other way around," he is committed to the notion of art as personal revelation—hence his dislike of the reader or the critic who "won't give a damn about how you got there."

The reduction of the author to mechanical parts of speech exposes the danger of defacement in the text and thus challenges the cliché of modern theory that the author must be banished from his writing. Once the author departed, the text will be forgotten, misunderstood, or appropriated. As Brodsky notes in "The Child of Civilization,"

> Whatever a work of art consists of, it runs to the finale which makes for its form and denies resurrection. After the last line of a poem nothing follows except literary criticism. So when we read a poet, we participate in his or his works' death. In the case of Mandelstam, we participate in both. A work of art is always meant to outlast its maker. Paraphrasing the philosopher, one could say that writing poetry, too, is an exercise in dying. (*Less Than One* 123)

The reader's participation in a work's death entails participation in the author's death if the work of art is intimately connected to the poetic self.[113]

As Brodsky observes in "Footnote to a Poem" (1979), a poet's death "is a drama of language as such: that of inadequacy of linguistic experience vis-à-vis existential experience" (*Less Than One* 198). Though the rhetoric is somewhat de Man's, the meaning is both Brodskian and familiar from the romantics onward: language fails to capture existential experience in all of its richness. The drama of language is actually the drama of the individual whose verbal expression holds value insofar as it reflects something of his personality and life. A genuine "complicity in the creative process" (Mandelstam's "sympathetic understanding") would entail recognition by the reader of the origins of speech (the saying), not his self-indulgent play with words (the said). This complicity is all too often frustrated by verbal occlusion, resulting in a destructive fragmentariness. The self, in the words of Brodsky's beloved Eliot, "is reduced to fragments, dispersed in space, whirled Beyond the circuit of the shuddering Bear in fractured atoms," a dance of atoms that has no Dantean air.[114]

In Maurice Blanchot's observation, if the modern writer has nothing to say,

> it is not for lack of means, but because everything he can say is controlled by the nothingness that dread makes appear to him as his own object among the temporary objects that dread gives itself. It is towards this nothingness that all literary powers flow back, as towards the spring that must exhaust them, and this nothingness absorbs them not in an effort to be expressed by them, but rather to consume them with neither aim nor result.[115]

Brodsky's depiction of an existential and verbal void falls in line with this modern absurdist verbal skepticism—the feeling that poetic efforts cede to nothingness "with neither aim nor result."

Compared to Mandelstam, the existential darkness intensifies in Brodsky. "Conversation with a Celestial Being" converts the view of language in "The Horseshoe Finder" as a reductive relic that still functions as a good luck charm as well as the ambivalent vision of the poetic word in "The Slate Ode" into meaningless verbal "dross." "I was born and grew up in the Baltic marshland" moves from the romantic/pantheist notion of the poet's word as inferior to nature's language but still partaking of its beauty in "The Seashell" to the view of poetry as dull as infinity. In turn, ". . . and when 'the future' is uttered," carries the problematic of the oblivious word and fragmentariness in the Lethean poems and "The Horseshoe Finder" to its extreme—words devour memories and end up as mechanized, semantically void parts of speech.

Brodsky's intensification of the ontological absurd can be seen no less vividly in later poems such as "Bagatelle" (1987) and "The Newt" ("Triton," 1994). The former, à la "Silentium," searches for universal music but meets only silence: it "seeks notes / to being outside the self, in colloquial language—to its soundlessness" (*podbiraet kliuchi / k bytiiu vne sebia, v prostorech'i—k ego bezgolos'iu*) (Brodskii 4:38). The latter, like "The blue island is great by its potters," hears "yes" in "water," but this is testimony to cosmic indifference, not harmony: at deciphering *voda* "will produce . . . 'infinity-o-yes'; / that is, that the world is not at all / created for us" (*dast . . .*

"beskonechnost'-o-da"; / to est' chto mir otniud' / sozdan ne radi nas) (Brodskii 4:190).

Verbal skepticism dominates in Brodsky's work, and the corollaries of this verbal skepticism—themes such as the failure of memory, the repudiation of immortality (in a Derzhavinesque vein of the part of the poet "surviving his mortal coil"), and exile as an unavoidable existential condition—are stronger than faith and logocentrism. He expresses his apprehension regarding the depersonalizing power of language in his poetry and essays alike. Indeed, for Brodsky language does not merely fail in its recuperatory aspirations; rather, there exists an essential antagonism between the poet and the word. So, in "Verses on the Death of T. S. Eliot," "death chooses from its bulging catalogue / the poet, not his words, however strong / but just—unfailingly—the poet's self" (*iz vsekh shchedrot Bol'shogo Kataloga / smert' vybiraet ne krasoty sloga, / a nepremenno samogo pevtsa*) (Brodskii 2:115).[116]

Other poems portray loss of meaning in the text and the poet's disappearance in the reader. In "Great Elegy to John Donne" ("Bol'shaia elegiia Dzhonu Donnu," 1963) with Donne's death one cannot distinguish between strong and weak syllables, just as one cannot distinguish between good and evil in his verses: "John Donne fell asleep. / His poems lie in slumber. / The images, the rhythms, strong or weak, / cannot be found. Vice, melancholy, sin / are silent all. They lie, mere syllables" (*Dzhon Donn usnul. / Usnuli, spiat stikhi. / Vse obrazy, vse rifmy. Sil'nykh, slabykh / naiti nel'zia. Porok, toska, grekhi, / ravno tikhi, lezhat v svoikh sillabakh* (Brodskii 1:231).[117] In "Elegy to W. H. Auden" (1974) poetry is only the reader without the deceased poet: "Poetry without you / equals only us" (Brodsky, *Collected Poems in English* 117).[118] "York: In Memoriam W. H. Auden" ("Iork," 1976) describes the transformation of the deceased poet into words: "Subtracting the greater from the lesser—time from man—/ you get words, the remainder, standing out against their / white background more clearly than the body / ever manages to while it lives" (*Vychitaia iz men'shego bol'shee, iz cheloveka—Vremia, / poluchaesh' v ostatke slova, vydeliaiushchiesia na belom / fone otchetlivei, chem udaetsia telom / eto sdelat' pri zhizni*) (Brodsky, *Collected Poems in English* 139; Brodskii 3:165).[119] Like "York," "Elegy: For Robert Lowell" (1980) describes language that survives its creator as emptied of spirit and meaning: "On the Charles's bank / dark, crowding, printed letters / surround their sealed tongue. / A child, comma-like, loiters / among dresses and pants / of vowels and consonants / that don't make a word. The lack of pen spells / their uselessness" (Brodsky, *Collected Poems in English* 148).

Finally, "The Hawk's Cry in Autumn" literally transforms a dead bird (bard's) body into writing, playing with the graphic likeness of feathery patterns, and script: "And in a twinkling / Once more one makes out circles, eyelets, strings, / rainbow like, multicolored, blurred / commas, ellipses, spirals, linking / heads of barley, concentric rings—/ the bright doodling pattern the feather once possessed" (*I na mgnoven'e / vnov' razlichaesh' kruzhki, glazki, veer, raduzhnoe piatno, / mnogotochiia, skobki, zven'ia, / koloski, voloski– / byvshii privol'nyi uzor pera*) (Brodsky, *Collected Poems in English* 262; Brodskii 3:106).[120] These lines turn on the punning of *pero* as "feather" and "pen," and children misinterpret the remnants of the bird's / poet's body as inanimate matter—"parts of speech"—snow. The hawk of poetry disappears in, and from, the text.[121]

Chapter Four

"A Poet Is Less Than a Poet": Timur Kibirov's Merry Logophobia

WHAT HAPPENS WHEN the hawk of poetry turns bird non grata in the stratosphere, however icy? Monuments not made by hand may not exactly stand on Alexandrine pillars, but they do crumble fast in a mass-consumer Elysium. As the former Soviet Union joined the family of market economies, Russian Logos, tempered and pampered by an extended autocratic tradition, left the era of worship for one of recreation. The poet, once "more than a poet," as in Evgeny Evtushenko's "Prayer Before a Poem" ("Molitva pered poemoi," 1964), becomes an equivalent of self, and, frequently, less than that.

This chapter focuses on Timur Kibirov's antiverbal parry as representative of a larger trend of verbal skepticism occupying center stage in conceptualism and postmodernism. With the lofty stature of Russian letters problematized as never before, verbal skepticism emerges full force in post-Soviet poetry. Kibirov, one of the most popular post-Soviet poets, conveys his skepticism more light-heartedly than his predecessors, but his critique is no less expansive.

Taking the lengthy poem-epistle "To Igor Pomerantsev" as my base text, I would like to consider the heteroglossia that is its hallmark. The polyphony of languages in the poem—Golden Age diction, modern slang, loan words, parodic quotation—creates a back-and-forth of mockery. Kibirov moves beyond play with multiple tongues to a scathing ridicule of language, an exercise that communicates his resentment of verbal masks. If verbal skepticism reaches its emotional apogee in Brodsky's portrayal of parallel verbal and existential catastrophe, in Kibirov tragedy subsides into slapstick. Yet this slapstick also powerfully dramatizes the language crisis. Kibirov uses verbal masks for comic purposes and ridicules multiple languages to question verbal clichés and, more widely, language as such. Words, ossified into banalities, do not express thought and emotion but inhibit them; they are vulgarized under the new order; and they are impotent against evil.

As I extend my analysis to other Kibirov poems, I consider whether his work suffers from the disappearance of the lyrical center (the "death of the author") as a result of the numerous languages employed, which seem to take over and make the poet their will-less instrument. But Kibirov is in fact determined to establish a lyrical center amidst the heteroglossic bacchanalia—for example, by interspersing details from his private life in his poems. For this poet there is a genuine poetic interiority, just as there remain genuine sentiments in this world, and moral values. An unwilling conceptualist and postmodernist, Kibirov, like his poetic predecessors, resists verbal self-effacement.

L(AUGHING) O(UT) L(OUD): THE CONCEPTUALIST LINEAGE OF VERBAL SKEPTICISM

The point of the concluding lines of Brodsky's "Funeral of Bobo" is that death is inexpressible: "Now Thursday. I believe in emptiness. / There, it's like hell, but shittier, I've heard. / And the new Dante, pregnant with his message, / bends to the blank space and writes a word" (*Idet chetverg. Ia veriu v pustotu. / V nei kak v adu, no bolee kherovo. / I novyi Dant skloniaetsia k listu / i na pustoe mesto stavit slovo*) (Brodsky, *Collected Poems in English* 57; Brodskii 3:35). What if a postmodern poet were to write these words? The reader, Pierre Menard-like, would likely fasten on the double import of "blank space," with its interplay of the somber and the jocular, a posthumous emptiness and a colloquial idiomatic "having nothing in it" (*pustoe mesto*). Such wordplay would not cancel the gravity altogether, yet some of the emotional charge would be diverted toward an ironic jarring of remote semantic spheres and, consequently, would promote a less angst-ridden perception of the utterance. The jovial metaliterary facet of postmodern verbal inadequacy softens its negativity. At the same time postmodern verbal skepticism itself is anything but flippant and all-pervasive.

A form of verbal skepticism based on the grotesque, irony, and play, which comes to the fore in the postmodern antiverbal project, has among its antecedents the poetry of OBERIU. In a way akin to the apocalyptic vision of "The Horseshoe Finder," Oberiuty see verbal structures as incommensurate with the arbitrary brutality of being:

> Verbs are living out their age right before our eyes . . . Plot and action are disappearing. What actions there are in my poetry are illogical and pointless . . . Events do not coincide with time. Time has swallowed up events. Not a single bone of them is left.[1]

The works of Kharms and Vvedensky foreground communicative blockage, silences, and discontinuities. Reason-based language is found wanting since reality, ugly and chaotic, defies reason. Depersonalized language conveys the dehumanization of the subject. Iterations devoid of sense and interchangeable words, characters, and plots capture the sensation of disintegrating life. Semantic and situational hiatuses reinforce each other.

In the case of OBERIU a sense of existential urgency coexists with the comic absurd, a combination that anticipates tendencies of postmodern anti-art, and specifically conceptualism. The Kharmsian absurdist miniature, a Barthean writing degree zero *avant la lettre,* playfully subverts the validity of verbal art as, for instance, does his "Skavka" (1930): "Eight people sit on a bench / here is the end of my skavka" (*Vosem' chelovek sidiat na lavke / vot i konets moei skavke*).[2] The text advertises its contingency, its status as a purely linguistic construct. *Skavka,* a non-word, is used instead of "fairy tale" (*skazka*) for the sheer sake of rhyming. Writing, devoid of meaningful content, is aborted as soon as it starts. Its sole objective is to erase its own validity.[3] Kharms's communicative disturbances, a predilection for fragmentariness, dislocations, minimalism, arbitrariness, and primitivism suggest a radical questioning of language and art, yet familiar problems of incommunicability, and the disintegration of meaning are treated in a parodic manner. The bureaucratese that ousts an individualized authorial voice, destabilized semantic connections, collage, and parody foreshadow conceptualist verbal sabotage and play with verbal clichés.

Following OBERIU, the concrete poetry of Lianozovtsy and proto-conceptualism reject lyrical self-expression in favor of minimalism, stylistic polyphony, and irony. Ian Satunovsky's "Kh and V" ("Kha i Ve," 1967) offers an homage to OBERIU: "Kh and V / Kharms / and Vvedensky. / Easter. / The forest is being resurrected. / Even a rusty tree stump / has risen. / But these two / will not arise" (*Kha i Ve / Kharms / i Vvedensky. / Paskha. / Voskresaet les. / Rzhavyi pen' / i tot voskres. / No eti dvoe / ne voskresnut*).[4] This poem plays with verbal fragments such as a children's counting rhyme "A and B sat on the pipe" (*A i B sideli na trube*), and a song from a popular Soviet movie, "Spring" ("Vesna," 1947): "And even a stump / On a spring day / Dreams of becoming a birch" (*I dazhe pen' / V vesennii den' / Berezkoi snova stat' mechtaet*).

Poets like Ian Satunovsky and Vsevolod Nekrasov develop OBERIU's minimalist poetics.[5] For Nekrasov the artist must eliminate artsiness (*khudozhnichan'e*) since genuine lyricism is present only in the simplest of forms. But even this is not enough. The author must proceed to remove all the aspects of the artifact until nothing remains but a blank sheet that bears no traces of artsiness but preserves art: "One by one the drawing, the composition, the image are gone, at last representation—the frame is removed as well, only the sheet remains. There is nothing on the sheet. What—really nothing? Not exactly. Nothing artful remains but art remains."[6]

Conceptualism transposes the Tiutchevian motif of "be silent, be secret, and hide" into a playful key. Andrei Monastyrsky declares the need for silence in down-to-earth terms jarring with lofty romantic discourse: "Do not shout, do not sing, do not stamp your foot" (*Ne krichi, ne poi, ne stuchi nogoi*).[7] Nekrasov's "Shut your mouth" ("Rot zatknite," 1978–79) comically replays Tiutchev's imperative: "Shut your mouth / take / pull your tongue / it's hard to express / and not to express / and how should I tell you" (*Rot zatknite / voz'mite / potianite za iazyk / trudno vyskazat / i ne vyskazat' / i kak vam skazat'*).[8] The poem pushes forward the irony of talking about silence through its overt verbosity. "It's hard to express and not to express" echoes a popular song, "Evenings near Moscow," followed by a semantically empty "and how should I tell you." The hero, inspired by Tiutchev's famous formula, slips into parody.

Playfulness notwithstanding, of all the late twentieth-century poetic movements, conceptualism is especially intent on antiverbal critique and conducts its antiverbal thrust in ways characteristic of the wider postmodern antiverbal project. It exposes verbal emptiness, arbitrariness, and conventionality, the limitations of all existing linguistic systems, linguistic inflation, and the dystopian propensity of language to stifle consciousness. Language ossifies, bypasses, and obfuscates reality. The task of the conceptualist poet is to lay bare these destructive tendencies.

Mikhail Aizenberg, a spokesman and theoretician of conceptualism, formulates its approach to language:

> It is no secret that in a poetic work language is not merely a means but also a reference point, possibly the only one. An author's artistic solvency is wholly determined by his sensitivity to the processes at work in language. There is the sense of poetic language as a completely other language in which you can say only the right thing and only in a way you cannot in ordinary language. Here the possibilities diverge, though. There is the traditional path of individual, singular poetic language and the path of plural language, like a local Tower of Babel, a language of languages that is made "other" (that is, artistic) not by the qualitative level of its components but by the author's dismissive-creative attitude toward them. This is the path of conceptual art. To use someone else's [Ilya Kabakov's] definition, in conceptual art it is not the author expressing himself in his own language but languages, always someone else's, conversing among themselves.[9]

Aizenberg makes a distinction between "the individual, unique poetic language," or monologic language, and "plural language," or heteroglossia, a distinction that replicates the dichotomy constructed by Bakhtin in his studies of *raznorechie.* Alienation from language(s) is the movement's structural dominant, which governs and modifies its other components.[10] Sensitive to the limitations of languages, the conceptualist poet does not express himself in them but exhibits them as something reified. The poet-ventriloquist produces an accumulation of quotations, distancing himself from them; he creates a Barthean "space in which a variety of writing, none of them original, blend and clash."[11]

Leading conceptualists—Dmitry Prigov, Lev Rubinshtein—subvert models of communication and expose the dissonance between hackneyed verbal formulas and reality. Their texts are often constructed as assemblages of chaotic verbal fragments, as in Lev Rubinshtein's "Life Is Everywhere" ("Vsiudu zhizn'," 1986): "Life is given to man only once. / Do not overlook it, my friend. . . / Life is not given to man without reason. / You need to deserve it, my dear" (*Zhizn' daetsia cheloveku tol'ko raz. / Ty smotri ee, moi drug, ne prozevai . . . / Zhizn' daetsia cheloveku nesprosta. / Nado byt' ee dostoinym, milyi moi*).[12] Meaningless iterations of Nikolai Ostrovsky's formula, "Life is given to man only once, and one needs to live in such a way as not to feel terrible pain for wasted years," lay bare the reification of Sovietspeak. Various attempts to finish the statement "life is given to man only once" result in textual noise that exposes the failure of words to adequately address the pain of life: "There is nothing in our life the way we want to. / So it's better to hide and say nothing" (*V nashei zhizni vse ne tak, kak my khotim. / Tak chto luchshe zataimsia i smolchim*).[13] Slowly building emotional tension, the poem in its latter section focuses on death, which "withered words" (*uviadshie slova*) cannot describe.

Conceptualism's antiverbal thrust surpasses the boundaries of sots art, the mockery of socialist realist discourse. For Ilya Kabakov, classical Russian literature suffers from empty verbosity no less than Sovietspeak with its hackneyed ideologemes. Dostoevsky's and Chekhov's works expose the neurosis of nonstop speech, self-realization in words and not in deeds: "One has to speak, speak without interruption, weave a ceaseless web of words, phrases, and opinions which are from the very beginning devoid of sense."[14] As Dmitry Prigov summarizes the movement's antiverbal stance,

> I took Soviet language as the most functional, clearest, and accessible language of the time, the one representing ideology and presenting itself as the absolute truth from heavens. Man was oppressed by this language not externally but from within. Any ideology that aims to own you completely, any language, has a totalitarian aspiration to capture the world, cover it with its terminology, and show that it is absolutely true. I wanted to show what freedom is. Language is only language, not ultimate truth, and once we comprehend that, we achieve freedom.[15]

The language of Soviet ideology is only a vivid instance of totalitarian aspirations inherent in language as such. *The Appearance of Verse After Its Death:*

Verses (*Iavlenie stikha posle ego smerti: Stikhi,* 1995), the title of a collection by Prigov, is telling. In a by now familiar paradox writ large, the task of conceptualism is to subvert the word through the word.

KIBIROV'S MECHANICS OF VERBAL SUBVERSION

"To Igor Pomerantsev. Summer Reflections on the Fate of Belles Lettres. Second Edition" ("Igoriu Pomerantsevu. Letnie razmyshleniia o sud'bakh iziashchnoi slovesnosti. Vtoraia redaktsiia," 1992) shows the ways in which Kibirov, one of the best-known conceptualists, engages with the language crisis.[16] It opens a collection of poems entitled *Paraphrasis* (*Parafrazis,* 1997). The collection's title, like Brodsky's *A Part of Speech,* is a "dictionary of literary terms" appellation, suggestive of the book's metaliterary concerns. The word presents a hybrid of two terms—"paraphrase" (*parafraza*) and "periphrasis" (*perifrazis*), anticipating what is in store in several ways. First, the collection is concerned with hybridization. Second, it explores metaliterary themes; more specifically, issues of intertextuality ("paraphrase"). Third, it proceeds in an indirect, roundabout manner ("periphrasis"). Finally, this play with words prefigures the ironic and the ambiguous dimensions of the cycle. It may very well be that Kibirov is engaging the New Criticism notion of the "heresy of paraphrase." Is he then going against the notion that a paraphrase cannot capture the original text's essential meaning, or is he employing a frankly misleading title for comic effect? Similarly, is "paraphrase" to be understood as a restatement of an idea that fully retains its meaning, or is it meant to be deliberately misleading?

Leaving these questions unanswered for the moment, let's consider the title of its first poem. "To Igor Pomerantsev. Summer Reflections on the Fate of Belles Lettres. Second Edition" is the first instance of Kibirov using a device one may term a syncretic allusion. This title simultaneously calls up Lomonosov's "Morning Contemplation of Divine Greatness" and "Night Contemplation of Divine Greatness," Dostoevsky's *Winter Notes on Summer Impressions* (*Zimnie zametki o letnikh vpechatleniiakh,* 1863), and Derzhavin's "To Eugene. Life at Zvanka" ("Evgeniiu. Zhizn' zvanskaia," 1807).[17] The latter is emulated thematically, since the poem describes a single summer day in the country in the form of an epistle to a friend. Compared to the more habitually homogeneous practice of allusion, such hybridity foregrounds the text's intertextual nature, with intertextuality conceived not so much as a work's linkage to specific prior texts but as an indicator of its participation in the space of literature at large. The technique of syncretic allusions has a double function: it accents the text's dialogic relationship to concrete prior utterances and to the overall literary enterprise, and acts as a mark of literariness, or, in the term's comically degraded sense, of bookishness (*literaturshchina*). Kibirov uses a traditional genre and offers ("properly") an epigraph to dramatize literariness.

The words "belles lettres" (*iziashchnaia slovesnost'*) sound pointedly old-fashioned; they are removed from their indigenous environment and transplanted onto the foreign ground of contemporaneity. As such, they assume an ironic tinge.[18] Just as the title is the first example of Kibirov's syncretic allusions, "belles lettres" is the first instance of Kibirov employing words with an "aura," as Bakhtin would term it.[19] In this case, he chose an expression with conspicuously classicist or Golden Age overtones, at once period bound and socially bound. The designation "second edition" injects a strain of romantic irony, underscoring the text's status as a literary piece and playing with the split between "letter" as a spontaneous private composition and "letter" or "epistle" as a formal designation. Kibirov's use in the title of a conventional genre ("epistle"), a period-bound rhetoric, a syncretic allusion, and romantic irony initiates a game with languages that he will sustain throughout the work.

The poem is written in iambic hexameter, or alexandrines. The meter is doubly appropriate —solemn and formal, again dramatizing play with lofty poetic discourse. On a higher structural level, the notion of ambience applies to locales or motifs no less than to stylistic details on the lexical plane. Hence a highly reified chronotope is chosen.[20] Different fields limit parameters with varying degrees of strictness, or, to put it differently, just as words may have a more or less marked "aura," chronotopes may be more or less typified. Kibirov's choice of a hyper-typologized locale (countryside), time (summer), and theme (contemplations on literature) amplifies three intertwined motifs: heteroglossia, bookishness, and the conventionality of the word.

Having positioned his work as a belated utterance in a literary dialogue, Kibirov engages heteroglossia on the literary level, mixing and mingling discourses of different schools and movements, as well as on the extraliterary level, toying with dialects of divergent social and professional groups.[21] All these languages are forms for conceptualizing the world in words, characterized by particular meanings and values.[22] This poem-hybrid abruptly switches from an elevated archaic tongue, to socialist realist clichés, sots-lingo, contemporaneous post-Soviet jargon, popular advertisements, political slogans, Anglicisms, and profanities. The poem presents a polyphony of voices, with sustained Pushkinesque or Derzhavinesque stylizations at one end of the spectrum and an impressive range of vulgarity at the other. On the level of literary stratification, one moves along the intertextual continuum from outright quotations through more or less obvious allusions to parodic reworkings and expressions that could not be connected to a single source but that carry a strong remembrance of things past—words with an aura.

The first stanza will illustrate Kibirov's technique of the heteroglossic maze:

Нелепо сгорбившись, застыв с лицом печальным,
овчарка какает. А лес как бы хрустальным
сияньем напоен. И даже песнь ворон
в смарагдной глубине омытых ливнем крон
отнюдь не кажется пророческой. Лесною
дорогой утренней за влагой ключевою
иду я с ведрами. Июль уж наступил.
Дней знойных череда катится в даль, и пыль,
прибитая дождем, ступню ласкает. Томик,
Руслана верного бессмысленный потомок,
мчит, черной молнии подобный, за котом
ополоумевшим. Навстречу нам с мешком
полителеновым, где две рыбешки вяло
хвостами шевелят, бредет рыбарь бывалый
Трофим Егорович: "Здорово, молодежь!
Ну, у тебя кобель! Я, чай, не напасешь
харчей для этакой орясины!" Докучный
рой комаров кружит над струйкой сладкозвучной
источника. Вода в пластмассовом ведре
прохладна и чиста. И Ленка во дворе
пеленки Сашкины полощет, напевая

Awkwardly stooping, stiffened with a sad face,
the German shepherd poops. And the forest is as if
suffused with crystal shine. And even the song of ravens
in the emerald depth of trees washed with rain
does not at all seem prophetic. Along a morning
forest road I walk, carrying buckets
for spring water. July has already come.
A train of sultry days rolls in the distance,
and dust, laid by rain, caresses my foot. Tomik,
the faithful Ruslan's senseless progeny,
sprints like black lightning
after a crazed cat.
Toward us moving with a polyethylene bag
where two small fishes limply move their tails,
the skilled fisherman Trofim Egorych plods:
"Hello, young people! What a male dog you
have! Methinks you will not have enough grub for such a rod!" An annoying
swarm of gnats whirls over the mellifluous
stream. The water in the plastic bucket
is cool and pure. And Lenka in the yard
rinses Sashka's nappies, singing

мелодью Френкеля покойного. Цветная	the deceased Frenkel's music. Cauliflower
капуста так и прет, свекольная ботва	pushes forward, beet tops are thick . . .
пышна . . . Любезный друг, картина не нова:	My dear friend, the picture is not new:
дубравы мирной сень, дубровы шум широкий,	the peaceful grove's canopy, the grove's wide murmur,
сребристых ив гряда, колодезь кривобокий	a line of silver willow trees, a crooked well,
и, словно фронтиспис из деревенских проз,	and, like a frontispiece from village prose,
в окне рябины гроздь и несколько берез.	a bunch of ash-berry and several birches in the window.[23]
(Kibirov, *Stikhi* 221–22)	

Kibirov opens the poem in a melancholy, lyrical tone: "Awkwardly stooping, stiffened with a sad face." He disrupts the lyrical tone at the beginning of the second line by throwing in the vulgar "poops" and then (lines 2–3) resurrects it with an echo of Tiutchev's "At the very beginning of autumn there is" ("Est' v oseni pervonachal'noi," 1857): "And the forest is as if suffused with crystal shine." Next, lines 3–5 ("the song of ravens . . . does not at all seem prophetic") contain a less specific allusion, which may have to do with Pushkin's "Raven flies to raven" ("Voron k voronu letit," 1828) or Edgar Allan Poe's "The Raven" (1845), since Kibirov does not confine his intertextual play to the realm of Russian literature. The expression could also be employed more generally as a poetic cliché. In the latter case, the image, like the title, would derive its energy from dramatized bookishness as such. The reference is negative ("does not at all seem"), both indicating entry into dialogue with prior utterances and stressing the utterance's denial of previous statements. Such indications that an utterance is a rejoinder in a dialogue, positive or negative, but mostly the latter, run throughout the poem.

Proceeding in the direction of increasing intertextual blurriness, Kibirov engages a customarily nineteenth-century, possibly Nekrasovian, stylization in lines 5–7: "Along a morning forest road / I walk, carrying buckets / for spring water." In these lines what Tynianov calls "the second plane" of the composition, or Bakhtin's external contexts behind the words of the work, "diffuses into a common notion of style."[24] The second half of line 7, "July has already come," again zeroes in on a concrete but modified utterance, this time from Pushkin's "Autumn" ("Osen'," 1833): "October has already come" (*Oktiabr' uzh nastupil*).[25] Another Golden Age cliché (line 8) follows.

The tone is again disrupted by a change of diction from the elevated to the everyday, with a down-to-earth image of "dust, laid by rain, / caresses my foot" (lines 8–9). At this point Kibirov modernizes the dialogic sphere, adding a quotation from Gorky's "Song About the Stormy Petrel" ("Pesn' o burevestnike," 1901) and a reference to Vladimov's novel *Faithful Ruslan* (*Vernyi Ruslan,* 1964) (lines 9–11): "Tomik, / the faithful Ruslan's senseless progeny, / sprints like black lightning." He makes another unexpected switch from the exalted, with Gorky's "Song About the Stormy Petrel" as a staple of revolutionary romanticism, to the mundane and humorous (lines 11–12), with "after a crazed cat."[26]

Subsequent switches play out as follows:

Line 13: contemporary, everyday detail "polyethylene";

Lines 14–17: Golden Age, Nekrasovian in particular, with a disruption of "male dog" (*kobel'*), vulgar usage; [27]

Lines 18–23: Golden Age: "annoying" (*dokuchnyi*); "over the mellifluous stream" (*nad struikoi sladkozvuchnoi*). Contemporary / everyday disruptions of "plastic" and "Frenkel," and a vulgarity interference "pushes forward" (*pret*);

Line 24: a dialogic indicator "the picture is not new";

Lines 25–26: Pushkinian: "the peaceful grove's canopy, the grove's wide murmur" (*dubravy mirnoi sen', dubrovy shum shirokii*);[28] silver (*srebristykh*), as opposed to *serebristykh. Dubravy* and *dubrovy,* repetition with variation, draw attention to the signifier and evolves in the direction of mounting bookishness;[29]

Lines 27–28 end the first stanza with a characteristic postmodernist reversal of the conventional relationship between life and literature, as life now becomes mediated by art: "and, like a frontispiece from village prose, / a bunch of ash-berry and several birches in the window."

Rather than writing in a unitary and singular language that directly expresses authorial individuality, Kibirov employs these multiple languages to parodic effect. In "From the Prehistory of Novelistic Discourse" (1940) Bakhtin goes into a detailed exploration of the linkage between parody and heteroglossia. He stresses parody's key role in paving the way for the novelistic discourse of modernity as well as for literary evolution in general, concurring in this respect with the ideas of the formalists.[30] Bakhtin depicts parodic discourse as "two styles coming together: the language being parodied and the language that parodies," with the latter "not entering as such into parody, but invisibly present in it." The language that parodies is "that 'normal' language, that 'normal' style, in light of which the given parody was created," and that presents "an actualizing background for creating and perceiving."[31] According to Tynianov, parody is characterized by the presence of an additional, parodied plane behind the surface of the work. Thus both Tynianov in "Dostoevsky and Gogol (Towards a Theory of Parody)" ("Dostoevskii i Gogol' [k teorii parodii]," 1921) and Bakhtin in "From the Prehistory of Novelistic Discourse" indicate the existence of the two levels as a principal feature of parody. Whereas Tynianov understands the second layer to be the object of parody, or parodied language, Bakhtin sees it as the opposite—language that parodies.

In Kibirov's case, the mechanics of heteroglossia's deployment in antiverbal critique does not exactly follow either scheme. Instead it involves reciprocal mockery: heteroglot languages enter the text, revealing one another's synthetic nature through coexistence. Language becomes "a language" when perceived alongside another tongue, and it is the relationship of the text's heterogeneous verbal components to one another that compromises them, exposing verbal inadequacy and transforming languages into masks.[32] The poem engages a multiplicity of discourses, arranged in such a way that their mutual incongruity is highlighted. It is not enough for an author to engage a multitude of tongues. A haphazard pairing of languages, seen in relation to each other, will not necessarily ridicule, though they may relativize, each other. Everything hinges on an improper, absurd juxtaposition of languages that are incompatible. Kibirov challenges the existence of a healthy linguistic norm (though one may still need the reader's expectation of an implied "normal" language as the background against which incongruity in the text can be discerned).

The deeper the chasm between neighboring languages, the more intense the verbal mockery. This is why Kibirov switches unexpectedly from an archaic lofty stylization to "the language of the day," from Pushkinian or Derzhavinian simulations to contemporary political jargon or advertisements. The peculiar positioning of Gorky (an arch-Soviet writer) and Vladimov (a dissident) side by side is an illustration of this technique. Drawing on an understanding of languages as bound to particular ideological systems, Kibirov chooses two contrasting discourses, to a strong parodic effect.

An appearance of structural disorder in Kibirov is deceptive. According to Douwe Fokkema, postmodern compositions transfer the modernist themes of alienation and discontinuity onto the level of structure.[33] In this view, to reverse a well-known formalist slogan, new material gives rise to new form. A work of art that speaks of disorder, fragmentation, and absurdity in an organized, orderly manner gives way to a composition that is messy both thematically and structurally. Not so with "To Igor Pomerantsev." Like "The Horseshoe Finder" and "A Part of Speech," Kibirov's poem is concerned with fragmentation. Likewise, it conforms to a specific method of conveying fragmentariness. Kibirov attains cacophony through his orchestration of heteroglossic polyphony. Like the practitioners of sots art (e.g., Ilya Kabakov with his installations of heterogeneous objects), Kibirov in his juxtapositions creates a gestalt with parodic properties none of its constituents possess.

This explains how this procedure diverges from Bakhtin's characterization. This method differs from Tynianov's as well, since the parodied languages, rather than being background to parody, themselves enter the text and are arranged to effect mutual buffoonery. Tynianov allows parody to be directed "not only at a specific composition, but also at a specific series of compositions, with a common genre, author, or even literary movement," but Kibirov goes beyond this.[34] "To Igor Pomerantsev" does not limit itself to exposing the conventions of an established school, genre, or author, much less a particular piece. Its intertextual interests encompass and play upon a profusion of authors and movements.

LIKE ROTTEN FISH: BEYOND LAUGHTER IN KIBIROV

While parodic and comic aspects of the poem are conspicuous, "To Igor Pomerantsev" has its less amusing facets as well. A few words should be said here about the relationship between the parodic and the ironic in this work. Analyses of parodic compositions tend to focus on the way the technique affects the target of parody. How parody functions with respect to the parodic subject is often overlooked, but an examination of the parodic subject reveals that frequently there occurs a backward loop effect, directing derision at the perpetrator of parody as well as at its victim. The words may enclose themselves in quotation marks regardless of the speaker's intent, or they may be put in quotation marks deliberately. Moreover, it is often hard to determine the degree to which the parodic subject acts freely as a perpetrator of ridicule, and how much the words enclose themselves in quotation marks against the erstwhile perpetrator's will.

In either case, the subject, too, acquires a comic coloration. This is exactly what happens in "To Igor Pomerantsev," where alien, inappropriate languages shove one another into parody and also give the ventriloquist's life a humorous cast. Parody approaches self-parody. The authorial persona, conscious of this side effect, welcomes it as a means to look with ironic detachment at himself as well as others. Indeed, parody may be subordinate to self-parody in Kibirov, rather than self-parody being a by-product of parody. His employment of the classical idiom introduces incongruity with respect to the contemporary state of affairs and functions as a means of postmodern self-distancing, making light of the author's all too genuine concerns.

Like Pushkin's "To a Grandee" ("K vel'mozhe," 1830), as well as Mandelstam's "The Horseshoe Finder," "To Igor Pomerantsev" responds to drastically changing times, people, and values. "To a Grandee" employs the same genre (epistle) and meter (the alexandrines). The use of alexandrines, in keeping with the subject matter, carries Pushkin's lament at the departure of the regal Age of the Enlightenment:

Всё новое кипит, былое истребя.	All new things rage, having destroyed what came before.
Свидетелями быв вчерашнего паденья,	Having been witnesses of yesterday's fall,
Едва опомнились младые поколенья.	The young generations barely recovered.
Жестоких опытов сбирая поздний плод,	Gathering a late harvest of cruel trials,
Они торопятся с расходом свесть приход.	They rush to make meet income and expenditure.
Им некогда шутить, обедать у Темиры,	They have no time for joking, dining at Temira's,
Иль спорить о стихах.[35]	Or arguing about verses.

Like "To a Grandee," "To Igor Pomerantsev" focuses on cultural rupture. Kibirov's hero recalls an earlier age, and ponders harsh novel realities. He muses on the striking cultural and ideological transformations that have taken place in post-Soviet Russia. He wants "to equal his age in enlightenment" (*v prosveshchenii stat' s vekom naravne*) (Kibirov, *Stikhi* 227) but cannot embrace the artist's situation in a newly formed consumer society.

In the first section of the poem the hero depicts a summer day in the countryside; following this, he offers a detailed, satirically charged portrayal of the sociocultural milieu of the early 1990s, playing on the market economy and invoking a multitude of allusions to high and pop culture. Lines 20–21 of stanza 2, for example, allude to Pushkin's "Conversation Between Bookseller and Poet," a poem that considers the problem of the commercialization of poetry: "and booksellers / no longer undertake conversations with the poet" (*i knigoprodavtsy / s poetom razgovor uzhe ne zatevaiut*) (Kibirov, *Stikhi* 223).[36] The Pushkinian and Lermontovian theme of selling the self in art is a key issue for Kibirov. The hero's "timid spirit is troubled by / inflation" (*robkii dukh smushchaet / infliatsiia*), he "craves gold" (*alchet zlata*) (Kibirov, Stikhi 222–24) and half in jest, half earnestly, agonizes about the problem of earning his living through words. Lines 46–47 state that, with the crushing of the old order, literature, degradingly called "little literature" (*literaturochka*), has become utterly trivialized. Reality, by contrast, has acquired new somberness. The artist's "weeping and reproach, with its studied tune" (Lermontov) pales before real life even more forcefully in the post-Soviet age.

The vulgarization of verbal art under the new order, its subversion by greed, is portrayed in stanzas 6–9, which supply a sarcastic catalogue of invented current bestsellers, commencing with detective fiction (the sixth stanza):

Итак, даешь рубли! Посмотрим на лоток.
Что нынче хавают? Так. Понял. Перспективы
ясны. Наметим план. Во-первых, детективы:
"Смерть в Красном Уголке," "Ухмылка мертвеца,"
"Поручик Порох прав," "Кровавая маца,"
"Хореныч и Кузьмин," "Так жить нельзя, Шарапов!"
"В пивной у Коваля," "Блондинка из гестапо,"
"Последний миллилитр," "Цикады," "Дело Швах,"
"Каплан, она же Брик и Айседора," "Крах
коньковской мафии," "Прозренье Левы," "Драма
в Скотопригоньевске," "Месть Бусикеллы," "Мама
на антресолях," "Кровь не пахнет, миссис Мэйн!,"
"Видок и Фантомас," "Таинственный нацмен,"
"Наследник Бейлиса," "Огонь на пораженье,
или 600 секунд," "Сплетенье рук, сплетенье
ног," "Красное пятно," "Не спи в саду, отец!,"
"Гроб на колесиках," "Крантец на холодец,"
"Фас, Томик, фас!" Хорош.
(Kibirov, *Stikhi* 227–28)

So give me rubles! Let's look at the book-stall.
What is guzzled now? Ah, I get it. The view
is clear. Let's map it out. First, thrillers:
Death in the Red Corner, Dead Man's Grin,
Lieutenant Powder Is Correct, Bloody Matzos,
Khorenych and Kuzmin, One Cannot Live this Way, Sharapov!,
At Koval's Tavern, The Blonde from Gestapo,
The Final Milliliter, Cicadas, The Shvakh Affair,
Kaplan, Who Is Also Brik and Isadora, Konkovo
Mafia's Collapse, Leva's Insight, Drama
in Skotoprigon'evsk, Busikella's Revenge, Mama
on the Mezzanine, Blood Does Not Smell, Mrs. Maine,
Vidok and Fantomas, The Enigmatic Alien,
The Heir of Beilis, Hit to Kill,
or 600 Seconds, Interlacing of Hands,
Interlacing of Feet, The Red Stain, Do Not Sleep in the Garden, Father!,
Coffin on Wheels, Death to Jellied Meat,
Get Him, Tomik, Get Him! Enough.

It is exclusively the commercial value of a book that matters now.[37] The Russian writer, the conscience of the people, has been replaced by the literary hack. Hence Kibirov's inventory of trashy thrillers, historical novels, sci-fi, the occult, and pornography. Even the highest cultural achievements of the nation are not immune from commercial degradation. For instance, *Drama in Skotoprigon'evsk,* an allusion to Dostoevsky's *The Brothers Karamazov,* is placed in the thriller section together with *Interlacing of Hands, Interlacing of Feet,* evoking Pasternak's "Winter Night" ("Zimniaia noch'") from *Doctor Zhivago* (*Doktor Zhivago,* 1957), and *Do Not Sleep in the Garden, Father!* (Shakespeare's *Hamlet*). Analogously, Pushkin's "Song About the Prophetic Oleg" ("Pesn' o veshchem Olege," 1825) has been rewritten as a pulp historical novel, *Revenge on the Khazars* (*Mest' khazaram*) (stanza 7) and his "Egyptian Nights" ("Egipetskie nochi," 1835) becomes a porn novel, *The Chamber Shined* (*Chertog siial*) (Stanza 9) (Kibirov, *Stikhi* 228–29).

Besides highlighting the humiliation of verbal art under these new conditions, the lengthy bestseller inventory dramatizes the language crisis through the contingency of Kibirov's output. In the words of "The Horseshoe Finder," "not a single word is better than another." It is precisely because all words have become devalued that Kibirov suppresses semantics and uses sheer formal similarities as the organizing principle of this catalogue of bestsellers. The inventory progresses mechanically, through words linked primarily on the phonic level. For instance, *Kaplan, Who Is Also Brik and Isadora* appears because Kaplan and Duncan are formally similar (though both Lilya Brik and Isadora Duncan are famous as poets' loves). *Death to Jellied Minced Meat* (*Krantets na kholodets*) is an analogous device. Additional jokes include *The Shvakh Affair,* playing with the German word for "feeble," which also sounds like a German or Jewish surname; *The End of the Star Ovir* (*Konets zvezdy Ovir*), with Ovir designating the Soviet Visa Department, the destination for the immigrating Soviet Jewry, and also resembling the name of a distant star from an Ivan Efremov space-travel novel; and Dar Veter (the hero's pseudonym as a potential sci-fi writer) resonating with the German *Der Vater* and Darth Vader, the villain of *Star Wars,* and ironically the sort of name to be given a Soviet space explorer in a novel by Efremov (Kibirov, *Stikhi* 228). "The Star Ovir" and "Dar Veter" again comically thrust together incompatible semantic spheres through formal linkage.

The language crisis captured in "To Igor Pomerantsev" is akin to the situation described by George Steiner when language becomes an obstacle to thought. Language shows that it has in it the germ of dissolution in several ways:

> Actions of the mind that were once spontaneous become mechanical, frozen habits (dead metaphors, stock similes, slogans). Words grow longer and more ambiguous. Instead of style, there is rhetoric. Instead of precise common usage, there is jargon. Foreign roots and borrowings are no longer ab-

> sorbed into the blood stream of the native tongue. They are merely swallowed and remain an alien intrusion. All these technical failures accumulate to essential failure: the language no longer sharpens thought but blurs it.[38]

Kibirov engages in tautologies, for example, "As for the strict Teheran, it is probably too strict" (*A strogii Tegeran, pozhalui, slishkom strog*) (Kibirov, *Stikhi* 227) and a profusion of jargon and Anglicisms. Thus "the broker," "the dealer," "the distributor," and "the computer" (*broker, diler, distrib'iuter, komp'iuter*) all appear in stanza 2, lines 33–34 (Kibirov, *Stikhi* 223), and are shown to be jarringly alien to the Russian language and spirit. Steiner's conclusion that "a civilization is imprisoned in a linguistic contour which no longer matches, or matches only at certain ritual, arbitrary points, the changing landscape of fact," aptly describes the situation of "To Igor Pomerantsev."[39]

Kibirov recycles clichés and worn tropes, the frozen habits of our language—a project going, like Rubinshtein's card catalogues, beyond mere comedy. Parody is not limited exclusively to the comical, which is only one of its functions.[40] The serious subtext varies but commonly involves the exposition of literary conventions. In this respect, parody, like the technique of defamiliarization, supplies a novel point of view that defies petrification. Both techniques revolt against the ossified lyrical vocabulary, and both (parody always, defamiliarization frequently) accomplish this by resorting to the incongruous. Unlike defamiliarization, however, which seeks an unusual point of view to make the familiar seem strange, parody aims at making the familiar seem clichéd.

Kibirov recycles textbook quotations to point at both the "dead words" themselves and at our clichéd perception of "dead words." The predominance of Pushkin's voice in "To Igor Pomerantsev" brings this home. Although here we also encounter, among others, Derzhavin, Krylov, Lermontov, Tiutchev, Baratynsky, Nekrasov, Gorky, Pasternak, and Vladimov, as well as several non-Russians (e.g., Coleridge, Wilde, and the Marquis de Sade), it is Pushkin who leads the chorus. Besides "Conversation Between Bookseller and Poet," stanza 2, lines 39–42, refer to *Eugene Onegin,* chapter 1, stanza 18. Stanza 3, lines 4–5 (an illustration of the link between parody and self-parody in Kibirov) invoke *The Little Tragedies* (*Malen'kie tragedii,* 1830) and *The Queen of Spades* (*Pikovaia dama,* 1834). Stanza 3, lines 29–30 again allude to *Eugene Onegin,* chapter 8, stanzas 1–7.

Apart from quoting, misquoting, echoing, and generally taking Pushkin's texts in vain, Kibirov engages a number of Pushkinian trademark devices, most frequently from *Eugene Onegin.* Stanzas 6–9 depict the lyrical hero looking at books and punctuate his movement from one stall to another with a series of strophic enjambments like Pushkin's "and breathless on the bench / Fell" (*i zadykhaias' na skam'iu / Upala*) (*Eugene Onegin*, chapter 3, stanzas 38–39).[41] At one point (stanza 9, line 1) this device is laid bare, with "Now, Igor, let's cross over" (*Zdes', Igor', perekhod*) (Kibirov, *Stikhi* 229) designating at once the hero's movement from one bookstall to the next one, and Kibirov's poetic technique. Chatty, everyday language and catalogues of things are also characteristic of mock epics such as *Eugene Onegin, Count Nulin* (*Graf Nulin*, 1825), *House in Colomna* (*Domik v Kolomne*, 1830), and other works by Pushkin. Kibirov chooses Pushkin on account of his iconic status. First, insofar as the poem's parodic effect depends on the recognizability of the second plane, Pushkin is by far the strongest candidate. Second, the oeuvre of this officially accepted national poet has become more heavily encrusted than that of any other Russian man of letters. Thus Kibirov aims less at conventionalizing the famous utterances than at making the reader sharply conscious of their state of petrifaction. Third, the employment of Pushkin as a littérateur par excellence and a metonymic representation of Russian belles lettres permits Kibirov to target literariness as a whole.

What would motivate one to spoof Literariness with a capital "L"? The poem conveys a post-Soviet weariness at being bombarded with lofty discourses, whatever their ideological underpinnings. And yet, explaining Kibirov's verbal skepticism in specifically political terms—for example, through the distortion of thought in Orwellian, totalitarian languages—may throw considerable light on antiverbalism, especially in its twentieth-century versions, but it does not take in the larger picture. Kibirov's work must be understood in a more sweeping (post)modern context of antiverbal verbal art. Conforming to Prigov's view that conceptualism extends beyond mockery of socialist realist ideologemes, Kibirov distrusts "grand narratives" in general, including the grand narrative of classical Russian literature. Such a distrust, characteristic of the post-Soviet mentality in particular, is a case of postmodern sensibility marked by an anti-authoritarian impulse.

Kibirov's narrative is expressive of the verbal nausea that attends the disintegration of meaning when language is utterly inflated, "not a single word is better than another," as everything "cracks and sways" in a dizzying onslaught of words. Ironically, verbal nausea is one of the most salient features of modern literature. All discourses present themselves as alien, as in Aizenberg's "languages themselves, always someone else's, conversing among themselves." The problem is not simply that "all languages were masks, and no language could claim to be an authentic, incontestable face." Rather, verbal masks evoke resentment as they make one feel trapped amidst a linguistic bacchanalia. Words ossified into banalities can only depersonalize the personal.

As Fredric Jameson observes, there is no way for a contemporary writer to speak in his own tongue:

> With the collapse of the high-modernist ideology of style . . . unique and unmistakable as your fingertips . . . the producers of culture have nowhere to turn but to the past: the imitation of dead styles, speech through all the masks and voices stored up in the imaginary museum of a now global culture.[42]

Aizenberg, while appearing to disagree with such a pessimistic view, relies on authorial alienation as the means of making heteroglossia artistic. Negation itself is made to function positively and becomes the chosen way to deal with fetid dead words. Yet can negativity yield anything like its opposite? Can code switching and verbal relativism permit greater cognitive and emotional freedom? Where tyrannies appear often to be characterized by linguistic fundamentalism, postmodern market economies come packaged with verbal relativism and pluralism. In the latter case, any liberating potential may be trumped by "an equal distribution of heat." When one language and value system is judged to be no better and no worse than any other, aesthetic and ethical entropy is likely to ensue.

Another somber aspect of heteroglossia in the poem should not be overlooked. The ambivalent dimensions of the cycle hinted at in its title have to do first and foremost with reverse mimesis (stanza 1, lines 27–28). As noted before, the conclusion of stanza 1 reverses the conventional relationship between life and literature, with the latter interceding between the perceiver and the object of perception. As a result, reality appears to be fictitious. These lines reveal the now-standard "simulacrum" approach to reality. Neither the ash-berries nor the birch trees are seen as authentic but are perceived as a picture in a book, "a copy for which no original has ever existed." The theme of life as a paraphrase of art, although addressed before, has become ubiquitous in postmodern writing. The question arises as to what degree it is possible to fashion an utterance that is not constrained (influenced, contaminated, distorted, enfeebled) by prior utterances. Reverse mimesis, like verbal leftovers, diminishes one's sensibilities, endowing reality with the quality of a "glossy mirage."[43] When reality is sensed to be artifice, and when life is experienced as a conglomeration of verbal clichés, how can one construct, as Aizenberg claims to do, "the other (that is, artistic) language"?

BAD INFINITY AND ETERNAL RECURRENCE

Kibirov articulates verbal skepticism in many of his poems as well as interviews. As he puts it in "The Rules of the Game" ("Pravila igry," 1996), "as soon as you start formulating something, you inevitably decline into this or that kind of kitsch and vulgarize what you feel."[44] When asked whether life and literature are mutually exclusive, and whether an increase in creativity means a decrease in life, Kibirov suggests that this is a stereotype, but like any stereotype, it has ample grounding:

> Indeed, a poetic occupation makes normal life more difficult—in particular, fulfilling civic, familial, or any other duty. This occupation inevitably stimulates the development of rather unpleasant character traits. Let me cite Nabokov. In *Pale Fire,* one of the main characters, the wonderful poet John Shade, says that creativity provokes the development of at least three deadly sins: vanity, lust, and sloth. I am afraid that "the vices of creativity" are not limited to these. I would add infantilism, irresponsibility, the deafness of being "not of this world," depicted by the very same Nabokov in *Luzhin's Defense.*[45]

The verbal artist's impotence against evil, his falsehoods, infantilism, moral deafness, and estrangement from reality are persistent themes of Kibirov's oeuvre. These, for instance, become the focus of "School Progress Report" ("Tabel'," 1999). True to Tiutchev's topos of the falsehoods of the word, making up a song equals lying:

В сущности, я не люблю жить.
Я люблю вспоминать.
Но я не могу вспоминать не по лжи.
Но все норовлю я песню сложить,
То-есть, в сущности, лгать.
Лгать, сочинять, буквы
   слагать.
Ответственность тоже слагать.
Уд за старательность. Неуд за жизнь.
По пению—с минусом пять.
   (Kibirov, *Stikhi* 400)

Actually, I do not like living.
I like recollecting.
But I cannot recall without lies.
But I still strive to compose a song,
That is, actually, to lie.
To lie, to compose, to write down
   letters.
To lay down responsibility as well.
"C" for diligence. "F" for life.
For singing an "A–."

This poem, like Nekrasov's "Shut your mouth," is a playful conceptualist version of "Silentium!" It succinctly restates the aporia between life and art. The poet is unable to fully experience the living moment and prefers the state of recollection. Like Brodsky, Kibirov notes the distortion of memories: "I cannot recall without lies." From memory, intimately connected to the creative process, the poem moves to the process itself. Although his recollections are false, the poet nevertheless strives to make up a song. The rhyme *lgat'—slagat'* formally equates poetry with lies. Similarly, Kibirov's pun on *slagat'* ("composing" [a song] and "laying down" [responsibility]) conveys the idea of the artist's moral untrustworthiness. The conclusion is both mocking and sad. A failure in life and a mediocre pupil as far as his diligence goes, the hero gets an "A–" for singing, one of the least important school subjects.

"Give an answer! It does not give an answer!" ("Dai otvet! Ne daet otveta!" 2000) denigrates poetry as self-indulgent clamor:

И потоками мутных пророчеств	With torrents of muddy prophecies
Заливает он матушку почву.	He inundates mother earth.
Так и так, мол. Иначе никак.	That's how it is, he says. Otherwise no way.
Накричавшись, уходит в кабак.	Having shouted his fill, he goes off to a bar.

(Kibirov, *Stikhi* 535)

The poem's title, a mocking Gogolian allusion, refers to the classic patriotic passage at the end of *Dead Souls* (*Mertvye dushi,* 1842): "Rus, whither are you speeding to? Answer me. No answer. The middle bell trills out in a dream its liquid soliloquy; the roaring air is torn to pieces and becomes wind; all things on earth fly by and other nations and states gaze askance as they step aside and give her the right of way."[46] Kibirov denies the prophetic Gogolian posture, epitomized by the narrator's expression of faith in his special mission vis-à-vis Rus', and instead shows the poet to be an impotent babbler.

"The Jubilee of the Lyrical Hero" ("Iubilei liricheskogo geroia," 2000) develops the themes of artistic impotence and the meaninglessness of language:

И что же? Где она, блаженная усталость,	So what? Where is the blessed weariness?
и умудренность где? Где-где— в узде,	and where is wisdom? Where?—under the bridle,
которой взнуздан я мирскими суетами—	curbed by worldly vanities—
тщеславьем, леностью, а паче словесами	conceit, laziness, and more than all the rest—
хитросплетенными, игрою роковой	by words woven cunningly, by a fatal game
фонем бессмысленных с нагрузкой смысловой,	of senseless phonemes with a load of meaning,
и возбешеньем блудным.	and lecherous frenzy.

(Kibirov, *Stikhi* 548)

The author has not grown wise with experience because of words and the vices attending verbal creation. Wisdom is curbed by, more than anything else, words. The bridle recalls Brodsky's "My quiet craft" with its conceit of verbal compulsion, and "words woven cunningly" evoke Old Russian *pletenie sloves.*[47] These lines insist that phonemes (signifiers) are senseless and that the load of meaning (signified) is artificially and arbitrarily imposed upon them. Poetry is a game of senseless sounds and lust.

The problems of linguistic arbitrariness and poetic powerlessness are rendered in "Know-Nothing in the Sunny City" ("Neznaika v solnechnom gorode," 2002). This poem claims that poetry is but a means to sublimate lust and reduce fear, and transforms Pushkin's "greetings, new generation" (*zdravstvui, plemia molodoe*) ("Vnov' ia posetil," 1835) into "greetings, young udder" (*zdravstvui, vymia molodoe*) (Kibirov, *Stikhi* 563–64).[48] The lyric concludes:

Ибо впрямь настало время.	Since the time has truly come.
Ибо исчерпалась тема.	Since the theme is exhausted.
Ибо бремя . . . ибо семя . . .	Since burden . . . since seed. . .
Ибо . . . ибо . . . потому . . .	Since . . . since . . . because. . .
Окончается на у-у-у-у . . .	Ends with u-u-u-u. . .
(Kibirov, *Stikhi* 564)	

In structuralist holistic interpretations the text is a gestalt in which the relationship between semantic aspects and formal devices is necessary, not a projection of device on the plane of semantics, but a full coherence between form and meaning. For instance, words that are equivalent phonetically as well as lexically may be selected from the paradigmatic axis of language, and, projected onto the axis of combination, rhymed with each other.[49] The principle of Kibirov's poem, as in the bestseller inventory of "To Igor Pomerantsev," is the reverse of this—a mechanical production of signifiers unfolding through formal linkage, with one *-mia* word ("generation") replaced by another *-mia* word ("udder"). At its conclusion the poem disintegrates into rhymed gibberish with a string of other heteroclitic *–mia* words one memorizes in school, haphazardly thrown on the page.

Kibirov's mechanical conglomeration of signifiers presents the text as meaningless. Poetry, a highly structured discourse, is especially suspect for sacrificing substance for the sake of formal flourish. The rhymed *vremia–tema–bremia–semia,* a more extreme version of Kharms's *lavka–skavka,* lay bare the vacuity of the aesthetic structure.[50] The poet has nothing to say ("since the theme is exhausted") but is caught in a graphomaniac spinning out of signs. *Potomu chto konchaetsia na 'u'* is a children's idiom employed when one fails to supply a meaningful response to a query. This fobbing-off phrase ("The answer is a lemon") is a non sequitur and a non-answer. What constitutes a pretense of reference is *u* as a segment of the signifier *potomu.* This is the opposite of Mandelstam's "The blue island is great by its potters." In Mandelstam *voda* says *da,* a segment of its signifier, and is a testament to verbal organicity and consequently ontological meaningfulness; in Kibirov the hypertrophy of the signifier denies the possibility of meaning.

The purging of semantics is Kibirov's ironic exposé of verbal creativity. According to Viacheslav Kuritsyn, "Kibirov himself once conveyed to the author of these lines a bitter observation that the texts printed in columns and rhymed at the ends of the lines now call forth a sense of almost physical revulsion in him."[51] The production of nonsense is his response to verbal negativity. Given the persistence of verbal inflation and the artist's degradation in contemporaneity, should one surrender to the pleasurable game of deconstruction, the Derridian dance of signifiers? Or, perhaps, simply be reduced to silence?

Importantly, Kibirov, like Brodsky though in a lighter key, resists self-effacement in language. His play with verbal masks does not altogether efface authorial voice, and his poetic subjectivity manages to express itself even in the midst of such a game. Lower discourse and new primitivism both function as modes of poetic deconstruction. Like the romantics, for instance Wordsworth (and much later concrete poetry), Kibirov strives to reject the extravagant rhetoric of his predecessors in favor of a simple, "authentic" language. As he puts it in "I do not prophesy—I chatter" ("Ia ne veshchaiu—ia boltaiu," 1998), "there was no life beyond them [well-written verses]. I am firmly convinced that poetry's antonym is not prose but poeticity."[52] Definition via opposition to others' words, through negative indicators of dialogism, is another strategy of resistance.

A proliferation of genuine biographical data is one more distinctive feature of Kibirov's oeuvre that resists Barthes's notion of the impersonal script. The poet's oeuvre depicts his private life, his simple everyday existence in meticulous detail. The reader of his works is well aware of how his wife looks and what her name is, what his daughter Sasha Zapoeva thinks about Russia and Italy, with whom his dog Tomik plays, and what happens in the village of Shil'kovo on a particular summer day.[53] Kibirov and the other members of his circle parade before the reader as heroes of friendly epistles, in the manner of Pushkin and his friends. The titles like "To Igor Pomerantsev," "To Misha Aizenberg. An Epistle on Poetry" ("Mishe Aizenbergu. Epistola o stikhotvorstve," 1989), or "To Serezha Gandlevsky. On Some Aspects of the Present Socio-Cultural Situation" ("Serezhe Gandlevskomu. O nekotorykh aspektakh nyneshnei sotsiokul'turnoi situatsii," 1990) are characteristic of his oeuvre. "A Message to Lenka" ("Poslanie Lenke," 1990) and "Twenty Sonnets to Sasha Zapoeva" ("Dvadtsat' sonetov Sashe Zapoevoi," 1995), a pointed retort to Brodsky's "Twenty Sonnets to Mary Queen of Scots," are of the same kind. The genre of the epistle, of course implying communicability, also endows Kibirov's renditions of the antiverbal topos with an inner tension characteristic of Tiutchev's "Silentium!" and other lyrics involving the operative paradox.

Kibirov attempts to resolve the linguistic predicament in yet another key in "To Igor Pomerantsev." Concurrent verbal pleasure and frustration constitute one of the work's central ambiguities. Whether moved to parody by appreciation or resentment of prior articulations, or by the sheer enjoyment of playing with the device, Kibirov offers positive intimations of "life being good when all is said and done" in the first part of the poem. The "pure water" in the plastic bucket is pure, and the plastic does not annihilate that. The old women with their moderate *mat* suggest a humor-tinged idyll. Lenka washing Sasha's diapers is a positive image that prevails over verbal confusion. His use of Golden Age diction indicates not only the impotence of modern poetic language and the need for recourse to a dead tradition, but also the knowledge that having a valid heritage may overcome the verbiage of modern times, when fused with what Kibirov and his generation can offer in the way of straight and modest praise of everyday life.

In the latter section of the poem, a change in Kibirov's diction becomes pronounced. The technique remains the same—constructing the text as a mosaic of quotations—but the tone is quite different. Here the ridicule is largely replaced by something that is, if not quite reverential, then seemingly earnest. In the final stanzas the poet portrays an evening in Shil'kovo. He seeks respite from the crude realities of contemporary life in the traditional ideals of freedom and artistic harmony:

И в наш жестокий век нам, право, не пристало	And, really, in our cruel age, it does not suit us
скулить и кукситься. Пойдем. Кремнистый путь	to whine and sulk. Let's go. The stony path
все так же светел. Лес, и небеса, и грудь	is still as bright as ever. The forest, heavens, the chest
прохладой полнятся. Туман стоит над прудом.	are full of coolness. A mist stands over the pond.
Луна огромная встает. Пойдем. Не будем	The huge moon rises. Let us go. Let us not
загадывать. Пойдем. В сияньи голубом	guess at what will come. Let us go. In a blue shine
спит Шильково мое. Мы тоже отдохнем,	sleeps my Shil'kovo. We, too, will rest,
немного погоди. В рябине филомела,	just wait a little. Do you hear? Philomela,
ты слышишь, как тогда, проснулась и запела,	as before has awaken and started singing in ash-berries,
и ветр ночной в листве плакучих ив шумит,	and the night wind rustles in the willows,

стволы берез во тьме мерцают, и блестит
бутылки горлышко у полусгнивших кладей.
Душа полна тоской, покоем и прохладой.
И черный Том бежит за тению своей
красиво и легко, и над башкой моей,
от самогоночки слегка хмельной, сияют
светила вечные, и вдалеке играет
(в Садах, наверное) гармоника. Пойдем.
Не бойся ничего. Мы тоже отдохнем.
Кремнистый путь блестит, окно горит в сельмаге.
Вослед за кошкой Том скрывается в овраге.
(Kibirov, *Stikhi* 230-31)

the trunks of birches glimmer in the darkness,
and the neck of a bottle shines by half-rotten haystacks.
The soul is full of melancholy, calm, and coolness.
And black Tom runs after his shadow
handsomely and lightly, and over my block-head,
a little tipsy from samogon, there shine
eternal luminaries, and far away
(likely, in the gardens) an accordion plays. Let's go.
Be not afraid of anything. We, too, will rest.
The stony path shines, a window is lit in the shop,
Tom hides in the ravine, chasing after the cat.

Critics have noted the permeability of the boundary that separates parody from straightforward quotation. Tynianov observed in "Dostoevsky and Gogol" that "it is one step from stylization to parody."[54] Similarly, in "From the Prehistory of Novelistic Discourse" Bakhtin remarked that in medieval literature the transitions between various nuances on the spectrum between piety and parody were so subtle that it was often hard to decide whether the sacred word was reverently invoked or travestied.[55] Mikhail Epstein's characterization of post-conceptualist aesthetics is analogous:

> This "post-post-postmodern" neo-sentimental aesthetics is defined not by the sincerity of the author or the quotedness of his style, but by the mutual interaction of the two. What is characteristic is the elusive border of their difference, which allows even the most sincere utterance to be perceived as a subtly quoted imitation, while a commonplace quotation may sound like a piercingly lyrical confession.[56]

The word of the other in Kibirov begins to sound like one's own heartfelt expression; cliché turns into wisdom; the "bad infinity" of literariness presents itself as eternal recurrence (stanza 12, lines 1–4). The lines continue to be interspersed with indicators of dialogism, now positive ones (e.g., "we, too, will rest," an allusion to Chekhov's *Uncle Vanya* [*Diadya Vanya,* 1897]), but the changed intonation makes their function the opposite of what it used to be. Whereas previously such elements underscored aesthetic weariness and denial, they now appear to convey a realization of emotional and poetic continuity. Pushkin's voice no longer leads the heteroglossia chorus. Instead, Lermontov, Chekhov, and Mandelstam take center stage.[57] The change may reveal less of the author's literary preferences than the fact that Pushkin's oeuvre, given the extent to which it has become ossified in the Russian literary consciousness, is particularly difficult to "dis-alienate."

As Kibirov puts it in "Where should we sail?" ("Kuda zh nam plyt?" 1999):

Картина та еще! Все то же и все те же.	What a picture! Everything and everyone are the same.
Сюжет—ни то, ни се. Пегас—ни тпру, ни ну.	The plot is neither here nor there. Pegasus won't budge.
Но глаз не оторвать! Но сколько же нюансов	But one cannot tear oneself away! But how many nuances
досель не знали мы, еще не знаем мы!	We have not known till now, how many we still do not know!

(Kibirov, *Stikhi* 430)

"Where should we sail" refers to the conclusion of Pushkin's "Autumn" when the lyrical persona pauses just on the verge of translating the perceptions of the day in the actuality of a poem. The sense is that of inspiration, which counters the notion of verbal skepticism, but at the same time harbors uncertainty. Pushkin, in yet another marine metaphor, compares his process of creation to a ship setting sail to an unknown land, and finishes his poem with a question followed by several lines of dots. Analogously, there is a tension in Kibirov's poem between a weary postmodernist perception of reality as derivative and a cheerful recognition that there are in fact "new things under the sun," and that novelty has to do with shades of color, with the small and the seemingly insignificant. The poet's task is to try to capture these subtle traits that may so easily be missed, whether they be of a personal mood or of the epoch.

A similar tension informs "A Postmodern Poem" ("Postmodernistskoe," 1999), which starts with the requisite admission that, as much as you may lie, everything has been said, but concludes with the observation that everything has been described, but not like this:

Не мной. Не тебе адресовано.	Not by me. Not to you addressed.
Кустарники, звезды, вода.	Bushes, stars, water.

Все сказано, все стилизовано. Но это, дружок, не беда!	Everything has been said and stylized. But this, my little friend, does not matter!

(Kibirov, *Stikhi* 429–30)

When the bad infinity of life and language petrifies the self, one seeks an authentic expression in nuances. "Poetry!—big fucking deal" ("Poeziia!—big fucking deal," 1999), similarly, concludes on a paradox, with a simultaneous acknowledgment of the Tiutchevian poetic lie and a suggestion that, only through this lie, can something genuine be discerned in life:

Гляди ж, пацан, сквозь эту ветошь, сквозь эту мишуру и ложь, авось, хоть что-нибудь заметишь, глядишь, хоть что-нибудь поймешь.	So watch, lad, through these rags, through this trumpery and lie, perhaps you will notice at least something, maybe you will understand at least something.

(Kibirov, *Stikhi* 398)

Asked whether he resents the present situation in which the Russian poet, for the first time in history, has lost his exceptional status, Kibirov offers an attenuated response that betrays his yearning for a logos that has not been dwarfed:

> No. I like it. It is much healthier this way . . . But there arises another problem, an opposite complex of ideas comes into fashion: the writer does not influence anything, does not bear any responsibility, and his occupation is merely a game. My heart opposes this as well. It is sad to think that your only life is wasted on monkey tricks.[58]

As he admits in another interview,

> I have always loved very much this poem by Akhmatova: "If only you knew from what trash / Verses grow, knowing no shame." But in the past, this seemed to be an absolute truth about poetry, whereas now it seems to me that there is no trash. On the contrary, the very thing I want is for this same trash to be engraved in my verses. I see my task as an attempt to salvage, almost to conserve everything.[59]

All the irony notwithstanding, it becomes evident that Kibirov not only subscribes to the traditional humanistic notion of poetry as a repository of memories, both private and historical, but also holds on to the nostalgic Russian vision of the poetic vocation as "more than itself." As he puts it in "To Igor Pomerantsev," he "still attempts / to hook refined chatter to Truth and Goodness" (*Ottochennye liasy / vse tshchus' ia pritsepit' i k pravde, i k dobru*) (Kibirov, *Stikhi,* 227). Parody, ever present, serves not so much to undermine the poet's sentiments as, on the contrary, to salvage them from sliding into degradation and vulgarity. Kibirov's polyphonic play is something like the other side of silence, an equivalent of the inexpressibility topos. The Bakhtinian author expresses himself through silence, but this silence is not literal. Rather, it manifests itself covertly, through a dialogized style (irony, parody). Because he is unable to find language that would be worthy of his most cherished sentiments, to safeguard them he slips into parody, a roundabout manifestation of silence. Kibirov chooses, to paraphrase Shakespeare's Cordelia, "to love and be parodic."

By attending to the intricacies of Kibirov's play with verbal masks one may discern the presence of poetic subjectivity in the text. Negative dialogic indicators, subdued modulations of attitude toward "bad-smelling words," and oscillation back and forth between mockery and reverence must be carefully observed. Kibirov's texts are exercises in lyrical ventriloquism since they are powered by a tension between the depersonalizing technique of multiple quotations and a drive for poetic self-expression. Insofar as they engage in ventriloquism, they correspond to the notion of the authorless text. Yet because this ventriloquism is lyrical, it cannot conform to the doctrine of the death of the author. The author strives to salvage something of the self and his epoch in his texts.

Kibirov treads a fine line between the repudiation and dis-alienation of logos. The main body of "To Igor Pomerantsev" manipulates language by parodic design. Until the poem's conclusion, accordingly, the collection's title, *Paraphrasis,* is perceived by the reader in an ironic light. The poem, a parody, is the opposite of a paraphrase. The former changes the content while retaining the form; the latter retains the content while changing the form. Likewise, until its conclusion "To Igor Pomerantsev" presents a critique of periphrasis in a negative sense, as a critique of empty verbosity. The poem's end attempts to reverse matters. Parody, having exhausted itself, seeks to become both periphrasis in its positive connotation and paraphrase, another iteration of the "freedom and peace" of Russian literature. The author's rendition of Russian logos at once competes with the poetics of the "sacred" text and longs to reinvigorate it. Whether the bad infinity of language and life can indeed be transformed into eternal recurrence is yet to be seen.

Conclusion

Logophobia in the Land of Logos

IN ACT 2, SCENE 2 of *Hamlet* the following exchange takes place between the Danish prince and Polonius:

> Polonius: What do you read, my lord?
> Hamlet: Words, words, words.
> Polonius: What is the matter, my lord?
> Hamlet: Between who?
> Polonius: I mean, the matter that you read, my lord.[1]

Polonius deems Hamlet's reply nonsensical. Believing that the "insane" prince did not comprehend his questions, he rephrases them. In reality it is Ophelia's father who remains in the dark regarding the purport of this exchange. As Hamlet dissembles a naive, literal understanding of the questions, he plays with one of the most fundamental philosophical problems—that of the relationship between language and reality. One tends to forget that whatever one reads is first and foremost "words, words, words," and that their connection to the "matter" is not to be taken for granted. In Ludwig Wittgenstein's words, "How am I supposed to know what he means, all I can see are merely his symbols."[2] For obvious reasons, Hamlet's insight is not couched in terms of symbolic logic, yet the issue at hand is very much the same. What is the connection of language and verbal art to the realities that they allegedly depict?

Hamlet's pretense of madness involves a continual sabotage of communication, an obsessive language game in which he juggles literal and figurative meanings of words. This game serves well his purpose since mental illness is frequently accompanied by a seemingly illogical, unorthodox usage of language. "Though this be madness, yet there is method in it." Not only does a similarly unconventional employment of language characterize literary art; more importantly, Hamlet's verbal games—like the one above—contain insights about the word and its ambiguities, its ability to communicate and to subvert communication, to refer to things and to obscure them. Does language communicate external or internal realities or only itself? Does it have access to "true essences," or does it provide artificial oppositions, misleading labels, and an illusion of understanding the world?

Amply investigated in western European settings, the antiverbal paradigm had been inviting adequate scrutiny in the Russian context—not to challenge the Russian preoccupation with the power of the word but to explore the understudied, yet equally important, antiverbal trend. Logocentrism and logophobia coexist within a single poet's oeuvre. David Bethea's description of Brodsky as consistently inconsistent, something that makes perfect sense for a poet, applies well to the other heroes of my story. Challenging cerebral habits such as the axiom of non-contradiction is what we laymen understand under *droit du poèt* —along with other rights (duties) of grasshopperish Don Juanism, departing before one tastes pleasures of healthy aging, and rhyming *slezy* and *morozy*. "You know him then?—Well, yes and no."

And yet, the tension between logocentrism and logophobia presents not a discrepancy but a powerful dynamic. It is precisely because forces more substantial than those of literary theory will the Russian poet dead that he has the right to speak with the authority of the nation. Likewise, it is precisely because poetry is perceived not as a species of entertainment removed from the exigencies of being, but as a form of revelation that the aesthetic act requires "an utter destruction in earnest" (*polnoi gibeli vser'ez*), as Pasternak puts it in "If I only knew it happens this way" ("O znal by ia, chto tak byvaet," 1932), or "a height above the word, in colloquial language—a spiritual height" (Brodskii 5:339).[3] Answerability and non-alibi in existence, Bakhtin's key ethical categories, apply to the poet "answerable for every word as his" more than other verbal practitioners.[4] The force of verbal art, and poetry especially, then, has to do neither with a modernist or structuralist focus on the message, nor with the postmodern dance of signifiers, but with the close bond between word, life, and self, which alone could vouchsafe that "an uttered thought is not a lie." To meet this demanding imperative, poets must push against the boundaries of language and self alike.

Russian antiverbal lyrics are compelling statements of verbal skepticism that impact the culture at large. Many of them are programmatic works in the context of a given poet's oeuvre and in the Russian poetic tradition as a whole. These poems are key texts that represent entire periods of creativity, and draw other works into their orbit. Anything but aberrations, they inscribe verbal skepticism onto a structure of motifs and imagery that are typical of their creators and encapsulate their existential preoccupations and artistic visions. A poet's version of verbal skepticism relates to his worldview. Verbal skepticism also determines the features of one's poetics. The novel stress on the uniqueness of selfhood and the concurrent distrust of the word as unable to capture the inimitable self drives the transition from the normative poetic system of classicism to romantic individualized poetics. The word as incommensurate with the sublime ("The Inexpressible") motivates Zhukovsky's poetics of suggestiveness and the polyvalence observable throughout his oeuvre. Tiutchev's "Silentium!" bears on key issues of the poet's Weltanschauung, such as the dichotomy between the individual and the universal and the inimitability of the individual, which leads to his alienation from others and from the cosmos. Mandelstam's "Silentium" and "The Horseshoe Finder" distill, in concentrated form, the major motifs and poetic principles of his art, from the pre-acmeist period and the 1920s, respectively. Brodsky's "Conversation with a Celestial Being" and the cycle "A Part of Speech" embody both the key existential problematic and the core features of his poetics. His attitude to the word throws light on signature Brodskian devices such as reverse personification, linguistic metaphor, enjambments, convoluted syntax, gaps, and silences. Kibirov's sensitivity to the language crisis drives his (post-)conceptualist wordplay.

Poetry's push against language is inherently paradoxical—Wittgenstein's over-cited tautology "what we cannot speak about we must consign to silence" rarely applies here. Though sometimes poets do fall silent (Batiushkov later in life, Zhukovsky intermittently, Mandelstam in the 1920s, Brodsky after he moved to the United States), generally they expostulate on the inadequacy of words in words, an operative paradox that becomes especially fraught when the best poets denigrate language in their most powerful poems. Contrary to the Pushkinian ideal that "poetry must be a little dumb," these poets know well what they do. By dramatizing the operative paradox just as they override it, they further advance their anti-discursive thrust.

I have argued that the poet's relation to the word is linked to his worldview, and that both these issues are historically conditioned. One can more accurately talk about verbal "skepticisms" rather than "skepticism" since there exist disparate historically bound approaches to the issue. As we move into the twentieth century, an earlier idealistic inexpressibility is ousted by absurdist verbal skepticism that aligns its critique of the word with an existential critique. The topos of verbal skepticism is multifaceted. As it is conceptualized in specific contexts, it is informed by divergent worldviews. Poets and theorists alike deploy the antiverbal paradigm in response to specific situations, and history introduces variations in antiverbal discourse. Still, while different writers conceive of verbal inadequacy in polyvalent terms, they all share the key belief that language is not fully commensurate with reality and human experience.

One more brief comparison, of Mandelstam's "On the Addressee" and Brodsky's "A Letter in a Bottle," will elucidate the points above. Mandelstam's essay has been traditionally read as an article of his faith in the transcendental future addressee. A corrective to that reading is in order. The essay begins by alluding to Baratynsky's "My gift is poor, my voice is not loud" to express a fear of incommunicability: "There is nothing as terrifying for a man as another person who does not at all care about him" (Mandel'shtam 1:182). It proceeds to imagine communication with a future interlocutor through the metaphor of a bottle thrown by the sailor-poet into the waves. Why start with Baratynsky's apprehensions vis-à-vis incommunicability, and why engage a metaphor that exposes the sailor-poet's solitude and danger? Can one indeed claim that "the notion of poetry as a letter in a bottle necessarily implies the poetic missive's eventual landfall and arrival in the hands of its reader"?[5] In commonsense terms, a bottle cast into the sea is hardly a FedEx.

I am not disputing a logocentric reading of this essay for, in contrast to many of Mandelstam's clearly antiverbal poems, the essay does posit a strong hope for the existence of the providential future interlocutor. Instead I am pointing out that this logocentrism has a darker undercurrent—a vision of the poetic word that emerges in the face of destruction and embarks on an uncertain path toward a receiver who must fulfill the existential imperative of responding to the drowning (dying) poet. Fighting this undercurrent of uncertainty, Mandelstam postulates the existence of the future addressee. In a revealing slip on the part of the translator, this addressee is someone "in whose existence the poet has no doubt, not doubting in himself."[6] In fact, the Russian original has it as someone "whose existence the poet cannot doubt without doubting himself" (*v sushchestvovanii kotorogo poet ne mozhet somnevat'sia ne usomnivshis' v sebe*) (Mandel'shtam 1:188). Rather than stating that the poet does not doubt his future interlocutor's existence, Mandelstam says that the poet stakes his faith in himself and his vocation on the eventual appearance of this interlocutor. One must believe in communicability for otherwise one would lose faith in the poetic word. Just as tellingly, the future addressee is "providential"—someone who will find the bottle (the poem) in spite of empirical odds against finding it. The meaningfulness of the poetic word again predicates itself on theology.

Brodsky's "A Letter in a Bottle" reimagines a more benign, though by itself not unproblematic, scenario of Mandelstam's transcendental future reader as a breakdown of communication:

(размыто) Так вспоминайте ж меня, мадам, при виде волн, стремящихся к Вам,	(washed out) Remember me, madam, whenever the sea comes hurrying toward you in crashing spray;

при виде стремящихся к Вам
валов
в беге строк, в гуденьи
слов . . .

Море, мадам, это чья-то
речь . . .
Я слух и желудок не смог
сберечь:
я нахлебался и речью
полн . . .
(размыто)
(Brodskii 1:184)

remember me, madam, when
verses pound,
remember me, madam, when
words resound.

The sea, my dear madam, is
someone's talk
I'm deaf and my stomach is past all
hope.
I've now drunk my fill and I'm
choked with speech . . .
(washed out)[7]

Brodsky's lyric literalizes Mandelstam's metaphor of the poem-bottle thrown into the waves (as well as Derrida's description of writing as an "essential drifting"), and questions the existence of a providential posthumous reader. Subtitled "entertainment for Mary" (*razvlechenie dlia Meri*), that is, Marina Basmanova, the poem trivializes its own message. The "washed out" that appears multiple times indicates the inadequacy of the author's communication with the recipient of his missive. The poet highlights the problem of incommunicability by bidding farewell to Morse, Popov, Marconi, and other inventors of modern means of communication. He acknowledges his defeat: he "has lost his trial" (*proigral protsess*) (Brodskii 1:178). If "On the Addressee" exemplifies the tug of verbal exaltation and verbal critique, and the bond between ontology and word-view, "A Letter in a Bottle" demonstrates the progression to absurdist verbal skepticism in later poetry.

SPECIFICITIES OF THE RUSSIAN PARADIGM

What makes the Russian version unique and distinct from Western antiverbal thought?[8] Modern intellectuals tend to focus on linguistic mediation as a site of falsehood. At the end of the Nietzschean line, post-structuralism comes to see language not as organic and necessary but as constructed and arbitrary; not defining human essence, but dehumanizing; not securing our place of honor in the universe, but deluding us into thinking that we occupy that place; not giving birth to consciousness, but operating in defiance of it. In a telling move, the conception of the word as sacred Logos is replaced by the vision of language as an omnipotent demiurge. At its limit, the self is conceived as both a victim and an illusion of linguistic practice: due to language "there is, in a very radical sense, no such thing as human."[9] This problematic entity constitutes the only "reality" and circumscribes humans within its bounds.

These are compelling charges. No less forceful is the subversion of expressive agency under the "death of the author" theory, even if prepared for by earlier considerations of junctures and disjoints between life and art in Russian formalism, American New Criticism, and Prague structuralism, and coexisting with less categorical analyses of the same, for example, by the Lotman-Tartu school.[10] It is when the "death of the author" no longer problematizes the relationship between the text and its origin and postulates in absolute terms that the text not be treated in terms of expressive agency—but becomes prescriptive, a staple of modern critical etiquette—that it loses some of its force.[11] The various permutations of the Barthean battle cry that proscribes reconstituting the ties between author and text are by now most familiar. Furthermore, the "death of the author" exhibits a tension between the notions of voluntary and involuntary depersonalization. Inasmuch as it is heartening to observe the presence of agency, if only one prepared to self-annihilate, the author's eager submission to an omnipotent linguistic power may seem superfluous. Nonetheless, the critic's vision of language as an inexorable power is matched on the part of the modern author by a self-inflicted depersonalization. Not accidentally, Barthes's "death of the author" manifesto singles out Mallarmé and other French modernists who welcome the autonomy of the word.

Alain Badiou's peculiar reading of "The Horseshoe Finder" will illustrate how these critical notions get projected onto Russian poetry—a charged sphere where rhetorical gestures of the "anonymity-of-poetry" kind do not quite hold sway. After listing instances of twentieth-century Western poets who deny personal agency in their textual production, Badiou summons Mandelstam as an example of a Russian poet who shares the belief that poetry must be impersonal:

> In "The Horseshoe Finder" Mandelstam, having spoken of coins the past had left to us, shows the present as gnawing into the past, one which can be discerned only when "there is no longer enough of me for me" . . . For Mandelstam the thought of the thought of poetry is nothing other than a search for some kind of a cut, shift, lack from which an anonymous and uncontrollable speech emanates . . . This consequence of thought cut by the age, this slippage of the fullness of being throws the poetic act back to some kind of an earthly anonymity, some kind of a petrification.[12]

For Badiou Mandelstam's poetry strives for depersonalization as a state that imparts special poetic powers.[13] To support his contention that a deliberately exercised anonymity is called for, he reads cause and effect where none are stated: the past "can be discerned only when 'there is no longer enough of me for me.'" By the time we read this "Pindaric fragment," the poet's words have fossilized: "What I am saying now is not said by me, / But is dug out of the earth like grains of petrified wheat." Petrification, brought on by time and language, is likewise reinterpreted as a kind of earthly anonymity in the initial poetic act. The lines that express the dangers of reducing the poetic self are recast to fit the critical paradigm of voluntary depersonalization.

Critics like Svetlana Boym, David Bethea, and Clare Cavanagh have pointed out that the Western "death of the author" does not translate seamlessly in the Slavic context. As Boym notes, the "poet without a biography" and the "autonomy of art and life" are less applicable to countries like Russia, where, for an array of political and cultural reasons, the myth of the phatic bard has endured, and the figurative death of the poet is trivialized by "actual human death[s] during the Stalinist purges of intellectuals."[14] Bethea continues this line of thought: scholars of Russian poetry "are made frightfully uncomfortable by notions of the 'death of the author' and the 'pleasure of the text' when applied, say, to Mandelstam, perhaps the greatest of all twentieth-century poets, who died a terrible death in a Stalinist camp and was last seen alive foraging about in refuse in a state bordering on insanity."[15] Clare Cavanagh, in turn, offers a corrective to Western postmodern theories from the Russianist and Polonist perspectives. Foucault's announcement that the work murders its author "is bound to give the Slavist pause, not least because such metaphors have had, in recent Russian history, an uncomfortable habit of realizing themselves as they pass from theory into practice."[16]

I align myself with these correctives, but—and this is worth emphasizing—would point out that a circumspect attitude to the post-structuralist model in the Russian case is not only context-sensitive but prompted by a self-conscious resistance to the "death of the author" doctrine on the part of Russian poets. While it is true that poets' literal and violent deaths "undo our capacity to conceive of language as mere metaphoricity," poets themselves (not only their lives and deaths) resist slippery metaphoricity at the heart of critical language, a rift between all-too-serious being and all-too-flippant words.[17] Russian renditions of the antiverbal topos parallel Western theoretical and literary works to a significant extent, yet the Russian paradigm departs from its Western counterparts in the twentieth century by placing a heavier emphasis on resistance to verbal depersonalization rather than deliberately and voluntarily yielding to disappearance in language.

To read someone like Brodsky or Kibirov in their portrayal of the language crisis means reading them against the grain of the post-structuralist critique of the subject. Nor are such readings called forth solely by Russian history that, as more tragic or more "authentic," suggests a commonsense corrective to post-structuralist rhetoric. Rather, it is how these poets demand to be read on their own terms. Kibirov's "Piroskaf" (2002) will exemplify this point:

И поскольку всё,	And since everything
Что я любил, что я хранил,	That I loved, that I kept,
В чём сердце я похоронил,	Where I buried my heart,
Сброшено с корабля	Is thrown from the ship
(Или у футуристов	(Or is it "steamship" with the
"с парохода"?)	Futurists?)
Современности—	Of modernity—
Сигану-ка и я за борт . . .	I will also leap overboard. . .
Конечно, спасти никого не удастся,	Of course, no one will be saved,
Но хотя бы недолго ещё	But at least I will flounder for
побарахтаюсь,	a little,
Побуду в приличном обществе,	Will stay in decent society,
В роковом его просторе . . .	In its fatal expanse . . .
А "Титаник" пусть себе плывёт,	And let "Titanic" swim,
И приблатнённый Ди Каприо	And let the thieving Di Caprio
Пусть себе ставит раком	Take doggy style
Всех пассажирок и членов	All the female passengers and
команды . . .	crew members. . .
Молодцу плыть недалечко.	That fine fellow will not swim far.
(Kibirov, *Stikhi* 571)	

"Piroskaf" manages to squeeze in allusions to Pushkin's *Eugene Onegin,* chapter 1, stanza 50, the futurist manifesto "A Slap in the Face of Public Taste" ("Poshchechina obshchestvennomu vkusu," 1912), the folk song "Glorious sea, sacred Baikal" ("Slavnoe more, sviashchennyi Baikal"), Nikolai Iazykov's "Swimmer" ("Plovets," 1829), and the 1997 Hollywood blockbuster *Titanic,* among others. In Kibirov's typical cento technique the text is constructed as a multiplicity of parodically reworked discourses, mixed incongruously and countering each other. The procedure ostensibly replicates Barthes's depersonalized writing as a tissue of quotations drawn from divergent cultural centers.

Yet Kibirov does not present himself as a Barthean scripter without feelings and impressions, a conduit of a gigantic dictionary from which writing is drawn. The lyric engages an established trope "ship-death." The title repeats that of Baratynsky's poem of 1844 published posthumously, a poem mailed by Baratynsky to Russia several days before his death. In mock defiance of "A Slap in the Face of Public Taste" demanding that Pushkin, Dostoevsky, Tolstoy, and so forth be thrown overboard from the ship of modernity, Kibirov sends his lyrical hero overboard. Decent company—dead Russian classics—are preferable to the Leviathan of pop culture. The lyrical persona asserts his will to flounder in the elite society of Russian writers.

The boat-death trope (shipwreck as death-threat) governs Mallarmé's "A throw of the dice will never abolish chance" ("Un coup de dés jamais n'abolira le hasard," 1897), a paradigmatic modernist foregrounding of autonomous language. According to Mallarmé ("Crisis of Verse"), the poetic text should be driven not by lyrical subjectivity (will, emotion, voice of the poet) but by structural relationships inherent among the words.[18] The unusual typographical layout of "A throw of the dice" fragments syntax and interrupts the narrative flow, drawing attention to the materiality of the text. The text seeks to achieve the impersonality of the constellation described at its conclusion, one in which there is no trace of the original thought and feeling that gave rise to the act of writing.[19]

Kibirov's "Piroskaf" turns the "ship-death" cliché upside down by claiming the trope's, the lyrical hero's, and his own literal and literary vitality. In de Man's terms, "Piroskaf" represents a funeral urn. The reader imposes the meaning on the text, interpreting it primarily as an allegory of the author's demise. Kibirov's poem, on the contrary, asserts the life of the author. In "Piroskaf" and elsewhere Kibirov goes precisely against a self-imposed lack of the personal. His invocation of multiple biographical details in these texts is a refusal to exercise poetic impersonality. Neither selfhood nor external reality is dismissed, however tritely they may be represented. Rather, the contamination of the authentic by verbal waste engenders yearning for reality and for selfhood.

Kibirov's texts display a conspicuous poetic subjectivity in defiance of the "death of the author" doctrine, only superficially corresponding to Barthes's vision of a multidimensional space of quotations focused on the reader in their multiplicity. While he may play with the Derridian existence outside the myth of a pure native language in "a certain laughter and a certain step of the dance," his verbal skepticism is predicated on the endangered value of elusive lyrical subjectivity.[20] It is the surplus of signifier over signified, or Mallarméan *signe,* that is ridiculed, for example, in the string of non sequiturs in "Know-Nothing in the Sunny City." "Generation–udder–burden–seed" (*plemia–vymia–bremia–semia*) carries to the absurd the privileging of verbal medium over content, "the dialectic that belongs to poetry alone."[21]

Lest one consider Kibirov, a suspect conceptualist, to be an imperfect example of a larger trend, it is instructive to juxtapose Barthes's "Death of the Author," American New Language poetics, and Aizenberg's conceptualist manifesto. In the case of Barthes and New Language poetics, the self is challenged; in the case of Russian conceptualists, the self is promoted, though in an unorthodox way. For Barthes, "the scripter no longer bears with him passions, humors, feelings, impressions but rather this immense dictionary from which he draws a writing that can know no halt."[22] The New Language manifesto, "Aesthetic Tendency and the Politics of Poetry" (1988) by Ron Silliman, Carla Harryman, Lyn Hejinian, Steve Benson, Bob Perelman, and Barrett Watten addresses the concerns of the more traditional critics:

> Isn't it [our work] written without a stable authorial center or perceptible narrative "voice," in an anonymous, collective environment? The individual is seen as under attack, and this is largely true: the self as the central and final term of creative practice is being challenged and exploded in our writing in a number of ways.[23]

To reiterate Aizenberg's characterization of conceptualist poetry, it is art in which "not the author expresses himself in his own language but languages, always someone else's, converse among themselves." The description seemingly mirrors Barthes's notion of the authorless text as well as Language Poetry's dismissal of the self as the locus of creativity. Yet textual uniqueness is defined via an authorial stance: the language of languages "is made 'other' (that is, artistic) not by the qualitative level of its components but by the author's dismissive-creative attitude toward them." This dismissive-creative attitude toward the word, not the relegation of agency to language, is the novel means of self-expression. Likewise, arch-conceptualist Prigov bolsters the movement's antiverbal disposition by positing (in the spirit of Brodsky for whom aesthetics is valuable as fostering human autonomy) the value of freedom and, consequently, personal agency: "Language is only language, not ultimate truth, and once we comprehend that, we achieve freedom."

Kibirov's work subscribes to the traditional vision of lyrical subjectivity. In this he follows Brodsky, who perceived the reduction of the self in the text as threatening, and, of course, Mandelstam, whose notion of the autonomous word was embedded in anything but the impersonal—the vision of acmeism that entails the filling of emptiness by human agency. Granted that Russian Orthodox post-structuralists and Western postmodernists who surreptitiously hold on to the notion of expressive agency do appear, much is at stake in this divergence. Whether laughing off verbal entrapment (Kibirov) or lamenting a textual self-effacement in existentially urgent terms (Brodsky), these late twentieth-century poets follow Mandelstam and the Russian tradition at large by remaining nostalgic for the poet at his fullest stature in life and in art.

Russian and Western antiverbal narratives diverge in ways that hinge on differences between (post-)romantic distrust of the word and post-Nietzschean/post-structuralist critique of logocentrism. To juxtapose Wordsworth and Blanchot, both used the metaphor of clothing to state their positions: "If words be not (recurring to a metaphor before used) an incarnation of the thought but only a clothing for it, then surely they will prove an ill gift"; "Who then is speaking here? Is it 'the author'? But to whom can such a word refer since anyhow he who writes is no longer Beckett but . . . the vacant site where speaks the redundancy of idle words under the ill-fitting cloak of a porous, agonizing I."[24] Wordsworth gives priority to inner experience over language. Casting the word as clothes points up its inorganic, deceptive quality, its incapacity to embody human thought. In contrast, Blanchot praises Beckett's *The Unnamable* (*L'Innommable,* 1953) as a text that conceptualizes personal agency as a decrepit cover for linguistic structures. In the former case the self is privileged, and the expression of the individual self is occluded by the wrong kind of word. In the latter case the self is a sham, on a par with the ontological structures Derrida resists in Meister Eckhart's apophasis: "Is it arbitrary to still call truth or hyper-truth this unveiling which is perhaps no longer an unveiling of being? . . . I do not believe so."[25]

From the perspective of this investigation, romantic inexpressibility set the tenor for the entire narrative of Russian verbal skepticism, all the way to contemporary poetry. The romantic mythologeme of the phatic bard flourished with the dire circumstances of the twentieth century, and resistance to depersonalization became vital to writers like Mandelstam. The literal annihilation of Russian poets created resistance among their descendants to toying with the "death of the author" notion. Hence Brodsky's "in the case of Mandelstam we participate in both [his death and his works' death]." Hence also "death . . . from a figure of speech became a figure that leaves you speechless," Brodsky's wry if unintentional reversal of de Man's "death is a displaced name for a linguistic predicament." Late twentieth-century poets, familiar with the post-structuralist critique of logocentrism, and apprehensive of the word's defacing qualities, all the more honor the centrality of the individual artist. In other words, they do not "guilelessly" believe that they non-problematically control their texts and communicate what they have in mind. Rather, even as they engage in acts of verbal criticism, they challenge theory. Words are found wanting as locuses of personal agency or ethical principles, but neither selfhood nor ethics are deconstructed as discursive shams—hence Brodsky's characterization of Akhmatova's impact on him as a moral and ethical one, "an unprinted fragment of the text." The self may be disfigured by the word and the world, but it will not yield without a struggle. Indeed, poetry bereft of a binding lyrical subjectivity and ethical force remains a dystopian notion in the Russian context.

Initially somewhat derivative, Russian verbal skepticism has evolved into an independent tradition that takes issue with Western notions. One of the earliest Russian lyrics of the antiverbal topos, Batiushkov's "There is enjoyment in a wilderness of forests," used a Byronic model, but already introduced some changes. Later Russian antiverbal poetry became progressively more original. Whether adherence to a lyrical subjectivity—an "essentialist" argument about the bond between feeling and lyric—be deemed antiquated or refreshing is a matter of one's critical allegiance. As the heyday of deconstruction recedes into the past, and its articles of faith are critically reexamined not only by adherents of other critical paradigms but by scholars committed to deconstruction as well as by the seminal figures of deconstruction themselves, the wary Russian attitude to the post-structuralist abyss of language strikes one not so much as a sign of naiveté as a healthy engagement with critical stereotypes.[26]

DICHTEN UND DENKEN

Throughout this work, I have considered the philosophical and theoretical views most relevant to the Russian poetic tradition of verbal skepticism; these have variously served as sources of inspiration or targets of critique: German idealist philosophy, Russian Silver Age philosophy, Nietzsche and the post-structuralist line and so on. Some poets adhered to certain philosophical ideas (e.g., Zhukovsky—transcendental idealism), while others problematized them (e.g., Brodsky—theological ineffability; Brodsky and Kibirov—modern theory). Poets may have been directly influenced by philosophers (e.g., Tiutchev and Baratynsky—by Schelling; Mandelstam and Brodsky—by Shestov), or may have responded to the general intellectual context. Conceptual and rhetorical linkages between theorists and poets permit one to reconstruct a broader cultural framework for verbal skepticism.

As much as philosophical influences are illuminating, Russian poetry of verbal skepticism is no stepchild of philosophy. Late twentieth-century Russian antiverbal poetry challenged important assumptions of modern theory. Nor did Russian poetry quite track Russian philosophical developments for, although Russian poetry and the philosophy of verbal skepticism shared resistance to post-humanist views, the former, unlike the latter, combated them mainly on secular terms. If recent poets (Brodsky, Kibirov) interacted with the philosophical tradition in a critical way, earlier poetry (of the romantic age in particular) exhibited more compliance. But as early as the 1830s, Russian poets produced works that deviated from established discourse and anticipated twentieth-century tendencies (Tiutchev, Baratynsky, Lermontov).

The relationship between antiverbal poetry and philosophy suggests not neat genetic attributions but a dynamic interplay that opens novel aspects of the problem. Clearly, the progression from benign ineffability to absurdist verbal skepticism describes a tendency and a matter of degree. Not to exaggerate coherence, one can usefully characterize particular periods, but poets are often more complex than the labels they suggest. They may have anticipated future trends (e.g., the late romantics), or may have harkened back to an earlier form but in a nonpareil manner (e.g., Mandelstam). The poets both fit into temporal taxonomies and were less determined by the spirit of the age, free to access one or another of the antiverbal topoi. Each time the articulation of verbal skepticism was a little different. As the topos developed, it acquired more semantic depth and complexity. Thus Mandelstam's antiverbal lyrics showed affinities with various philosophical notions. However, philosophical discourse was engaged obliquely. Philosophical ingredients, sometimes incompatible, were idiosyncratically intertwined and imaginatively reworked.

Russian poetry does not subordinate itself to philosophy but engages in dialogue with it. The traffic between poetry and philosophy of verbal skepticism is bilateral. Just as philosophers impact poets, poets make a significant contribution to the philosophical tradition. And, in a distinctly Russian twist, poetry often dominates philosophy. Solovyev's "F. I. Tiutchev's Poetry," one of the first works to launch his mystical doctrine, claims Tiutchev as a key predecessor of his metaphysics. Lotman's culminating work of semiotic theory, *Culture and Explosion,* quotes Zhukovsky's "and only silence speaks understandably" at the opening of the book, and later employs Blok's "The Artist" ("Khudozhnik," 1913) to illustrate the notion of inspiration followed by a catastrophic reduction.[27] Florensky's "Antinomy of Language" ("Antinomiia iazyka," 1918) (*By the Watersheds of Thought* [*U vodorazdelov mysli*]) quotes something like a dozen poems from the very context discussed in this study, including, within the space of a few pages, Pushkin's "Echo," Lermontov's "Do not trust yourself" and "There are speeches—meaning" and Fet's "Like midges at twilight," and "How poor our language is!" The Zhukovsky quotation, "and only silence speaks understandably," attributed to Tiutchev by Lotman, shows the extent to which the narrative of verbal skepticism is unified in cultural consciousness.[28]

Russian philosophy's manner of drawing on poetry is noteworthy. As a contrasting example, I will use de Man's analysis of Wordsworth's "Essays upon Epitaphs" in "Autobiography as De-Facement." De Man cites the following passage from Wordsworth:

> Words are too awful an instrument for good and evil to be trifled with: they hold above all other external powers a dominion over thoughts. If words be not . . . an incarnation of the thought but only a clothing for it, then surely they will prove an ill gift; such as those poisoned vestments, read of in the stories of superstitious times, which had power to consume and to alienate from his right mind the victim who put them on. Language, if it do not uphold, and

> feed, and leave in quiet, like the power of gravitation or the air we breathe, is a counterspirit . . .[29]

The citation omits "recurring to a metaphor before used" that follows "if words be not . . . " as well as the end of the passage after "counterspirit": "unremittingly and noiselessly at work to derange, to subvert, to lay waste, to vitiate, and to dissolve."[30] De Man expresses surprise as regards Wordsworth's condemnation of language: why does the poet contrast flesh and clothing if "incarnate flesh and clothing have at least one property in common, in opposition to the thoughts they both represent, namely their visibility?"[31] Wordsworth's critique of language verges on the distinction (familiar from Plato on) between words as organic ("incarnation of thought"), and words as shells covering primary essences ("clothes"). To object that "garb-body-soul is in fact a perfectly consistent metaphorical chain" is to disregard this clear opposition.[32] Next de Man wonders why Wordsworth condemns figurative language inasmuch as the language of tropes "is indeed like the body, which is like its garments, the veil of the soul as the garment is the sheltering veil of the body."[33] "By means of the problematic expression 'is indeed like'—technically, a simile, but with an excessive logic of persuasion that makes it almost an equation—de Man designs a metaphorical chain of linguistic garments, covering up the singularity of their folds and cultural tensions, to say nothing of all the potentially erotic excesses of the body."[34] But the problem is not only that of disregarding differences (or *différances,* if one so prefers). "Is indeed like," a trope, enables de Man to occlude Wordsworth's distinction between verbal organicity and non-organicity. Finally, he articulates his main insight: as figuration, language is always privative, "the picture of the thing and, as such, it is silent, mute as pictures are mute."[35] Wordsworth's observation that evil language works incessantly and silently applies to the poet's own language.

Given the ultimate conclusion of "Autobiography as De-Facement" that figurative language is privative, the critic's initial bewilderment as to why Wordsworth condemns figuration is bewildering indeed. De Man performs the requisite deconstructive move of demonstrating the failure of the text's structuring trope (Wordsworth's language subverts its message), one which is all too easy in the case of texts which themselves challenge the word as does Wordsworth's "Essays upon Epitaphs." The omission of "recurring to a metaphor before used" from the quotation allows de Man, by the conclusion of the essay, to present language as figure (as metaphor or prosopopeia) as his own exposure of the rupture in Wordsworth's text, rather than Wordsworth's self-reflexive acknowledgment of his text's metaphoricity.

As de Man is quick to point out, earlier questionings of language themselves fall prey to the operative paradox. Thus Nietzsche's disparagement of tropes in his Basel lecture notes and "On Truth and Lying in an Extra-Moral Sense" is itself subject to the mendacity of specularity: "The deconstruction of the self as a metaphor does not end in the vigorous separation of the two categories (self and figure) from each other but ends instead in an exchange of properties that allows for their mutual persistence at the expense of literal truth . . . By calling the subject a text, the text is made to seem a subject."[36] Similarly, Locke, Condillac, and Kant's attempts to control figures by acknowledging their existence and circumscribing their impact fail since these attempts prove unable to extricate themselves from figuration (de Man, "The Epistemology of Metaphor," 1978). For Locke we can banish rhetoric from philosophy through "an ethical determination of high seriousness coupled with an alert eye for interlopers"; for Condillac the solution is to abstain from taking rhetoric for reality; for Kant "the entire question seems to lack urgency." However, "in each case, it turns out to be impossible to maintain a clear line of distinction between rhetoric, abstraction, symbol, and all other forms of language."[37] The resulting undecidability "is due to the asymmetry of the binary model that opposes the figural to the proper meaning of the figure," and "the manifest effacement of such anxiety-traces in the texts is much less important than the contradictory structures of the texts themselves, as it is brought out by a reading willing to take their own rhetoric into consideration."[38]

To be fair to Locke, all speeches may carry specularity but some speeches are more specular than others. It is by employing figuration more liberally than many a romantic poet that "Autobiography as De-Facement" obscures Wordsworth's opposition between language as organic and nonorganic. Metaphorization, including anthropomorphizing metaphors of language, so that the text is indeed "made to seem a subject," is something de Man both denigrates and overindulges in. So does he both denigrate, and display a penchant for, manifesto-like rhetoric, slogans of the "death is a displaced name for a linguistic predicament" kind. Equally, the essay's didactic emphasis on its reading as correct (it opens with "the theory of autobiography is plagued by a recurrent series of questions and approaches that are not only simply false . . . but . . . confining") goes against deconstruction's problematization of binary oppositions such as "truth" and "falsehood."[39]

Still at issue in "Autobiography as De-Facement" are not only operative paradoxes such as hyper-rhetoricity or didacticism. The charge of inflated rhetoric, while hardly dismissable altogether, could be allayed by the critic's self-reflexive acknowledgment of performative paradoxes in his own work. Such an acknowledgment would indeed make his analysis not only "willing to take their own [analyzed texts'] rhetoric into consideration" but also willing to consider his own rhetoric—albeit this does not take place.[40] Nor are offshoots of hyper-rhetoricity merely at issue—restatements of the problem of organicity versus non-organicity of language in the most incendiary terms possible and an overly complicated idiom both divert attention from this problem's ancient lineage.[41] Nor is one unsettled merely by the predictability of the deconstructive procedure, with its foregone conclusion that Wordsworth's text subverts its own logic from within.[42] Even putting aside religious and ethical concerns that underlie Wordsworth's thinking on words (the miracle of the Incarnation, language as a "counterspirit" and "too awful an instrument for good and evil to be trifled with") is not most contestable either. What, in my view, is especially problematic is the vulnerability of the target (language that questions language) and the recasting of the insight proper to Wordsworth's doubts about words as the workings of language against authorial will—or, more precisely, as the insight of the critic who exposes textual rupture. Indeed, the omitted finale of the passage from Wordsworth, "at work to derange, to subvert, to lay waste, to vitiate, and to dissolve," employs some of de Man's and deconstructive criticism's favorite terms to highlight the instability of language.[43]

Given that articulations of verbal skepticism are too easy to subvert; that, insofar as writers are well aware of the pitfalls of their endeavor, exposing the contradiction rending the text is a gratifying but hardly essential procedure; and that deconstructive procedures are themselves liable to deconstruction—it makes sense that Russian theorists do not destabilize antiverbal poems. Moreover, nowhere do they even offer sustained interpretations of poetry. Supplying very little or typically no commentary at all, they posit poems as self-explanatory and impeccable articulations of their own argument. Poetic pronouncements speak for themselves, and so philosophers invoke the authority of poets to support their visions.

While the dialogue between poetry and philosophy is important, and philosophy has recourse to poetry no less than poetry to philosophy, intrapoetic dialogue dominates. Zhukovsky's participation in preparing Batiushkov's "There is enjoyment in a wilderness of forests" for publication in *Northern Flowers* (*Severnye tsvety*) was in this sense typical. The romantics relied on German idealism but even more on each other; Fet echoed Tiutchev and Nadson; symbolists responded to Zhukovsky, Tiutchev, Lermontov, and Fet; Mandelstam drew on Batiushkov, Tiutchev, Baratynsky, Fet, and Ivanov; Brodsky engaged Baratynsky, Lermontov, Tiutchev, and Mandelstam, among others. Tiutchev's "Silentium!" became the focal point for Russian poetry of verbal skepticism, as is attested by the poem's influence on authors ranging from Mandelstam to Kibirov. By the time Kibirov enters the scene, the accumulated energy of the topos is so potent that a slight intertextual vibration (e.g., "to lie, to compose" in "School Progress Report") resonates throughout the poetic system. Russian verbal skepticism has generated a long and rich literary lineage.

Russian antiverbal narrative displays a high degree of coherence. Romantic lyrics of verbal skepticism erected a cogent conceptual and figurative framework within which later transpositions of the topos developed. Some works departed markedly from preceding lyrics in the ways they conceptualized the foibles of the word. However, whether texts echoed, modified, or inverted earlier works, the evolution of the antiverbal narrative proceeded within a configuration of stable motifs and recurrent imagery. Whatever the degree of creative transformation of earlier lyrics in later texts, the very polemics occurring were undertaken within, and facilitated by, a forceful intertextual field. Russian logophobic verse is a Mandelstamian "philology as family" par excellence.

WIDENING THE SPACE OF INEFFABILITY

As Russian poetry entered the new millennium, the topos of verbal skepticism continued to thrive. Recent work by Timur Kibirov, Pavel Peppershtein, Yuri Leiderman, Alexander Skidan, Dmitry Vodennikov, and many others contributed to the ongoing narrative. Kibirov forges on with his interrogations of the modern world and word in the collections *Kara-baras* (2006), *On the Margins of "A Shropshire Lad"* (*Na poliakh "A Shropshire Lad,"* 2007), *Three Narrative Poems* (*Tri poemy,* 2008), *Poems About Love* (*Stikhi o liubvi,* 2008), and "Greek and Roman-Catholic Little Songs and Ditties" ("Greko- i rimsko-kafolicheskie pesenki i poteshki," 2009). Younger poets like Skidan poeticize the foibles of the word in books like *Red Displacement* (*Krasnoe smeshchenie,* 2005) and the cycles "Russian Hebrew" ("Russkii ivrit," 2008), and theorize them in *The Resistance to Poetry: Researches and Essays* (*Soprotivlenie poezii: Izyskaniia i esse,* 2001).

Verbal skepticism is, of course, not limited to poetry, as examples from prose, drama, fine art, and film show. Viktor Pelevin's *Generation 'П'* (1999), a celebrated turn-of-the-millennium Russian novel, narrates the adventures of one Vavilen Tatarsky coming of age as the Soviet Union disintegrates. As a youngster, he was an aspiring poet and a student at the Moscow Literary Institute. With the collapse of the country, Tatarsky becomes first a lowly shop assistant, and later an advertising copywriter whose job is to concoct Russian advertisements patterned on up-to-date American advertising technologies. As he prospers in the advertising business, there unfolds a savage spoof of Russia's transformation into consumer society. In Pelevin's satire of cultural decline and rampant consumerism, the degradation of language plays a pivotal role. To circumscribe the individual fully within the social norm, language is redefined in operational terms, and the concept of the subject is now identified with its function. The systematic brainwashing of the populace by publicity is grounded in debasement of the Russian language by advertising jingles, which recycle once potent cultural statements and disgorge them as white noise.

From a historical perspective, some of the most renowned Russian prose works contain a wealth of material on verbal inadequacy. Why does Dostoevsky cite Tiutchev's "Silentium!" again and again in his work (*The Adolescent* [*Podrostok,* 1875], *Diary of a Writer* [*Dnevnik pisatelia,* 1873–81], *The Brothers Karamazov*), albeit rewriting Tiutchev's fluid formula for his own ideological ends as in the case of Mitya Karamazov's kenotic "suffer, be humble, and be silent"?[44] Why has the indispensable Raskolnikov killed the requisite old pawnbroker? One suspects that no two randomly chosen critical investigations of *Crime and Punishment* (*Prestuplenie i nakazanie,* 1866) will agree on the protagonist's motives. One also suspects there was a rationale for Dostoevsky making it this way—that is, one beyond philanthropic inclinations toward future needy academicians. Why does Christ keep silent throughout the Grand Inquisitor's effusive monologue, merely kissing this Satan-serving, verbiage-discharging old cleric in the end, and why does Alyosha "plagiarize" his actions in *The Brothers Karamazov*? Why is the Underground Man so critical of rationalist explanations of human behavior in *Notes from Underground* (*Zapiski is podpol'ia,* 1864)? What is the nature of the entangled relationship between Prince Myshkin, Nastas'ia Filippovna, and Aglaia in *The Idiot* (*Idiot,* 1868), and what keeps Myshkin from answering when asked whether he truly claimed that beauty would save the world? Are Dostoevsky's dialogism (advanced by Bakhtin) and Bakhtin's investment in dialogic theory both indebted to the conviction intrinsic to the Russian tradition, that humans are endlessly complex, contradictory, and not locatable (*vnenakhodimy*) in the word? More generally, why is the reader left with the impression that Dostoevsky never resolves the problems he deals with in his oeuvre, and why is this seeming inability to resolve them so mesmerizing?

We need not exploit Dostoevsky's philanthropy excessively. What did Levin mean in Tolstoy' s *Anna Karenina* (1873–77) by not knowing whether he was acting well or badly and even avoiding thinking about this issue? Why is Tolstoy so bent on denying the connection between reason, language, and ethics in this novel and elsewhere? What is the basis for his struggle to capture the living continuum of overlapping events and unnecessary episodes in *War and Peace* (*Voina i mir,* 1865–69)? What makes him reject the traditional equation of poetry, beauty, and goodness and assert the quest for artistic pleasure to be subservient to Christian goodness in *What Is Art?* (*Chto takoe iskusstvo?*, 1897–98)? What are the implications of his definition of genuine art as a human activity by which one human, by way of external signs, consciously communicates to others his feelings, in such a way that other people are infected with them?

Why does Treplev note bitterly in Chekhov's *The Seagull* (*Chaika,* 1895) that he spoke a great deal about innovative forms of art but feels himself sliding into routine? What are the reasons and effects of his death offstage? What is the purport of Dorn's remark on the quiet angel that has flown over the scene? Why is Gaev's and other characters' incessant chatter interrupted in *The Cherry Orchard* (*Vishnevyi sad,* 1904) by silence giving birth to a sound of a torn string from far away that the characters are unable to comprehend but are perturbed by? What makes Brodsky's "My quiet craft" similar to Chekhov's story of incommunicability and loss, "Grief" ("Toska," 1886)? Why is there so much silence, incoherence, and fragmentation in Chekhov's oeuvre overall, and what makes these gaps and ruptures so charged, felt to be more meaningful than words? In Brodsky's non-idiomatic phrasing, "so forth."[45]

At the heart of these, and numerous other scenes in Russian classical literature, lies the issue of the word in its existential implications. For Ivan Kireevsky, Semyon Frank, Nikolai Lossky, and the heyday of Russian idealist philosophy in general, establishing an indigenous Russian school of philosophy meant the conceptualization of man and being as not absorbable by the expressible aspect of thought or by the logical cohesion of verbal expression. Analogously, the lion's share of what has come to be regarded as the special mystique of nineteenth-century Russian classical literature is predicated on its engagement of inexpressibility.

The novel of the Golden Age opened up a space beyond the written text and forged, *via negativa,* a locus of lyrical and cognitive power. By foregrounding an essential ineffability of man, being, and the divine, authors like Dostoevsky and Tolstoy not only framed their insights as superior to the corpus of Western rationalist tradition but developed a unique poetics where what is said is aggrandized by the unsaid and the unsayable. The reader closes an expansive volume spellbound not only by the "truth and beauty" in the narrative but by hints at something—more beautiful and more genuine—beyond the pages. The fascination lies not only in the "accursed questions" but in the inimitable way of treating them: silences, enigmas, denials, the apophatic rhetoric of Dostoevskian and Tolstoyan "that's not it" and "could not explain why."

Nor is verbal skepticism confined to the written medium. There exist a multitude of canvases entitled "Silence." Isaak Levitan's "Silence" ("Tishina," 1898) strives to communicate his discernment of inexpressible sublimity. The bell in the background of Mikhail Nesterov's "Silence" ("Molchanie," 1903), which presents two monks, an elderly man, and a youngster on a lake, offers the promise of sound, perhaps even harmony, but not language. Nikolai Roerich's "Silence" ("Molchanie [Tishina]," 1964) depicts a lone human figure high in the mountains of Tibet. A monk or philosopher, this man is contemplating the ineffable. Multiple twentieth-century paintings entitled "Silence" present fragmented human figures with blocked mouths and cut-out tongues. For Vasily Kandinsky "black is like the silence of the body after death, the close of life," and for Kazimir Malevich "the end of music is silence."[46] Malevich's monochromatic squares are renditions of ineffability—the void beyond the image. And what about film? Appalled by the savagery encountered in his travels in fifteenth-century Tatar-torn Russia, the protagonist of Andrey Tarkovsky's *Andrei Rublev* (1966) eschews painting and takes a vow of silence. Silence on the narrative plane coexists in *Andrei Rublev* with silence as a structural device. Why are there prolonged stretches of mute action in a Tarkovsky or a Sokurov movie?

Explored and exploited by Russian classics, the enigma of being irreducible to verbal expression displays one more engaging facet. Kibirov's "Give an answer! It does not give an answer!" references the lyrical paean to Rus' in the last chapter of the first volume of Gogol's *Dead Souls.* The first lyrical address sketches a sublime mountain landscape only to negate it—this is no Russia. The narrator confesses his inability to capture Russia in his vision, but the country's huge empty space produces a song. Characteristically, music proves more meaningful than concepts. The narrator realizes that Russia wants something from him but is unsure what he is summoned to accomplish. Overwhelmed by the vast expanse, he does not believe himself to be up to the task of grasping the country's essence. Like Neoplatonists, he experiences a loss of identity and a fusion with this infinite space. Traditional ineffability epithets like "boundless," "illimitable," "mighty," "motionless," "strange," and "spectral" abound in the text. Finally the earthly carriage is transfigured into an incorporeal spirit, bird–troika–Rus' leaping into the beyond.

The ineffability topoi typically aggrandizes its subject, and this is precisely what Gogol achieves, promoting national uniqueness as Russia's transcendence of the limits of verbal representation. The same may be said of "Russia is not to be understood by the mind" ("Umom Rossiiu ne poniat'," 1866), penned by the author of "Silentium!" That verbal skepticism defines the Slavophile mythologeme of Russian uniqueness testifies once again to its centrality. With Russian inexpressibility meeting the inexpressibility of Russia, I conclude this study of the peregrinations of the great, powerful, truthful, and free Russian logophobia.

Notes

INTRODUCTION

1. Turgenev, *Sobranie sochinenii v dvenadtsati tomakh,* 10:45.

2. For example, Franke, ed., *On What Cannot Be Said,* an expansive collection of apophatic writings from Plato to Derrida and beyond, does not include a single Russian writer, philosopher, or theologian. Mikhail Epstein's *Slovo i molchanie* discusses the problem of the word and silence, but, rather than concentrating on this issue exclusively, considers it among multiple metaphysical problems and paradoxes of Russian literature: the great and the little, being and nothingness, demonism and apophaticism, the unconscious in religion and art, atheism and secularization, utopia and the apocalypse. On the word and silence, see Epshtein, *Slovo i molchanie,* 179–210, and "Slovo i molchanie v russkoi kul'ture."

3. The tension between laudatory and degrading views of language falls in line with the culture's essential polarity as analyzed in Lotman's and Uspensky's "Binary Models in the Dynamics of Russian Culture." My study avoids a binary bind since "both sides of the paradigm are glued together in an ultimately complicitous fashion: there is a structural agreement between the contesting and the contested forms" (Barthes, *Pleasure of the Text,* 55). Rather than emphasizing binary oppositions or privileging one element at the expense of the other, I seek to enrich the overall picture of Russian logology by focusing a bright light on the less explored element.

4. Dante, *Paradiso,* XIII, 19, 123.

5. Celan, *Gesammelte Werke in fünf Bänden,* 2:31.

6. My principle of selection resembles Franke's: "Among countless poets of the unsayable, a few [Dante, Holderlin, Dickinson, Rilke, Eliot, Celan, Stevens] distinguish themselves for the programmatic way in which the theme of the unsayable emerges at the center of their work and at the core of their act of making poetry" (Franke, ed., *On What Cannot Be Said,* 2:37).

7. Pushkin, *Polnoe sobranie sochinenii,* 3:420.

8. This coverage is of necessity selective. For a more detailed survey of theories of verbal skepticism, see my doctoral thesis, *Silence and the Rest: Verbal*

Skepticism in Russian Poetry, 1–84. For book-length Western analyses of verbal skepticism, see especially Gibson, *The Limits of Language;* Waldrop, *Against Language;* Hawkins and Schotter, eds., *Ineffability;* Budick and Iser, eds., *Languages of the Unsayable;* Blodgett and Coward, eds., *Silence, the Word, and the Sacred;* Scharfstein, *Ineffability;* Grabher and Jessner, eds., *Semantics of Silences in Linguistics and Literature;* Scharlemann, ed., *Negation and Theology;* Wolosky, *Language Mysticism;* Carabine, *The Unknown God;* Bulhof and Laurens, eds., *Flight of the Gods;* Bruns, *Modern Poetry and the Idea of Language;* Harpham, *Language Alone;* Franke, ed., *On What Cannot Be Said;* and Reisner, *Milton and the Ineffable.* Such prominent theoreticians as Blanchot, Bataille, Foucault, Derrida, de Man, Iser, Kermode, and Culler, among others, have focused on the antiverbal paradigm in western European settings. See, for example, Blanchot, *Sirens' Song* and *The Gaze of Orpheus;* Bataille, *Inner Experience;* Foucault, *Language, Counter-Memory, Practice;* Derrida, *Margins of Philosophy* and "How to Avoid Speaking"; de Man, *Allegories of Reading* and *The Rhetoric of Romanticism;* Iser, "The Play of the Text"; Kermode, "Endings, Continued"; and Culler, "On the Negativity of Modern Poetry."

9. John 1:1.

10. The conceptualization of humans as fundamentally verbal creatures also appears in Hesiod, Aristotle, Socrates, Isocrates, and other philosophers of antiquity, as well as later in Descartes, Humboldt, and Hegel. Just as the essence of humanity is seen in speech, thought is also defined through language. Humboldt claims, as Sapir and Whorf would do later, that conceptualization depends on language, which is an inseparable part of being human: "Where the raw materials of inner perception and sensation are to be imprinted with conceptualization, everything depends on the individual way of looking at things of an individual human being whose language is an inseparable part of him." See Humboldt, *Humanist Without Portfolio,* 245.

11. In *The Homeric Hymn to Apollo,* the Deliads, maidens who serve Apollo, are endowed with the ability to imitate human dialects. Just as human incommunicability is the effect of divine anger, the command of all languages is a sign of divine power. See also the episode of the apostles and fiery tongues (Acts of the Apostles, chap. 2).

12. Humans "wandered in confusion the whole of their long life" until Prometheus discovered for them "letters and their combination, an art that fosters memory of all things, the mother of the Muses' arts." See Morford, *Classical Mythology,* 74. In Shelley's *Prometheus Unbound* (1820), the protagonist "gave man speech, and speech created thought, / Which is the measure of the universe." See Shelley, *Shelley's Poetry and Prose,* 72.

13. The winged horse Pegasus, symbol of poetic inspiration, springs from the corpse of Medusa, who was beheaded by Perseus; Athena's invention of the flute is inspired by the lamentations of the surviving Gorgons; the satyr Marsyas picks the flute, challenges Apollo to a musical contest, and is flayed alive, and so

on. The tale of Orpheus being torn to pieces by crazed Thracian women is a classic narrative that links poetry, music, suffering, and death.

14. Plato also prefigures a later critique of language by underscoring the dangers of misnaming. Language may or may not be divinely sanctioned, just as it may or may not reveal things, and humans will never be able to solve the riddle of how language came to them. In Socrates's view, names are not arbitrary phenomena but are "integrally connected to the objects they denote." See Plato, *Cratylus,* 435. While Hermogenes promotes the notion of conventional referentiality, Plato insisted that essences be known on their own terms. For Plato's critique of poetry, see *The Republic.*

15. Plato, *Phaedrus,* 247.

16. "In our writing and telling we are but urging toward it; out of discussion we call to vision; to those desiring to see, we point the way." See Plotinus, *The Enneads,* 617–18. Although any depiction of the One is provisional, negations are more useful than assertions since "assertions slice up reality, whereas negations tend to simplify them from distinction and definition in the direction of being uncircumscribed and from being set apart by their proper boundaries in the direction of being unbounded." See Proclus, *A Commentary on the First Book of Euclid's Elements,* 427.

17. Schoenberg, *Moses and Aaron,* 38.

18. Saint Augustine, *De Doctrina Christiana,* 2:254. The philosophical implications of modern physics suggest a similar operative inconsistency: since the nature of knowledge does not permit us to say anything definite about the world, we cannot say that there exists a world beyond our knowledge. According to Gödel's incompleteness theorem, any formal system at least as complicated as arithmetic contains statements that cannot be proved either true or false—by analogy, to think fundamentally about language, one would have to go outside language. For more on the operative paradox, see Meise, "On Talking About Silence in Conversation and Literature," 47–48; and Gibson, *The Limits of Language,* 22.

19. Dante, *Paradiso,* XIII, 19–24, 123. Even the prowess with which Dante portrays the sphere of the Sun turns out to be inadequate to convey his vision. The constellation "is as far beyond our experience as the motion of the heaven that out-speeds all the rest is beyond the motion of the Chiana." See Dante, *Paradiso,* XIII, 24, 123.

20. Milton's images "communicate tone and other such musical values, stirring emotion which may lead the reader to inward apprehensions of an unarticulated and inarticulable truth." See Franke, "Blind Prophesy," 91.

21. Wittgenstein, *Tractatus Logico-Philosophicus,* 151.

22. Garber, "The Rest Is Silence," 32–35. Conventional expressions of verbal skepticism like the ineffability topos are themselves testimonies to the failure of the word.

23. The Sophist Gorgias underscores the distinction between words and

things and is skeptical about the ability of language to communicate reality: "That with which we communicate is speech, and speech is not the same thing as the things that exist, the perceptibles. So that we communicate not the things which exist, but only speech." See Freeman, *Ancilla to the Pre-Socratic Philosophers,* 129. Gorgias focuses on style as a power in itself, as distinct from the rhetorician's purpose in court. His power of delivery (*hypocrisis*) leads him to question the relation between language and truth. See also Sprague, *The Older Sophists,* 42–46.

24. Shakespeare, *King Lear,* 1.1.3–4.

25. For darker inexpressibility in Shakespeare, see, for example, "the worst is not so long as we can say 'This is the worst.'" Shakespeare, *King Lear,* 4.1.57.

26. "Since every appearance contains a manifold, thus different perceptions by themselves are encountered dispersed and separate in the mind, a combination of them, which they cannot have in sense itself, is therefore necessary." See Kant, *The Critique of Pure Reason,* 238–39. The active faculty of this synthesis is imagination. The view of imagination as the agency that synthesizes variegated elements of experience in the act of knowledge led the romantics to exalt it as a focal point of poetic consciousness.

27. On apophasis in Kant, see Kant, *The Critique of Pure Reason,* pt. 2, bk. 2, chap. 3, sec. 7.

28. Kant, *The Critique of Judgment,* 91. On negativity and the sublime, see Hertz, *The End of the Line.*

29. Kant, *The Critique of Judgment,* 314.

30. Schopenhauer, *Philosophical Writings,* 101.

31. Schopenhauer, *The World as Will and Representation,* 1:243.

32. Schopenhauer, *Philosophical Writings,* 98.

33. Ibid., 123.

34. Works of art intensify the experience of the will, so that people perceive it and are temporarily freed from its clutches.

35. Some aspects of Nietzsche's verbal skepticism, such as his critique of the mercenary nature of poetry, are long-established themes, but he goes further than earlier thinkers in his attack on the word.

36. Nietzsche, *The Will to Power,* 427.

37. Nietzsche, *Thus Spake Zarathustra,* 329.

38. Nietzsche, *The Joyful Wisdom,* 337.

39. Nietzsche, *Friedrich Nietzsche on Rhetoric and Language,* 21.

40. Ibid., 15.

41. Nietzsche, *Thus Spake Zarathustra,* 410.

42. Nietzsche, *Friedrich Nietzsche on Rhetoric and Language,* 244.

43. Ibid., 240.

44. Artists are not men of great passion for two reasons: "they have no shame before themselves (they observe themselves while they live; they lie in wait for

themselves, they are too curious), and they have no shame before great passion (they exploit it artistically). Secondly, their vampire—their talent—generally begrudges them any such squandering of energy as is involved in passion . . . One is finished with it [passion] when one represents it." See Nietzsche, *The Will to Power,* 431.

45. Nietzsche, *The Twilight of the Idols,* 530–31. See also Heidegger on Nietzsche's claim that he can no longer communicate his philosophy (at least not in print): "The internal limit of all thinking . . . is that the thinker can never say what is most his own . . . because the spoken word receives its determination from the ineffable." Heidegger, *Nietzsche,* 484. On the unsayability of being, see Heidegger, *On the Way to Language.*

46. Nietzsche, *The Twilight of the Idols,* 483.

47. Ibid., 483; Nietzsche, *Beyond Good and Evil,* 49.

48. Derrida, "How to Avoid Speaking," 7–8.

49. Ibid., 32.

50. Derrida, *Of Grammatology,* 158. Some critics have claimed important similarities between Derrida's thought and negative theology. For example, for Caputo "negative theology is nothing negative, no more than deconstruction itself, but rather, just like deconstruction itself, is a deeply affirmative irruption . . . a passion for the impossible, for trespassing and transgression." See Caputo, *The Prayers and Tears of Jacques Derrida,* 27. "A passion for the impossible . . . " seems too broad a description to suggest a compelling link between deconstruction and negative theology. That traditional apophatic theology "is nothing negative" is true, but in what way is apophatic theology (a matter of faith) transgressive, and in what way exactly is deconstruction affirmative? The claim that deconstruction "repeats the passion of the messianic promise and messianic expectations, sans the concrete mechanisms of the positive religions that wage endless war" (Caputo, *The Prayers and Tears of Jacques Derrida,* xxi) is too vague as well. Nor does "the indeterminate faith and open-ended hope in what is coming, in the incoming of the tout autre, the passion for which deconstruction is all about" seem to adequately characterize "the religious structure of experience" (Caputo, *The Prayers and Tears of Jacques Derrida,* 47–48). That apophatic theology broadens the horizon of unknowability and potentially leads to the hollowing out of the divine is true. This trait prompts Mikhail Epstein to suggest connections between apophasis, Russian nihilism, and Soviet atheism. See Epshtein, *Slovo i molchanie,* 271. In contrast to Epstein who sees the negative potential of indeterminacy, Caputo posits indeterminacy and denial as the crux of faith. That is not so, not even in the case of apophatic theology that envisions the transcendent splendor of the divine. I would rather side with those critics who question the association of deconstruction and negative theology. For instance, Shira Wolosky objects to Caputo relying on Derrida's "How to Avoid Speaking" with the observation: "Negation does not in itself guarantee such an

escape [of negative theology from ontology], does not necessarily deontologize theological structures." See Wolosky, "An 'Other' Negative Theology," 264. It stands to reason that negative theology does not escape ontology—it is a version of ontology. Derrida's "rescue for theology" in my view entails an unwarranted projection of deconstruction's deontologizing impulse on matters of faith.

51. Derrida, *Of Grammatology,* 14.

52. Derrida, "How to Avoid Speaking," 29.

53. De Man, *The Rhetoric of Romanticism,* 4–6. "The 'speech' privileged in logocentrism is not literal but is a figure of speech: a figure, ultimately, of God." See Johnson, "Writing," 47.

54. Derrida, *Limited Inc,* 62.

55. Derrida, *Margins of Philosophy,* 316.

56. Barthes, *Image, Music, Text,* 146–47.

57. Foucault, *Language, Counter-Memory, Practice,* 121.

58. De Man, *The Resistance to Theory,* 122.

59. Derrida, *Margins of Philosophy,* 27.

60. De Man, *The Rhetoric of Romanticism,* 76.

61. Ibid., 81.

62. De Man, *The Resistance to Theory,* 122. "No ethical evaluation for or against this deplorable fate can be made. The subject is not its agent but is generated by it, automatically, by a mechanical process." See Miller, *Others,* 228. The text is able "to configure or subvert every system and position it is thought to manifest." See Culler, *On Deconstruction,* 220.

63. De Man, *The Resistance to Theory,* 96.

64. Language is limited as an object of knowledge, for it is "an imponderably vast, contradictory, and amorphous mass that defeats rational inquiry by its unsorted immensity." As such, language has come to function as a buffer between humankind and its self-imposed hardships in a post-humanist climate. See Harpham, *Language Alone,* 56.

65. Pseudo-Dionysius, *The Divine Names* and *Mystical Theology,* 217–18.

66. Pseudo-Dionysius proposes to make up a list of the names and characteristics of God in the Bible, and to show that all these names and properties are inadequate. He concludes that the divine itself is not conceptual. On Pseudo-Dionysius, see also Blans, "Cloud of Unknowing," 58–77.

67. Sorsky, *The Complete Writings,* 46.

68. Important hesychast works by Pseudo-Dionysus, Symeon the New Theologian, Saint Gregory of Sinai, John Chrysostom, and others were translated into Church Slavonic during the fourteenth and the fifteenth centuries. In *On Stillness and Prayer,* Saint Gregory demands a complete shedding of images, words, and thoughts, and argues that those who "have attained the state of illumination, should cultivate silence." See Plamer, Shepard, and Ware, eds., *Philocalia,* 268. See also Saint Symeon the New Theologian's *Practical and Theological Chapters and Three Theological Discourses.*

69. Zenkovsky, ed., *Medieval Russia's Epics, Chronicles, and Tales,* 208. Epiphanius blames verbal art for its exteriority. He begins *The Life of St. Stefan of Perm'* (*Zhitie sv. Stefana, episkopa Permskogo,* 1417–18) with apologia for his inability "to write invisibly on the tablets of the mind and the heart." His meager skill only allows him "to write on perceptible charters." See Epifanii, *Zhitie sv. Stefana, episkopa Permskogo,* 1.

70. The 1793 translation of *The Philocalia,* an anthology of hesychast writings, played a large role in a major religious revival. Toward the close of the nineteenth century, *The Candid Narrations of a Pilgrim to His Spiritual Father* popularized the hesychast prayer. See Fedotov, *The Russian Religious Mind,* 2:200–202.

71. The Slavophiles "were the first thinkers in Russia to philosophize specifically as Russians and to generate a self-conscious Russian intellectual tradition." See Scanlan, "The Nineteenth Century Revisited," 24.

72. Aristotle's system tore the unity of mental self-consciousness and transferred the root of man's inner convictions outside of moral and aesthetic meaning. See Kireevskii, *Izbrannye stat'i,* 250.

73. Ibid., 271.

74. Earlier Tolstoy's *What Is Art?* (1897–98) questioned the validity of art as a mode of apprehending truth. Conventional art is found wanting as a frivolous undertaking not concerned with moral improvement. Genuine art must be subservient to Christian goodness.

75. Solov'ev, *Sobranie sochinenii,* 2:331. See also Solov'ev, *Filosofiia iskusstva i literaturnaia kritika.*

76. Lossky, *The World as an Organic Whole,* 67.

77. To remedy this problem, Lossky offers a distinction between the absolute as such and the absolute in its relation to the world. The former is the ineffable of negative theology; the latter appears as a living personal God: "It must not be thought . . . that this is a positive definition of the nature of God as such, i.e. of God as the Absolute. Like all positive definitions of the Absolute, it has meaning only in relation to the world." See Lossky, *The World as an Organic Whole,* 75–76.

78. Ibid., 75. Rather than demonstrating that the absolute is not hostile to the world, Lossky claims the supposition of hostility to be impossible on the grounds that the ineffable absolute transcends finite being.

79. Frank, *The Unknowable,* 279. To clear himself of the charge of operative inconsistency, Frank warns the reader that "the author would have no right to consider himself a philosopher and would betray his own thesis if he thought his work anything more than a mere hint, a 'babbling indication' of the truth of genuine, ineffable, unutterable reality." See ibid., xi.

80. Ibid., xvi, xiii.

81. Shestov, *In Job's Balances,* 207–8.

82. Ibid.

83. Shestov, *Potestas Clavium,* 132.

84. Shestov, *All Things Are Possible,* 34; Shestov, *Penultimate Words,* 170.

85. Bakhtin, *Speech Genres and Other Late Essays,* 148. On Bakhtin and theology, see, for example, Felch and Contino, eds., *Bakhtin and Religion.*

86. Bakhtin, *The Dialogic Imagination,* 299. At issue here is not the disputed Bakhtinian notion of the monologicity of poetry versus the dialogicity of prose but his emphasis on linguistic relativism. For an argument that poetry displays dialogic features, see Boym, "Dialogue as 'Lyrical Hermaphrodism'"; Shapiro, *The Sense of Form in Literature and Language,* 97–116; Eskin, *Ethics and Dialogue in the Works of Levinas, Bakhtin, Mandel'shtam, and Celan,* 113–25.

87. Bakhtin, *The Dialogic Imagination,* 273.

88. This observation is credited to O. Ostrogorskii's "Gnoseological Foundations of the Byzantine Argument on Sacred Icons" ("Gnoseologicheskie osnovy vizantiiskogo spora o sv. ikonakh"). See Jakobson, *Language in Literature,* 528.

89. Jakobson, *Language in Literature,* 378.

90. Ibid., 68.

91. Lotman, *Kul'tura i vzryv,* 176.

92. Lotman and Uspensky, "'Agreement' and 'Self-Giving' as Archetypal Models of Culture," 128.

93. "The sordid and opportunistic character of arbitrary signification emanates from its source in the original satanic compact." See Mandelker, "Lotman's Other," 69.

94. Epstein, "Like a Corpse in the Desert," 136–37.

95. Epshtein, *Slovo i mochanie,* 317.

96. Foucault, *The Order of Things,* 386–87.

97. Pushkin, *Polnoe sobranie sochinenii,* 2:47.

98. Ibid., 2:47.

99. Nepomniashchii, "Prorok," 205–13.

100. If Pushkin talks about incommunicability, as, for example, in "Conversation Between Bookseller and Poet," "The Poet" ("Poet," 1827), "The Poet and the Crowd" ("Poet i tolpa," 1828), and "To the Poet" ("Poetu," 1830), he tends to couch it as a conventional romantic opposition of "the poet versus the mob." For an argument that Pushkin does not question the powers of language, see Ginzburg, *O lirike,* 235–36; Nepomniashchii, "Prorok," 205–13; Etkind, *"Vnutrennii chelovek" i vneshniaia rech',* 82–83. Monika Greenleaf, on the other hand, places Pushkin among romantic ironists for whom perception is sustained by the language that determines the categories of thought: in *Eugene Onegin* "there is no consistent, dialectical development from an illusory, partial language to an authentic one." See Greenleaf, *Pushkin and Romantic Fashion,* 207. Many discussions of Russian philosophical poetry have claimed that Pushkin stands outside the main line of its arguments. By contrast, Andrew Kahn challenges this traditional resistance to reading Pushkin as a poet of ideas, as well as sug-

gests that Pushkin's poems on poetry, creativity, and communication "express claims for authority rather than its possession." See Kahn, *Pushkin's Lyrical Intelligence,* 11. Removing the cultural filter "makes it possible to appreciate the impact of a poem ["The Prophet"] that is strikingly violent and even ugly" (ibid., 202). For a challenge to mainstream readings of "The Prophet," see Davidson, "The Moral Dimension of the Prophetic Ideal." On the poem's historical context, see Sandler, *Commemorating Pushkin,* 5–21; and Bocharov, *Siuzhety russkoi literatury,* 230–45.

CHAPTER ONE

1. Herder, *Herders Sämtliche Werke,* 4:162; Wackenroder, *Confessions and Fantasies,* 118; Humboldt, *On Language,* 92.

2. Coleridge, *Collected Works,* 166; Wordsworth, *Prose Writings,* 184.

3. Batiushkov, *Nechto o poete i poezii,* 91; Venevitinov, *Polnoe sobranie sochinenii,* 217.

4. Zhirmunskii, *Nemetskii romantizm i sovremennaia mistika,* 33–36. This approach has been taken by later commentators, for example, Pigarev, *Zhizn' i tvorchestvo Tiutcheva,* 181–84; Mann, *Dinamika russkogo romantizma,* 20–30; Toporov, "Ob istochnikakh stikhotvoreniia Zhukovskogo 'Nevyrazimoe,'" 39–51.

5. De Staël, *De l'Allemagne,* 140–44.

6. Schelling posits an accord of human consciousness and physical reality that justifies an appeal to external nature to express inexpressible inner feelings. This is likely the way Mme de Staël conceives of the mind-nature relationship, although one cannot exclude the possibility that she views the relationship as the mind projecting itself onto the world. In romantic poetry "the impressions of the senses are to be hallowed by a mysterious connection with higher feelings and the soul embodies its forebodings and indescribable intuitions of infinity in types and symbols borrowed from the visible world." See Schlegel, *Vorlesungen über dramatische Kunst und Literatur,* 34. By contrast, Hazlitt relies on subjective idealism: poetry "conforms the shows of things to the desires of the soul, instead of subjecting the soul to external things." See Foakes, ed., *Romantic Criticism 1800–1850,* 111. For Coleridge the lyrical subject "infuses the thoughts and passions of man into everything that is the object of his contemplation." See Coleridge, *Miscellaneous Criticism,* 215.

7. For an early version of this analysis, see Khagi, "Silence and the Rest." I see German idealism as more important to the Russian romantics than the hesychast tradition. At the same time Orthodoxy offers a congenial ground for idealist philosophy. On a common belief in the inadequacy of the senses that binds Orthodox apophaticism and the evening meditation of sensibility of the English Sentimentalists, see Pratt, *Nikolai Zabolotsky,* 208. On Zhukovsky and Schelling's objective idealism, see Gukovskii, *Pushkin i russkie romantiki,* 33–

41. On Venevitinov and German idealism, see Ginzburg, *O lirike,* 52–61. On Tiutchev, Baratynsky, and German idealism, see Pratt, *Russian Metaphysical Romanticism,* 19–36. On Tiutchev and Schopenhauer, see Korovin, "Tiutchev i Shopengauer." On Schelling's apophatic thinking, see his *Philosophy of Revelation* (1841).

8. Lomonosov's "Morning Contemplation of Divine Greatness" ("Utrennee razmyshlenie o Bozh'em velichestve") and "Evening Contemplation of Divine Greatness" ("Vechernee razmyshlenie o Bozh'em velichestve," 1743) note man's inability to grasp the greatness of the Creator: "The end of creatures is unknown to you? / Then say how great the Creator Himself is?" (*Nesvedom tvarei vam konets?/ Skazhite zh, kol' velik tvorets?*) ("Evening Contemplation"). See Lomonosov, *Polnoe sobranie sochinenii,* 8:203. Derzhavin's "God" ("Bog," 1784) contemplates the inadequacy of human understanding vis-à-vis God: "Spirit omnipresent and unified, / Who needs no place or reason, / Whom none could ever comprehend" (*Dukh vsiudu sushchii i edinyi, / Komu net mesta i prichiny, / Kogo nikto postich' ne mog*). See Derzhavin, *Sochineniia,* 158.

9. Batiushkov, *Polnoe sobranie stikhotvorenii,* 187. Other examples include "A Message to My Verses" ("Poslanie k stikham moim," 1804–05) and "A Dream" ("Mechta," 1817). At the age of thirty-four Batiushkov falls literally silent.

10. Batiushkov, *Polnoe sobranie stikhotvorenii,* 237. For quotations, unless indicated otherwise, I am using my literal translations of Russian poems. I borrowed some of the locutions from *An Age Ago.*

11. Byron's original reads:

> There is a pleasure in the pathless woods,
> There is a rapture on the lonely shore,
> There is society, where none intrudes,
> By the deep sea, and music in its roar:
> I love not Man the less, but Nature more,
> From these our interviews, in which I steal
> From all I may be, or have been before,
> To mingle with the Universe, and feel
> What I can ne'er express, yet cannot all conceal.

See Byron, *Childe Harold's Pilgrimage,* 197. As any secondhand handling of signs, Batiushkov's translation sensitizes the author to verbal problems.

12. Many Russian romantic lyrics link the subject of inexpressibility to that of music, including Batiushkov's, Tiutchev's, and Baratynsky's lyrics discussed here.

13. Byron, *Childe Harold's Pilgrimage,* 197.

14. Ibid., 197.

15. Pratt, *Nikolai Zabolotsky,* 220.

16. Byron, *Childe Harold's Pilgrimage,* 197.

17. Zhukovsky participated in preparing Batiushkov's "There is enjoyment

in a wilderness of forests" for publication in *Northern Flowers* (*Severnye tsvety*). See Vatsuro, *Zapiski kommentatora,* 164–65. Zhukovsky's poems about inspiration such as "Night" ("Noch'," 1823) and "I used to encounter a youthful muse" ("Ia muzu iunuiu byvalo," 1824) are examples of his logocentrism. For an analysis of these poems, see, for example, Ianushkevich, *V mire Zhukovskogo.*

18. Zhukovskii, *Sobranie sochinenii,* 1:37. The addressee, Anna Turgeneva, retorts that "The more you feel the more you talk (*Chem bol'she chuvstvuesh', tem bol'she govorish'*). Zhukovsky replies: "Let's leave the art of speech to the intellect, / Let the heart feel, sigh, and be silent" (*Ostavim razumu iskusstvo govorit', / Pust' serdtse chuvstvuet, vzdykhaet i molchit*). See Veselovskii, *V. A. Zhukovskii,* 38.

19. Zhukovskii, *Sobranie sochinenii,* 1:390, 1:306–7.

20. On the importance of "The Inexpressible" in the context of Zhukovsky's oeuvre and in the context of romantic inexpressibility, see Gukovskii, *Pushkin i russkie romantiki;* Toporov, "Ob istochnikakh stikhotvoreniia Zhukovskogo 'Nevyrazimoe'"; Mann, *Dinamika russkogo romantizma;* Vatsuro, *Zapiski kommentatora.*

21. Zhukovskii, *Sobranie sochinenii,* 2:129–30.

22. Gukovskii, *Pushkin i russkie romantiki,* 36.

23. There are two languages—of nature and of man, with the former inadequate to the latter. See Toporov, "Ob istochnikakh stikhotvoreniia Zhukovskogo 'Nevyrazimoe'," 45. See also Pyotr Viazemsky's "Evening" (To Ekaterina Fedorovna Tiutcheva) ("Vecher" [Ekaterine Fedorovne Tiutchevoi], 1865).

24. For August Schlegel "the literature of the ancients has its foundation in the physical world, while ours [romantic literature] hovers between recollection and hope." See Schlegel, "Vienna Lecture on Literature #1," 34. According to Schiller in "Treatise on Naive and Sentimental Poetry" (1795), "the sentimental poet is always involved with two conflicting representations and perceptions—with actuality as a limit and with his idea as infinitude; and the mixed feelings that he excites will always testify to this dual source." See Schiller, *On Naive and Sentimental Poetry and on the Sublime,* 116.

25. It has been argued that Zhukovsky's poem promotes art's portrayal of inner, not external, reality. See Gukovskii, *Pushkin i russkie romantiki,* 35. It has also been claimed that the poem laments poetry's powerlessness "to adequately convey 'the wonderful life of nature.'" See Iezuitova, *Zhukovsky i russkaia kul'tura,* 18.

26. Schlegel, *Lucinde and the Fragments,* 261.

27. Mann, *Dinamika russkogo romantizma,* 23. The true philosopher "sees everything as an eternal becoming, an uninterrupted process of creation." See Schlegel, *Vorlesungen über dramatische Kunst und Literatur,* 59.

28. Schlegel, *Lucinde and the Fragments,* 212. On romantic fragments, see Greenleaf, *Pushkin and Romantic Fashion,* 1–55. On Tieck, Wackenroder, and

Zhukovsky, see Toporov, "Ob istochnikakh stikhotvoreniia Zhukovskogo 'Nevyrazimoe.'" On Zhukovsky's attempts to portray the soul as a whole, see Fleishman, *Ot Pushkina k Pasternaku*, 10.

29. Schlegel, *Vorlesungen über dramatische Kunst und Literatur*, 59.

30. Wordsworth, *The Complete Poetical Works*, 110.

31. Ibid., 92.

32. On the analogy in British romantic poetry, see Abrams, *The Mirror and the Lamp*, 52–60.

33. Compare the inexpressible being conceptualized more subjectively, as an ineffable property of Fichtean ego producing non-ego. On Zhukovsky's poetry suggesting the presence of the divine in nature, see Vinitskii, *Dom tolkovatelia*, 15.

34. Punctuation here follows Zhukovsky's own. See Zhukovskii, *Sobranie sochinenii*, 1:129–30.

35. Gukovskii, *Pushkin i russkie romantiki*, 38.

36. Zhukovskii, *Sobranie sochinenii*, 2:536.

37. According to August Schlegel, "the modern can do justice to its endeavors . . . after what is infinite by approximation." See "Vienna Lecture on Literature #1," 34. No modern work of art is perfect, while each is striving for perfection.

38. Venevitinov, *Sobranie sochinenii*, 97–98. Venevitinov engages the theme of inexpressibility in lyrics such as "Poet" ("Poet," 1826–27), "Consolation" ("Uteshenie," 1827), and "Poet and Friend" ("Poet i drug," 1827).

39. Zhukovsky's conclusion, "and only silence speaks understandably," introduces the issue of incommunicability. The shift, therefore, is a matter of degree. Nor should this shift be understood in the sense that Venevitinov replaces the problem of the inexpressible with that of the incommunicable. Rather, he appends the issue of incommunicability to that of inexpressibility, and brings the former into sharper focus.

40. Some later philosophers (Nietzsche, Frank) veer between the view that one purposefully conceals one's true experiences and the view that these experiences are incommunicable.

41. All references to Tiutchev, *Polnoe sobranie sochinenii i pisem v 6 tomakh*, are abbreviated as (Tiutchev volume: page) and placed in the main text.

42. Gregg, *Fedor Tiutchev*, 30.

43. As man is expelled from Eden, his language falls as well. The notion that language is evil in its doubling up of matter resembles Plato's critique of the poetic word in *The Republic* as doubly removed from ideal essences—as material copies of copies.

44. For an analysis of "A Vision" in the context of Tiutchev's works on the poet and poetry, see Pratt, *Russian Metaphysical Romanticism*, 104–20.

45. For an analysis of "Insomnia" and the night theme in Russian poetry, see Ginzburg, "F. I. Tiutchev."

46. The image of the deaf-mute is "strongly foreshadowed by repeated use of negative sound Imagery." See Pratt, *Russian Metaphysical Romanticism,* 47. On this poem, see also Goldberg, "Christianity and Romanticism in Tjutcev's 'Pevuchest' est' v morskich volnach.' "

47. Tiutchev's poetic world lies outside the limits of the word. See Lotman, "Poeticheskii mir Tiutcheva," 860. Poems like "When with a sympathy to our word" and "We cannot foresee" show the interplay between verbal idealism and verbal skepticism. For an expression of idealism in Tiutchev, see, for example, "Poetry" ("Poeziia," 1850).

48. On the lyric's translations into English, see Girivenko and Charysheva, "Angliiskie versii stikhotvoreniia F. Tiutcheva 'Silentium!' kak perevodcheskii kommentarii." The Latin title means "be silent!," and was used into the twentieth century in Germany to begin meetings (Michael Wachtel, personal communication).

49. Iambic quatrains of alternating rhyme are the most conventional prosodic form of the period. Iambic couplets would be perceived as archaic. At the same time, all masculine rhymes are odd, as are six-line stanzas. On the ubiquity of iambic tetrameter during the period, see Gasparov, *Ocherk istorii russkogo stikha,* 112–15.

50. *Zvezdý, zakhodiát,* and *razgoniát* were not acceptable alternative stresses. Following the first publication, the Turgenev–Sushkov edition published the poem in the corrected form, with all the lines written in regular iambs. Mikhail Gasparov explains Tiutchev's metrical irregularities as "attempts to introduce rhythmical variations characteristic of Latin (this time French) syllabics to Russian iambs." See Gasparov, *Ocherk istorii russkogo stikha,* 149. On the deviations as "an iconic image of a different order . . . reigning in 'the depth of the soul,'" see Shcheglov, "Eshche raz o metricheskikh otstupleniiakh v 'Silentium!' Tiutcheva," 685.

51. What is distinctive about Coleridge and Wordsworth "is not the attribution of a life and soul to nature, but the repeated formulation of this outer life as a contribution of, or else as in constant reciprocation with, the life and soul of the man observer." See Abrams, *The Mirror and the Lamp,* 64.

52. Among the German romantics, Herder commended music instead of words as a more powerful means of expressing feelings. See Herder, *Herders Sämtliche Werke,* 4:162.

53. Fraize and Zailer, "Paradoks kak oruzhie poezii dlia osvobozhdeniia iz tiur'my dvoinoi sviazi," 50.

54. Pigarev, *Zhizn' i tvorchestvo Tiutcheva,* 183.

55. Mann, *Dinamika russkogo romantizma,* 26.

56. Schlegel, *Lucinde and the Fragments,* 167. On the self-creation and self-destruction of romantic irony, see ibid., 167, 176, 200. For an analysis of the romantic crisis lyric, see Quinney, *The Poetics of Disappointment.*

57. Greenleaf, *Pushkin and Romantic Fashion,* 46.

58. Schlegel, *Lucinde and the Fragments,* 177.

59. Pratt, "Tiutchev's Poetic Admonitions," 527.

60. Eikhenbaum, *Melodika russkogo liricheskogo stikha,* 24–25. "Silentium!" "is built around no fewer that eleven imperatives . . . with the imperative most directly related to the title 'Silentium!,' 'molchi,' occurring as both the first and last words of the poem, and twice in the middle of the poem for good measure." See Pratt, "Tiutchev's Poetic Admonitions," 527. The poem "has the nature of an appeal, conviction." See Markova, "Formirovanie kategorial'nogo apparata refleksii 'bezmolviia' v ramkakh khudozhestvennogo tselogo," 116. For a twentieth-century visual dramatization of the operative paradox, see Gomringer, "Silence" ("Silencio," 1954).

61. Tiutchev retained regard for the eighteenth century, when high lexicon was required for an elevated subject matter. See Pumpianskii, "Poeziia F. I. Tiutcheva," 56.

62. Badiou, "Vek poetov," 12.

63. On paradoxes as the testing ground of verbal limits, see Brooks, *The Well-Wrought Urn.*

64. It is likely that Tiutchev deliberately made his maxim enigmatic. If the poet had a certain version of inexpressibility in mind, he did not specify it.

65. In August Schlegel's observation on the semantics of the word "expression" (*Ausdruck*), the word is strikingly chosen: "The inner is pressed out as though by a force alien to us." See Schlegel, *Vorlesungen über dramatische Kunst und Literatur,* 91. Although the same etymological relationship does not obtain between "*vyrazit', vyskazat',* or *izrech',* Schlegel's observation illustrates a common romantic conceptualization of poetry as the internal pressed out involuntarily, something Tiutchev could have known if he read Schlegel. Individualism "was so strong in Tiutchev, and he was so burdened by it, that he tried to demean it philosophically as much as he was capable." See Lavretskii, "Vzyskuiushchii blagodati," 366.

66. See, for example, Shelley's "A Defense of Poetry."

67. Baratynskii, *Polnoe sobranie stikhotvorenii,* 1:78.

68. Ibid., 1:201.

69. Ibid., 1:235.

70. On these poems, see Rassadin, "Vozvrashchenie Baratynskogo"; Sandler, "Baratynskii, Pushkin, and Hamlet"; Pratt, *Russian Metaphysical Romanticism,* 125–41 and 170–83; Mann, "Neobkhodimost' Baratynskogo." "Song heals a sick spirit" ("Boliashchii dukh vrachuet pesnopen'e," 1834) and "Always only thought and more thought! Poor artist of the word!" ("Vse mysl' da mysl'! Khudozhnik bednyi slova," 1840) are examples of Baratynskii's verbal idealism.

71. Unlike shorter poems, poems that are several pages in length are not quoted in full in this book. The full text of "Autumn" can be accessed in Baratynskii, *Polnoe sobranie stikhotvorenii,* 188–93. For a comprehensive analysis of the

poem, see Pratt, *Russian Metaphysical Romanticism,* 80–94. For my translation I borrowed some of the expressions from Pratt's book, 84–87.

72. Pratt, *Russian Metaphysical Romanticism,* 90.

73. Baratynskii, *Polnoe sobranie stikhotvorenii,* 191–92.

74. "With the decline of the ode, the odic 10-line stanza disappears from usage, remaining only as a deliberate allusion to the eighteenth-century tradition." See Gasparov, *Ocherk istorii russkogo stikha,* 157. The epithet "lofty" (*prevysprennii*) became less common in the nineteenth century.

75. The idea that "there is a music whose modes are the elements, the concord of the planetary orbits, the chime of water and blood, is ancient as Pythagoras and has never lost its metaphoric life." See Steiner, *Language and Silence,* 42.

76. The romantics perceive "not a grim amorphous infinity but a grandiose harmony of the universe, its secret organic unity." See Vaiskopf, "Oliva mira," 40.

77. Baratynskii, *Polnoe sobranie stikhotvorenii,* 190. The affinity between Baratynsky and Schopenhauer likely stems from the common German romantic context. *The World as Will and Representation* and other works by Schopenhauer grew popular in Russia in the mid-nineteenth century, influencing Tiutchev, Turgenev, Fet (the translator of the work into Russian), and Tolstoy.

78. In George Herbert's "Grief" (1633), poetry is unfit to express intense suffering which "excludes both measure, tune, and time." See Herbert, *George Herbert,* 32.

79. Baratynskii, *Polnoe sobranie stikhotvorenii,* 191.

80. Ibid., 192.

81. On the star and Pushkin's death, see Sandler, "Baratynskii, Pushkin, and Hamlet," 87.

82. Baratynskii, *Polnoe sobranie stikhotvorenii,* 190.

83. Lermontov, *Sochineniia,* 1:178.

84. Ibid., 1:230.

85. Shelley, *Shelley's Poetry and Prose,* 306.

86. Lermontov, *Sochineniia,* 2:144.

87. Ibid., 2:144.

88. Ibid., 2:146.

89. For analyses of Lermontov's poems on writing and communication, see Ginzburg, *Tvorcheskii put' Lermontova;* Powelstock, *Becoming Mikhail Lermontov,* 32–33, 231–38, 289–290, and 439–48; Markova, "Opyt refleksii fenomena bezmolviia v lirike A. S. Pushkina i M. I. Lermontova." "Journalist, Reader, and Writer" combines verbal skepticism and logocentrism.

90. Lermontov, *Sochineniia,* 2:122.

91. Manuilov, ed., *Lermontovskaia Entsiklopediia,* 336; Belinskii, *Polnoe sobranie sochinenii,* 3:190–91.

92. These lines subvert genuine, not false inspiration. See Vatsuro, "Chuzhoe 'ia' v lermontovskom tvorchestve," 511.

93. "Silentium!" was first published in *Rumor* (*Molva* [no. 32, 1833]), and subsequently in *The Contemporary* (*Sovremennnik,* vol. 3, p. 16, 1836), signed "F. T." Lermontov published some of his poems in *The Contemporary,* and could have been familiar with "Silentium!"

94. There is a tension in the poem between incommunicability and shamefulness of poetic expression. Evidently the self can be expressed at least to such an extent that the issue of denigrating self-exposure would arise. According to Mattias Freise, this poem exposes the degradation of turning intimate feelings into public ones: the muse as "a sign of heavens" is turned into "a furious friend," "sounds" become "noise," and "sadness and passion" turn into communicatively oriented "anger and pain." See Freise, "'Ne ver' sebe'—a komu zhe verit'?" 267. In my reading, the muse is negated from the onset as a sign of heaven, and "anger and pain" are hardly more communicatively oriented than "sadness and passion."

95. There is a tension between the idea that poetry makes profane one's precious sentiments and the notion that poetic sentiments are not genuine.

96. Foakes, ed., *Romantic Criticism,* 35.

97. Vickery, *M. I. Lermontov,* 181.

98. Ginzburg, *Tvorcheskii put' Lermontova,* 85.

99. Lermontov neither belongs to romanticism nor anticipates realism but "at once reveres, doubts, and departs from his most eminent model, along with the ideals of the era he is inexorably leaving behind, as he drifts into the uncharted cultural waters ahead." See Allen, *A Fallen Idol Is Still a God,* 57. For more on the change from Barbier, see Manuilov, ed., *Lermontovskaia entsiklopediia,* 336; Brown, *A History of Russian Literature of the Romantic Period,* 170; Lermontov, *Major Poetical Works,* 523–24. For an account of the poem's dialogic ironies, see Powelstock, *Becoming Mikhail Lermontov,* 324–27.

100. Nemoianu, *The Taming of Romanticism,* 35; Ginzburg, *Tvorcheskii put' Lermontova,* 127–60.

CHAPTER TWO

1. All references to Mandelstam, *Sobranie sochinenii,* are abbreviated as (Mandel'shtam volume: page) and placed in the main text.

2. With the fading of romanticism, and with prose dislodging poetry from its central place in Russian literary culture from the 1840s onward, fewer poems took on verbal inadequacy. Those that did mainly rehashed romantic notions of the inexpressible and were not particularly compelling artistically. Ivan Nikitin's "Forest" ("Les," 1849), Aleksei Pleshcheev's "Silence" ("Molchanie," 1861), and Semyon Nadson's "Dear friend, I know, I know deeply" ("Milyi drug, ia znaiu, ia gluboko znaiu," 1882) are some examples of this trend. There also appears fertile prose material on the topos.

3. Fet, *Polnoe sobranie stikhotvorenii,* 308–9.

4. Fet combines allusions to Tiutchev's "Silentium!" and Nadson's "Dear friend, I know, I know deeply." See Ronen, *An Approach to Mandelstam,* 258. Fet's "On the Poetry of F. Tiutchev ("O stikhotvoreniiakh F. Tiutcheva," 1859) gives examples of imagery and thought in Tiutchev's poetry that go beyond words. This article is Fet's first proper attempt at reviewing another writer. See Aizlewood, "Fet on Tiutchev," 15–21.

5. The tendency to boost prosody's musicality can be observed in Zhukovsky and Lermontov, but Fet goes further in the direction of turning poetry into "music."

6. Fet, *Polnoe sobranie stikhotvorenii,* 447.

7. For Botkin Fet sometimes falls into obscurity and indefiniteness, but there is "an inner, musical perspective that his verse leaves in the soul of the reader." See Botkin, "A. A. Fet," 40–51. On Fet's acquaintance with Schopenhauer, see Gustafson, *The Imagination of Spring,* 7, 27, 189–95; Stammler, "Metamorphoses of the Will," 35–58; and Bukhshtab, "A. A. Fet," 27. Fet's lyrics express "an unclear emotional experience, which is not defined plot-wise, and is not analyzed psychologically." See Bukhshtab, "A. A. Fet," 36. See also Blagoi, "Mir kak krasota," 579–81; Bukhshtab, "A. A. Fet," 36–42; Klenin, *The Poetics of Afanasy Fet,* 6, 29–30, 121, and "On Groups of Poems by Fet," 297. Fet's verbless poetry prompts the reader to experience emotion without mediation: "There are no recounted events and there are no explicit human event participants, but rather the experience of events that themselves lie outside the domain of the poems' verbal expression." See Klenin, *The Poetics of Afanasy Fet,* 135.

8. See also "In vain" ("Naprasno," 1852), "No, do not wait for a passionate song" ("Net, ne zhdi ty pesni strastnoi," 1858), "If I meet a bright dawn in the sky" ("Vstrechu l' ia iarkuiu v nebe zariu," 1882), "I will not say anything to you" ("Ia tebe nichego ne skazhu," 1885), "Should you desire to divine my soul" ("Esli zakhochesh' ty dushu moiu razgadat'," 1888), and "Human words are so coarse" ("Liudskie tak gruby slova," 1889).

9. Zhirmunskii, *Voprosy teorii literatury,* 179. On Tiutchev as one of the main precursors of Russian symbolism, see Peterson, *A History of Russian Symbolism,* 31.

10. Ivanov, *Sobranie sochinenii,* 1:712.

11. Ibid., 1:606. On Ivanov and Tiutchev, see Malmstad, "Mandelstam's 'Silentium'"; and Wachtel, *Russian Symbolism and Literary Tradition,* 13, 30, 79, 116, 120–21. On "The Alpine Horn," see Wachtel, *Russian Symbolism and Literary Tradition,* 81–84; and Janecek, "Viacheslav Ivanov's 'Alpine Horn' as a Manifesto of Russian Symbolism," 30–45. On Ivanov's "revitalization of the Christian roots through a rediscovery of its mystical roots," see Davidson, *The Poetic Imagination of Viacheslav Ivanov,* 27f.

12. Ivanov, *Sobranie sochinenii,* 2:262.

13. Ibid. On Ivanov's silence as a surplus of sense, see Ghidini, "Zvuk i

smysl," 76. On other "silence" poems in Ivanov, see, for example, Sobolevskaia, "Transformatsiia motiva 'molchaniia' kak edinstvo poeticheskogo konteksta," 205–7.

14. Ivanov, *Sobranie sochinenii,* 2:262. Merezhkovsky's "Silence" ("Molchanie," 1893), Fyodor Sologub's "You were gleaming sadly" ("Ty pechal'no mertsala," 1897), Konstantin Balmont's collection *Silence* (*Tishina,* 1898), Ivanov's "Silence" ("Molchanie," 1904–07), Valery Briusov's "Angel of Blissful Silence" ("Angel blagogo molchaniia," 1908), and many other symbolist poems took on the theme of inexpressibility. Among these, Sologub's "You were gleaming sadly" describes a Tiutchevian and symbolist silence of the night, Merezhkovsky's "Silence" posits modesty and muteness as one's best emotions, and Briusov's "Angel of Blissful Silence" resembles the weaving of words and the Jesus prayer in its invocation of "the angel of blissful silence." As Ivanov remarks in "The Poet and the Mob," "Our most recent poets do not weary of celebrating Silence." See Ivanov, *Sobranie sochinenii,* 1:712.

15. Ivanov, *Sobranie sochinenii,* 4:301.

16. Ibid., 2:630.

17. Belyi, *Simvolizm,* 430.

18. Ivanov, *Sobranie sochinenii,* 2:607.

19. Terras, *Poetry of the Silver Age,* 392.

20. Ivanov, *Sobranie sochinenii,* 2:552.

21. Belyi, *Simvolizm,* 438.

22. Ivanov, *Rodnoe i vselenskoe,* 48.

23. In "The Stranger" ("Neznakomka," 1906), the poet begins to perceive the mysteries of the universe. They are enigmatic in a dark, bewildering way—silent, mute (*glukhie*). See Blok, *Sobranie sochinenii,* 1:87.

24. Ibid., 5:327–29.

25. Peterson, *A History of Russian Symbolism,* 151.

26. Blok, *Sobranie sochinenii,* 5:329, 5:332.

27. Idiosyncratic word usage, bolder associations and metaphors, semantic complexity, the privileging of media-bound intransitivity over reference, and greater sensitivity to the verbal load of the past have all widened the scope of inexpressibility and incommunicability in modernist poetry.

28. Lawton, ed., *Russian Futurism Through Its Manifestoes,* 290.

29. This is the case in the final piece of the collection, *Death to Art* (*Smert' iskusstvu,* 1913), by Vasilisk Gnedov. The self-sufficient word is a reaction against conceptual and conventional language, the futurists' analogue of symbolist semantic vagueness and musicality. What is novel is the degree of vehemence with which the avant-garde rejects any word of the Other.

30. Khlebnikov, *Sobranie sochinenii,* 1:198. "Every sound, every letter by itself would carry all the fullness of meaning." See Vinokur, *Filologicheskie issledovaniia,* 252. The linkage of letters and colors, however, does not eliminate the conventionality of the sign: "The color signification of a sound is no less con-

ventional than the word's denotative value, and gives an unlimited space for the asymmetry of the verbal sign." See Shapir, "O 'zvukosimvolizme' u rannego Khlebnikova," 38.

31. On Khlebnikov's views of language, see, for example, Cooke, *Velimir Khlebnikov,* 67–103.

32. Janecek, *Zaum,* 127.

33. For more on Kuzmin, see, for example, Bogomolov and Malmstad, "U istokov tvorchestva Mikhaila Kuz'mina," 109–11.

34. Annenskii, *Knigi otrazhenii,* 465.

35. Ibid., 467, 466.

36. Ibid., 367.

37. Ibid., 53.

38. Ibid., 107.

39. Ibid., 121. "My Anguish" ("Moia toska," 1909) depicts pain that spurs on the lyrical persona's poetry in apophatic terms: "Annensky does not define *toska* . . . He approaches it by apposition . . . negation . . . opposition." See Pollak, "Annensky's Anguished Muse," 148. The essay "The Portrait" ("Portret," 1906) contrasts the compassion that one experiences in art and in life. The former is simulated and pleasurable, the latter causes genuine pain and calls for action. See Annenskii, *Knigi otrazhenii,* 24.

40. The acmeists did not aim "to expel mysticism from poetry but wanted to balance the 'mystical' and the 'earthly.'" See Lekmanov, "Akmeisty: Poety kruga Gumileva II," 149.

41. Gumilev, *Sobranie sochinenii,* 3:28.

42. Ibid., 1:71. Compare Gumilev's "dead words" to Andrei Bely's "putrefaction" (*razlozhenie*) and "death of the word" as the result of the loss of its visual and phonic imagery. See Belyi, *Simvolizm,* 436.

43. On Mandelstam and Gumilev, see Goldberg, "The Shade of Gumilev in Mandel'shtam's *Kamen'*." The symbolists and the avant-garde recast Tiutchev in ways that promoted their respective poetics. The acmeists, in turn, claimed the poet as their predecessor by positing novel, unorthodox readings of his maxim. In Osip Mandelstam's reading, the idea of verbal inadequacy, which is epitomized by Tiutchev's aphorism, serves not to safeguard the inner being from the constrictions of language, but to safeguard the Russian language that "thus protects itself from unceremonious attempts upon its life." See Mandel'shtam 1:221.

44. On Mandelstam's verbal idealism, see Broyde, *Osip Mandelstam and His Age;* Przybylski, *Essay on the Poetry of Mandelstam,* esp. 46–78; Toddes, "Mandel'shtam i Tiutchev"; Taranovsky, *Essays on Mandelstam;* Terras, *Poetry of the Silver Age,* 184–218, and "Osip Mandel'shtam i ego filosofiia Slova."

45. On "On The Addressee," see Segal, *Osip Mandel'shtam,* 81–83; MacKay, *Inscription and Modernity,* 189–190; Eskin, *Ethics and Dialogue in the Works of Levinas, Bakhtin, Mandel'shtam, and Celan,* 125–35; Glazov-Corrigan, *Mandelstam's Poetics,* chap. 4; Glazova, "Vozdushno-kamennyi Kristal," 86, and "Poetry

of Bringing About Presence," 1109–12; Olschner, "Poetic Mutations of Silence"; Brinkley and Kostova, "Posthumous Writing." On the poetics of the addressee in "Conversation About Dante," see Glazov-Corrigan, *Mandelstam's Poetics,* 75–107. Like Mandelstam's essay, Marina Tsvetaeva's "From the Seaside" ("S moria," 1926) employs seaside imagery to explore issues of communication and conceptualizes communicability as a triumph in defiance of physical laws. See Tsvetaeva, *Sochineniia,* 4:247. "The action of the sea provides a metaphor for the use of literary material observed throughout Tsvetaeva's poetry," and "a fragment of poetry is found (inherited) by one poet (the narrator) and passed on to another poet (the addressee, Pasternak), for him to complete." See Makin, *Marina Tsvetaeva,* 301.

46. Epstein interprets Mandelstam's nominalism in the following way: "Russian language resists the naming and informative function precisely because real life takes place not outside it . . . but in it—it lives at the expense of all the other kinds of being." Russian nominalism "leads toward the overabundance of language in its own 'sounding and speaking flesh' and the inadequacy of its 'naming and applied qualities' that show through semantic emptiness." See Epshtein, *Slovo i molchanie,* 184.

47. In "The Slate Ode," "the river of time cannot be stopped, but the form it gives to objects it touches on its course is varied and has permanence." See Terras, *Poetry of the Silver Age,* 207. In "January 1st, 1924," "if the right word is not found, the poem cannot be finished; on a larger scale, without the sense of poetic rightness, the poet falls silent." See Pollak, *Mandelstam the Reader,* 13. For analyses of these poems, see Ronen, *Approach to Mandelstam,* 37–223 and 225–329. On the plot of "The Slate Ode" in the drafts and intermediate versions that is "much more tragic than in the final version," see Semenko, *Poetika pozdnego Mandel'shtama,* 29.

48. On "And still on Mount Athos" in the context of *imiasliavie,* see Przybylski, *An Essay on the Poetry of Mandelstam,* 62–65; Paperno, "O prirode poeticheskogo slova," 31; Surat, "Prevrashcheniia imeni," 156, and *Mandel'shtam i Pushkin,* 97–100. It is "as if he greets the 'beautiful' heresy of *imiabozhnichestvo,* however, equating faith and love . . . asserts that love/faith is nameless, and a heretic pronouncement of the name of the beloved/God's name is lethal." See Paperno, "O prirode poeticheskogo slova," 31.

49. The following passage captures this tension between idealism and skepticism:

> Naming is associated with binding in M's poetry, and the name itself is a verbal incarnation of musical harmony ("Otchego dusha tak pevucha") . . . In "Mne stalo strashno zhizn' otzhit' " namelessness is a result of separation, while the threads tying the poet to all the living are identified with a name . . . In . . . "Kak oblakom serdtse odeto" the naming of objects is compared to a caress

> and to the sacrament of matrimony . . . In other poems ("Silentium," "I ponyne na Afone," "Sestry—tiazhest' i nezhnost'") love itself is unnamable because it remains an unbreakable bond as long as it is nameless.

See Ronen, *An Approach to Mandelstam,* 202–3. Gregory Freidin contextualizes Mandelstam's logocentric/logophobic tension: at the turn of the century, "the age of differentiation had commenced and with it the nagging questions about the special, all-embracing position of Russian letters . . . There cannot be a better environment for the dispersal of charisma than the time when old convictions, even if undermined, continue to coexist side by side with new uncertainties." See Freidin, *A Coat of Many Colors,* 18–19.

50. The young Mandelstam "used a persistent cluster of ideas, a cluster for which we might adopt the title 'Silentium' as the occasion for some of his best poetry." See Brown, *Mandelstam,* 165. On Mandelstam's artistic will as a kind of negativism, see Averintsev, "Rannii Mandelstam," 207. On Mandelstam's verse "expressing Apophaticism in its full sense—in the sense of 'unnameability' and inexpressibility of the given content in positive categories," see Levin, *Izbrannye trudy,* 55–61.

51. Segal, *Osip Mandel'shtam,* 89.

52. Terras, *Poetry of the Silver Age,* 191.

53. Gasparov, "Poet i kul'tura," 8.

54. Taranovsky, *Essays on Mandelstam,* 122.

55. Cavanagh, *Osip Mandelstam and the Modernist Creation of Tradition,* 41.

56. Epshtein, *Slovo i molchanie,* 203.

57. Panova, *"Mir," "prostranstvo," "vremia" v poezii Osipa Mandel'shtama,* 436.

58. Malmstad, "Mandelstam's 'Silentium,'" 237. For analyses of *Stone*'s "silentium" poems, see Taranovsky, *Essays on Mandelstam,* 120; Malmstad, "Mandelstam's 'Silentium,'" 238; Cavanagh, *Osip Mandelstam and the Modernist Creation of Tradition,* 40–41. For analyses of "Silentium" specifically, see Gumilev, *Sobranie sochinenii,* 4:363; Brown, *Mandelstam,* 164–67; Taranovsky, *Essays on Mandelstam,* 120–21; Przybylski, *An Essay on the Poetry of Mandelstam,* 78–90, and "Osip Mandel'shtam i muzyka," 104–13; Terras, "The Time Philosophy of Osip Mandelstam," 351; Malmstad, "Mandelstam's 'Silentium,'" 236–52; Segal, *Osip Mandel'shtam,* 86–91; Cavanagh, *Osip Mandelstam and the Modernist Creation of Tradition,* 41–47, 57–58; Paperno, "O prirode poeticheskogo slova," 31; Doherty, *The Acmeist Movement in Russian Poetry,* 217; Iun, *Organicheskaia poetika Osipa Mandel'shtama,* 204–5. For "Silentium's" link to "Silentium!," see Taranovsky, *Essays on Mandelstam,* 121–24; Ronen, *An Approach to Mandelstam,* 203, 257; Cavanagh, *Osip Mandelstam and the Modernist Creation of Tradition,* 41–44; Frolov, *O rannikh stikhakh Osipa Mandel'shtama,* 167–68. Tiutchev's influence on Mandelstam has been discussed by Toddes in

"Mandel'shtam i Tiutchev." "The most simple cases are those when Mandelstam proclaims his text's connection with Tiutchev's, duplicating the title . . . or relying on obligatory associations of an educated reader." See Toddes, "Mandel'shtam i Tiutchev," 79. On the history of this poem's publication, see Frolov, *O rannikh stikhakh Osipa Mandel'shtama,* 165–67. On Mandelstam and Tiutchev, see also Segal, *Osip Mandel'shtam,* esp. 45–59, 118–19, 143–48, 201–17.

59. Rothe, "Mandelstam and Motifs from Classical Antiquity," 309.

60. Gasparov, "Kommentarii," 728.

61. Brown, *Mandelstam,* 165–66.

62. Taranovsky, *Essays on Mandelstam,* 4.

63. Levin et al., "Russkaia semanticheskaia poetika kak potentsial'naia kul'turnaia paradigma," 60.

64. A history of clashing interpretations and the poem's discrepant translations into English (compare, e.g., those by James Greene and by Burton Raffel and Alla Burago) are a testament to its complexity. See divergent translations of the first line: "It has not yet been born" (Brown, *Mandelstam,* 165); "It has not yet been born" (Mandelstam, *Modernist Archaist,* 39); "It has not yet come into being" (Mandelstam, *Osip Mandelstam,* 27); "She has not yet been born" (Cavanagh, *Osip Mandelstam and the Modernist Creation of Tradition,* 42); "She has not yet been born" (Mandelstam, *Poems from Mandelstam,* 63); "She's still unborn" (Mandelstam, *Complete Poetry of Osip Emilevich Mandelstam,* 37). The seemingly inappropriate "madman" in reference to the "bright day" could be understood if one recalled Tiutchev's preference for "azure" night over "golden" day in, for example, "A Vision" and "You saw him in the circle of high society" ("Ty zrel ego v krugu bol'shogo sveta," early 1830s). Hence the puzzling "but": the sea is tranquil and azure while the day is insanely bright. Hence also the "black-azure" vessel. This explanation, however, is merely one option. The list of questions may be easily continued. The "murkiness itself, as Russian modernists believed, constituted a major factor in the effectiveness of a verbal charm." See Freidin, *A Coat of Many Colors,* 201. See also Gurvich, "Mandel'shtam i problema 'bessmyslennogo slova,'" 174.

65. An admirer of Viacheslav Ivanov, in 1909 Mandelstam sent him letters and copies of his poems, in which he discussed Verlaine, prosody, and Tiutchev. The similarity between Mandelstam and the symbolists would of course hold less for the later material. On Ivanov and Mandelstam, see also Mets, "*Kamen'*"; Lekmanov, *Kniga ob akmeizme,* 122–31; Lekmanov and Glukhova, "Osip Mandel'shtam i Viacheslav Ivanov."

66. The poem asks "to be made one with the unformed source of all being." See Cavanagh, *Osip Mandelstam and the Modernist Creation of Tradition,* 42. It imagines "the primeval harmony of the universe" (Taranovsky, *Essays on Mandelstam,* 122), and longs for a pre-historic existence when there was no duality to overcome, no opposition of Music and Word, no chaos or Cosmos" (Malm-

stad, "Mandelstam's 'Silentium,'" 243). The "Belinskian-Dostoevskian notion of 'happiness' or 'unhappiness' is sublated in the ultimate creative act of the kenotic abjuration of creativity in a return to the ultimate source of being (Taranovsky 1976: 122)." See Ronen, "Sublation / [Aufhebung] in the Poetics of Acmeism," 327. Blok's "The Artist" ("Khudozhnik") describes the capture and murder of pre-creative music in the language of poetry.

67. Shelley, *Shelley's Poetry and Prose,* 306.

68. Brown, *Mandelstam,* 166.

69. Christiansen, *Italian Painting,* 182–84. For a reading of *Stone* based on emblemata, see Nesterov, "Ikonografiia i poeziia."

70. Ivanov, *Sobranie sochinenii,* 4:344.

71. Eliot, *Complete Poems and Plays,* 27. "Silentium" belongs to the tradition of Russian sea poetry from Pushkin and Tiutchev to the Silver Age poets such as Marina Tsvetaeva. On the sea and language, see "On the Nature of the Word." On the sea and inspiration, see "The Seashell" and "Insomnia. Homer. Taut Sails. . ." ("Bessonnitsa. Gomer. Tugie parusa . . . ," 1915).

72. Stevens, *The Collected Poems of Wallace Stevens,* 101.

73. Solov'ev, "Beauty in Nature," 267. Mandelstam's lyrics reverberate with the notions of Schopenhauer, Solovyev, Florensky, and Shestov, among others. The intellectual interest in Schopenhauer in Russia "was not to flag until the outbreak of the First World War as Grusenberg's (rather incomplete) Schopenhauer bibliography of 1914 demonstrates." See Stammler, "Metamorphoses of the Will," 36. Nadezhda Mandelstam notes Mandelstam's dedication to Florensky. Solovyev enters via symbolism, and Ivanov especially. The principle of existential uncertainty "has been absorbed from Annenskii, Shestov, and, ultimately, Nietzsche." See Freidin, *A Coat of Many Colors,* 185.

74. Solov'ev, "Beauty in Nature," 267.

75. On Dante's "l'amor che move il sole e l'atre stele" in Mandelstam, see Przybylski, *An Essay on the Poetry of Mandelstam,* 68–69. See also Mandelstam's "Insomnia. Homer. Taut Sails . . ." Note the distinction between Aphrodite as the goddess of physical versus spiritual love in classical mythology.

76. On the meaning of Mandelstam's images transferring from one poem to the next, see Ginzburg, *O lirike. 2–e, rasshirennoe izdanie,* 353.

77. Stevens, *The Collected Poems of Wallace Stevens,* 100.

78. This poem is a poetic analogue of Vrubel's "Swan Princess" ("Tsarevna-lebed'," 1900), which presents a fantastic creature, half-girl and half-swan, a nebulous figure as if made of foam.

79. On "The Seashell" and "Silentium," see Brown, *Mandelstam,* 166. See also "Insomnia. Homer. Taut Sails . . .": "On the heads of kings—divine foam" (*Na golovakh tsarei—bozhestvennaia pena*) (Mandel'shtam 1:115). On glass as the image of eternity, see "I am given a body—what to do with it" ("Dano mne telo—chto mne delat' s nim," 1909).

80. “Ancient people respected the silent poet as the woman who prepares to become a mother is respected.” See Gumilev, *Sobranie sochinenii,* 4:160. The theme of prenatal life with its long invisible biological path of development until one emerges into the world attracted the attention of many artists of the Silver Age. See Baschmakoff, “V prostranstve do mira,” 37. On Khlebnikov’s “Chertezh do mira” as “an image of the purely semantic energy of the world, prior to its material incarnation,” see Duganov, “Velimir Khlebnikov,” 172.

81. Mandelstam’s poetics “relies on scrutinizing the crystallized, monadic instance in which it detaches from the deceptively linear sequence of historical unfolding.” See Pavlov, “Killing Time,” 450. Such a suspension of movement is represented in “Silentium” via the crystallization of sound.

82. Shklovskii, *O poezii i zaumnom iazyke,* 22.

83. Freidin, *A Coat of Many Colors,* 162; Paperno, “O prirode poeticheskogo slova,” 32.

84. *Gasparov,* “Poet i kul’tura,” 31–32. “The ‘blessed senseless word” (*blazhennoe bessmyslennoe slovo*) in “We will meet again in Petersburg” (“V Peterburge my soidemsia snova,” 1920) “is senseless because it has not yet found its object, ‘the sounding mold of form’ preceding verse (‘The Word and Culture’).” See Gasparov and Ronen, “Pokhorony solntsa v Peterburge,” 210. See also Brodsky’s reading of the Mandelstam passage (*Less Than One* 140).

85. Nadezhda Mandelstam, *Vospominaniia,* 74.

86. The relative metaphysical optimism of “Silentium” goes against the Schopenhauerian mood, but its pure contemplation of beauty and loss of the self parallel Schopenhauer’s ideas. Other *Stone* lyrics reverberate with Schopenhauer’s metaphysical pessimism.

87. Florenskii, *U vodorazdelov mysli,* 263.

88. Tsvetaeva, *Sochineniia,* 2:438; Brown, *Mandelstam,* 174.

89. Gasparov, “Kommentarii,” 607. The fruit is an intruder in the forest, “like Tiutchev’s ‘thinking reed,’ whose rustling disrupts nature’s ‘common chorus.’ ” See Cavanagh, *Osip Mandelstam and the Modernist Creation of Tradition,* 36. For the forest as a metaphor for music and poetry, see Surat, “Etiudy o Mandel’shtame.” In a letter of 1909 written to Maximilian Voloshin, Mandelstam expressed his sense of being alienated from the Russian language and its practitioners: “Torn off from the medium of the Russian language—more than at any other time, I am forced to make up a clear view of myself on my own” (Mandel’shtam 4:16).

90. Through the various senses of *glukhoi* “runs the notion of blockage and impediment, the result of which is silence.” See Brown, *Mandelstam,* 174–75. See also the mute pendulum of “Today is a bad day” (“Segodnia durnoi den’,” 1911), the deaf Beethoven of “Ode to Beethoven” (“Oda Betkhovenu,” 1914), the mute years of “The Twilight of Freedom,” the mute Judaic night of “Return to the incestuous womb” (“Vernis’ v smesitel’noe lono,” 1920), the deaf-mute of

The Egyptian Stamp, and the spidery deafness of "Lamarck" (1932). For occurrences of the root *glukh-* in Mandelstam, see Kouborlis, ed., *A Concordance to the Poems of Osip Mandelstam,* 100. "The sound cautious and muted" resonates with Pushkin's "as a nightly sound in dense forest" (*kak zvuk nochnoi v lesu glukhom*) from "What is there for you in my name?" ("Chto v imeni tebe moem?" 1830) as well as "Echo." See Ronen, "A Beam upon the Axe," 159; and Pollak, "Mandelstam's 'First' Poem," 107. On sound effects in the poem that embody the theme of the "mute sound," see Segal, *Osip Mandel'shtam,* 11

91. The laws of reality are evoked in the neighboring poems such as "When a blow meets blows" ("Kogda udar s udarami vstrechaetsia," 1910), "Inexorable words" ("Neumolimye slova," 1910), and "Today is a bad day" ("Segodnia durnoi den' "). The antinomy of art–reality is a persistent motif in Mandelstam. In contrast to his theoretical writings where it tends to be resolved as art's victory, most of his lyrics treat the theme more ambivalently. See also the toy wolves and miniature emotions of "With tinsel gold burn" ("Susal'nym zolotom goriat," 1908), as well as the toy thicket of "Why is the soul so melodious" ("Otchego dusha tak pevucha").

92. Cavanagh, *Osip Mandelstam and the Modernist Creation of Tradition,* 40.

93. On Penates as Mandelstam's poetic ancestors, see Ronen, *An Approach to Mandelstam,* xv.

94. Terras, *Poetry of the Silver Age,* 187.

95. Segal, *Osip Mandel'shtam,* 32.

96. Keats, *Complete Poems and Selected Letters,* 232. Multiple *Stone* lyrics preserve this tension between the poetic word's miniature beauty and safety, and its artificiality and transitoriness: "On pale-blue enamel" ("Na bledno-goluboi emali," 1909), "A fine decay is made thin" ("Istonchaetsia tonkii tlen," 1909), and "In the calm of my gardens." "On pale-blue enamel" views art not as a means to overcome death but as a way to forget it, if only for a brief moment. The artist, an artisan working with delicate faience (Stratanovskii, "Tvorchestvo i bolezn'," 211), creates "conscious of a momentary strength, / oblivious of sad death" (*v soznanii minutnoi sily, / v zabvenii pechal'noi smerti*) (Mandel'shtam 1:35). "I am given a body—what to do with it" describes an imprint of poetry that is not to be crossed out, but the value of which vis-à-vis poetic interiority is problematized because the pattern becomes unrecognizable: "A pattern will be imprinted on it [the glass of eternity], / Unrecognizable from recent times" (*Zapechatleetsia na nem uzor, / Neuznavaemyi s nedavnikh por*) (Mandel'shtam 1:37).

97. See also "On pale-blue enamel," "On the dark sky as ornament" ("Na temnom nebe, kak uzor," 1909), "Through a wax curtain" ("Skvoz' voskovuiu zanaves'," 1909), and "The keen ear strains a sail."

98. Gasparov, "Poet i kul'tura," 10.

99. Przybylski, *An Essay on the Poetry of Mandelstam,* 74.

100. Terras, "The Black Sun," 55.

101. "It is transparent and dark in the enormous pool" ("V ogromnom omute prozrachno i temno," 1910) "outlines a strategy for distancing the poetic self from the 'actual ego' by transforming it into aesthetic material." See Freidin, *A Coat of Many Colors*, 50. This procedure resembles Schopenhauer's transcendence of the will through art with Nietzschean sardonic implications.

102. "Prophetic breathing is in my poems" ("Dykhan'e veshchee v stikhakh moikh," 1909) also employs the image of the seashell to raise the issue of (in)communicability. It wonders whether the "life-giving spirit" (*zhivotvoriashchii dukh*) of the poetic word will touch the reader's heart or whether the poet's singing will remain more obscure than "seashells that sing in the sand" (*tekh rakovin, v peske poiushchikh*) (Mandel'shtam 1:44). "You should not talk about anything" ("Ni o chem ne nuzhno govorit'," 1909), another poem that articulates the motif of silence in the context of sea imagery, envisions silence as a return to a free, instinctive condition when the soul "does not know at all how to speak / And swims like a young dolphin / On the gray depths of the world" (*ne umeet vovse govorit' / I plyvet del'finom molodym / Po sedym puchinam mirovym*) (Mandel'shtam 1:45).

103. See "Implacable words" ("Neumolimye slova," 1910), which depicts the Crucifixion. On kenosis of the poetic word, see Ronen, *Poetika Osipa Mandel'shtama*, 106.

104. Blok, *Sobranie sochinenii*, 1:87.

105. Breathing often stands for poetic production in Mandelstam. See "Concert at the Railway Station." "At the bedstead a black crucifix" ("V izgolov'i chernoe raspiat'e," 1910) also treats silence in the context of religious doubt. Frightening silence is drowned in bliss, not a lucid delight of faith but a sickly languor of delirium. The cross is "cursed" by a trace of dust. Nature (frosty smoke) and religion (church mosaic) mirror each other, both drug-like, lulling the hero into a stupefied condition. The conclusion of the poem identifies the source of the hero's doubt, "the underwater stone of faith" (*podvodnyi kamen' very*), an allusion to Tiutchev's "Problème" (1833) (Mandel'shtam 1:60). See also "When the reproach of the bells" ("Kogda udar kolokolov," 1910): "And my soul is overfilled / With ineffable wormwood" (*I mne perepolniaet dushu / neiz'iasnimaia polyn'*) (Mandel'shtam 1:55).

106. Terras, *Poetry of the Silver Age*, 195.

107. Paperno, "O prirode poeticheskogo slova," 31.

108. In the Hebraic tradition the name of God "is completely withdrawn into the realm of the Ineffable." See Scholem, "The Name of God and the Linguistic Theory of the Kabbalah," 67. On God's name "uttered as a substitute for the palpable image," see Ronen, *An Approach to Mandelstam*, 203. *Gospodi* "is a mere interjection but it is at the same time a substitute of the most important, unutterable Biblical name of God, so-called Tetragrammaton." See Averintsev, "Sud'ba i vest' Osipa Mandel'shtama," 27. If the image of the bird is inspired by

the mythological motif of the bird-soul leaving the body (Paperno, "O prirode poeticheskogo slova," 31), uttering the forbidden name is equated with death. For discussions of silence and Judaism in Mandelstam, see Taranovsky, *Essays on Mandelstam,* 153; and Pollak, *Mandelstam the Reader,* 6, 33–34. On the connection with the *imiaslavie* debate, see Freidin, *A Coat of Many Colors,* 356. Florensky's "Imiaslavie as a philosophical premise" ("Imiaslavie kak filosofskaia predposylka," 1922) argues that the name of God manifests His essence but does not encompass or comprehend it. On the poem, see also Surat, "Prevrashcheniia imeni," 154; Segal, *Osip Mandelstam,* 103; Edmond, "From Pathos to Parody." On modern Jewish negative theology (Rosenzweig, Benjamin, and Levinas), see, for example, Franke, ed., *On What Cannot Be Said,* 2:14–24, 21–33, 121–24, 139–41, 406–10.

109. Averintsev, *Sud'ba i vest' Osipa Mandel'shtama,* 221.

110. Mandelstam inscribed his first collection to Akhmatova with "To Anna Akhmatova—flashes of consciousness in the unconsciousness of days" (Mandel'shtam 1:8).

111. Ginzburg, *O lirike. 2–e, rasshirennoe izdanie,* 350. "Beginning with a 'quiet' declaration of his rootedness in space and time, the lyrical hero of *Stone* is then tempted to deny art and the very self to, in the book's final poems, come to a firm awareness of his place in life and literature." See Lekmanov, *O pervom "kamne" Mandel'shtama,* 4.

112. See, for example, "We cannot bear an intense silence," "I start from the cold" ("Ia vzdragivaiu ot kholoda," 1912), "The Pedestrian" ("Peshekhod," 1912), and "The Lutheran" ("Liuteranin," 1912). "I start from the cold" conveys the poet's desire to fall silent: "I want to grow mute! / But gold dances in the sky—/ Orders me to sing" (*Mne khochetsia onemet'! / A v nebe tantsuet zoloto—/ Prikazyvaet mne pet'*) (Mandel'shtam 1:87). In "The Pedestrian," poetry and music lose their salvific powers: "And truly sadness sings in me; / Truly there is an avalanche in the mountains! / And all of my soul—is in the bells—/ But music will not save from the abyss!" (*I podlinno vo mne pechal' poet; / Deistvitel'no lavina est' v gorakh! / I vsia moia dusha—v kolokolakh—/ No muzyka ot bezdny ne spaset!*) (Mandel'shtam 1:74). "The Lutheran" advises against "orating" (*vitiistvovat' ne nado*) (Mandel'shtam 1:78). In "We cannot bear an intense silence" "the reader is gladly paid attention to not so much because of the meaning of his words as because of the calming quality of a smoothly flowing speech" (Epshtein, *Slovo i molchanie,* 191). Even "I hate the light" ("Ia nenavizhu svet," 1912), Mandelstam's acmeist manifesto, wonders: "But where will the arrow / Of a living thought go?" (*No kuda uidet / Mysli zhivoi strela*) (Mandel'shtam 1:71); the poet "counts himself among the modernists who, like Mallarmé, know that their quest will ultimately end in failure" (Terras, *Poetry of the Silver Age,* 192). For analyses of these poems, see Mets, "Kommentarii," 532–33; Ginzburg, *O lirike. 2–e, rasshirennoe izdanie,* 335–37; Taranovsky, *Essays on Mandelstam,* 17,

19; Paperno, "O prirode poeticheskogo slova," 32; Przybylski, *An Essay on the Poetry of Mandelstam,* 114; Segal, *Osip Mandel'shtam,* 109–11, 113–17; Lekmanov, "Akmeisty: Poety kruga Gumileva I," 177, "Akmeisty: Poety kruga Gumileva II," 151, and *Kniga ob akmeizme,* 36–38, 76; Magun, "Poetika revoliutsionnogo vremeni," 52–55; Stratanovskii, "Tvorchestvo i bolezn'," 214–217; Frolov, *O rannikh stikhakh Osipa Mandel'shtama,* 170–73.

113. Broyde, *Osip Mandelstam and His Age,* 175–76.

114. Cavanagh, *Osip Mandelstam and the Modernist Creation of Tradition,* 188. I'd agree that "The Horseshoe Finder" "illustrates both the thesis of the deadliness of linear time" and the thesis that "nothing disappears entirely" (Panova, *"Mir," "prostranstvo," "vremia" v poezii Osipa Mandel'shtama,* 621) but see the former as prevailing. In more hopeful readings, "a horse dies, but the horseshoe becomes a talisman which protects the human home" (Ronen, *An Approach to Mandelstam,* 84) or a sign of Nietzschean "eternal recurrence" (Panova, *"Mir," "prostranstvo," "vremia" v poezii Osipa Mandel'shtama,* 577). For analyses of this poem, see Brown, *Mandelstam,* 287–95; Broyde, *Osip Mandelstam and His Age,* 169–99; Cavanagh, *Osip Mandelstam and the Modernist Creation of Tradition,* 157–92; Freidin, *A Coat of Many Colors,* 112–13 and 215–16; Myers, "The Hum of Metaphor and the Cast of Voice"; Panova, *"Mir," "prostranstvo," "vremia" v poezii Osipa Mandel'shtama,* 607–715; Smoliarova, "Pindar i Mandel'shtam."

115. Pindar's odes were traditionally translated into free verse. See Gasparov, "Kommentarii," 770. "The Horseshoe Finder" is the only poem by Mandelstam written in free verse. See Gasparov, *Izbrannye trudy,* 3:494.

116. On the lack of cosmic harmony in "Concert at the Railway Station," see Ginzburg, *O lirike. Izdanie 2-e, rasshirennoe,* 373; Przybylski, *An Essay on the Poetry of Osip Mandelstam,* 90–102, and "Mandel'shtam i muzyka," 118–21; Taranovsky, *Essays on Mandelstam,* 1–20; Freidin, *A Coat of Many Colors,* 190–92; Nillsen, "Osip Mandelstam and His Poetry," 47; Surat, *Mandel'shtam i Pushkin,* 36–39.

117. The full text of "The Horseshoe Finder" can be accessed in Mandel'shtam 2:42-45. I have borrowed some locutions from Mandelstam and Willett, "The Horseshoe Finder," 90–93; and Cavanagh, *Osip Mandelstam and the Modernist Creation of Tradition,* 158–60.

118. "The word 'fragment' of the subtitle was especially suitable . . . for the dominant theme of the second part, where all the operative images are residua." See Brown, *Mandelstam,* 292. "The verbal fragment [the poem] echoes the physical fragment [the horseshoe], and both are metonyms for a cultural unity that is, perhaps, lost forever." See Cavanagh, *Osip Mandelstam and the Modernist Creation of Tradition,* 165. On modernist fragments, see Greenleaf, "Through the Lens of Montage." On fragmentation in Eliot, see, for example, Wolosky, *Language Mysticism,* 28.

119. Eliot, *Complete Poems and Plays,* 126.

120. The Christian era, represented by a hollow golden sphere, rings and is supported by no one because its values are genuine. It is hollow perhaps because humanity has exited it. See Panova, *"Mir," "prostranstvo," "vremia" v poezii Osipa Mandel'shtama,* 657.

121. Tynianov, *Poetika. Istoriia literatury. Kino,* 189–90. Cavanagh draws attention to "The Interval" in her discussion of "The Horseshoe Finder." She suggests that, in Tynianov's view, Mandelstam "prefers poetic 'promissory notes' to the literary equivalent of hard cash." See Cavanagh, *Osip Mandelstam and the Modernist Creation of Tradition,* 179.

122. On "The Twilight of Freedom" painting a brighter picture of revolutionary changes but still "oversaturated with ambivalent images," see Gasparov and Ronen, "O. Mandel'shtam: 'Sumerki svobody,'" 4. Scholars still disagree as to whether Mandelstam meant "dawn" or "dusk" by *sumerki.* See Lekmanov, *Mandelstam,* 61.

123. Freidin, *A Coat of Many Colors,* 112. "And new buds will still swell, / Green shoots will sprout, / But your spine is cracked, / My beautiful, pitiful age" (*I eshche nabukhnut pochki, / Bryznet zeleni pobeg. / No razbit tvoi pozvonochnik, / Moi prekrasnyi zhalkii vek*) (Mandel'shtam 2:42). Also compare "time cuts me like a coin" to "And time cuts me / Like your heel" (*I menia srezaet vremia, / Kak skosilo tvoi kabluk*) (Mandel'shtam 2:37).

124. The likely subtext of "responded 'yes' and 'no'" is the Sermon on the Mount: "But let your communication be, Yea, yea; Nay, nay: for whatsoever is more than these cometh of evil" (Matthew 5:37). See Panova, *"Mir," "prostranstvo," "vremia" v poezii Osipa Mandel'shtama,* 661. On this phrase, see also Myers, "The Hum of Metaphor and the Cast of Voice," 33. For Mandelstam's critique of the overusage of metaphors by the imagists, see "Letter on Russian Poetry" ("Pis'mo o russkoi poezii," 1922): "Young Moscow savages have discovered another America—the metaphor, simple-mindedly confused it with the image, and enriched our literature with a whole brood of unnecessary tattered metaphorical likenings" (Mandel'shtam 2:239–40). For commentary on this, see Myers, "The Hum of Metaphor and the Cast of Voice," 15.

125. Nietzsche, *Friedrich Nietzsche on Rhetoric and Language,* 250.

126. For more on this passage in Nietzsche, see, for example, Schrift, *Nietzsche and the Question of Interpretation,* 127. "Poets and thinkers like Stéphane Mallarmé, Friedrich Nietzsche, Henri Bergson, and Ferdinand de Saussure phrased their most pressing meditations on the nature of language in terms of currency." See Cavanagh, *Osip Mandelstam and the Modernist Creation of Tradition,* 190.

127. Freidin, *A Coat of Many Colors,* 369.

128. Florenskii, *Stolp i utverzhdenie istiny,* 35–38. This translation comes from Florensky, *The Pillar and the Ground of the Truth,* with modifications. For

analyses of the second letter, see Pyman, *Pavel Florensky,* 74–75; Cassedy, *Flight from Eden,* 539–40; Iakovenko, "Filosofiia otchaianiia," 252–56.

129. Hofmannsthal, *The Lord Chandos Letter and Other Writings,* 118. Hofmannsthal's work "documents a crisis that coincides with a growing awareness of the dissolution of self . . . and the self-referentiality of texts." See Boker, " 'A Raid on the Inarticulate,' " 76. On apophasis in the letter, see also Franke, ed., *On What Cannot Be Said,* 2:90–92.

130. Hofmannsthal, *The Lord Chandos Letter and Other Writings,* 118.

131. Ibid., 119.

132. Lotman and Uspensky, " 'Agreement' and 'Self-Giving' as Archetypal Models of Culture," 137.

133. The world is "inhuman, even demonic, where 'the master has been chased out of his house and no longer dares to enter' (CPL, 129)." See Cavanagh, *Osip Mandelstam and the Modernist Creation of Tradition,* 178.

134. Pushkin, *Polnoe sobranie sochinenii,* 2:30–32.

135. Mallarmé, *Oeuvres complètes,* 368.

136. "The vehicle [ship] is reduced in dimensions . . . the boundless sea is replaced by the limited track of the racecourse, having a direction but leading nowhere . . . 'Dvukolki' implies a pot-holed track and, unlike chariots, they cannot ascend into the heavens." See Myers, "The Hum of Metaphor and the Cast of Voice," 18. See also the ambivalent usage of "gold" (*zoloto*) in "I start from the cold." What is happening is "not only the transformation of the eternal into the momentary and the united into the diffuse and ephemeral but also the breakdown of the poetic personality into the cheapest bronze coins." See Segal, *Osip Mandelstam,* 110–11; and Edmond, "From Pathos to Parody," 367.

137. Mallarmé, *Oeuvres complètes,* 368.

138. On Mallarmé's analogy between language and money, see Mitchell, "Rodin and the Baudelairean Legacy," 75; Cassedy, *Flight from Eden,* 72; Hoffer, *Reflets réciproques,* 88. See also Mandelstam's conversation with Rudakov on "The Horseshoe Finder": "Life and death are taken away, pawned—pawn tickets are given . . . And a conversation is conducted with the assistance of receipts while all the real is hidden, ends in the water." See Gershtein, *Novoe o Mandel'shtame,* 204. "The direct connection between a man and his life is lost. In similar fashion . . . the bond between the word and the thing is lost, and the word as 'living speaking flesh' is replaced by an empty sign, a 'receipt.' " See Myers, "The Hum of Metaphor and the Cast of Voice," 13.

139. Saussure, *Course in General Linguistics,* 113. Though Mandelstam's nominalism ("Word and Culture," "On the Nature of the Word") points to Saussure's theory, it prompts an etymological reading "as the capacity for magical nomination (*nomen est omen*), for affecting the world with the word." See Freidin, *A Coat of Many Colors,* 173.

140. Cavanagh, *Osip Mandelstam and the Modernist Creation of Tradition,* 187.

141. "I have forgotten the word that I wanted to say" (*Ia slovo pozabyl, chto ia khotel skazat'*) ("The Swallow") (Mandel'shtam 1:146); "What pain it is to search for the forgotten word" (*Kakaia bol'—iskat' poteriannoe slovo*) ("January 1st, 1924") (Mandel'shtam 2:51).

142. Florenskii, *Stolp i utverzhdenie istiny,* 18.

143. "Among grasshoppers the word is without memory" (*Sredi kuznechikov bespamiatstvuet slovo*) (Mandel'shtam 1:146). On the theme of the forgotten word in the Lethean poems, see Ginzburg, *O lirike. 2–e, rasshirennoe izdanie,* 350; Przybylski, *An Essay on the Poetry of Osip Mandelstam,* 51–57, 66; Taranovsky, *Essays on Mandelstam,* 76–78; Ronen, *An Approach to Mandelstam,* 256–59; Terras, *Poetry of the Silver Age,* 203; Pollak, *Mandelstam the Reader,* 13; Freidin, *A Coat of Many Colors,* 197–206, 212–13; Levin, *Izbrannye trudy,* 77–97; Surat, *Mandel'shtam i Pushkin,* 345–47; Gronas, *Cognitive Poetics and Cultural Memory,* 110–16. On the problematic relation of memory to the scene of writing in *The Noise of Time* and *The Egyptian Stamp,* see Pavlov, ". . . Tem zvuchashchim slepkom formy. . . . ," and "Memory and the Scene of Writing in Mandelstam's *Egipetskaia marka.*" On "grains of petrified wheat," see Toddes, "Stat'ia 'Pshenitsa chelovecheskaia' v tvorchestve Mandel'shtama 20–kh godov." For a more affirmative image of the earth as preserving spiritual treasures, see "The Word and Culture."

144. "Take for joy from my palms" depicts "a plain dry necklace / Of dead bees" (*nevzrachnoe sukhoe ozherel'e / Iz mertvykh pchel*) (Mandel'shtam 1:147).

145. Smoliarova, "Mandel'shtam i Pindar," 1–2.

146. Cavanagh, *Osip Mandelstam and the Modernist Creation of Tradition,* 173–86.

147. On radio sets, see Taranovsky, *Essays on Mandelstam,* 130.

148. On ineffability in the Stalin ode ("Oda," 1937), see Freidin, *A Coat of Many Colors,* 259–60; and Coetzee, "Osip Mandelstam and the Stalin Ode." To extend their observations, the ode's conditional beginning, "Were I to take up the charcoal for the sake of supreme praise" (*Kogda b ia ugol' vzial dlia vysshei pokhvaly*) (Mandel'shtam 3:112) is a version of the humility topos as, for example, at the start of Epiphanius's "Panegyric to St. Stephen of Perm.'" Given that Stalin appears as a version of the ineffable, the claim that Mandelstam "fabricates the body of an ode without actually inhabiting it" (Coetzee, "Osip Mandelstam and the Stalin Ode," 80) seems to me well-intended but unconvincing.

149. Taranovsky, *Essays on Mandelstam,* 123. For more on political versus mystical silence, see Epshtein, *Slovo i molchanie,* 200–204. See also Taranovsky, "Dva 'molchaniia' Osipa Mandel'shtama," 118. Mandelstam "adjures himself with the words made famous by Tiutchev a century before. He had learned to keep his counsel, contenting himself with the creative miracle of his own poetry which had at last returned to him." See Baines, *Mandelstam,* 118–19.

150. Epshtein, *Slovo i molchanie,* 217.

151. On these poems, see Taranovsky, *Essays on Mandelstam,* 123–24;

Baines, *Mandelstam,* 10, 20, 22, 36, 113, 118–19, 225–26; Terras, *Poetry of the Silver Age,* 215, and "Osip Mandelstam i ego filosofiia slova," 459; Pollak, *Mandelstam the Reader,* 14; Surat, *Mandel'shtam i Pushkin,* 43–44, 197–98. On the act of communication in Mandelstam's late verse, see Levin, *Izbrannye trudy,* 126–41. Like Mandelstam's later poetry, Akhmatova's *Requiem* (*Rekviem,* 1935–40) strives to articulate extreme suffering. As Adorno writes on Celan, this poetry "is imbued with the shame of art in view of the suffering that withdraws from both experience and sublimation." See Adorno, *Aesthetic Theory,* 444. On Celan's language as "in a state of shock," see Franke, "The Singular and the Other at the Limits of Language," 632.

CHAPTER THREE

1. Kline, "Variations on the Theme of Exile," 73.

2. Bethea, "To My Daughter," 240. On Brodsky's verbal idealism, see Kreps, *O poezii Iosifa Brodskogo;* Polukhina, *Joseph Brodsky,* esp. 146–95, "Poeticheskii avtoportret Brodskogo," "Similarity in Disparity," and other articles; Loseff's miscellaneous essays, for example, "On the Centenary of Anna Akhmatova"; Glushko, "Lingvoditseia Iosifa Brodskogo"; Plekhanova, *Preobrazhenie tragicheskogo,* 2:144–89; Beaver, "Time in the Lyric Poetry of Joseph Brodsky," esp. 16–38 and 383–431; Khairov, "'Esli bog dlia menia i sushchestvuet, to eto imenno iazyk'"; Williams, *Defending Poetry,* 53–98. Kreps stresses Brodsky's belief in the poetic word's power over time. Polukhina and Loseff concur: for Brodsky "the word is capable of protecting man not only from things, but even from time" (Polukhina, *Joseph Brodsky,* 177); "through the act of poetry one becomes a 'part of speech,' that is, 'more than one'—this is Brodsky's paradoxical reinterpretation of Horace's 'Non omnis moriar, multiquae pars mei vitabit Libitinam'" (Loseff, "On the Centenary of Anna Akhmatova," 229). Brodsky's key notions of self-value and self-sufficiency of language appear as early as 1963 in his letter about the forthcoming language reform. See Gordin, *Pereklichka vo mrake,* 139.

3. Auden, *Another Time,* 93. On Brodsky being inspired by "time . . . worships language," see his essay on Auden, "To Please a Shadow" (1983) (*Less Than One* 362–63). Auden opted to excise the concluding lines of "In Memory of W. B. Yeats" for his 1958 Penguin Poets volume. Brodsky dismisses the weight of the final skeptical lines of Auden's elegy by seeing a "touch of irrelevance . . . in the falling intonation" and suggesting that these lines merely offset the seriousness of the key remark, "time . . . worships language" (*Less Than One* 364).

4. Fading of faith in the word "is the most important and the most touching, even tragic, development during the last decade of Brodsky's life." See Smith, "Joseph Brodsky: Summing Up," 408. However, doubts in the power of the word arise in Brodsky much earlier. I see Bethea's ambivalent reading as insightful: "The poet is tested by a Yahweh, the Yahweh of language, who is not a loving

parent and has not made man in his own image, but has given him, in the wilderness of an arbitrary world order, speech." See Bethea, "To My Daughter," 254. As Beaver discusses Brodsky's lyric-temporal strategies (*athanasia, atomization, povtorenie, apophasis, keddah, kataphasis*), he examines both sides of this issue. For example, Brodsky's "faith in language, while it remains steadfast, leads him to write poems of *positive kataphasis*"—asserting a belief that language "lies beyond nature and transcends the limits of ordinary knowledge and experience"; "when his faith in language fails, Brodsky's poems insist on the transience of language or on a dread final silence that will follow after language" (*negative kataphasis*). See Beaver, *Time in the Lyric Poetry of Joseph Brodsky,* 382–83.

5. All references to Brodsky, *On Grief and Reason,* are abbreviated as (*On Grief and Reason* page), and placed in the main text. Brodsky's comparison of the exiled writer in the same essay to "a dog or a man hurtled into space in a capsule (more like a dog than a man, because they will never bother to retrieve you)," with "your capsule—your language" (*On Grief and Reason* 32), like Mandelstam's "message in a bottle" metaphor ("On the Addressee") both places high stakes on the poetic word and stresses the verbal practitioner's precarious condition.

6. All references to Brodskii, *Sobranie sochinenii,* and Brodsky, *Collected Poems in English,* are abbreviated as (Brodskii volume: page) and (Brodsky, *Collected Poems in English* page) respectively and placed in the main text. On "the poetic word that, in Brodsky's world, is capable of overcoming separation, ruins, and unrepeatability of the moment," see Zholkovskii, "'Ia vas liubil . . . .,'" 51). A number of Brodsky's poems harbor both logocentric and logophobic polarities. For example, "Lullaby of Cape Cod" ("Kolybel'naia treskovogo mysa," 1975) transmits a stifling atmosphere, the fear of silence, the asphyxiation of the word, and yet also the poet's and the word's desire for self-preservation.

7. On verbal power to access realities outside the sphere of ordinary cognition (infinity, the inanimate), see Plekhanova, *Preobrazhenie tragicheskogo,* 2:119–43; and Beaver, *Time in the Lyric Poetry of Joseph Brodsky,* 209–21. While I agree that Brodsky's language "does not so much balance the destructive power of time with its own creative will as lays claim to a universal affinity with it," I do not see how "the equation of infinity with emptiness removes the problem of destructiveness altogether" (Plekhanova, *Preobrazhenie tragicheskogo,* 2:144).

8. See, for example, Kreps's and Polukhina's monographs, and Gordin, *V storonu Stiksa,* esp. 1–33. However, note the following word choice: "The poet is not even so much a puppet of his gift as a puppet of language." See Polukhina, "Grammatika metafory i khudozhestvennyi smysl," 64.

9. Brodsky, "Nobel Lecture," 10.

10. In Mikhail Epstein's view, this passage from the Nobel speech shows "first and foremost the demonism of language." See Epshtein, *Slovo i molchanie,* 527.

11. Brodsky, "Nobel Lecture," 6.

12. Brodskii, *Bol'shaia kniga interv'iu,* 447. All references to Brodsky, *Less Than One,* are abbreviated as (*Less than One* page) and placed in the main text. "The surest defense against Evil . . ." comes from Brodsky's "Commencement Address" (1984). Poetry "makes us individually response-able and responsible, separated from the coercion of the collective." See Williams, *Defending Poetry,* 97.

13. The claim that the poet's role as mediator (through whom language cognizes itself), and not creator, "removes one of the most tragic problems of creativity—the problem of the inexpressible, so torturous for nineteenth-century lyricists." See Plekhanova, *Preobrazhenie tragicheskogo,* 2:155. This contention is contradicted by statements like the one from "In the Shadow of Dante." For a different take on synthetic versus analytic languages, see Brodsky's preface to Platonov's *Foundation Pit* (*Kotlovan,* 1929–30), where the writer is dependent "on the synthetic (or, more precisely, non-analytical) essence of the Russian language itself, something which . . . determines the formation of concepts which are devoid of any real content" (Brodsky, "Preface," x). The Russian nation falling "victim of its language" (ibid., x) is clearly meant in a negative sense—not in the sense of verbal modeling "as the gates of freedom to the fullness of comprehended meaning" (Plekhanova, *Preobrazhenie tragicheskogo,* 2:170). On the superiority of inflected languages, see Humboldt, *On Language,* 44.

14. The full text of "Conversation with a Celestial Being" can be accessed in Brodskii 2:361–67. For close readings of this poem, see Polukhina, *Joseph Brodsky,* 263–78; Ranchin, *Na piru Mnemoziny,* 147–63; Sluzhevskaia, *Tri stat'i o Brodskom,* 39–56; Beaver, *Time in the Lyric Poetry of Joseph Brodsky,* 437–43; Ozherel'eva, "Bog i chelovek v stikhotvorenii Iosifa Brodskogo 'Razgovor s nebozhitelem,'" 65–89.

15. Polukhina, *Joseph Brodsky,* 263.

16. Ranchin, *Na piru Mnemoziny,* 152–61.

17. Loseff, "Iosif Brodsky's Poetics of Faith," 191.

18. Noks, "Ierarkhiia drugikh v poezii Brodskogo," 165–66.

19. Zholkovskii, *Izbrannye stat'i o russkoi poezii,* 302.

20. Sluzhevskaia, *Tri stat'i o Brodskom,* 41.

21. Ozherel'eva, "Bog i chelovek v stikhotvorenii Iosifa Brodskogo 'Razgovor s nebozhitelem,'" 65. Beaver's reading of the poem as asserting language's non-transcendent character and Ranchin's observations on the points of contact and divergence between Brodsky's thought and religious existentialism seem most compelling to me, though I would part from Ranchin's view that Brodsky conceptualizes language in terms of a conventional religious ineffability. Brodsky's readings in the 1960s, "especially in the latter half, were Shestov, then Berdyaev, Lossky, and Frank." See Volkov, *Conversations with Joseph Brodsky,* 178. Brodsky "held in esteem Kierkegaard, Dostoevsky, Shestov, Kafka, Camus, and Beckett." See Losev, *Iosif Brodskii,* 174. On Brodsky and Shestov, see Brod-

skii, *Bol'shaia kniga interv'iu,* 204–5; MacFadyen, *Joseph Brodsky and the Baroque,* 23–59; Volkov, *Conversations with Joseph Brodsky,* 178; Plekhanova, *Preobrazhenie tragicheskogo,* 1:34–40, 2:208–11. On Brodsky and Kierkegaard, see Beaver, *Time in the Lyric Poetry of Joseph Brodsky,* 380–431, and "Brodsky and Kierkegaard, Language and Time"; and Plekhanova, *Preobrazhenie tragicheskogo,* 1:18–21, 2:218–22. On Brodsky and religious existentialists, see also Polukhina, *Joseph Brodsky,* 263–75; Noks, "Ierarkhiia drugikh v poezii Brodskogo"; Ranchin, *Na piru Mnemoziny,* 146–74; Sluzhevskaia, *Tri stat'i o Brodskom,* 49; Kelebai, *Poet v dome rebenka,* 106–218; Losev, *Iosif Brodskii,* 174–77; Plekhanova, *Preobrazhenie tragicheskogo,* 1:56–66, 2:211–24.

22. Most poets prefer to place short lines after long ones but Brodsky starts with a short line. See Scherr, "Strofika Brodskogo," 278. There is also an uneven layout in "The Butterfly" ("Babochka," 1972), but for different reasons: the poem reproduces the movement of the butterfly. Similar to Zhukovsky's hero unable to compete with nature, the poet in "The Butterfly" is unable to compete with the painter—God—but writes to assuage the pain of life "whose spasm reaps no pollen, / but eases hearts" (*ne pyl' s tsvetka snimaia, / no tiazhest' s plech*) (Brodsky, *Collected Poems in English* 76; Brodskii 3:23). Compare Zhukovsky's and Baratynsky's convoluted syntax of inexpressibility.

23. Ranchin, *Na piru Mnemoziny,* 224.

24. "Some pages showed through like onion peel. Measles, scarlet fever, and chicken pox lived in them" (Mandel'shtam 2:490). On Brodsky and Mandelstam, see, for example, Venclova, "Brodskii o Mandel'shtame" and Burnett, "Complicity of the Real." In Burnett's argument, "for Mandelstam, the language of the poet offers the precursion to the possibility of communication—and communion—with the future, while Brodsky denies that the poem "is a communion through time (between the poet and the 'distant, unknown addressee')." See Burnett, "Complicity of the Real," 14–15.

25. Luke 6:20–21.

26. Matthew 5:3.

27. In "Presentation for a Symposium" ("Doklad dlia simpoziuma," 1989), "aesthetic feeling is / a mold made from the instinct of self-preservation" (*esteticheskoe chut'e / sut' slepok s instinkta samosokhraneniia* (Brodskii 4:62). The "mold from the instinct of self-preservation" echoes the "mold from a sad gift."

28. Donne, *The Complete Poems,* 33.

29. Polukhina, *Joseph Brodsky,* 278.

30. "Language is not a tool of cognition but one of assimilation . . . The human being is a natural bourgeois and uses language for the same ends as he uses housing and clothing" (*Less Than One* 56). In "Strophes" the proliferation of writing turns one indifferent to the past and the future, and the proximity of the void "merely increases the speed / the pen picks up on paper" (*lish' uskoriaet begstvo / po bumage pera*) (Brodsky, *Collected Poems in English* 153; Brodskii 3:184).

31. Kreps, *O poezii Iosifa Brodskogo,* 237.

32. Lermontov's "Gratitude" ("Blagodarnost'," 1840) expresses a similar defiant sentiment. See Ranchin, *Na piru Mnemoziny*, 163. These lines are also akin to the conclusion of Brodsky's "1972": "Beat the drum about your trust / into shears in which the fate of matter / is hidden. Only the size of the loss / makes man equal to God" (*Bei v baraban o svoem doverii / k nozhnitsam, v koikh sud'ba materii / skryta. Tol'ko razmer poteri i / delaet smertnogo ravnym Bogu*) (Brodsky, *Collected Poems in English* 70; Brodskii 3:19). In "May 24th, 1980" ("24 maia 1980") Brodsky states his determination to utter only words of gratitude (Brodskii 3:191). See also "Lullaby of Cape Cod," in which the poet hesitates to confess pain and doubts that there will be a response: "the vast obscurity / of darkness and heavy heat (may one add, grief?)" (*gruz / temnoty, zhary i—skazat' li—goria*) (Brodsky, *Collected Poems in English* 124; Brodskii 3:87).

33. For transcendental needlework, see "Great Elegy to John Donne."

34. Sluzhevskaia, *Tri stat'i o Brodskom*, 45.

35. Ranchin, *Na piru Mnemoziny*, 153.

36. Compare "one should not orate" in Mandelstam's "The Lutheran."

37. The theme of verbal infection recurs in "Letters from the Ming Dynasty" ("Pis'ma dinastii Min'," 1977): "And the meaninglessness, like a plague, / spreads from words onto numbers" (*I zaraza bessmyslennosti so slova / perekidyvaetsia na tsifry*) (Brodsky, *Collected Poems in English* 143; Brodskii 3:154). Comparing human speech to smallpox "reflects an extremely skeptical and ambiguous opinion regarding the possibility of an at least limited dialogue with God." See Noks, "Poeziia Iosifa Brodskogo," 221. On death and snow, see "Verses on the Death of T. S. Eliot," "Great Elegy to John Donne," and "The Hawk's Cry in Autumn."

38. On the rhythmical outline of the poem, see Polukhina, *Joseph Brodsky*, 280.

39. On the cycle, see, among others, Kreps, *O poezii Iosifa Brodskogo*, 246–54; Polukhina, *Joseph Brodsky*, 39, 229–36, 241–48; Piarli, "Sintaksis i smysl"; Polukhina and Piarli, *Slovar' tropov Brodskogo;* Bel'skaia, "'Chast' rechi' Iosifa Brodskogo"; Semenova, "Poema Iosifa Brodskogo 'Chast' rechi'"; Kim, "Poeticheskii perenos v tsikle 'Chast' rechi' I. Brodskogo"; Broitman and Kim, "O prirode khudozhestvennoi real'nosti v tsikle I. Brodskogo 'Chast' rechi"; Fomenko et al., "Opyt rekonstruktsii mirooshchushcheniia I. Brodskogo ('Chast' rechi')"; Sluzhevskaia, *Tri stat'i o Brodskom*, 57–139; Beaver, *Time in the Lyric Poetry of Joseph Brodsky*, 53–58, 290–303; Akhapkin, *Iosif Brodskii posle Rossii*, 37–47.

40. Brodsky "wished to create a visual impression of sparseness by presenting each laconic poem against a void." See Wachtel, *Cambridge Introduction to Russian Poetry*, 154.

41. For my analysis of this cycle I employ both Brodsky's auto-translations and my own literal translations since in his auto-translations Brodsky frequently departs from the original in significant ways. My translations borrow some locu-

tions from Daniel Weissbort's rendition of "A Part of Speech" (March 1978 issue of *Poetry*). In his auto-translations Brodsky "deliberately simplified the contents but refused to simplify the form. In the first place, he wanted to preserve rhymes, then—rhythm, and then—other features of versification." Such translations "are not equivalents but, rather, interpretations, prompting us to return to the original." See Wachtel, "Joseph Brodsky chitaet Iosifa Brodskogo," 602. "Translation—because of its explanatory nature—somehow catches up with the original by clarifying those things that could be regarded by the author as self-evident and thus elude the native reader" (*Less Than One* 99). On Brodsky's (auto-)translations, see also Volgina, "Iosif Brodskii / Joseph Brodsky"; and Kline, "Revisiting Brodsky."

42. Polukhina, *Joseph Brodsky*, 232.

43. Compare Mandelstam's "Zamolchi! ni o chem, nikogda, nikomu" and Emily Dickinson's Lyric 1251, in which the syllepsis of the last line dramatizes contortion: "Silence is all we dread. / There's ransom in a Voice—/ But silence is infinity. / Himself have not a face" (Dickinson, *The Complete Poems*, 548). "All the expressions, by the way maximally prosaic in themselves . . . are broken up and taken apart, beginning in one, ending in the neighboring line." See Sluzhevskaia, *Tri stat'i o Brodskom*, 64. On communicative quandaries in Brodsky, see Artemova, "O zhanre pis'ma v poezii I. Brodskogo"; and Venclova, "A Journey from Petersburg to Istanbul," 137.

44. Poetry is transformed into a shriek in "A wooden laocoon, for a while casting the mountain off" ("Dereviannyi laokoon, sbrosiv na vremia goru s") and "From the point of view of air, the end of earth" ("S tochki zreniia vozdukha, krai zemli"). In the former lyric, "a voice / pitches high, keeping words on a string of sense" (*golos / staraetsia uderzhat' slova, vzvizgnuv, v predelakh smysla*) (Brodsky, *Collected Poems* 111; Brodskii 3:130). Beneath Brodsky's estranged tone, "one hears grief that has not been, and cannot be, overcome, a 'howl' that he does not permit himself." See Sedakova, "Volia k forme," 235. See also Allen Ginsberg's "Howl" (1955).

45. The lyric "bares the poetic process." See Kulle, "Struktura avtorskogo 'ia' v stikhotvorenii Iosifa Brodskogo 'Niotkuda s liubov'iu,'" 141. "As it is not said below at least—" "attempts to obscure suffering by irony" (Sluzhevskaia, *Tri stat'i o Brodskom*, 67); it was "precisely this split into 'the one who writes and the one who suffers' that Brodsky had in mind in connection with Akhmatova's *Requiem*" (Semenova, "Poema Iosifa Brodskogo 'Chast' rechi'," 81). The dash in "as it is not said below at least—" (given the erotic context) may also be a gesture of self-censorship. For Emily Dickinson, "the dash—invariably ambiguous, often inscrutable—comes close to the all-inclusive unutterable word." See Fagan, "Emily Dickinson's Unutterable Word," 70. On the dash as indicative of unutterability, see Polianskii, "Formy i funktsii neizrechennogo v tekstakh khudozhestvennoi literatury," 56.

46. Volkov, *Conversations with Joseph Brodsky,* 227.

47. In "The Lithuanian Nocturne: To Thomas Venclova" ("Litovskii noktiurn: Tomasu Venclova," 1974) the home of poetry is eternity. For an analysis of this poem, see Venclova, "Lithuanian Nocturne."

48. The fossil also appears in "The Lagoon" ("Laguna," 1973) and "Less Than One." The objective of the concluding stanza's convoluted inversion is "not to disclose oneself until the last line . . . and only at the very end to utter a complaint—and to lower the curtain." See Sluzhevskaia, *Tri stat'i o Brodskom,* 79. On Brodsky's (self-)estrangement, see Polukhina, "The Myth of the Poet and the Poet of Myth," 147; and Kozitskaia-Fleishman, "'Ia byl kak vse.'" On death as the realm of deafness and muteness, see, for example, "Nunc Dimittis" ("Sreten'e," 1972).

49. Ranchin, *Na piru Mnemoziny,* 330.

50. William Butler Yeats in "The Sad Shepherd" (1885) uses imagery similar to Mandelstam's to depict the hero singing to a seashell that transforms his complaints into an inarticulate moan: "But the sad dweller by the sea-ways lone / Changed all he sang to inarticulate moan / Among her wildering whirls, forgetting him" (Yeats, *The Poems,* 9). Like Yeats, Brodsky notes the lack of response in the world.

51. In the poetry of the last Soviet decades, accentual verse was used "more often to stress the vast and chaotic nature of the object portrayed or the artless prosiness of the authorial intonation." See Gasparov, *Ocherk istorii russkogo stikha,* 281. On Brodsky's early verse as refashioning Soviet materialist rhetoric to articulate metaphysical issues, see MacFadyen, *Joseph Brodsky and the Soviet Muse.*

52. On New Year's Eve by the sea, see Volkov, *Conversations with Joseph Brodsky,* 247.

53. See "Lullaby of Cape Cod." Compare T. S. Eliot's "The Love Song of J. Alfred Prufrock" (1917).

54. Polukhina, "Similarity in Disparity," 166.

55. "In Memory of My Father: Australia" ("Pamiati ottsa: Avstraliia," 1989) "stridently enforces these laws [of space and time]." See Beaver, "Lyricism and Philosophy in Brodsky's Elegiac Verse," 594. The elegy brings to consciousness the gap between printed word and spoken language. See Sandler, "On Grief and Reason, on Poetry and Film," 668.

56. "In the Shadow of Dante" characterizes Eugenio Montale's poetry as marked by "a deliberately monotonous intonation that is occasionally made shrill by the addition of feet or is muted by their omission—one of the many techniques he employs in order to avoid prosodic inertia" (*Less Than One* 98). See also Brodsky on Auden: "He achieved a neutrality of sound, a neutrality of voice. This neutrality comes at a high price. It comes not when the poet becomes objective, dry, and restrained. It comes when he merges with time. Because time is

neutral." See Volkov, *Conversations with Joseph Brodsky,* 142. Or, as he puts it in his essay on Thomas Hardy, "Wooing the Inanimate" (1995), "language flows into the human domain from the realm of nonhuman truths and dependencies . . . it is ultimately the voice of inanimate matter" (*On Grief and Reason* 333).

57. See, for example, "The Slate Ode." Mandelstam's "Bursts of round harbors, and cartilage, and blueness" ("Razryvy kruglykh bukht, i khriashch, i sineva," 1937) likens seaweed to hair, describing the former as "false-haired and smelling of a long lie" (*lozhnovolosaia—i pakhnet dolgoi lozh'iu*) (Mandel'shtam 3:120). The poem alludes to Pushkin's "From Pindemonte" ("Iz Pindemonti," 1836), itself quoting Shakespeare's "words, words, words." Mandelstam's symbolism-inspired ideas, expressed in his 1909 letter to Ivanov, resonate with Brodsky's conception of the impersonal nature of prosody: "This poem ['On the dark sky as ornament'] was supposed to be a 'romance sans paroles' . . . 'Paroles,' that is, intimate-lyrical, personal: I tried to restrain, to bridle it with the bridle of rhythm . . . I can't help remembering your remarks on the anti-lyrical nature of iambics" (Mandel'shtam 4:18).

58. Shklovskii, *Literatura i kinematograf,* 11.

59. Brodsky, "Joseph Brodsky's 'Verses on the Death of T. S. Eliot,'" 196. "The theme of the poet who lives in the memory of generations is explicit in Auden's elegy: 'The words of a dead man / Are modified in the guts of the living.'" See Polukhina, *Joseph Brodsky,* 87. For similar readings, see Gillespie, "Joseph Brodsky (Iosif Aleksandrovich Brodsky)," 27; and Beaver, *Time in the Lyric Poetry of Joseph Brodsky,* 32–33 and 393–95. However, "The words of a dead man / Are modified in the guts of the living," preceded in Auden by "Now he is scattered among a hundred cities / And wholly given over to unfamiliar affections; / To find his happiness in another kind of wood / And be punished under a foreign code of conscience" (Auden, *Another Time,* 93), indicate a problematic transformation of the dead poet's words in the reader and loss of authorial control. I agree that in "Verses on the Death of T. S. Eliot" the dead poet is moving away from the addressee, with irony inherent in the opening where "the end of a life comes at the beginning of a new year, and the difference between the one and the other is a caesura." Analogously, in the process of Yeats becoming his poems ["In Memory of W. B. Yeats"] "that active, difficult, protean self that gave birth to the poems is, in a sense, exiled from them." See Bethea, *Joseph Brodsky and the Creation of Exile,* 129–31.

60. Brodsky, *Selected Poems,* 64. "The ship is ice-bound, the passenger freezes, drowns. But this plot is merely a frame around principal content—a farewell to the world, which cannot come to help." See Loseff, "Politics/Poetics," 37. On this poem, see also Eskin, *Poetic Affairs,* 104–5; and Beaver, *Time in the Lyric Poetry of Joseph Brodsky,* 27–29. See also Brodsky's grim image of the reader in "The Condition We Call Exile" as well as Grünbein's negative trans-

position of Mandelstam's "message in a bottle" metaphor. See Grunbein, *Antike dispositionen,* 46; and Eskin, *Poetic Affairs,* 142.

61. Alexander Levitsky, unpublished.

62. This conceit is present in "The Horseshoe Finder" and in the Mandelstam letter to Ivanov. In "The Horseshoe Finder" the hero's bird-driven cart gets torn competing with the other horses. In Virginia Woolf, "words and words and words . . . gallop . . . , lash their long manes and tails," but "for some fault in him" the hero "cannot give himself to their backs." See Woolf, *The Waves,* 61.

63. The color yellow is traditionally associated with madness. See also Blok's "The Stranger" where the moon "looks on with a mindless leer" (*bessmyslenno krivitsia disk*) (Blok, *Sobranie sochinenii,* 1:87).

64. Celan, *Gesammelte Werke in fünf Bänden,* 2:31. On the neologism *tikhotvorenie,* see Polukhina, *Joseph Brodsky,* 247.

65. *A Part of Speech* (1977) was Brodsky's first book published in the United States (1977). *Chast' rechi* (1990) was the title of Brodsky's first collection published in the Soviet Union.

66. Loseff, "On the Centenary of Anna Akhmatova," 229. This point is made more assertively in the Russian version of the article: "Man in life is 'less than himself' ('less than one'), but man in verbal art, man as 'part of speech' is 'more than himself' (cf. Derzhavin's translation of Horace *'chast' menia bol'shaia,'* which means not 'a big part of me' but 'a part of me that is bigger than me')." See Losev, "Na stoletie Anny Akhmatovoi," 205. "Chast' menia bol'shaia" has not meant (in the eighteenth century) "a part that is larger than me" (Alexander Levitsky, personal communication).

67. Polukhina, *Joseph Brodsky,* 39.

68. Sluzhevskaia, *Tri stat'i o Brodskom,* 135–36; Plekhanova, *Preobrazhenie tragicheskogo,* 2:168.

69. On Brodsky as an exilic writer, see Bethea, *Joseph Brodsky and the Creation of Exile;* Kline, "Variations on the Theme of Exile"; Loseff, "Home and Abroad in the Works of Brodskii"; Glazunova, *Iosif Brodskii;* Turoma, *Brodsky Abroad.* On theories of exile, see Seidel, *Exile and the Narrative Imagination;* Said, *The Edward Said Reader;* Tabori, *The Anatomy of Exile;* Robinson, ed., *Altogether Elsewhere;* Rose, ed., *The Dispossessed.* On the linguistic consequences of the condition, see Beaujour, *Alien Tongues;* and Steiner, *After Babel.*

70. For an analysis of "1972" in the context of Brodsky's exile, see Kline, "Variations on the Theme of Exile," 67–70, 81–83.

71. Turoma faults Brodsky for "remaining imprisoned in his Arnoldian understanding of the ethical hierarchy between literature and society . . . Instead of re-politicizing or re-historicizing modernist exile, Brodsky de-politicizes and dehistoricizes it." See Turoma, *Brodsky Abroad,* 21.

72. Rather than claiming Brodsky's familiarity with specific poststructuralists, I have in mind an exposure to the general critical context (Susan

Sontag and Roland Barthes are likely exceptions). On Brodsky's essays as throwing into relief the difference between philosophy and literature, see Eskin, "Who Is Speaking?"

73. Compare Nadezhda Mandelstam's description of Mandelstam's poetry emerging from music and Brodsky's auto-description: "Usually everything starts from some kind of sound in the head. Confidence arises. This is similar to touching the tuning fork . . . This is about having meaning fit the melody sounding in your head. This melody has not only a phonic but a psychological aspect as well, that's why I feel which key must be touched." See Brodskii, *Bol'shaia kniga interv'iu,* 611. Note, though, how, for example, "Singing Without Music" ("Pen'e bez muzyki," 1970) reverses the dream of pre-verbal music shared by the romantics and "Silentium." On this, see Smith, "Singing Without Music," 23.

74. "Inanimate and animate are no longer categories that matter." See Wachtel, *Cambridge Introduction to Russian Poetry,* 153.

75. Derrida, "How to Avoid Speaking," 45; De Man, *The Rhetoric of Romanticism,* 81.

76. Blok, *Sobranie sochinenii,* 1:87.

77. Wachtel, *Cambridge Introduction to Russian Poetry,* 154.

78. Polukhina, *Joseph Brodsky,* 118.

79. Pushkin, *Polnoe sobranie sochinenii,* 3:250. "While Pushkin's poem traces the path from uncertainty to control, Brodsky's leads only to increasing fragmentation and disintegration." See Wachtel, *Cambridge Introduction to Russian Poetry,* 152.

80. Allusions to mice occur in many poems by Brodsky; for example, in "Great Elegy to John Donne" "a thieving mouse pleads guilty" (*mysh' idet s povinnoi*) (Brodsky, *Elegy to John Donne and Other Poems* 64; Brodskii 1:232); in "The Torso" a mouse leaves a ruined statue of the lyrical hero (Brodskii 3:36).

81. Brodsky, *Joseph Brodsky,* 59.

82. In *The Iliad* (1.39) Apollo is called "Mouse Apollo" by his favorite priest Smintheus. The temples of the Sminthean Apollo contain images of sacred mice. On the mouse-muse mythologeme see Maksimilian Voloshin, "Apollo and the Mouse" ("Apollon i mysh'," 1911). This essay was discussed by Polukhina, Strizhevskaia, and Ranchin in connection with Brodsky's poem. See also Mandelstam's "What the clock-grasshopper sings" ("Chto poiut chasy-kuznechik," 1918), with its linkage of the destructive forces of mice and poetry.

83. Strizhevskaia, *O Poezii Iosifa Brodskogo,* 282.

84. Polukhina, *Joseph Brodsky,* 177.

85. Akhapkin, "'Filologicheskaia metafora' v poetike Iosifa Brodskogo," 229.

86. MacFadyen, *Joseph Brodsky and the Baroque,* 53. For MacFadyen "words gobble up things" means language's "ability to overpower existence's dumb tendency to objectify." However, he then acknowledges that "although words are building blocks toward a paradoxical expression of ineffable faith,

they often cannot help but express what is expressible, creating things by naming them; a name does objectify a signified with its unchanging signifier when it gobbles it." See ibid., 53.

87. This self-consuming verbal predatoriness is negative, not a productive "submission to the imperative of cognition grounded in language" (Plekhanova, *Preobrazhenie tragicheskogo,* 2:156). *Pozhrat'* occurs in Derzhavin's death-door poem "The river of time in its flowing": "It will be devoured by the crater of eternity" (*To vechnosti zherlom pozhretsia*) (Derzhavin, *Sochineniia,* 281).

88. John 1:1.

89. Dante's and Mandelstam's poetry "is testimony to the belief that not only could the word become flesh but that, in their cases, it had. The hidden meaning of Brodsky's poem is precisely the opposite, that the flesh has become word." See Bethea, *Joseph Brodsky and the Creation of Exile,* 71.

90. The theme of the failure of memory is foregrounded in many lyrics of this cycle. While some of the poems reminisce over the past, as does "A dark-blue morning in a frame covered with hoar-frost" ("Temno-sinee utro v zaindevevshei rame"), most are obsessed with forgetting: "Because the heel leaves prints—it is winter" ("Potomu chto kabluk ostavliaet sledy—zima"); "You forgot the village lost in the marshlands" ("Ty zabyla derevniu, zateriannuiu v bolotakh"); "It is not that I grow mad, but I grew tired during the summer" ("Ia ne to chto skhozhu s uma, no ustal za leto"); "So, it gets warmer, in memory as on a boundary path" ("Itak, prigrevaet, v pamiati kak na mezhe"); "I recognize this wind lying on the grass" ("Uznaiu etot veter, lozhashchiisia na travu").

91. Glazunova, *Iosif Brodskii,* 276. Kozlov's analysis is analogous to Glazunova's: "His memory, his inner world are inseparably connected to the Russian language. That's why, if memory in the future will be getting impoverished, that same will be happening to the Russian language as well as the lyrical hero's inner world." See Kozlov, "Neperevodimye gody Brodskogo," 177. As I see this, exile provides an added rationale for verbal skepticism and fear of memory loss preexisting in Brodsky. On the opposition between Russian and English in Brodsky, see Akhapkin, "Iosif Brodskii—poeziia grammatiki"; Khairov, " 'Esli bog dlia menia i sushchestvuet, to eto imenno iazyk' "; Burnett; "Galatea Encore"; Kozlov, "Neperevodimye gody Brodskogo."

92. Compare Lotman: "The process of narration pushes out of our memory the real imprints of the dream." See Lotman, *Kul'tura i vzryv,* 61.

93. Scherr, "To Urania," 96.

94. The idea that memories are damaged in the text is not confined to Brodsky's work. The motif of the ineffability of memory, touched by Batiushkov and Zhukovsky, becomes more prominent in Mandelstam. Vladimir Nabokov writes: "I have often noticed that after I had bestowed on the characters of my novels some treasured item of my past, it would pine away in the artificial world where I had so abruptly placed it" (Nabokov, *Speak, Memory,* 95). In the words of Italo

Calvino, "memory's images, once they are fixed in words, are erased" (Calvino, *Invisible Cities,* 87). On the theme of memory in Brodsky, see, for example, Weststeijn, "'The Thought of You Is Going Away . . . "; Beaver, *Time in the Lyric Poetry of Joseph Brodsky,* 304–31; Day, "The Optics of Memory in Brodsky's 'Fifth Eclogue.'"

95. In English Brodsky "removed both cases of pronominal usage. Yet these depersonalized uses of 'you' in the Russian poem make the absence of humanity more palpable than their complete omission. They raise the possibility of human contact only to annul it." See Wachtel, *Cambridge Introduction to Russian Poetry,* 154. See also "A Dedication" ("Posviashchenie," 1987) where the author and the reader are mutually absent: "You do not exist for me; in your eyes I am Cyrillic letters, titles" (*Ty dlia menia ne sushchestvuesh'; ia / v glazakh tvoikh—kirillitsa, nazvan'ia*) (Brodskii 4:29).

96. Wachtel, *Cambridge Introduction to Russian Poetry,* 153.

97. In Milton's sonnets such a moment of syntactic slide invites the reader to make a certain kind of sense only to discover (at the beginning of the next line) that the sense he has made is either incomplete or simply wrong. The significant word or phrase occurs at a line break where a reader is invited to place it first in one and then in another structure of syntax and sense. See Fish, *Is There a Text in This Class?* 147. Enjambments appear in Brodsky's work more often than in the work of any other Russian poet, perhaps even Tsvetaeva. See Batkin, *Tridtsat' tret'ia bukva,* 48. On enjambments in "A Part of Speech," see Kim, "Poeticheskii perenos v tsikle 'Chast'rechi' I. Brodskogo."

98. On regular enjambments, see Zubova, *Sovremennaia russkaia poeziia v kontekste istorii iazyka,* 314.

99. The changes occurring in English are not explained by a different relation between Brodsky and his readership. Brodsky was simply unable to replicate the same effect in the English version. For critical reviews of Brodsky's English-language poetry, see, for example, Volgina and Kiust, "Plokhoi poet Iosif Brodskii."

100. One of the functions of the enjambment is to "raise a word serving a structural function to the status of a word equally important to other words." See Tynianov, *Problema stikhotvornogo iazyka,* 209.

101. On Brodsky's usage of a linguistic term in its non-technical meaning, see Akhapkin, "Iosif Brodskii: 'Glagoly,'" 32.

102. In Brodsky's recitation of the poem (December 18, 1980) the third *chast' rechi* is read as a cadence, a toned-down representation of mechanized language. Repeating the same words, "Brodsky seems to hammer nails in the lid of the coffin ready to accept the body." See Sluzhevskaia, *Tri stat'i o Brodskom,* 130. See also multiple repetitions of "I said" (*ia skazal*) in "Gorbunov and Gorchakov." On this, see Verkheil, "'Enei i Didona' Iosifa Brodskogo," 135; Beaver, *Time in the Lyric Poetry of Joseph Brodsky,* 451; Plekhanova, *Preobrazhenie*

tragicheskogo, 2:270; Monas, "Words Devouring Things," 1069. Silence in "Gorbunov and Gorchakov" is "a metaphor replacing death." See Polukhina, *Grammatika metafory i khudozhestvennyi smysl,* 86. On language losing meaning, see also Brodsky's "Infinitive" (1994).

103. For the claim that this poem is an apotheosis of the word, see Semenova, "Poema Iosifa Brodskogo 'Chast' rechi'," 83.

104. Lomonosov, *Polnoe sobranie sochinenii,* 8:184; Derzhavin, *Sochineniia,* 144.

105. Scherr, "Beginning at the End," 191.

106. "Verses on the Death of T. S. Eliot" and "Roman Elegies" ("Rimskie elegii," 1981) mention Horace. The latter poem echoes *griadushchee* from ". . . And when 'the future' is uttered": "And a sultry, porous / cavity of a mouth scatters around / cold pearls of Horace. / I've never built that cloud-thrusting stony / object / that could explain clouds' pallor. / I have learned about my own, and any / fate, from a letter, from its black color" (*I v goriachei / polosti gorla kholodnym perlom / perekatyvaetsia Goratsii. / Ia ne vozdvig ukhodiashchei k tucham / kamennoi veshchi dlia ikh ostrastki. / O svoem—i o liubom—griaduschem / ia uznal u bukvy, u chernoi kraski*) (Brodsky, *Collected Poems in English* 276; Brodskii 3:229). In my view, these lines do not so much bespeak "the power of Word, in the best Mandelstamian sense, that came before the poet" (Torlone, *Russia and the Classics,* 188), as reaffirm the theme of non-lionization in poetry and premonition of death in language. Compare "My words, I think, will die" ("Moi slova, ia dumaiu, umrut," 1963), an early version of a hopeless *griadushchee.*

107. Browning, *The Complete Poetic Works,* 280. Brodsky "constantly looks both ways, both to the West and to Russia . . . His vision can be called triangular in that a Russian source, say Mandelstam, is subtly implanted within a Western source, say Dante, so that each source comments on the other, but as they do so they also implicate a third source—Brodsky himself." See Bethea, *Joseph Brodsky and the Creation of Exile,* 49. Browning's poem was included in *Antologiia novoi angliiskoi poezii,* a book with which Brodsky was familiar. See Volkov, *Conversations with Joseph Brodsky,* 129; Polukhina, *Brodskii glazami sovremennikov,* 159. On *Antologiia,* see Polukhina, "Beseda s L'vom Losevym," 165–66.

108. "Even the opening ellipsis suggests that we have already missed some of the essential presuppositions." See Wachtel, *Cambridge Introduction to Russian Poetry,* 152. Robert Graves's "Leaving the Rest Unsaid" ends in mid-sentence: "So now, my solemn ones, leaving the rest unsaid, / Rising in the air as on a gander's wing / At a careless comma," (Graves, *Complete Poems,* 126). Compare Dickinson Fr. 479: "Because I could not stop for death—." See also the destructive apotheosis of particles in Brodsky's "Only ashes know what it means to be burned out . . ." ("Tol'ko pepel znaet, chto znachit sgoret' dotla . . . ," 1986).

109. Donne, *The Complete Poems,* 207.

110. In a "de Manian" reading of Brodsky's marble imagery, the marble toga

is "oblique unveiling of the body, modesty eternalized in stone—and total impersonalization—solidification of life, a decapitated body which does not 'speak,' save through the scarcely disclosed contours of its inner self." See Nivat, "The Ironic Journey into Antiquity," 89.

111. Meilakh, "'Poet sam uznaet po temperament svoego predshestvennika . . . ,'" 283.

112. On authorial will in Brodsky, see Zholkovskii, *Bluzhdaiushchie sny i drugie raboty,* 214. On transformation into a closed and self-sufficient object of thought as Brodsky's dream, see Kiust, "Brodskii kak predmet issledovaniia," 160.

113. The implication of Brodsky's argument is that "in essence Mandelstam's art, life, and death form a single whole." See Reynolds, "Feathers and Sons," 555.

114. Eliot, *Complete Poems and Plays,* 234.

115. Blanchot, *The Gaze of Orpheus,* 7.

116. Brodsky, "Joseph Brodsky's 'Verses on the Death of T. S. Eliot,'" 196. Although these lines have been interpreted as suggesting that "while death chooses the poet, the implication is that it could have chosen his words" (Rigsbee, *Styles of Ruin,* 45), Brodsky insists that it is invariably the poet, not poetry, that is taken by death. The eternity of art "does not compensate for, but, as it were, provokes the poet's perishability." See Levinton, "Smert' poeta," 202.

117. Brodsky, *Elegy to John Donne and Other Poems,* 65.

118. This point of irony comes from Auden's "In Memory of W. B. Yeats"—"He became his admirers" (Auden, *Another Time,* 93). This line shows "Auden the proto-deconstructionist losing control over his poems." See O'Neill and Reeves, *Auden, MacNeice, Spender,* 159. "It was his last afternoon as himself" means that "he is about to become a disembodied reputation, a name in literary history." See Robinson, *Poetry, Poets, Readers,* 35.

119. The poet's language may "continue on, in time, and, dialectically, in eternity" (Beaver, "Brodsky and Kierkegaard, Language and Time," 432), but, just as importantly, language is stronger than earthly love, and the dead poet is objectified in the word. On "York," see also Beaver, *Time in the Lyric Poetry of Joseph Brodsky,* 30–31; and Sokolov, "'Brodskii=Oden.'"

120. "The price of this rise is disembodiment and transfiguration into sound, as the transformation of being into non-being, and return into being is also the transformation of sound into the word . . . In the interval between the sound of pain and the word-time there play reflections of the bird's disintegrating flesh and the former word that absorbs this body." See Plekhanova, *Preobrazhenie tragicheskogo,* 2:138.

121. Brodsky's last poem "August" ("Avgust," 1995), like ". . . And when 'the future' is uttered," avoids the first-person singular, underscores a sense of victimization through the prepositional case *u vas,* and depersonalizes the lyrical persona, "an anonymous man inhabiting a nameless setting." See Smith, "Long

Growing Dark," 253. On Brodsky's last poem as "both an elegy for the tradition and its poets and a self-elegy," see Reynolds, "Returning the Ticket," 314.

CHAPTER FOUR

1. Vvedenskii, *Polnoe sobranie sochinenii,* 2:81.
2. Kharms, *Sobranie sochinenii,* 2:40.
3. Mikhail Iampolsky explains a predilection for fragmentariness and ultrashort works by amnesiac roots of Kharms's oeuvre. Jean-Philippe Jaccard elucidates the same formal peculiarities as a problem of speech. For Jaccard, Kharms systematically disrupts the conditions of communication. He conducts "an uncompromising quest for the means to undermine his own stories, or to facilitate their self-destruction." See Cornwell, *The Absurd in Literature,* 163. On the problem of adequate self-expression in Kharms, see also Klebanov, "The Dilemma of Amnesia and Alalia." On Kharms's minimalism, see Wanner, "Russian Minimalist Prose."
4. Satunovskii, *Khochu li ia posmertnoi slavy,* 38.
5. On Vsevolod Nekrasov's minimalism, see Janecek, "Minimalism in Contemporary Russian Poetry."
6. Nekrasov, "Kak eto bylo (i est') s konceptualizmom," 8.
7. Monastyrsky, *Nebesnomu nosatomy domiku po puti v Pagan,* 17.
8. Nekrasov, "Stikhi iz zhurnala," 32.
9. Aizenberg, "In Lieu of an Introduction," 10.
10. On the dominant as "the focusing component of a work of art: it rules, determines, and transforms the remaining components," see Jakobson, *Language in Literature,* 41. Mark Lipovetsky presents Mikhail Bakhtin's theory of dialogism, along with chaos theory, as the two major conceptual models for the elucidation of Russian postmodernism. See Lipovetsky, *Russian Postmodernist Fiction,* 24.
11. Barthes, *Image, Music, Text,* 146. On alienation from language as characterizing American Language poetry, see Perloff, "Language Poetry and the Lyric Subject."
12. Rubinshtein, *Stikhi,* 58.
13. Ibid., 63.
14. Kabakov, *Zhizn' mukh,* 130.
15. Gandlevskii and Prigov, "Mezhdu imenem i imidzhem," 5.
16. For an earlier discussion of this poem, see Khagi, "Art as Aping." For a book-length study of sots art, see Balina, Condee, and Dobrenko, eds., *Endquote.* Kibirov's works from the 1990s onward are post-conceptualist. On post-conceptualism, see Mikhail Epstein, "On the Place of Postmodernism in Postmodernity," 456–68.
17. For a brief discussion of Kibirov's connections to Derzhavin in his earlier poems, see Falikov, "Glagol vremen."

18. The usage of archaisms in an ironic function has been discussed by Tynianov in "On Literary Evolution" ("O literaturnoi evoliutsii," 1927).

19. Bakhtin, *Speech Genres and Other Late Essays,* 88.

20. On the chronotope, see Morson and Emerson, *Mikhail Bakhtin,* 370; and Holquist, *Dialogism,* 110.

21. For a discussion of heterogeneous stylistic registers in Kibirov's poems other than "To Igor Pomerantsev," see Wachtel, "The Youngest Archaists," 270–86; Platt, *History in a Grotesque Key,* 171–86; Weststeijn, "Timur Kibirov," 271–72; Freidin, "A Farewell Elegy for Soviet Civilization," 123–45.

22. Bakhtin, *The Dialogic Imagination,* 291–92.

23. The full text of "To Igor Pomerantsev" can be accessed in Kibirov, *Stikhi,* 221–31. All references to Kibirov, *Stikhi* are abbreviated as (Kibirov, *Stikhi* page) and placed in the main text.

24. Tynianov, *Poetika. Istoriia literatury. Kino,* 212; Bakhtin, *The Dialogic Imagination,* 275.

25. Pushkin, *Polnoe sobranie sochinenii,* 3:318.

26. "Only the brave stormy petrel / Hovers boldly and freely / Over the gray plain of the sea" (*Tol'ko gordyi burevestnik / Reet smelo i svobodno / Nad sedoi ravninoi moria*). See Gor'kii, *Polnoe sobranie sochinenii,* 67.

27. Compare Nekrasov's "Father Frost" ("Moroz, Krasnyi Nos," 1862–64), and "In the Village" ("V derevne," 1853).

28. See, for example, Pushkin's "Demon" ("Demon," 1823): "In those days when all the impressions / Of being were new to me—/ And the girls' glances, and the murmur of the forest" (*V te dni, kogda mne byli novy / Vse vpechatlen'ia bytiia—/ I vzory dev, i shum dubrovy*) (Pushkin, *Polnoe sobranie sochinenii,* 2:299).

29. Some of Kibirov's allusions further enrich his poetry's dialogic milieu by involving second-degree intertext, the works that made these allusions in the past. For example, "Piroskaf" quotes "in its fatal space" (*v rokovom ego prostore*) a line from Iazykov's "Swimmer," which made an appearance in Chernyshevsky's *What Is to Be Done?* (*Chto delat'?* 1863). In a similar manner, "Titanic" of the same poem refers to the infamous doomed liner and the Hollywood production of the 1990s.

30. Tynianov, *Poetika. Istoriia literatury. Kino,* 198–226, 293–94.

31. Bakhtin, *The Dialogic Imagination,* 75–76.

32. Postmodern heteroglossia relates to the carnivalesque since it entails the ridicule of authorities and the erosion of hierarchies. On the carnival, see Bakhtin, *Rabelais and His World.*

33. Fokkema, *Literary History, Modernism, and Postmodernism,* 5.

34. Tynianov, *Poetika. Istoriia literatury. Kino,* 279.

35. Pushkin, *Polnoe sobranie sochinenii,* 3:217.

36. For discussions of references to Pushkin in other poems by Kibirov, see Wachtel, "The Youngest Archaists," 281; and Weststeijn, "Timur Kibirov," 272.

Russia's "first love" (Tiutchev) has been "tempered by irritation, bickering, and a desire for distance." See Sandler, *Commemorating Pushkin*, 4.

37. Major political upheavals of the twentieth century instigated a progression to more politically charged verbal skepticism as exemplified by Mandelstam's later work as well as by conceptualism. In Steiner's characterization of mass-consumer literacy, "the constant inflation of verbal counters has so devalued the once numinous act of written communication that there is almost no way for the valid and the genuinely new to make themselves heard." See Steiner, *Language and Silence*, 53.

38. Ibid., 96.

39. Steiner, *After Babel*, 241.

40. The parodic and the comic are not necessarily the same. For example, Tynianov in "Dostoevsky and Gogol" disputes a conception of the parodic genre as essentially comic. See Tynianov, *Poetika. Istoriia literatury. Kino*, 226.

41. Pushkin, *Polnoe sobranie sochinenii*, 6:71.

42. Jameson, *Postmodernism*, 17–18.

43. Ibid., 21.

44. Kibirov, "Pravila igry," 215.

45. Ibid., 224.

46. Gogol', *Polnoe sobranie sochinenii*, 6:247.

47. On poets like Aigi, Monastyrsky, Dragomoschenko, and Abdullaev "departing from Hesychasm or approaching it," see Ioffe, "Liki tishiny," 295–96.

48. Pushkin, *Polnoe sobranie sochinenii*, 3:400.

49. Jakobson, *Language in Literature*, 71; Mukařovský, *The Word and Verbal Art*, 137–38.

50. This technique also carries to the limit Pushkin's clichéd "roses-frost" (*rozy–morozy*) rhyme in *Eugene Onegin*, ch. 4, stanza 42. See Pushkin, *Polnoe sobranie sochinenii*, 6:90.

51. Kuritsyn, "3 debiuta Timura Kibirova v 1997 godu," 36.

52. Kibirov, "Ia ne veshchaiu—ia boltaiu," 12.

53. To be sure, correspondence between life and literature is not to be taken wholly for granted.

54. Tynianov, *Poetika. Istoriia literatury. Kino*, 201.

55. Bakhtin, *The Dialogic Imagination*, 69–70.

56. Epstein, "On the Place of Postmodernism in Postmodernity," 457.

57. For example, Kibirov invokes Mandelstam's "There is an unshakable cliff of values" ("Est' tsennostei nezyblemaia skala," 1914) (stanza 11), "Midnight in Moscow" (stanza 11) as well as "To German Speech" (stanza 10): "Not to ask, not to complain! Hush! Not to whine!" (Mandel'shtam 3:52); "God Nakhtigal, I am still being recruited / For new pestilences, for seven-year slaughters, / Sound has narrowed. Words hiss and rebel, / But you live, and I am calm with you" (*Bog Nakhtigal', menia eshche verbuiut / Dlia novykh chum, dlia semiletnikh*

boen. / Zvuk suzilsia. Slova shipiat, buntuiut, / No ty zhivesh', i ia s toboi spokoen) (Mandel'shtam 3:69).

58. Kibirov, "Pravila igry," 215.

59. Kibirov, "Interv'iu s Filippom Nikolaevym i Katei Kapovich," 2.

CONCLUSION

1. Shakespeare, *Hamlet,* 77.

2. Wittgenstein, *MS 108,* 277.

3. Pasternak, *Sobranie sochinenii,* 1:415.

4. Bakhtin, *Voprosy literatury i estetiki,* 110.

5. Eskin, "Of Sailors and Poets," 320.

6. Mandelstam, *The Complete Prose,* 46.

7. Brodsky, *Selected Poems,* 114.

8. These remarks do not aspire at a sustained critique of post-structuralist thought, but only at suggesting how Russian verbal skepticism diverges from modern Western verbal skepticism, and that of post-structuralist critique of logocentrism in particular.

9. De Man, *The Resistance to Theory,* 96.

10. On this issue in New Criticism, Russian formalism, and Soviet semiotics, see, for example, Boym, *Death in Quotation Marks,* 14–15, 25–26.

11. For an example of a circuitous argument resulting from an a priori acceptance of deconstructive theory, see Kamuf on de Man's *The Rhetoric of Romanticism:* "Such disruptive or defacing acts [in texts] cannot easily be attributed to a deliberate intentionality because what is at issue is the very possibility of making language submit to intention." See Kamuf, "Monumental De-Facement," 237.

12. Badiou, "Vek poetov," 15.

13. A notion likely transferred onto "The Horseshoe Finder" from Mandelstam's essays such as "End of the Novel" ("Konets romana," 1922).

14. Boym, *Death in Quotation Marks,* 10.

15. Bethea, *Joseph Brodsky and the Creation of Exile,* 11.

16. Cavanagh, *Lyric Poetry and Modern Politics,* 110. For more on the argument that "the death of the author" does not quite work in the Russian context, see Boym, *Death in Quotation Marks,* 1–36. On the Russian belief in the bond between the suffering poet and people, see Freidin, *A Coat of Many Colors,* 1–33.

17. Cavanagh, *Lyric Poetry and Modern Politics,* 111.

18. Mallarmé, *Oeuvres complètes,* 366.

19. On these features of the poem, see Staudt, "The Poetics of Black on White," 158–59; and Bruns, *Modern Poetry and the Idea of Language,* 117. Baudelaire, Rimbaud, and Mallarmé "have been treated as founders of a dis-

tinctively negative modern style. Nevertheless, the focus on style for its own sake and on language itself fights shy of the Apophatic passion for what lies beyond language." See Franke, ed., *On What Cannot Be Said,* 2:38–39. On Rimbaud's images having no grounding in reality, see Perloff, *The Poetics of Indeterminacy,* 45.

20. Derrida, *Margins of Philosophy,* 27.

21. Mallarmé, *Oeuvres complètes,* 333.

22. Barthes, *Image, Music, Text,* 147.

23. Silliman et al., "Aesthetic Tendency and the Politics of Poetry," 263.

24. Wordsworth, *Prose Writings,* 2:84; Blanchot, *Sirens' Song,* 195.

25. Derrida, "How to Avoid Speaking," 45.

26. For example, Barthes's *Pleasure of the Text* (1973) and *Roland Barthes* (1977) reconsider some of his earlier notions including the "death of the author." On the shift toward an acknowledgment of subjectivity in Barthes's and Foucault's later writings, see Boym, *Death in Quotation Marks,* 19–20. In *The Pleasure of the Text* the body of the text "gradually opens the space for the erotic figuration of the author who is 'dead as an institution' but alive as the object of the reader's desire"; in *Roland Barthes* Barthes "attempts to capture what he calls the 'unfashionable subject'—the subject 'subtracted from the book'—and the subject 'not banalized by literature.'" See Boym, *Death in Quotation Marks,* 19. "I do not know how to reverse it [my discourse], organize it, stud it with glances, quotation marks; I always speak in the first degree; I persist in a dutiful, discreet, conformist delirium, tamed and banalized by literature" suggests resistance to textualization. See Barthes, *A Lover's Discourse,* 177. On the autobiographical mode in *Roland Barthes,* see also, for example, Ungar, "RB: The Third Degree." Bennington's and Derrida's *Jacques Derrida* (1991) has Derrida's *Circumfession,* an autobiographical account modeled after Saint Augustine's *Confession,* printed along with Bennington's "Derridabase," that seeks to produce a code for Derrida's writings. Derrida falls back on the notion of singularity to resist Bennington's attempts to circumscribe him.

27. Lotman, *Kul'tura i vzryv,* 8, 37–39.

28. Ibid., 8.

29. De Man, *The Rhetoric of Romanticism,* 79.

30. Wordsworth, *Prose Writings,* 2:84. The phrase "unremittingly and noiselessly" is cited later.

31. De Man, *The Rhetoric of Romanticism,* 79.

32. Ibid., 80.

33. Ibid.

34. Boym, *Death in Quotation Marks,* 16.

35. De Man, *The Rhetoric of Romanticism,* 80. In De Man's analysis of Baudelaire's "Correspondences," "the serenity of the diction celebrates the power of tropes or 'symboles' that can reduce any conceivable difference to a

set of polarities and combine them in an endless play of substitution and amalgamation, extending from the level of signification to that of the signifier." The success of the project "can be measured by the unquestioned acceptance of a paradox such as "Vaste comme la nuit et comme la clarté," and "the seamlessness of articulation distracts attention from the poem's stitch marks and from a syntax that cannot always dissimulate semantic rupture" such as occurs "with the final 'comme' that is syntactically ambiguous: does it function as an analogy or as enumeration?" See de Man, *The Rhetoric of Romanticism,* 244. De Man's deconstructive reading of Baudelaire applies to his own "Autobiography as De-Facement.": The "power of tropes" ("is indeed like") "reduces any conceivable difference" between verbal organicity and non-organicity. The success of the project "can be measured by the unquestioned acceptance" of language as "indeed like the body, which is like its garments, the veil of the soul as the garment is the sheltering veil of the body." Lastly, "the seamlessness of articulation distracts attention from the poem's stitch marks and from a syntax that cannot always dissimulate semantic rupture." This effect occurs with "is indeed like" that is problematic as a simile that stages itself as an equation.

36. De Man, "Nietzsche's Theory of Rhetoric," 40. See also Derrida on the operative paradox: "The modality of apophasis, despite its negative and interrogative value, is often that of the sentence, verdict, or decision, of the statement." See Derrida, "Post-Scriptum," 283.

37. De Man, "The Epistemology of Metaphor," 28.

38. Ibid., 28–29.

39. De Man, *The Rhetoric of Romanticism,* 67. The compromised notions of truth and falsehood do find their way into de Man's scholarship: "The deconstruction of the self as a metaphor . . . ends in an exchange of properties that allows for their mutual persistence at the expense of literal truth." But what is "literal truth" if language as such is specular?

40. In Derrida's acknowledgment, "we cannot utter a single destructive proposition which has not already slipped into the form, the logic, and the implicit postulations of precisely what it seeks to contest." See Derrida, "Structure, Sign, and Play in the Discourse of Human Sciences," 250. Language and interpretations, however, are not uniformly authoritative.

41. Complex idiom, for example, prompts Culler's paraphrase of "the asymmetry of the binary model that opposes the figural to the proper meaning of the figure" as one "that opposes the figural to the literal." See Culler, *On Deconstruction,* 148. This is a helpful gloss, but what exactly is "the proper meaning of the figure" in its opposition to the "figural"?

42. That deconstructive procedures are too predictable is a charge frequently advanced by critics. See, for example, Ellis, *Against Deconstruction,* 137–52; and Wellek, "The New Nihilism in Literary Studies," 82–83. On the ways deconstruction restates familiar tenets of the language crisis in the most polemical way pos-

sible, see, for example, Ellis, *Against Deconstruction,* 37–39, 67–96, 157. For other critiques of deconstruction, see Jameson, *The Prison House of Language;* Graff, *Literature against Itself* and "Deconstruction as Dogma." For possible misreadings of deconstruction, see Rapaport, *The Theory Mess.*

43. Deconstructive critics such as Jonathan Culler, J. Hillis Miller, and Barbara Johnson modulate some of the earlier statements. For Johnson the deconstructive method means "a teasing out of warring forces of signification within the text." See Johnson, *The Critical Difference,* 5. Culler claims in his preface to the twenty-fifth anniversary edition of *On Deconstruction* that the text is not deconstructed by the critic but deconstructs itself. More precisely, the text "does not just contain or perform a self-deconstruction but is about self-deconstruction, so that a deconstructive reading is an interpretation of the text, an analysis of what it says or means." See Culler, *The Pursuit of Signs,* 17. The shift, according to Culler, is inaugurated in de Man's critique of Derrida's reading of Rousseau ("The Rhetoric of Blindness") where, as de Man argues, Rousseau's text itself carries out the deconstructive operations which Derrida claims to perform on it. In his own analysis of apostrophic poems, Culler maintains that these poems "display in various ways awareness of the difficulties of what they purport to seek." See Culler, *The Pursuit of Signs,* 144. For Miller, the dismantling is not performed "from the outside by the critic on a piece of language which remains innocently mystified about its own status . . . The 'unreadability' is always thematized in the text in the form of metalinguistic statements." See Miller, *Theory Now and Then,* 108. Culler also notes that de Man's writing is "striking in its emphasis on truth and error; there is no question to stand out above or outside the play of truth and falsity and pluralistically allow each competing view a validity of sorts." See Culler, *On Deconstruction,* 274. Miller concedes that "words are not, strictly speaking, mad. People are mad. The phrase is a prosopopeia . . . It is the one trope he [de Man] cannot expunge from his own work." See Miller, *Others,* 228.

44. On the fate of Tiutchev's citations in Dostoevsky's novels, see Gacheva, "'Silentium!' F. I. Tiutcheva v khudozhestvennom mire F. M. Dostoevskogo," 15–16.

45. On the Grand Inquisitor and Christ's silence, silence in *The Cherry Orchard,* and Gogol's negative aesthetics, see Epshtein, *Slovo i molchanie,* 194, and 106–32.

46. Kandinskii, *O dukhovnom v iskusstve,* 96; Malevich, *Essays on Art,* 111.

Bibliography

Abrams, Meyer, *The Mirror and the Lamp: Romantic Theory and the Critical Tradition* (Oxford, 1953).

Adorno, Theodor, *Aesthetic Theory*, ed. Gretel Adorno and Rolf Tiedemann (London, 1984).

Aizenberg, Mikhail, "In Lieu of an Introduction," *Russian Studies in Literature: A Journal of Translations* 29, no. 4 (Fall 1993): 8–24.

———, "The Possibility of Expression," *Russian Studies in Literature: A Journal of Translations* 32, no. 2 (Spring 1996): 67–81.

———, "Vmesto predisloviia," in *Ponedel'nik: Sem' poetov samizdata*, 7–26 (Moscow, 1990).

Aizlewood, Robin, "Fet on Tiutchev," in *Russian Writers on Russian Writers*, ed. and intro. Faith Wigzell, intro. Robin Aizlewood, 15–25 (Oxford, 1994).

Aizlewood, Robin, and Diana Maiers, eds., *Stoletie Mandel'shtama: Materialy simpoziuma* (Tenafly, N.J., 1994).

Akhapkin, Denis, "'Filologicheskaia metafora' v poetike Iosifa Brodskogo," *Russkaia Filologiia* 9 (1998): 228–38.

———, "Iosif Brodskii: *Glagoly*," in *Poetika Iosifa Brodskogo: Sbornik nauchnykh trudov*, ed. Valentina Polukhina, I. V. Fomenko, and A. G. Stepanov, 28–38 (Tver', Russia, 2003).

———, "Iosif Brodskii: Poeziia grammatiki," in *Iosif Brodskii i mir: Metafizika, antichnost', sovremennost'*, ed. Iakov Gordin and Irina Murav'eva, 269–75 (St. Petersburg, 2000).

———, *Iosif Brodskii posle Rossii: Kommentarii k stikham 1972–1995* (St. Petersburg, 2009).

Akhmatova, Anna, *Sobranie sochinenii v shesti tomakh* (Moscow, 1998–2002).

Allen, Elizabeth Cheresh, *A Fallen Idol Is Still a God: Lermontov and the Quandaries of Cultural Transition* (Stanford, Calif., 2007).

An Age Ago: A Selection of Nineteenth-Century Russian Poetry, trans. Alan Myers, foreword and notes Joseph Brodsky (New York, 1988).

Andrew, Joe, and Robert Reid, eds., *Neo-Formalist Papers: Contributions to the Silver Jubilee Conference to Mark 25 Years of the Neo-Formalist Circle* (Amsterdam, 1998).

Annenskii, Innokentii, *Knigi otrazhenii,* ed. N. Ashimbaeva et al. (Moscow, 1979).

Annensky, Innokenty, "On Contemporary Lyricism," in *The Russian Symbolists: An Anthology of Critical and Theoretical Writings,* ed. and trans. Ronald Peterson, 127–42 (Ann Arbor, Mich., 1980).

Antologiia novoi angliiskoi poezii, intro. M. Gutner (Leningrad, 1937).

Appelbaum, Stanley, ed., *English Romantic Poetry: An Anthology* (Mineola, N.Y., 1996).

Artemova, S., "O zhanre pis'ma v poezii I. Brodskogo," in *Poetika Iosifa Brodskogo: Sbornik nauchnykh trudov,* ed. Valentina Polukhina, I. V. Fomenko, and A. G. Stepanov, 128–38 (Tver', Russia, 2003).

Atanaszova-Szokolova, Denise, Anna Han, and A. Hollós, eds., *Sub Rosa: Koszonto konyv Lena Szilard tiszteletere* (Budapest, 2005).

Auden, W. H., *Another Time* (New York, 1940).

Augustine, Saint, *De Doctrina Christiana: A Select Library of the Nicene and Post-Nicene Fathers of the Christian Church* (Grand Rapids, Mich., 1974).

Averintsev, Sergei, "Rannii Mandel'shtam," *Znamya* 4 (1990): 207–12.

———, *Sud'ba i vest' Osipa Mandel'shtama,* in *Sobranie sochinenii v dvukh tomakh,* by Osip Mandel'shtam (Moscow, 1990).

Averintsev, Sergei, and Rosemarie Ziegler, eds., *Viacheslav Ivanov i ego vremia: Materialy VII mezhdunarodnogo simpoziuma, Vena 1998* (Frankfurt, 2002).

Badiou, Alain, "Vek poetov," *Novoe literaturnoe obozrenie* 63 (2003): 11–23.

Baines, Jennifer, *Mandelstam: The Later Poetry* (Cambridge, Eng., 1976).

Bakhtin, Mikhail, *Art and Answerability: Early Philosophical Essays,* ed. Michael Holquist and Vadim Liapunov (Austin, Tex., 1990).

———, *The Dialogic Imagination: Four Essays,* ed. Michael Holquist, trans. Caryl Emerson and Michael Holquist (Austin, Tex., 1981).

———, *Iz chernovykh tetradei,* ed. Vadim Kozhinov (Moscow, 1992).

———, *Rabelais and His World,* trans. Hélène Iswolsky (Bloomington, Ind., 1984).

———, *Speech Genres and Other Late Essays,* ed. Caryl Emerson and Michael Holquist, trans. Vern W. McGee (Austin, Tex., 1986).

———, *Voprosy literatury i estetiki: Issledovaniia raznykh let,* ed. S. Leibovich (Moscow, 1975).

Balina, Marina, Nancy Condee, and Evgeny Dobrenko, eds., *Endquote: Sots-Art Literature and Soviet Grand Style* (Evanston, Ill., 2000).

Bal'mont, Konstantin, *Stikhotvoreniia,* intro. and commentaries V. Orlov (Leningrad, 1969).

Baran, Kh., et al., eds., *Stikh. Iazyk. Poeziia. Pamiati Mikhaila Leonidovicha Gasparova* (Moscow, 2006).

Baratynskii, Evgenii, *Polnoe sobranie stikhotvorenii v 2 tomakh,* ed. and commentaries E. Kupriianova and I. Medvedeva, intro. D. Mirskii (Leningrad, 1936).

Barthes, Roland. *Image, Music, Text,* trans. Stephen Heath (New York, 1977).
———, *A Lover's Discourse: Fragments,* trans. Richard Howard (London, 1990).
———, *The Pleasure of the Text,* trans. Richard Miller (New York, 1975).
———, *Roland Barthes / by Roland Barthes,* trans. Richard Howard (London, 1977).
Baschmakoff, Natalia, "V prostranstve do mira," *Studia Slavica Finlandensia* 16, no. 1 (1999): 30–42.
Bataille, Georges. *Inner Experience,* trans. and intro. Leslie Anne Boldt (Albany, N.Y., 1988).
Batiushkov, Konstantin, *Nechto o poete i poezii,* ed., intro., and commentaries V. A. Koshelev (Moscow, 1985).
———, *Polnoe sobranie stikhotvorenii,* intro., ed., and commentaries N. V. Fridman (Moscow, 1964).
Batkin, Leonid, *Tridtsat' tret'ia bukva: Zametki chitatelia na poliakh stikhov Iosifa Brodskogo* (Moscow, 1996).
Baudelaire, Charles, *Oeuvres complètes,* intro. and commentaries Y.-G. Le Dantec, ed. and rev. Claude Pichois (Paris, 1961).
Baudrillard, Jean, *Simulations,* trans. Paul Foss, Paul Patton, and Philip Beitchman (New York, 1983).
Beaujour, Elizabeth, *Alien Tongues: Bilingual Russian Writers of the "First" Emigration* (Ithaca, N.Y., 1989).
Beaver, Aaron, "Brodsky and Kierkegaard, Language and Time," *Russian Review* 67, no. 3 (July 2008): 415–37.
———, "Lyricism and Philosophy in Brodsky's Elegiac Verse," *Slavic Review* 67, no. 3 (Fall 2008): 591–609.
———, *Time in the Lyric Poetry of Joseph Brodsky.* Dissertation Abstracts International, April 2004, http:// gateway.proquest.com.
Beckett, Samuel, *The Beckett Trilogy: Molloy, Malone Dies, The Unnamable* (London, 1979).
Belinskii, Vissarion, *Polnoe sobranie sochinenii v 13 tomakh* (Moscow, 1953–59).
Bel'skaia, L. L., "'Chast' rechi' Iosifa Brodskogo," *Russkaia rech'* 1 (1998): 21–27.
Belov, Andrei, "Tiutchevskoe 'kak by' v svete fenomena pretsedentnosti ("Tiutchev's 'kak by' as a Phenomenon of Precedency"), *Russian, Croatian and Serbian, Czech and Slovak, Polish Literature* 64, no. 2 (Aug. 2008): 157–65.
Belyi, Andrei, *Simvolizm* (Moscow, 1910).
Bennington, Geoffrey, and Jacques Derrida, *Jacques Derrida* (Chicago, 1999).
Berenshtein, E., "Iosif Brodskii i problema tragicheskogo," in *Poetika Iosifa Brodskogo: Sbornik nauchnykh trudov,* ed. Valentina Polukhina, I. V. Fomenko, and A. G. Stepanov, 95–106 (Tver', Russia, 2003).
Berlin, Isaiah, *The Hedgehog and the Fox: An Essay on Tolstoy's View of History* (New York, 1953).
Bethea, David, *Joseph Brodsky and the Creation of Exile* (Princeton, N.J., 1994).

———, "To My Daughter," in *Joseph Brodsky: The Art of a Poem,* ed. Lev Loseff and Valentina Polukhina, 240–57 (New York, 1999).

Blagoi, Dmitrii, "Mir kak krasota," in Afanasii Fet, *Vechernie ogni,* ed. D. D. Blagoi and M. A. Sokolova (Moscow, 1971).

Blanchot, Maurice, *The Gaze of Orpheus, and Other Literary Essays,* pref. Geoffrey Hartman, trans. Lydia Davis, ed. P. Adams Sitney (New York, 1981).

———, *Sirens' Song: Selected Essays,* ed. and intro. Gabriel Iosipovichi, trans. Sasha Rabinovitch (Bloomington, Ind., 1982).

Blans, Bert, "Cloud of Unknowing: An Orientation in Negative Theology from Dionysus the Areopagite, Eckhart, and John of the Cross to Modernity," in *Flight of the Gods: Philosophical Perspectives on Negative Theology,* ed. Ilse von Bulhof and Laurens ten Kate, 58–77 (New York, 2000).

Blodgett, E. D., and H. G. Coward, eds., *Silence, the Word, and the Sacred* (Calgary, 1989).

Blok, Aleksandr, *Sobranie sochinenii v vos'mi tomakh,* ed. V. N. Orlov, A. A. Surkov, and K. I. Chukovskii (Moscow, 1960–63).

Bloom, Harold, ed., *Romanticism and Consciousness: Essays in Criticism* (New York, 1970).

Boker, Uwe, "'A Raid on the Inarticulate': Hawthorne, Hopkins, and Hofmannsthal," in *Self-Reflexivitiy in Literature,* ed. Werner Huber, Martin Middeke, and Huber Zapf, 75–85 (Würzburg, 2005).

Bocharov, Sergei, *Siuzhety russkoi literatury* (Moscow, 1999).

Bogomolov, Nikolai, and John Malmstad, "U istokov tvorchestva Mikhaila Kuz'mina," *Voprosy Literatury* 3 (1993): 64–121.

Botkin, Vasily, "A. A. Fet," *Russian Literature Triquaterly* 17 (1982): 23–60.

Boym, Svetlana, *Death in Quotation Marks: Cultural Myths of the Modern Poet* (Cambridge, Mass., 1991).

———, "Dialogue as 'Lyrical Hermaphrodism': Mandelstam's Challenge to Bakhtin," *Slavic Review* 50, no. 1 (Spring 1991): 118–26.

Brinkley, Tony, and Raina Kostova, "Posthumous Writing: Mandelstam's Poetics," *Modernism / Modernity* 15, no. 4 (2008): 745–59.

Briusov, Valerii, *Sobranie sochinenii v semi tomakh* (Moscow, 1973–75).

Brodskii, Iosif, *Bol'shaia kniga interv'iu,* ed. V. Polukhina (Moscow, 2000).

———, *Chast' rechi: Izbrannye stikhi 1962–1989* (Moscow, 1990).

———, "A Part of Speech," *Poetry* (March 1978): 311–20.

———, *Sochineniia Iosifa Brodskogo,* ed. G. F. Komarov (St. Petersburg, 1997–2001).

Brodsky, Joseph, *The Academy of American Poets,* intro. and trans. Mark Strand (Donnell Library Center, New York Public Library).

———, *Collected Poems in English,* ed. Ann Kjellberg (New York, 2000).

———, *Elegy to John Donne and Other Poems,* sel., trans., and intro. Nicholas Bethell (London, 1967).

———, "Elegy to W. H. Auden," *New York Review of Books* 21, no. 20 (Dec. 12, 1974).

———, *Joseph Brodsky: Conversations,* ed. Cynthia L. Haven (Jackson, Miss., 2002).

———, "Joseph Brodsky's 'Verses on the Death of T. S. Eliot,'" trans. and intro. George Kline, *Russian Review* 27, no. 2 (1968): 195–98.

———, *Less Than One: Selected Essays* (New York, 1986).

———, "Nobel Lecture, 1987," in *Brodsky's Poetics and Aesthetics,* ed. Lev Loseff and Valentina Polukhina, 3–11 (New York, 1990).

———, *On Grief and Reason: Essays* (New York, 1995).

———, "Preface," in Andrei Platonov, *The Foundation Pit,* trans. Thomas P. Whitney, pref. Joseph Brodsky (Ann Arbor, Mich., 1973): ix–xii.

———, *Selected Poems,* trans. George Kline, foreword W. H. Auden (New York, 1973).

Broitman, S. and Kim Ien Kim, "O prirode khudozhestvennoi real'nosti v tsikle I. Brodskogo 'Chast' rechi'," in *Poetika Iosifa Brodskogo: Sbornik nauchnykh,* ed. Valentina Polukhina, I. V. Fomenko, and A. G. Stepanov, 329–42 (Tver', Russia, 2003).

Brooks, Cleanth, *The Well-Wrought Urn: Studies in the Structure of Poetry* (New York, 1968).

Brown, Clarence, *Mandelstam* (Cambridge, Eng., 1973).

Brown, Edward, *A History of Russian Literature of the Romantic Period,* vol. 4 (Ardis, Mich., 1986).

Browning, Robert, *The Complete Poetic Works of Browning* (Boston, 1960).

Broyde, Steven, *Osip Mandelstam and His Age: A Commentary on the Themes of War and Revolution in the Poetry 1913–1923* (Cambridge, Mass., 1975).

Bruns, Gerald, *Modern Poetry and the Idea of Language: A Critical and Historical Study* (Urbana-Champaign, Ill., 2001).

Budick, Sanford, and Wolfgang Iser, eds., *Languages of the Unsayable: The Play of Negativity in Literature and Literary Theory* (New York, 1989).

Bukhshtab, Boris, "A. A. Fet," in *Polnoe sobranie stikhotvorenii,* by Afanasii Fet (Leningrad, 1959).

Bulhof, Ilse von, and Laurens ten Kate, eds., *Flight of the Gods: Philosophical Perspectives on Negative Theology* (New York, 2000).

Burnett, Leon, "The Complicity of the Real: Affinities in the Poetics of Brodsky and Mandelstam," in *Brodsky's Poetics and Aesthetics,* ed. Lev Loseff and Valentina Polukhina, 12–33 (New York, N.Y., 1990).

———, "Galatea Encore," in *Joseph Brodsky: The Art of a Poem,* ed. Lev Loseff and Valentina Polukhina, 150–76 (New York, 1999).

Byron, George Gordon, *Childe Harold's Pilgrimage,* ed. William Rolfe (Boston, 1886).

Calvino, Italo, *Invisible Cities,* trans. William Weaver (New York, 1974).

Caputo, John, *The Prayers and Tears of Jacques Derrida: Religion Without Religion* (Bloomington, Ind., 1997).
Carabine, Deidre, *The Unknown God: Negative Theology in the Platonic Tradition: Plato to Eriugena* (Louvain, Belg., 1995).
Cassedy, Steven, *Flight from Eden: The Origins of Modern Literary Criticism and Theory* (Berkeley, Calif., 1990).
———, "Pavel Florenskij's Philosophy of Language: Its Contextuality and Its Context," *Slavic and East European Journal* 35, no. 4 (Winter 1991): 537–52.
Cavanagh, Clare, *Lyric Poetry and Modern Politics: Russia, Poland, and the West* (New Haven, Conn., 2009).
———, *Osip Mandelstam and the Modernist Creation of Tradition* (Princeton, N.J., 1995).
Caws, Mary Anne, ed., *Russian Writers Since 1980* (Detroit, Mich., 2004).
Celan, Paul, *Collected Prose,* trans. Rosemarie Waldrop (Manchester, Eng., 1986).
———, *Gesammelte Werke in fünf Bänden,* ed. Beda Allemann and Stefan Reichert, asst. Rudolf Bücher (Frankfurt am Main, Ger., 1983).
Chekhov, Anton, *Polnoe sobranie sochinenii i pisem v 30 t,* ed. N. F. Bel'chikov et al. (Moscow, 1974–82).
Chernyshevskii, Nikolai, *Polnoe sobranie sochinenii v piatnadtsati tomakh,* ed. V. Kirpotin (Moscow, 1939–53).
Chizhevsky, Dmitry, *History of Russian Literature from the Eleventh Century to the End of the Baroque* (The Hague, Neth., 1971).
Christiansen, Keith, *Italian Painting* (Peking, 1992).
Chudakova, Marietta et al., eds., *Tynianovskii sbornik: Tret'i tynianovskie chteniia* (Riga, Latvian S.S.R., 1988).
Coates, Paul, *Words After Speech: A Comparative Study of Romanticism and Symbolism* (New York, 1986).
Coetzee, J. M., "Osip Mandelstam and the Stalin Ode," *Representations* 35 (Summer 1991): 72–83.
Coleridge, Samuel, *Coleridge's Miscellaneous Criticism,* ed. Thomas Raysor (London, 1936).
———, *The Collected Works of Samuel Taylor Coleridge,* ed. Kathleen Coburn (Princeton, N.J., 1983).
Cooke, Raymond, *Velimir Khlebnikov: A Critical Study* (Cambridge, Eng., 1987).
Cornwell, Neil, *The Absurd in Literature* (Manchester, Eng., 2006).
Coward, Howard, and Tobey Foshay, eds., *Derrida and Negative Theology* (Albany, N.Y., 1992).
Culler, Jonathan, *On Deconstruction: Theory and Criticism after Structuralism,* 25th anniversary edition (Ithaca, N.Y., 2007).
———, "On the Negativity of Modern Poetry: Friedrich, Baudelaire, and the Critical Tradition," in *Languages of the Unsayable: The Play of Negativity*

in Literature and Literary Theory, ed. Sanford Budick and Wolfgang Iser, 189–208 (New York, 1989).

———, *The Pursuit of Signs: Semiotics, Literature, Deconstruction,* augmented edition, with a new preface by J. Culler (Ithaca, N.Y., 2002).

Dante, *Dante Alighieri's Divine Comedy,* vol. 5, *Paradise,* trans. and commentaries Mark Musa (Bloomington, Ind., 2004).

Davidson, Pamela, "The Moral Dimension of the Prophetic Ideal: Pushkin and His Readers," *Slavic Review* 61, no. 3 (Fall 2002): 490–518.

———, *The Poetic Imagination of Viacheslav Ivanov* (Cambridge, Eng., 1989).

Day, Jennifer, "The Optics of Memory in Brodsky's 'Fifth Eclogue,'" *Russian, Croatian, and Serbian, Czech and Polish Literature* 62, no. 1 (July 2007): 23–48.

Derrida, Jacques, "How to Avoid Speaking: Denials," in *Languages of the Unsayable: The Play of Negativity in Literature and Literary Theory,* ed. Sanford Budick and Wolfgang Iser, 3–70 (New York, 1989).

———, *Limited Inc.* (Evanston, Ill., 1988).

———, *Margins of Philosophy,* trans. and notes Alan Bass (Chicago, 1972).

———, *Of Grammatology,* trans. Gayatri Chakravorty Spivak (Baltimore, 1976).

———, *On The Name,* ed. Thomas Dutoit, trans. David Wood, John P. Leavey, Jr., and Ian McLeod (Stanford, Calif., 1995).

———, "Post-Scriptum: Aporias, Ways, and Voices," in *Derrida and Negative Theology,* ed. Howard Coward and Tobey Foshay, 283–323 (Albany, N.Y., 1992).

———, "Structure, Sign, and Play in the Discourse of Human Sciences," in *The Structuralist Controversy: The Languages of Criticism and the Sciences of Man,* ed. Richard Macksey and Eugenio Donato, 247–64 (Baltimore, 1972).

Derzhavin, Gavriil, *Sochineniia,* ed. V. P. Stepanov and G. P. Makogonenko (Leningrad, 1987).

Dickinson, Emily, *The Complete Poems of Emily Dickinson,* ed. Thomas H. Johnson (Boston, 1951).

Doherty, Justin, *The Acmeist Movement in Russian Poetry: Culture and the Word* (Oxford, 1995).

Donne, John, *The Complete Poems of John Donne,* ed. Roger E. Bennett (New York, 1949).

Dostoevskii, Fedor, *Polnoe sobranie sochinenii v 30–ti t.,* ed. V. G. Bazanov et al. (Leningrad, 1972–90).

Duganov, Rudol'f, *Velimir Khlebnikov: Priroda tvorchestva* (Moscow, 1990).

Edmond, Jacob, "From Pathos to Parody: Ambivalent Antithesis and Echoes of 'Vykhozhu odin ia na dorogu' in 'Obraz tvoi muchitel'nyi i zybkii' and 'Zolotoi' from Osip Mandel'shtam's *Kamen',*" *Russian, Croatian and Serbian, Czech and Slovak, Polish Literature* 58, no. 3–4 (2005): 353–73.

Eikhenbaum, Boris, *Melodika russkogo liricheskogo stikha* (Leipzig, 1973).

Eliot, T. S., *Complete Poems and Plays* (New York, 1952).

———, *The Sacred Wood : Essays on Poetry and Criticism* (New York, 1932).

Ellis, John M., *Against Deconstruction* (Princeton, N.J., 1989).

Emerson, Caryl, "Jurij Lotman's Last Book and Filiations with Bakhtin," *Welt der Slaven: Halbjahresschrift für Slavistik* 48, no. 2 (2003): 201–16.

Epifanii, *Zhitie sv. Stefana, episkopa Permskogo,* intro Dmitry Chizhevsky (The Hague, Neth., 1959).

Epshtein, Mikhail, *Slovo i molchanie: Metafizika russkoi literatury* (Moscow, 2006).

———, "Slovo i molchanie v russkoi kul'ture," *Zvezda* 10 (2005): 202–22.

Epstein, Mikhail. "Like a Corpse in the Desert: Dehumanization in the New Moscow Poetry," in *Russian Postmodernism: New Perspectives on Post-Soviet Culture,* ed. and trans. Mikhail Epstein, Alexander A. Genis, and Slobodanka M. Vladiv-Glover, intro. Thomas Epstein, 134–44 (New York, 1999).

———, "On the Place of Postmodernism in Postmodernity," *Russian Postmodernism: New Perspectives on Post-Soviet Culture,* ed. and trans. Mikhail Epstein, Alexander A. Genis, and Slobodanka M. Vladiv-Glover, intro. Thomas Epstein, 456–68 (New York, 1999).

Epstein, Mikhail, Alexander A. Genis, and Slobodanka M. Vladiv-Glover, eds., *Russian Postmodernism: New Perspectives on Post-Soviet Culture* (New York, 1999).

Eskin, Michael, *Ethics and Dialogue in the Works of Levinas, Bakhtin, Mandel'shtam, and Celan* (Oxford, 2000).

———, "Of Sailors and Poets: On Celan, Grunbein, and Brodsky," *German Life and Letters* 60, no. 3 (July 2007): 315–28.

———, *Poetic Affairs: Celan, Grunbein, Brodsky* (Stanford, Calif., 2008).

———, "Who Is Speaking? Brodsky, Heidegger, Wittgenstein, and the Question of Genre," in *Literature and Philosophy: A Guide to Contemporary Debates,* ed. David Rudrum, 163–69 (London, 2006).

Etkind, Efim, *"Vnutrennii chelovek" i vneshniaia rech': Ocherki psikhopoetiki russkoi literatury XVIII-XIX vv* (Moscow, 1999).

Evtushenko, Evgenii, *Pervoe sobranie sochinenii v vos'mi tomakh,* ed. and commentaries Evgenii Evtushenko (Moscow, 1997).

Fagan, Deidre, "Emily Dickinson's Unutterable Word," *Emily Dickinson Journal* 14, no. 2 (2005): 70–75.

Falikov, Il'ia, "Glagol vremen: G. Derzhavin i T. Kibirov: Opyt parallel'nogo prochteniia," *Literaturnaia gazeta* 42, no. 5522 (Oct. 19, 1994).

Fedotov, Georgy, *The Russian Religious Mind* (Cambridge, Mass., 1966).

Felch, Susan M., and Paul J. Contino, eds., *Bakhtin and Religion: A Feeling for Faith* (Evanston, Ill., 2001).

Fet, Afanasii, *Polnoe sobranie stikhotvorenii,* ed., intro., and commentaries B. Bukhshtab (Leningrad, 1959).

Fioretos, Aris, ed., *Readings of Paul Celan* (Baltimore, 1994).

Fish, Stanley, *Is There a Text in This Class? The Authority of Interpretive Communities* (Cambridge, Mass., 1980).

Fisher, Kuno, *Istoriia noveishei filosofii*, vol. 6, *Artur Shopengauer* (St. Petersburg, 1905–10).

Fleishman, Lazar', *Ot Pushkina k Pasternaku: Izbrannye raboty po poetike i istorii russkoi literatury* (Moscow, 2006).

Florenskii, Pavel, *The Pillar and the Ground of the Truth*, trans. Boris Yakim, intro. Richard Gustafson (Princeton, N.J., 1990).

———, *Stolp i utverzhdenie istiny* (Moscow, 1914).

———, *U vodorazdelov mysli* (Moscow, 1990).

Foakes, R. A., ed., *Romantic Criticism 1800–1850* (London, 1968).

Fokkema, Douwe, *Literary History, Modernism, and Postmodernism* (Philadelphia, 1984).

Fomenko, I. V., et al., "Opyt rekonstruktsii mirooshchushcheniia I. Brodskogo ('Chast' rechi')," in *Poetika Iosifa Brodskogo. Sbornik nauchnykh trudov*, ed. Valentina Polukhina, I. V. Fomenko, and A. G. Stepanov, 343–54 (Tver', Russia, 2003).

Foucault, Michel, *Language, Counter-Memory, Practice*, ed. and intro. Donald Bouchard, trans. Donald Bouchard and Sherry Simon (Ithaca, N.Y., 1977).

———, *The Order of Things: An Archaeology of the Human Sciences* (New York, 1973).

Fraize, Mattias, and Ulrike Zailer, "Paradoks kak oruzhie poezii dlia osvobozhdeniia iz tiur'my dvoinoi sviazi. Vklad v teoriiu psikhodiakhronologii," in *Paradoksy russkoi literatury: Sbornik statei*, 42–53 (St. Petersburg, 2001).

Frank, Semyon, *The Unknowable: An Ontological Introduction to the Philosophy of Religion*, trans. Boris Jakim (Athens, Ohio, 1983).

Franke, William, "Blind Prophecy: Milton's Figurative Mode in *Paradise Lost*," in *Through a Glass Darkly: Essays in the Religious Imagination*, ed. John C. Hawley, 87–103 (New York, 1996).

———, ed., *On What Cannot Be Said: Apophatic Discourses in Philosophy, Religion, Literature, and the Arts*, vol. 1, *Classic Formulations*, vol. 2, *Modern and Contemporary Transformations* (Notre Dame, Ind., 2007).

———, "The Singular and the Other at the Limits of Language in the Apophatic Poetics of Edmond Jabes and Paul Celan," *New Literary History* 36 (2005): 621–38.

Freeman, Kathleen, *Ancilla to the Pre-Socratic Philosophers* (Cambridge, Mass., 1957).

Freidin, Gregory, *A Coat of Many Colors: Osip Mandelstam and His Mythologies of Self-Presentation* (Berkeley, Calif., 1987).

———, "A Farewell Elegy for Soviet Civilization," in *Endquote: Sots-Art Literature and Soviet Grand Style*, ed. Marina Balina, Nancy Condee, and Evgeny Dobrenko, 123–45 (Evanston, Ill., 2000).

Freise, Mattias, "'Ne ver' sebe'—a komu zhe verit'? (Oratorskaia lirika Lermontova)," *Russian, Croatian and Serbian, Czech and Slovak, Polish Literature* 38, no. 3 (1995): 259–72.

Frolov, Dmitrii, *O rannikh stikhakh Osipa Mandel'shtama* (Moscow, 2009).

Frolov, N. K., ed., *Slavianskie dukhovnye tsennosti na rubezhe vekov* (Tyumen, Russ., 2001).

———, *Slavianskie istoki slovesnosti i kul'tury v Zapadnoi Sibiri,* vol. 2 (Tyumen, Russ., 2001).

Gacheva, Anastasiia, "'Silentium!' F. I. Tiutcheva v khudozhestvennom mire F. M. Dostoevskogo," *Russkaia rech'* 5 (2001): 14–25.

Gandlevskii, Sergei and Dmitrii Prigov, "Mezhdu imenem i imidzhem," *Literaturnaia gazeta* (May 12, 1993), no. 19: 5.

Garber, Marjorie, "'The Rest Is Silence': Ineffability and the 'Unscene' in Shakespeare's Plays," in *Ineffability: Naming the Unnamable from Dante to Beckett,* ed. Peter Hawkins and Anne Howland Schotter, 35–50 (New York, 1984).

Gasparov, Boris, "The Iron Age of the 1930s: The Centennial Return in Mandelstam," in *Rereading Russian Poetry,* ed. Stephanie Sandler, 78–103 (New Haven, Conn., 1999).

Gasparov, Boris, Robert Hughes, and Irina Paperno, eds., *Cultural Mythologies of Russian Modernism: From the Golden Age to the Silver Age* (Berkeley, Calif., 1992).

Gasparov, Mikhail, *Izbannye trudy, Tom III, O stikhe* (Moscow, 1997).

———, "Kommentarii," in *Stikhotvoreniia: Proza,* by Osip Mandel'shtam (Moscow, 2001).

———, "O. Mandel'shtam: 'Sumerki svobody': Opyt akademicheskogo kommentariia," *Izvestiia AN. Seriia literatury i iazyka* 58, no. 5–6 (1999): 3–9.

———, *Ocherk istorii russkogo stikha* (Moscow, 2000).

———, "Poet i kul'tura: Tri poetiki Osipa Mandel'shtama," in *Polnoe sobranie stikhotvorenii,* by Osip Mandel'shtam, 5–64 (St. Petersburg, 1997).

Gasparov, Mikhail, and Omry Ronen, "Pokhorony solntsa v Peterburge: O dvukh teatral'nykh stikhotvoreniiakh Mandel'shtama," *Zvezda* 5 (2003): 207–19.

Genova, Pamela, ed. and intro., *Twayne Companion to Contemporary World Literature: From the Editors of World Literature Today* (New York, 2003), 1066–71.

Gershtein, Emma, *Novoe o Mandel'shtame* (Paris, 1986).

Ghidini, Maria C., "Zvuk i smysl: Nekotorye zamechaniia po teme glossolalii u Viacheslava Ivanova," in *Viacheslav Ivanov i ego vremia: Materialy VII mezhdunarodnogo simpoziuma,* ed. Sergei Averintsev and Rosemarie Ziegler, 65–81 (Frankfurt am Main, 2002).

Gibson, Walker, *The Limits of Language* (New York, 1962).

Gillespie, Alyssa, "Joseph Brodsky (Iosif Aleksandrovich Brodsky)," in *Russian Writers Since 1980,* ed. Mary Anne Caws, 17–39 (Detroit, 2004).

Ginsberg, Allen, *Collected Poems* (Orono, Maine, 1992).

Ginzburg, Elizabeth, "F. I. Tiutchev: Variatsii na temu 'bessonnitsy nochnoi' (F. I. Tiutchev: Variation on the Theme of 'Nocturnal Insomnia')," *Russian, Croatian and Serbian, Czech and Slovak, Polish Literature* 66, no. 1 (2009): 1–35.

Ginzburg, Lidiia, *O lirike* (Leningrad, 1964).

———, *O lirike. 2–e, rasshirennoe izdanie* (Moscow, 1997).

———, *Tvorcheskii put' Lermontova* (Leningrad, 1940).

Girivenko, A. N., and Charysheva, I. R., "Angliiskie versii stikhotvoreniia F. Tiutcheva 'Silentium!' kak perevodcheskii kommentarii," *Russian, Croatian and Serbian, Czech and Slovak, Polish Literature* 57, no. 1–2 (2005): 25–41.

Glazova, Anna, "Poetry of Bringing About Presence: Paul Celan Translates Osip Mandelstam," *MLN* 123, no. 5 (December 2008): 1108–26.

———, "Vozdushno-kamennyi Kristal: Tselan i Mandel'shtam," *Novoe literaturnoe obozrenie* 63, no. 5 (2003): 83–100.

Glazov-Corrigan, Elena, *Mandelstam's Poetics: A Challenge to Postmodernism* (Toronto, 2000).

Glazunova, Olga, *Iosif Brodskii: Amerikanskii dnevnik: O stikhotvoreniiakh, napisannykh v emigratsii* (St. Petersburg, 2005).

Glushko, Anastasiia, "Lingvoditseia Iosifa Brodskogo," in *Iosif Brodskii: Tvorchestvo, lichnost', sud'ba,* ed. Iakov Gordin, 143–44 (St. Petersburg, 1998).

Gogol', Nikolai, *Polnoe sobranie sochinenii v 14 t,* ed. N. L. Meshcheriakov (Moscow, 1937–52).

Goldberg, Stuart, "Christianity and Romanticism in Tjutcev's 'Pevuchest' est' v morskich volnach'," in *Russian, Croatian and Serbian, Czech and Slovak, Polish Literature* 64, no. 2 (August 2008): 177–200.

———, "The Shade of Gumilev in Mandel'shtam's *Kamen'*," *Slavonic and East European Review* 87, no. 1 (2009): 39–52.

Gomringer, Eugen. *The Book of Hours, and Constellations,* pres. Jerome Rothenberg (New York, 1968).

Gordin, Iakov, ed., *Iosif Brodskii: Tvorchestvo, lichnost', sud'ba* (St. Petersburg, 1998).

———, *Pereklichka vo mrake: Iosif Brodskii i ego sobesedniki* (St. Petersburg, 2000).

———, *V storonu Stiksa: Bol'shoi nekrolog* (Moscow, 2005).

Gordin, Iakov, and Irina Murav'eva, eds., *Iosif Brodskii i mir: Metafizika, antichnost', sovremennost'* (St. Petersburg, 2000).

Gor'kii, Maksim. *Polnoe sobranie sochinenii* (Moscow, 1968).

Grabher, Gudrun, and Ulrike Jessner, eds., *Semantics of Silences in Linguistics and Literature* (Heidelberg, Ger., 1996).

Graff, Gerald, "Deconstruction as Dogma," *Georgia Review* 34 (1980): 401–21.

———, *Literature Against Itself: Literary Ideas in Modern Society* (Chicago, 1979).

Graves, Robert, *Complete Poems* (Manchester, Eng., 1995).

Greenleaf, Monika, "Found in Translation: The Subject of Batiushkov's Poetry," in *Russian Subjects: Empire, Nation, and the Culture of the Golden Age*, ed. and intro. Monika Greenleaf and Stephen Moeller-Sally, 51–79 (Evanston, Ill., 1998).

———, *Pushkin and Romantic Fashion: Fragment, Elegy, Orient, Irony* (Stanford, Calif., 1994).

———, "Through the Lens of Montage: Tynianov, Pushkin, and the Fragment," in *Cultural Mythologies of Russian Modernism: From the Golden Age to the Silver Age*, ed. Boris Gasparov, Robert Hughes, and Irina Paperno, 264–92 (Berkeley, Calif., 1992).

Greenleaf, Monika, and Stephen Moeller-Sally, eds. and intro., *Russian Subjects: Empire, Nation, and the Culture of the Golden Age* (Evanston, Ill., 1998).

Gregg, Richard, *Fedor Tiutchev: The Evolution of a Poet* (New York, 1965).

Gronas, Mikhail, *Cognitive Poetics and Cultural Memory* (New York, 2011).

Grünbein, Durs, *Antike Dispositionen: Aufsätze* (Frankfurt am Main, 2005).

Gudzii, Nikolai, "Tiutchev v poeticheskoi kul'ture russkogo simvolizma," *Izvestiia po russkomu iazyku i slovesnosti Akademii nauk SSSR* 3 (Leningrad, 1930): 465–549.

Gukovskii, Grigorii, *Pushkin i russkie romantiki* (Moscow, 1995).

Gumilev, Nikolai, *Sobranie sochinenii v chetyrekh tomakh*, ed. G. P. Struve and B. A. Filippov (Washington, D.C., 1968).

Gurvich, I., "Mandel'shtam i problema 'bessmyslennogo slova,'" *Russian Literature* 42, no. 2 (1997): 171–82.

Gustafson, Richard, *The Imagination of Spring: The Poetry of Afanasy Fet* (New Haven, Conn., 1966).

Harpham, Geoffrey, *Language Alone: The Critical Fetish of Modernity* (New York, 2002).

Harris, Jane G., *Osip Mandelstam* (Boston, 1988).

Hawkins, Peter, and Anne Howland Schotter, eds., *Ineffability: Naming the Unnamable from Dante to Beckett* (New York, 1984).

Heidegger, Martin, *Nietzsche* (Pfullingen, W.Ger., 1961).

———, *On the Way to Language*, trans. Peter D. Hertz (New York, 1971).

Herbert, George, *George Herbert: Poems: Selections*, ed. Louis Martz (New York, 1994).

Herder, Johann, *Herders Sämtliche Werke* (Berlin, 1877).

Hertz, Neil, *The End of the Line: Essays on Psychoanalysis and the Sublime* (New York, 1985).

Hesiod, *Theogony*, comm. Richard Hamilton (Bryn Mawr, Pa., 1990).

Hoffer, Pamela M., *Reflets Réciproques: A Prismatic Reading of Stéphane Mallarmé and Hélène Cixous* (New York, 2006).

Hofmannsthal, Hugo von, *The Lord Chandos Letter and Other Writings*, sel. and trans. Joel Rotenberg, intro. John Banville (New York, 2005).

Hölderlin, Friedrich, *Friedrich Hölderlins sämtliche Werke* (Leipzig, 1927).

Holquist, Michael, *Dialogism: Bakhtin and His World* (London, 1990).

Homer, *The Complete Works of Homer: The Iliad,* trans. Andrew Lang, Walter Leaf, and Ernest Myers (New York, 1950).

Horace, *The Complete Odes and Epodes,* trans., intro., and notes David West (New York, 1997).

Humboldt, Wilhelm, *Humanist Without Portfolio: An Anthology of the Writings of Wilhelm von Humboldt* (Detroit, 1963).

———, *On Language: The Diversity of Human Language-Structure and Its Influence on the Mental Development of Mankind,* trans. Peter Heath, intro. Hans Aarsleff (Cambridge, Eng., 1988).

Iakovenko, B. V., "Filosofiia otchaianiia," in *P. A. Florenskii, pro et contra: Lichnost' i tvorchestvo Pavla Florenskogo v otsenke russkikh myslitelei i issledovatelei,* ed. K. G. Isupov, 252–63 (St. Petersburg, 1996).

Iampol'skii, Mikhail, *Bespamiatstvo kak istok* (Moscow, 1998).

Ianushkevich, Aleksandr, *V mire Zhukovskogo* (Moscow, 2006).

Iazykov, Nikolai, *Stikhotvoreniia i poemy* (Leningrad, 1988).

Iezuitova, Raisa, ed., *Zhukovsky i russkaia kul'tura: Sbornik nauchnykh trudov* (Leningrad, 1987).

Ioffe, Denis, "Liki tishiny: Noveishaia istoriia russkogo eksperimental'nogo stikhoproizvodstva sub specie hesychiae: Tri skhematicheski vziatye poetiki umnogo delaniia," *Russian, Croatian and Serbian, Czech and Slovak, Polish Literature* 57, no. 3–4 (2005): 293–314.

Iser, Wolfgang, "The Play of the Text, " in *Languages of the Unsayable: The Play of Negativity in Literature and Literary Theory,* ed. Sanford Budick and Wolfgang Iser, 325–39 (New York 1989).

Isupov, K. G., ed., *F. I. Tiutchev: Pro et contra: Lichnost' i tvorchestvo Tiutcheva v otsenke russkikh myslitelei i issledovatelei* (St. Petersburg, 2005).

———, *P. A. Florenskii—Pro et contra: Lichnost' i tvorchestvo Pavla Florenskogo v otsenke russkikh myslitelei i issledovatelei: Antologiia* (St. Petersburg, 1996).

Iun, Pak Sun, *Organicheskaia poetika Osipa Mandel'shtama* (St. Petersburg, 2008).

Ivanov, Viacheslav, *Rodnoe i vselenskoe,* ed., intro., and commentaries V. M. Tolmachev (Moscow, 1994).

———, *Sobranie sochinenii v chetyrekh tomakh,* ed. D. V. Ivanov and O. Deshart (Brussels, 1971–87).

———, "Thoughts About Symbolism," in *Russian Symbolists: An Anthology of Critical and Theoretical Writings,* ed. Donald Peterson (Ann Arbor, Mich., 1980).

Jackson, Robert L., and Lowry Nelson Jr., eds., *Viacheslav Ivanov: Poet, Critic and Philosopher* (New Haven, Conn., 1986), 236–52.

Jakobson, Roman, *Language in Literature,* ed. Kristina Pomorska and Stephen Rudy (Cambridge, Mass., 1987).

Jakobson, Roman, C. H. Van Schooneveld, and Dean S. Worth eds., *Slavic Poetics: Essays in Honour of Kiril Taranovsky* (The Hague, Neth., 1973), 455–60.

Jameson, Fredric, *Postmodernism, or, The Cultural Logic of Late Capitalism* (Durham, N.C., 1991).

———, *The Prison House of Language: A Critical Account of Structuralism and Russian Formalism* (Princeton, N.J., 1975).

Janecek, Gerald, "Minimalism in Contemporary Russian Poetry: Vsevolod Nekrasov and Others," *Slavonic and East European Review* 70, no. 3 (1992): 401–19.

———, "Viacheslav Ivanov's 'Alpine Horn' as a Manifesto of Russian Symbolism," *Slavic and East European Journal* 45, no. 1 (2001): 30–44.

———, *Zaum: The Transrational Poetry of Russian Futurism* (San Diego, Calif., 1996).

Johnson, Barbara, *The Critical Difference* (Baltimore, 1980).

———, "Writing," in *Literary Theory: An Anthology,* 2nd editon, ed. Julie Rivkin and Michael Ryan, 340–47 (Malden, Mass., 2004).

Jost, Francois, ed., Melvin J. Friedman, asst., *Aesthetics and the Literature of Ideas: Essays in Honor of A. Owen Aldridge* (Newark, N.J., 1990).

Kabakov, Ilya, *Zhizn' much* (Kolnischer, Germ., 1992).

Kahn, Andrew, *Pushkin's Lyric Intelligence* (Oxford, 2008).

———, "Pushkin's Wanderer Fantasies," in *Rereading Russian Poetry,* ed. Stephanie Sandler, 225–47 (New Haven, Conn., 1999).

Kamuf, Peggy, "Monumental De-Facement: On Paul de Man's *The Rhetoric of Romanticism,*" *Comparative Literature* 38, no. 4 (Autumn 1986): 319–28.

Kandinskii, Vasilii, *O dukhovnom v iskusstve* (Moscow, 1992).

Kant, Immanuel, *The Critique of Judgment,* trans. James Creed Meredith (Oxford, 1952).

———, *The Critique of Pure Reason,* trans. and ed. Paul Glover and Allen Wood (Cambridge, Eng., 1998).

Keats, John, *Complete Poems and Selected Letters,* ed. Clarence De Witt Thorpe (Indianapolis, Ind., 1935).

Kelebai, Evgenii, *Poet v dome rebenka: Prolegomeny k filosofii tvorchestva Iosifa Brodskogo* (Moscow, 2000).

Kermode, Frank, "Endings, Continued," in *Languages of the Unsayable: The Play of Negativity in Literature and Literary Theory,* ed. Sanford Budick and Wolfgang Iser, 71–94 (New York, 1989).

Khagi, Sofya, "Art as Aping: The Uses of Dialogism in Timur Kibirov's 'To Igor Pomerantsev': Summer Reflections on the Fate of Belles Lettres," *Russian Review* 61, no. 4 (October 2002): 579–98.

———, "Silence and the Rest: The Inexpressible from Batiushkov to Tiutchev," *Slavic and East European Journal* 48, no. 1 (Spring 2004): 41–61.

———, *Silence and the Rest: Verbal Skepticism in Russian Poetry.* Dissertation Abstracts International, February 2007, http://proquest.umi.com.proxy.lib.umich.edu.

Khairov, Shamil', "'Esli bog dlia menia i sushchestvuet, to eto imenno iazyk': Iazykovaia refleksiia i lingvisticheskoe mifotvorchestvo Iosifa Brodskogo," *Novoe literaturnoe obozrenie* 67, no. 3 (2004): 198–223.

Kharms, Daniil, *Sobranie sochinenii,* Volumes 1–2 (Bremen, W. Ger., 1978).

Khlebnikov, Velimir, *Sobranie sochinenii v shesti tomakh,* ed. R. V. Duganov (Moscow, 2000–2004).

Kibirov, Timur, *Greko- i rimsko-kafolicheskie pesenki i poteshki* (Moscow, 2010).

———, "Ia ne veshchaiu—ia boltaiu . . ." Victor Kulle's conversation with Timur Kibirov, November 21, 1997, *Literaturnoe obozrenie* 1, no. 267 (1998): 10–16.

———, "An Interview with Philip Nikolaev and Katya Kapovich," 2002, http://imperium.lenin.ru/~verbit/Stihi-interview.html.

———, *Kara-baras: 2002–2005* (Moscow, 2006).

———, *Na poliakh "A Shropshire Lad"* (Moscow, 2007).

———, "Pravila igry," *Voprosy literatury* 4 (July–August 1996): 214–25.

———, *Stikhi* (Moscow, 2005).

———, *Stikhi o liubvi* (Moscow, 2009).

———, *Tri poemy: 2006–2007* (Moscow, 2008).

Kim, Khen En, "Poeticheskii perenos v tsikle 'Chast' rechi' I. Brodskogo," *Slavistica* 18 (2002): 150–66.

Kireevskii, Ivan, *Izbrannye stat'i,* ed., intro., and commentaries V. A. Kotel'nikov (Moscow, 1984).

Kiust, Ion, "Brodskii kak predmet issledovaniia: Vosem' let spustia," *Novoe literaturnoe obozrenie* 67, no. 3 (2004): 160–63.

———, "Plokhoi poet Iosif Brodsky: K istorii voprosa," *Novoe literaturnoe obozrenie* 45 (2000): 248–55.

Klebanov, Mikhail, "The Dilemma of Amnesia and Alalia on the Crossroads of Judgments on the Creative Methods and Creative Difficulties of Daniil Kharms," *Russian, Croatian and Serbian, Czech and Slovak, Polish Literature* 60, no. 3–4 (2006): 367–77.

Klenin, Emily, "On Groups of Poems in Books by Fet," *Elementa: Journal of Slavic Studies and Comparative Cultural Semiotics* 2, no. 3–4 (1996): 297–310.

———, *The Poetics of Afanasy Fet* (Cologne, 2002).

Kline, George, "Revisiting Brodsky," in *Translating Poetry: The Double Labyrinth,* ed. Daniel Weissbort, 95–106 (Iowa City, 1989).

———, "Variations on the Theme of Exile," in *Brodsky's Poetics and Aesthetics,* ed. Lev Loseff and Valentina Polukhina, 56–88 (New York, 1990).

Knox, Jane. See Noks, Dzhein.

Korovin, Vladimir, "Tiutchev i Shopengauer: K postanovke problemy," in *Pushkin v XXI veke: Sbornik v chest' Valentina Semenovicha Nepomniashchego,* ed.

and intro. A. B. Kudelin, V. M. Guminskii, V. E. Orlov, and S. S. Sazonova, 370–92 (Moscow, 2006).

Kouborlis, Demetrius J., ed., *A Concordance to the Poems of Osip Mandelstam,* foreword Clarence Brown (Ithaca, N.Y., 1974).

Kozitskaia-Fleishman, Ekaterina, "Ia byl kak vse': O nekotorykh funktsiiakh liricheskogo 'ty' v poezii I. Brodskogo," in *Poetika Iosifa Brodskogo: Sbornik nauchnykh trudov,* ed. Valentina Polukhina, I. V. Fomenko, and A. G. Stepanov, 107–27 (Tver', Russia, 2003).

Kozlov, Vladimir, "Neperevodimye gody Brodskogo: Dve strany i dva iazyka v poezii i proze I. Brodskogo 1972–77 godov," *Voprosy literatury* 3 (2005): 155–85.

Krasutkin, G., ed., *Pushkinist: Sbornik Pushkinskoi komissii Instituta mirovoi literatury* (Moscow, 1989).

Kreps, Mikhail, *O poezii Iosifa Brodskogo* (Ann Arbor, Mich., 1984).

Kruchenykh, Aleksei, *Izbrannoe,* ed. and intro. Vladimir Markov (Munich, 1973).

Kudelin, A. B., V. M. Guminskii, V. E. Orlov, and S. S. Sazonova, eds. and intro., *Pushkin v XXI veke. Sbornik v chest' Valentina Semenovicha Nepomniashchego* (Moscow, 2006).

Kulle, Viktor, "Struktura avtorskogo 'ia' v stikhotvorenii Iosifa Brodskogo 'Niotkuda s liubov'iu,'" in *Iosif Brodskii: Tvorchestvo, lichnost', sud'ba,* ed. Iakov Gordin, 136–42 (St. Petersburg, 1998).

Kuritsyn, Viacheslav, "3 debiuta Timura Kibirova v 1997 godu," *Literaturnoe obozrenie* 1, no. 267 (1998): 36–38.

Kuz'min, Mikhail, *Stikhotvoreniia* (St. Petersburg, 1996).

Lavretskii, Aleksandr, "Vzyskuiushchii blagodati (F. I. Tiutchev: poet i poeziia)," in *F. I. Tiutchev: Pro et contra: Lichnost' i tvorchestvo Tiutcheva v otsenke russkikh myslitelei i issledovatelei,* ed. K. G. Isupov, 278–300 (St. Petersburg, 2005).

Lawton, Anna, ed., *Russian Futurism Through Its Manifestoes, 1912–1928,* trans. Anna Lawton and Herbert Eagle (Ithaca, N.Y., 1988).

Lekmanov, Oleg. "Akmeisty: Poety kruga Gumileva I," *Novoe literaturnoe obozrenie* 17 (1996): 168–84.

———, "Akmeisty: Poety kruga Gumileva II," *Novoe literaturnoe obozrenie* 19 (1996): 148–61.

———, *Kniga ob akmeizme* (Moscow, 1998).

———, *Mandelstam,* trans. Tatiana Retivov, ed. Lazar Fleishman (Boston, 2010).

———, ed., *Mandel'shtam i antichnost'* (Moscow, 1995), 116–22.

———, *O pervom "Kamne" Mandel'shtama* (Moscow, 1994).

Lekmanov, Oleg, and E. Glukhova, "Osip Mandel'shtam i Viacheslav Ivanov," in *Bashnia Viacheslava Ivanova i kul'tura serebrianogo veka,* ed. V. S. Kizilo, preface A. B. Shishkin, 173–79 (St. Petersburg, 2006).

Lermontov, Mikhail, *Major Poetical Works,* trans. Anatoly Liberman (Minneapolis, Minn., 1983).

———, *Sochineniia: V shesti tomakh,* ed. N. F. Bel'chikov, B. P. Gorodetskii, and B. V. Tomashevskii (Moscow, 1954–57).

Levin, Iurii, *Izbrannye trudy: Poetika: Semiotika* (Moscow, 1998).

Levin, Iurii, et al., "Russkaia semanticheskaia poetika kak potentsial'naia kul'turnaia paradigma," *Russian Literature* 7/8 (1974): 47–82.

Levinton, Georgii, "Smert' poeta: Iosif Brodskii," in *Iosif Brodskii: Tvorchestvo, lichnost', sud'ba,* ed. Iakov Gordin, 190–215 (St. Petersburg, 1998).

Lipovetsky, Mark, *Russian Postmodernist Fiction: Dialogue with Chaos,* ed. Eliot Borenstein (Armonk, N.Y., 1999).

Lomonosov, Mikhail, *Polnoe sobranie sochinenii* (Moscow, 1950–83).

Loseff, Lev, "Home and Abroad in the Works of Brodskii," in *Under Eastern Eyes: The West as Reflected in Recent Russian Émigré Writing,* ed. Arnold McMillin, 25–41 (London, 1992).

———, "Iosif Brodskii's Poetics of Faith," in *Aspects of Modern Russian and Czech Literature: Selected Papers of the Third World Congress for Soviet and East European Studies,* ed. Arnold McMillin, 188–201 (Columbus, Ohio, 1989).

———, " 'On the Centenary of Anna Akhmatova' 'Na stoletie Anny Akhmatovoi,' " in *Joseph Brodsky: The Art of a Poem,* ed. Lev Loseff and Valentina Polukhina, 225–39 (New York, 1999).

———, "Politics/ Poetics," in *Brodsky's Poetics and Aesthetics,* ed. Lev Loseff and Valentina Polukhina, 34–55 (New York, 1990).

Loseff, Lev, and Valentina Polukhina, eds., *Brodsky's Poetics and Aesthetics* (New York, 1990).

———, eds., *Joseph Brodsky: The Art of a Poem* (New York, 1999).

Losev, Lev, *Iosif Brodskii: Opyt literaturnoi biografii* (Moscow, 2006).

———, "Na stoletie Anny Akhmatovoi," in *Kak rabotaet stikhotvorenie Brodskogo: Iz issledovanii slavistov na zapade,* ed. Lev Losev and Valentina Polukhina, intro. Lev Losev, 202–22 (Moscow, 2002).

———, ed., *Poetika Brodskogo: Sbornik statei* (Tenafly, N.J., 1986).

Losev, Lev, and Valentina Polukhina, eds., *Kak rabotaet stikhotvorenie Brodskogo: Iz issledovanii slavistov na zapade,* intro. Lev Losev (Moscow, 2002).

Lossky, Nikolai, *The World as an Organic Whole* (London, 1928).

Lotman, Iurii, " 'Agreement' and 'Self-Giving' as Archetypal Models of Culture," in *The Semiotics of Russian Cultural History: Essays by Iurii M. Lotman, Lidiia Ia. Ginsburg, Boris A. Uspenskii,* ed. Alexander Nakhimovsky and Alice Stone Nakhimovsky, 125–40 (Ithaca, N.Y., 1985).

———, *Kul'tura i vzryv* (Moscow, 1992).

———, "Poeticheskii mir Tiutcheva," in *F. I. Tiutchev: Pro et contra: Lichnost' i tvorchestvo Tiutcheva v otsenke russkikh myslitelei i issledovatelei,* ed. K. G. Isupov (St. Petersburg, 2005).

———, *The Structure of the Artistic Text,* trans. Ronald Vroon (Ann Arbor, Mich., 1977).

Lotman, Iurii, and Boris Uspenskii, "Binary Models in the Dynamics of Russian Culture (to the End of the Eighteenth Century)," in *The Semiotics of Russian Cultural History: Essays by Iurii M. Lotman, Lidiia Ia. Ginsburg, Boris A. Uspenskii,* ed. Alexander Nakhimovsky and Alice Stone Nakhimovsky, 30–66 (Ithaca, N.Y., 1985).

Lyotard, Jean-François, *The Postmodern Condition: A Report on Knowledge,* trans. Geoffrey Bennington and Brian Massumi (Manchester, Eng., 1984).

MacFadyen, David, *Joseph Brodsky and the Baroque* (Montreal, 1998).

———, *Joseph Brodsky and the Soviet Muse* (Montreal, 2000).

Macksey, Richard, and Eugenio Donato, eds., *The Structuralist Controversy: The Languages of Criticism and the Sciences of Man* (Baltimore, 1972).

Magun, Artemii, "Poetika revoliutsionnogo vremeni: G'ol'derlin i Mandel'shtam," *Novoe literaturnoe obozrenie* 63, no. 5 (2003): 39–58.

Maiakovskii, Vladimir. *Polnoe sobranie sochinenii v 12 tomakh,* ed. N. N. Aseev, L. V. Maiakovskaia, V. O. Pertsov, and M. I. Serebianskii (Moscow, 1939).

Makin, Michael, *Marina Tsvetaeva: Poetics of Appropriation* (Oxford, 1993).

Malevich, Kazimir, *Essays on Art* (Copenhagen, 1968–78).

Mallarmé, Stéphane, *Oeuvres complètes,* ed. and commentaries Henri Mondor and G. Jean-Aubry (Paris, 1945).

Malmstad, John, "Mandelstam's 'Silentium': A Poet's Response to Ivanov," in *Viacheslav Ivanov: Poet, Critic and Philosopher,* ed. Robert L. Jackson and Lowry Nelson Jr., 236–52 (New Haven, Conn., 1986).

Man, Paul de, *Allegories of Reading: Figural Language in Rousseau, Nietzsche, Rilke, and Proust* (New Haven, Conn., 1979).

———, *Blindness and Insight* (New York, 1971).

———, "The Epistemology of Metaphor," *Critical Inquiry* 5, no. 1 (Autumn 1978): 13–30.

———, "Nietzsche's Theory of Rhetoric," *Symposium* 28, no. 1 (1974): 33–51.

———, *The Resistance to Theory* (Minneapolis, Minn., 1986).

———, *The Rhetoric of Romanticism* (New York, 1984).

Mandelker, Amy, "Lotman's Other: Estrangement and Ethics in Culture and Explosion," in *Lotman and Cultural Studies: Encounters and Extensions,* ed. Andreas Schönle, 59–83 (Madison, Wis., 2006).

Mandel'shtam, Nadezhda, *Vospominaniia* (New York, 1970).

Mandel'shtam, Osip, *Kamen',* ed. L. Ginzburg, A. Mets, S. Vasilenko, I. Freidin (Leningrad, 1990).

———, *Kamen': Stikhi* (St. Petersburg, 1913).

———, *Polnoe sobranie stikhotvorenii,* ed. M. L. Gasparov and A. G. Mets (St. Petersburg, 1997).

———, *Sobranie sochinenii v chetyrekh tomakh,* ed. P. Nerler and A. Nikitaev (Moscow, 1993).

———, *Stikhotvoreniia: Proza,* commentaries Mikhail Gasparov (Moscow, 2001).

Mandelstam, Osip, *The Complete Critical Prose,* ed. Jane Harris, trans. Jane Harris and Constance Link (Ann Arbor, Mich., 1997).

———, *Complete Poetry of Osip Emilevich Mandelstam,* trans. Burton Raffel and Alla Burago, intro. and notes Sidney Monas (Albany, N.Y., 1973).

———, *Modernist Archaist: Selected Poems by Osip Mandelstam,* ed. and intro. Kevin M. F. Platt (Delray Beach, Calif., 2008).

———, *Osip Mandelstam,* trans. James Greene, forewords Nadezhda Mandelstam and Donald Davie (London, 1989).

———, *Poems from Mandelstam,* trans. Robert H. Morrison, intro. Ervin C. Brody (Cranbury, N.J., 1990).

Mandelstam, Osip, and Steven J. Willett, "The Horseshoe Finder: a Pindaric Fragment," *Arion,* third series, vol. 9, no. 2 (Fall 2001): 90–93.

Mann, Iurii, *Dinamika russkogo romantizma* (Moscow, 1995).

———, "Neobkhodimost' Baratynskogo," *Voprosy literatury* 1 (1994): 135–64.

Manuilov, V., ed., *Lermontovskaia Entsiklopediia* (Moscow, 1981).

Markova, Viktoriia, "Formirovanie kategorial'nogo apparata refleksii 'bezmolviia' v ramkakh khudozhestvennogo tselogo: 'Nevyrazimoe' V. A. Zhukovskogo, 'Silentium!' F. I. Tiutcheva," in *Slavianskie dukhovnye tsennosti na rubezhe vekov,* ed. N. K. Frolov (Tyumen, Russ., 2001).

———, "Opyt refleksii fenomena bezmolviia v lirike A. S. Pushkina i M. I. Lermontova," in *Slavianskie istoki slovesnosti i kul'tury v Zapadnoi Sibiri,* vol. 2, ed. N. K. Frolov, 128–37 (Tyumen, Russ., 2001).

Matejka, Ladislav, and Irwin W. Titunik, eds., *Semiotics of Art: Prague School Contributions* (Cambridge, Mass., 1976).

McKay, John, *Inscription and Modernity: From Wordsworth to Mandelstam* (Bloomington, Ind., 2006).

McMillin, Arnold, ed., *Aspects of Modern Russian and Czech Literature: Selected Papers of the Third World Congress for Soviet and East European Studies* (Columbus, Ohio, 1989).

———, *Under Eastern Eyes: The West as Reflected in Recent Russian Émigré Writing* (London, 1992).

Meilakh, Mikhail, "'Poet sam uznaet po temperament svoego predshestvennika . . .': Iz razgovorov s Iosifom Brodskim," *Novoe literaturnoe obozrenie* 79, no. 3 (2006): 273–85.

Meise, Katrin, "On Talking About Silence in Conversation and Literature," in *Semantics of Silences in Linguistics and Literature,* ed. Gudrun Grabher and Ulrike Jessner (Heidelberg, 1996).

Merezhkovskii, Dmitrii, *Polnoe sobranie sochinenii* (St. Petersburg, 1911).

Mets, Aleksandr, "*Kamen'* (k tvorcheskoi istorii knigi)," in Osip Mandelstam, *Kamen',* ed. L. Ginzburg, A. Mets, S. Vasilenko, and I. Freidin, 277–85 (Leningrad, 1990).

———, "Kommentarii," in Osip Mandel'shtam, *Polnoe sobranie stikhotvorenii,* ed. M. L. Gasparov and A. G. Mets (St. Petersburg, 1997).

Mikotin, Anthony, ed., *Western Philosophical Systems in Russian Literature: A Collection of Critical Studies,* University of Southern California Series in Slavic Humanities, no. 3 (Los Angeles, 1979), 35–58.

Miller, J. Hillis, *Others* (Princeton, N.J., 2001).

———, *Theory Now and Then* (Durham, N.C., 1991).

Mitchell, Claudine, "Rodin and the Baudelairean Legacy: Arthur Symons on the Sculptor as Poet," in *Rodin: The Zola of Sculpture,* ed. Claudine Mitchell, 73–94 (Aldershot, Eng., 2004).

———, *Rodin: The Zola of Sculpture* (Aldershot, Eng., 2004).

Monas, Sidney, "Words Devouring Things: The Poetry of Joseph Brodsky," in *Twayne Companion to Contemporary World Literature: From the Editors of World Literature Today,* ed. and intro. Pamela Genova, 1066–71 (New York, 2003).

Monastyrskii, Andrei, *Nebesnomu nosatomy domiku po puti v Pagan* (Moscow, 2001).

Morford, Mark, ed., *Classical Mythology* (White Plains, N.Y., 1995).

Morson, Gary Saul, and Caryl Emerson. *Mikhail Bakhtin: Creation of a Prosaics* (Stanford, Calif., 1990).

Mukařovský, Jan, *The Word and Verbal Art: Selected Essays,* ed. and trans. John Burbank and Peter Steiner, foreword René Wellek (New Haven, Conn., 1977).

Myers, Diana, "The Hum of Metaphor and the Cast of Voice: Observations on Mandel'shtam's 'The Horseshoe Finder,'" *Slavonic and East European Review* 69, no. 1 (1991): 1–39.

Nabokov, Vladimir, *Speak, Memory: An Autobiography Revisited* (New York, 1989).

———, *Three Russian Poets* (Stanford, Calif., 1947).

Nadson, Semen, *Polnoe sobranie stikhotvorenii,* intro. G. A. Blagoi (St. Petersburg, 2001).

Nakhimovsky, Alexander, and Alice Stone Nakhimovsky, eds., *The Semiotics of Russian Cultural History: Essays by Iurii M. Lotman, Lidiia Ia. Ginsburg, Boris A. Uspenskii* (Ithaca, N.Y., 1985).

Nekrasov, Nikolai, *Polnoe sobranie sochinenii i pisem v 15 tomakh,* ed. V. G. Bazanov et al. (Leningrad, 1982).

Nekrasov, Vsevolod, "Kak eto bylo (i est') s konceptualizmom," *Literaturnaia gazeta* no. 31 (August 1, 1990): 8.

———, *Stikhi iz zhurnala* (Moscow, 1989).

Nemoianu, Virgil, *The Taming of Romanticism: European Literature and the Age of Biedermeier* (Cambridge, Mass., 1984).

Nepomniashchii, Valentin, "Prorok," in *Pushkinist: Sbornik Pushkinskoi komissii Instituta mirovoi literatury,* ed. G. Krasutkin (Moscow, 1989).

Nesterov, Anton, "Ikonografiia i poeziia, ili kommentarii k nekotorym tekstam

Mandel'shtama, napisannyi na osnove emblemata," *Novoe literaturnoe obozrenie* 67, no. 3 (2004): 137–59.

Nietzsche, Friedrich, *Beyond Good and Evil: Prelude to a Philosophy of the Future,* trans. and ed. Marion Faber, intro. Robert Holub (Oxford, 1998).

———, *Friedrich Nietzsche on Rhetoric and Language,* ed., trans., and intro. Sander Gilman, Carole Blair, and David Parent (New York, 1989).

———, *Human, All-too-Human: A Book for Free Spirits,* trans. R. Hollingdale (Cambridge, Eng., 1996).

———, *The Joyful Wisdom,* trans. Thomas Common (Edinburgh, 1910).

———, *The Philosophy of Nietzsche,* ed. and intro. Geoffrey Clive (New York, 1965).

———, *The Portable Nietzsche,* trans. Walter Kaufmann (New York, 1954).

———, *Thus Spoke Zarathustra,* trans. Walter Kaufmann (New York, 1954.

———, *Twilight of the Idols, or, How to Philosophize with a Hammer,* trans. Walter Kaufmann (New York, 1954).

———, *The Will to Power,* trans. Walter Kaufmann and R. Hollingdale (New York, 1967).

Nikitin, Ivan, *Polnoe sobranie stikhotvorenii,* intro. L. A. Plotkin (Leningrad, 1965).

Nillsen, Nils A., "Osip Mandelstam and His Poetry," *Scando-Slavica* 9 (1993).

Nivat, Georges, "The Ironic Journey into Antiquity," in *Brodsky's Poetics and Aesthetics,* ed. Lev Loseff and Valentina Polukhina, 89–97 (New York, 1990).

Noks [Knox], Dzhein [Jane], "Ierarkhiia drugikh v poezii Brodskogo," in *Poetika Iosifa Brodskogo: Sbornik nauchnykh trudov,* ed. Valentina Polukhina, I. V. Fomenko, and A. G. Stepanov, 160–71 (Tver', Russia, 2003).

———, "Poeziia Iosifa Brodskogo: Al'ternativnaia forma sushchestvovaniia, ili novoe zveno evoliutsii v russkoi kul'ture," in *Iosif Brodskii: tvorchestvo, lichnost', sud'ba,* ed. Iakov Gordin, 216–23 (St. Petersburg, 1998).

Olschner, Leonard, "Poetic Mutations of Silence: At the Nexus of Paul Celan and Osip Mandelstam, in *Readings of Paul Celan,* ed. Aris Fioretos, 369–85 (Baltimore, 1994).

O'Neill, Michael, and Gareth Reeves, *Auden, MacNeice, Spender: The Thirties Poetry* (Basingstoke, Eng., 1992).

Ozherel'eva, Ekaterina, "Bog i chelovek v stikhotvorenii Iosifa Brodskogo 'Razgovor s nebozhitelem' (God and Man in Iosif Brodskii's 'Conversation with God')," *Russian, Croatian and Serbian, Czech and Slovak, Polish Literature* 62, no. 1 (2007): 65–89.

Panova, Lada, *"Mir," "prostranstvo," "vremia" v poezii Osipa Mandel'shtama* (Moscow, 2003).

Paperno, Irina, "O prirode poeticheskogo slova: Bogoslovskie istochniki spora Mandel'shtama s simvolizmom," *Literaturnoe obozrenie* 1 (1991): 29–36.

Pasternak, Boris, *Sobranie sochinenii v piati tomakh* (Moscow, 1989).

Pavlov, Evgeny, "Killing Time: Walter Benjamin, Osip Mandel'shtam, and the

Stalinist Metaphysics of History," *Russian, Croatian and Serbian, Czech and Slovak, Polish Literature* 63, no. 2–4 (2008): 443–60.

———, "Memory and the Scene of Writing in Mandelstam's *Egipetskaia marka*: Unrolling the Manuscript," *Slavic and East European Journal* 42, no. 4 (1998): 621–39.

———, "'. . . tem zvuchashchim slepkom formy . . .': Opyt Mandel'shtama," *Novoe literaturnoe obozrenie* 63, no. 5 (2003): 59–83.

Peer, Larry, ed., *The Romantic Manifesto: An Anthology* (New York, 1988).

Pelevin, Viktor, *Generation P* (Moscow, 1999).

Perloff, Marjorie, "Language Poetry and the Lyric Subject: Ron Silliman's Albany, Susan Howe's Buffalo," *Critical Inquiry* 25, no. 3 (Spring 1999): 405–34.

———, *The Poetics of Indeterminacy: Rimbaud to Cage* (Princeton, N.J., 1981).

Pesonen, P., J. Heinonen, and G. Obatnin, eds., *Modernizm i postmodernism v russkoi literature i kul'ture* (Helsinki, 1996).

Peterson, Ronald E., *A History of Russian Symbolism* (Amsterdam, 1993).

———, ed., *Russian Symbolists: An Anthology of Critical and Theoretical Writings* (Ann Arbor, Mich., 1980).

Piarli, Iulle, "Sintaksis i smysl: Tsikl 'Chast' rechi' I. Brodskogo," in *Modernizm i postmodernism v russkoi literature i kul'ture,* ed. P. Pesonen, J. Heinonen, and G. Obatnin, 409–18 (Helsinki, 1996).

Picchio, Riccardo, and Harvey Goldblatt, eds., *Aspects of the Slavic Language Question* (New Haven, Conn., 1984).

Pigarev, Kirill, "Poeticheskoe nasledie Tiutcheva," in *Lirika v dvukh tomakh,* by F. Tiutchev, vol. 1 (Moscow, 1965).

———, *Zhizn' i tvorchestvo Tiutcheva* (Moscow, 1962).

Plamer, G., P. Shepard, and K. Ware, eds. and trans., *Philocalia: The Complete Text,* Comp. St. Nikodimos of the Holy Mountain and St. Makarios of Corinth (London, 1979).

Plato, *Cratylus: The Laws,* trans. J. Sanders (Harmondsworth, Eng., 1970).

———, *Phaedrus,* trans. and intro. James Nichols (Ithaca, N.Y., 1998).

———, *The Republic,* trans. Benjamin Jowett, intro. Scott Buchanan (Cleveland, Ohio, 1946).

Platonov, Andrei, *The Foundation Pit,* trans. Thomas P. Whitney, pref. Joseph Brodsky (Ann Arbor, Mich., 1973).

Platt, Kevin, *History in a Grotesque Key: Russian Literature and the Idea of Revolution* (Stanford, Calif., 1997).

Plekhanova, Irina, *Preobrazhenie tragicheskogo,* parts 1 and 2, *Metafizicheskaia misteriia Iosifa Brodskogo: Pod znakom beskonechnosti: Estetika metafizicheskoi svobody protiv tragicheskoi real'nosti* (Irkutsk, Russia, 2001).

Pleshcheev, Aleksei, *Polnoe sobranie stikhotvorenii,* intro. M. I. Poliakov (Moscow, 1964).

Plotinus, *The Enneads,* trans. Stephen MacKenna (London, 1962).

Poe, Edgar Allan, *The Complete Poetical Works* (London, 1909).

Polianskii, A. N., "Formy i funktsii neizrechennogo v tekstakh khudozhestvennoi literatury," *Filologicheskie nauki* 2 (1990): 54–62.

Pollak, Nancy, "Annensky's Anguished Muse," in *Rereading Russian Poetry*, ed. Stephanie Sandler, 146–60 (New Haven, Conn., 1999).

———, *Mandelstam the Reader* (Baltimore, 1995).

———, "Mandelstam's 'First' Poem," *Slavic and East European Journal* 32, no. 1 (Spring 1988): 98–108.

Polukhina, Valentina, "Beseda s L'vom Losevym," *Zvezda* 1 (2005): 159–70.

———, *Brodskii glazami sovremennikov* (St. Petersburg, 1997).

———, "Grammatika metafory i khudozhestvennyi smysl," in *Poetika Brodskogo: Sbornik statei*, ed. Lev Losev, 63–96 (Tenafly, N.J., 1986).

———, *Joseph Brodsky: A Poet for Our Time* (Cambridge, Eng., 1989).

———,"The Myth of the Poet and the Poet of the Myth: Russian Poets on Brodsky," in *Russian Writers on Russian Writers*, ed. and intro. Faith Wigzell, 139–59 (Oxford, 1994).

———, "Poeticheskii avtoportret I. Brodskogo," in *Iosif Brodskii: Tvorchestvo, lichnost', sud'ba*, ed. Iakov Gordin, 145–53 (St. Petersburg, 1998).

———, "Similarity in Disparity," in *Brodsky's Poetics and Aesthetics*, ed. Lev Loseff and Valentina Polukhina, 150–75 (New York, 1990).

Polukhina, Valentina, I. V. Fomenko, and A. G. Stepanov, eds., *Poetika Iosifa Brodskogo: Sbornik nauchnykh trudov* (Tver', Russia, 2003).

Polukhina, Valentina, and Iulle Piarli, *Slovar' tropov Brodskogo: Na material sbornika "Chast' rechi"* (Tartu, Estonia, 1995).

Potebnia, Aleksandr, *Mysl' i iazyk* (Kiev, 1993).

Powelstock, David, *Becoming Mikhail Lermontov: The Ironies of Romantic Individualism in Nicholas I's Russia* (Evanston, Ill., 2005).

Pratt, Sarah, *Nikolai Zabolotsky: Enigma and Cultural Paradigm* (Evanston, Ill., 2000).

———, *Russian Metaphysical Romanticism: The Poetry of Tiutchev and Boratynsky* (Stanford, Calif., 1984).

———, "Tjutchev's Poetic Admonitions—with Some Help from Pushkin and Zabolockij," *Russian, Croatian and Serbian, Czech and Slovak, Polish Literature* 54, no. 4 (2003): 525–37.

Prigov, Dmitrii, *Iavlenie stikha posle ego smerti: Stikhi* (Moscow, 1995).

Proclus, *A Commentary on the First Book of Euclid's Elements*, trans. G. Morrow (Princeton, N.J., 1970).

Proffer, Ellendea, and Karl Proffer, eds., *The Ardis Anthology of Russian Futurism* (Ann Arbor, Mich., 1980).

Proffer, Karl. "Ostanovka v sumasshedshem dome: Poema Brodskogo 'Gorbunov i Gorchakov,'" in *Poetika Brodskogo: Sbornik statei*, ed. Lev Losev, 132–40 (Tenafly, N.J., 1986).

Przybylski, Ryszard, *An Essay on the Poetry of Mandelstam: God's Grateful Guest*, trans. Madeline G. Levine (Ann Arbor, Mich., 1987).

———, "Osip Mandel'shtam i muzyka," *Russian Literature* 2 (1972): 103–25.

Pseudo-Dionysius the Areopagite, *The Divine Names* and *Mystical Theology*, trans. and intro. John Jones (Milwaukee, Wis., 1980).

Pumpianskii, Lev, "Poeziia F. I. Tiutcheva (vstupitel'naia stat'ia)," in *Uraniia: Tiutchevskii al'manakh: 1803–1828* (Leningrad, 1928).

Pushkin, Alexander, *Collected Narrative and Lyrical Poetry*, trans. Walter Arndt (Ann Arbor, Mich., 1984).

———, *Polnoe sobranie sochinenii v shestnadtsati tomakh*, ed. Maksim Gor'kii et al. (Moscow, 1937–59).

Pyman, Avril, *Pavel Florensky: A Quiet Genius: The Tragic and Extraordinary Life of Russia's Unknown da Vinci*, foreword Geoffrey Hosking (New York, 2010).

Quinney, Laura, *The Poetics of Disappointment: Wordsworth to Ashbery* (Charlottesville, Va., 1999).

Ranchin, Andrei, *Na piru Mnemoziny: Interteksty Brodskogo* (Moscow, 2001).

Rapaport, Herman, *The Theory Mess: Deconstruction in Eclipse* (New York, 2001).

Rassadin, Stanislav, "Vozvrashchenie Baratynskogo," *Voprosy literatury* 7 (1970): 92–113.

Redfield, Mark, ed., *Legacies of Paul de Man* (New York, 2007).

Reisner, Noam, *Milton and the Ineffable* (Oxford, 2009).

Reynolds, Andrew, "Feathers and Suns: Joseph Brodsky's 'Dedal v Sitsilii' and the 'Fear of Replication,'" *Slavic and East European Journal* 51, no. 3 (2007): 553–82.

———, "Returning the Ticket: Brodsky's 'August' and the End of the Petersburg Text," *Slavic Review* 64, no. 2 (Summer 2005): 307–32.

Rigsbee, David, *Styles of Ruin: Joseph Brodsky and the Postmodernist Elegy* (Westport, Conn., 1999).

Rivkin, Julie, and Michael Ryan, eds., *Literary Theory: An Anthology*, 2nd ed. (Malden, Mass., 2004).

Robinson, Marc, ed., *Altogether Elsewhere: Writers in Exile* (Winchester, Mass., 2005).

Robinson, Peter, *Poetry, Poets, Readers: Making Things Happen* (Oxford, 2002).

Ronen, Omry, *An Approach to Mandelstam* (Jerusalem, 1983).

———, "A Beam upon the Axe: Some Antecedents of Osip Mandel'shtam's 'Umyvalsia noch'iu na dvore . . . ,'" *Slavica Hierosolymitana* 1 (1977): 158–76.

———, *Poetika Osipa Mandel'shtama* (St. Petersburg, 2002).

———, "Sublation [Aufhebung] in the Poetics of Acmeism," *Elementa* 2 (1996): 319–29.

Rose, Peter I., ed., *The Dispossessed: An Anatomy of Exile*, foreword Liv Ullmann (Amherst, Mass., 2005).

Rothe, Hans, "Mandelstam and Motifs from Classical Antiquity," in *Stoletie Mandel'shtama: Materialy simpoziuma*, ed. Robin Aizlewood and Diana Maiers, 308–18 (Tenafly, N.J., 1994).

Rubinshtein, Lev, *Stikhi* (St. Petersburg, 1996).
Said, Edward, *The Edward Said Reader,* ed. Moustafa Bayoumi and Andrew Rubin (New York, 2000).
Sandler, Stephanie, "Baratynskii, Pushkin, and Hamlet: On Mourning and Poetry," *Slavic Review* 42, no. 1 (1983): 73–90.
———, *Commemorating Pushkin: Russia's Myth of a National Poet* (Stanford, Calif., 2004).
———, "On Grief and Reason, on Poetry and Film: Elena Shvarts, Joseph Brodsky, Andrei Tarkovsky," *Russian Review* 66, no. 4 (2007): 647–70.
———, ed., *Rereading Russian Poetry* (New Haven, Conn., 1999).
Satunovskii, Ian., *Khochu li ia posmertnoi slavy: Izbrannye stikhi* (Moscow, 1992).
Saussure, Ferdinand. *Course in General Linguistics,* trans. and ed. Roy Harris (Chicago, 1986).
Scanlan, James, "The Nineteenth Century Revisited," in *Russian Thought After Communism: The Recovery of a Philosophical Heritage,* ed. James Scanlan, 23–30 (Armonk, N.Y., 1994).
———, ed., *Russian Thought After Communism: The Recovery of a Philosophical Heritage* (Armonk, N.Y., 1994).
Scharfstein, Ben-Ami, *Ineffability: The Failure of Words in Philosophy and Religion* (Albany, N.Y., 1993).
Scharlemann, Robert, ed., *Negation and Theology* (Charlottesville, Va., 1992).
Schelling, Friedrich, *Schelling's Philosophy of Mythology and Revelation: Three of Seven Books,* trans. and reduced, intro. Victor C. Hayes (Armidale, Australia, 1995).
Scherr, Barry, "Beginning at the End: Rhyme and Enjambment in Brodsky's Poetry," in *Brodsky's Poetics and Aesthetics,* ed. Lev Loseff and Valentina Polukhina, 176–93 (New York, 1990).
———, "Strofika Brodskogo," in *Poetika Brodskogo,* ed. Lev Losev, 97–120 (Tenafly, N.J., 1986).
———, "Strofika Brodskogo: Novyi vzgliad," in *Kak rabotaet stikhotvorenie Brodskogo: Iz issledovanii slavistov na zapade,* ed. Lev Losev and Valentina Polukhina, intro. Lev Losev, 269–99 (Moscow, 2002).
———, "To Urania," in *Joseph Brodsky: The Art of a Poem,* ed. Lev Loseff and Valentina Polukhina, 92–106 (New York, 1999).
Schiller, Friedrich, *On Naive and Sentimental Poetry and on the Sublime,* trans. Julius Elias (New York, 1984).
Schlegel, August, "Vienna Lecture on Literature #1," in *The Romantic Manifesto: An Anthology,* ed. Larry Peer (New York, 1988).
———, *Vorlesungen über dramatische Kunst und Literatur* (Stuttgart, W. Ger., 1966).
Schlegel, Friedrich, *Lucinde and the Fragments,* trans. Peter Firchow (Minneapolis, Minn., 1971).

Scholem, Gershom, "The Name of God and the Linguistic Theory of the Kabbalah," *Diogenes* 79–80 (1972): 59–80, 165–94.

Schönle, Andreas, ed., *Lotman and Cultural Studies: Encounters and Extensions* (Madison, Wis., 2006).

Schopenhauer, Arthur, *Philosophical Writings*, ed. Wolfgang Schirmacher (New York, 1994).

———, *The World as Will and Representation*. 2 vols, trans. E. Payne (New York, 1969).

Schrift, Alan D., *Nietzsche and the Question of Interpretation: Between Hermeneutics and Deconstruction* (New York, 1990).

Sedakova, Ol'ga, "Volia k forme," *Novoe literaturnoe obozrenie* 45 (2000): 232–36.

Segal, Dmitrii, *Osip Mandel'shtam: Istoriia i poetika* (Berkeley, Calif., 1998).

Seidel, Michael, *Exile and the Narrative Imagination* (New Haven, Conn., 1986).

Seifrid, Thomas, *The Word Made Self: Russian Writings on Language, 1860–1930* (Ithaca, N.Y., 2005).

Semenko, Irina, *Poetika pozdnego Mandel'shtama (ot chernovykh redaktsii k okonchatel'nomu tesktu)* (Rome, 1986).

Semenova, Ekaterina, "Poema Iosifa Brodskogo 'Chast' rechi,'" *Staroe literaturnoe obozrenie* 278, no. 2 (2001): 80–86.

Shakespeare, William, *Hamlet*, ed. R. Andrews and R. Gibson (Cambridge, Eng., 1994).

———, *The Tragedy of King Lear*, prep. and annot. Neil Freeman (New York, 2000).

Shapir, Maksim, "O 'zvukosimvolizme' u rannego Khlebnikova ('Bobeobi pelis' guby . . .': Fonicheskaia struktura)," *Izvestiia akademii nauk SSSR. Seriia literatury i iazyka* 51, no. 6 (1992): 37–42.

Shapiro, Michael, *The Sense of Form in Literature and Language* (New York, 1998).

Shcheglov, Iurii, "Eshche raz o metricheskikh otstupleniiakh v 'Silentium!' Tiutcheva," in *Stikh, Iazyk, Poeziia: Pamiati Mikhaila Leonidovicha Gasparova*, ed. Kh. Baran et al., 674–88 (Moscow, 2006).

Shein, Louis, ed. and trans., *Readings in Russian Philosophical Thought: Logic and Aesthetics* (The Hague, Neth., 1973).

Shelley, Percy B., *Shelley's Poetry and Prose*, sel. and ed. Donald H. Reimnan and Neil Fraistat (New York, 2002).

Shestov, Lev, *All Things Are Possible*, trans. S. S. Koteliansky, foreword D. H. Lawrence (New York, 1920).

———, *Athens and Jerusalem*, trans. and intro. Bernard Martin (Athens, Ohio, 1966).

———, *In Job's Balances: On the Sources of the Eternal Truths* (London, 1932).

———, *Penultimate Words and Other Essays* (Boston, 1916).

———, *Potestas Clavium* (Athens, Ohio, 1968).

Shklovskii, Viktor, *Literatura i kinematograf* (Berlin, 1923).

———, *Poetika: Sborniki po teorii poeticheskogo iazyka* (Petrograd, 1919).

Silliman, Ron, Carla Harryman, Lyn Hejinian, Steve Benson, Bob Perelman, and Barrett Watten, "Aesthetic Tendency and the Politics of Poetry," *Social Text* 19/20 (Fall 1988): 261–75.

Skidan, Aleksandr, *Krasnoe smeshchenie* (Moscow, 2005).

———, "Russkii ivrit," *Zerkalo* 29–30 (2007).

———, *Soprotivlenie poezii: Izyskaniia i esse* (St. Petersburg, 2001).

Sluzhevskaia, Irina, *Tri stat'i o Brodskom* (Moscow, 2004).

Smirnov, Igor', *Khudozhestvennyi smysl i evoliutsiia poeticheskikh system* (Moscow, 1977).

Smith, Gerald, "Joseph Brodsky: Summing Up," *Literary Imagination: The Review of the Association of Literary Scholars and Critics* 7, no. 3 (2005): 399–410.

———, "Long Growing Dark": Joseph Brodsky's August," in *Rereading Russian Poetry*, ed. Stephanie Sandler, 248–55 (New Haven, Conn., 1999).

———, "Singing Without Music" / "Pen'e bez muzyki," in *Joseph Brodsky: The Art of a Poem*, ed. Lev Loseff and Valentina Polukhina, 1–25 (New York, 1999).

———, "Stikhoslozhenie Iosifa Brodskogo, 1987, " in *Poetika Iosifa Brodskogo: Sbornik nauchnykh trudov*, ed. Valentina Polukhina, I. V. Fomenko, and A. G. Stepanov, 181–204 (Tver', Russia, 2003).

Smoliarova, Tatyana. "Pindar i Mandel'shtam," *Toronto Slavic Quarterly* 31 (2003), http://www.utoronto.ca.proxy.lib.umich.edu/tsq/13/smolyarova13.shtml.

Sobolevskaia, E. N., "Transformatsiia motiva 'molchaniia' kak edinstvo poeticheskogo konteksta (Pushkin—Viach. Ivanov—Tsvetaeva)," *Russkaia literatura* 1 (1996): 203–10.

Sokolov, Konstantin, "'Brodskii=Oden': Kommunikativnyi aspect stikhotvoreniia," in *Poetika Iosifa Brodskogo: Sbornik nauchnykh trudov*, ed. Valentina Polukhina, I. V. Fomenko, and A. G. Stepanov, 378–85 (Tver', Russia, 2003).

Sologub, Fedor, *Stikhotvoreniia*, ed. and commentaries M. I. Dikman (Leningrad, 1975).

Solov'ev, Vladimir, "Beauty in Nature," in *Readings in Russian Philosophical Thought: Logic and Aesthetics*, ed. and trans. Louis Shein (The Hague, Neth., 1973).

———, *Filosofiia iskusstva i literaturnaia kritika* (Moscow, 1991).

———, "Poeziia F. I. Tiutcheva," in *F. I. Tiutchev: Pro et contra: Lichnost' i tvorchestvo Tiutcheva v otsenke russkikh myslitelei i issledovatelei*, ed. K. G. Isupov (St. Petersburg, 2005).

———, *Sobranie sochinenii,* 10 vols. (Brussels, 1966–70).
———, *A Solovyev Anthology,* ed. S. Frank (London, 1950).
Sorsky, Nil, *The Complete Writings,* ed. and trans. George Maloney (New York, 2003).
Spieker, Sven, ed., *Gogol: Exploring Absence: Negativity in 19th-Century Russian Literature* (Bloomington, Ind., 1999).
Sprague, Rosamond, ed., *The Older Sophists* (Columbia, S.C., 1972).
Staël, Anne de, *De l'Allemagne* (Paris, 1930).
Stammler, Heinrich, "Metamorphoses of the Will: Schopenhauer and Fet," in *Western Philosophical Systems in Russian Literature: A Collection of Critical Studies,* ed. Anthony Mikotin, 35–58, University of Southern California Series in Slavic Humanities no. 3 (Los Angeles, 1979).
Staudt, Kathleen, "The Poetics of Black on White, Stéphane Mallarmé's 'Un Coup de dés,'" in *Ineffability: Naming the Unnamable from Dante to Beckett,* ed. Peter Hawkins and Anne Howland Schotter, 147–61 (New York, 1984).
Steiner, George, *After Babel: Aspects of Language and Translation* (New York, 1975).
———, *Language and Silence: Essays on Language, Literature, and the Inhuman* (New York, 1974).
Stevens, Wallace, *The Collected Poems of Wallace Stevens* (New York, 1982).
Stoekl, Allan, "De Man and the Dialectic of Being," *Diacritics* 15, no. 3 (Autumn 1985): 36–45.
Stratanovskii, Sergei, "Tvorchestvo i bolezn': O rannem Mandel'shtame," *Zvezda* 2 (2004): 210–21.
Strizhevskaia, Tat'iana, *O poezii Iosifa Brodskogo* (Moscow, 1997).
Surat, Irina, "Etiudy o Mandel'shtame," *Znamya* 5 (2007): 190–202.
———, *Mandel'shtam i Pushkin* (Moscow, 2009).
———, "Prevrashcheniia imeni," *Novyi mir* 9 (2004): 151–68.
Symeon the New Theologian, *The Practical and Theological Chapters and Three Theological Discourses,* trans. and intro. Paul McGuckin (Kalamazoo, Mich., 1982).
Tabori, Paul, *The Anatomy of Exile: A Semantic and Historical Study* (London, 1972).
Taranovsky, Kirill, "Dva 'molchaniia' Osipa Mandel'shtama," in *Mandel'shtam i antichnost',* ed. Oleg Lekmanov, 116–22 (Moscow, 1995).
———, *Essays on Mandelstam* (Cambridge, Mass., 1976).
Taylor, Mark C., "Non-Negative Atheology," *Diacritics* 20, no. 4 (Winter 1990): 2–16.
Terras, Victor, "The Black Sun: Orphic Imagery in the Poetry of Osip Mandelstam," *Slavic and East European Journal* 45, no. 1 (2001): 45–60.
———, "Osip Mandel'shtam i ego filosofiia slova," in *Slavic Poetics: Essays in Honour of Kiril Taranovsky,* ed. Roman Jakobson, C. H. Van Schooneveld, and Dean S. Worth, 455–60 (The Hague, Neth., 1973).

———, *Poetry of the Silver Age: The Various Voices of Russian Modernism* (Dresden, Ger., 1998).

———, "The Time Philosophy of Osip Mandel'shtam," *Slavonic and European Review* 17, no. 109 (1969).

Tiutchev, Fedor, *Polnoe sobranie sochinenii i pis'ma v 6 tomakh*, ed. N. N. Skatov et al. (Moscow, 2002–04).

Toddes, Evgenii, "Mandel'shtam i Tiutchev," *International Journal of Slavic Linguistics and Poetics* 17 (1974): 59–85.

———, "Stat'ia 'Pshenitsa chelovecheskaia' v tvorchestve Mandel'shtama 20–kh Godov," in *Tynianovskii sbornik: Tret'i tynianovskie chteniia*, ed. Marietta Chudakova et al., 184–217 (Riga, Latvian S.S.R., 1988).

Tolstoy, Leo, *Polnoe sobranie sochinenii v sta tomakh*, ed. G. I. Galagan et al. (Moscow, 2000).

Toporov, Vladimir, "Ob istochnikakh stikhotvoreniia Zhukovskogo 'Nevyrazimoe,'" *Slavica Hierosolymitana* 1 (1977).

Torlone, Zara M., *Russia and the Classics: Poetry's Foreign Muse* (London, 2009).

Tsvetaeva, Marina, *Sochineniia v dvukh tomakh* (Moscow, 1980).

Turgenev, Ivan, *Sobranie sochinenii v dvenadtsati tomakh* (Moscow, 1962).

Turoma, Sanna, *Brodsky Abroad: Empire, Tourism, Nostalgia* (Madison, Wis., 2010).

Tynianov, Iurii, *Poetika. Istoriia literatury. Kino* (Moscow, 1977).

———, *Problema stikhotvornogo iazyka* (Moscow, 1965).

Ungar, Steven, "RB: The Third Degree," *Diacritics*, vol. 7, no. 1 (Spring, 1977): 67–77.

Vaiskopf, Mikhail, "Oliva mira: Smert'-khudozhnitsa v poezii Boratynskogo," *Izvestiia RAN: Seriia literatury i iazyka* 63, no. 3 (2003): 38–46.

Vatsuro, Vadim, "Chuzhoe 'ia' v lermontovskom tvorchestve," *Russian, Croatian and Serbian, Czech and Slovak, Polish Literature* 33, no. 4 (1993).

———, *Zapiski kommentatora* (St. Petersburg, 1994).

Venclova, Thomas, "Brodskii o Mandel'shtame," in *Poetika Iosifa Brodskogo: Sbornik nauchnykh trudov*, ed. Valentina Polukhina, I. V. Fomenko, and A. G. Stepanov, 386–96 (Tver', Russia, 2003).

———, "A Journey from Petersburg to Istanbul," in *Brodsky's Poetics and Aesthetics*, ed. Lev Loseff and Valentina Polukhina, 135–49 (New York, 1990).

———, "Lithuanian Nocturne: To Thomas Venclova," in *Joseph Brodsky: The Art of a Poem*, ed. Lev Loseff and Valentina Polukhina, 107–49 (New York, 1999).

Venevitinov, Dmitrii, *Polnoe sobranie sochinenii*, ed. B. V. Smirenskii, intro. D. D. Blagoi (Moscow, 1934).

Verkheil, Keis, "'Enei i Didona' Iosifa Brodskogo," in *Poetika Brodskogo: Sbornik statei*, ed. Lev Losev, 121–31 (Tenafly, N.J., 1986).

Verlaine, Paul, *Oeuvres complètes* (Paris, 1922–23).

Veselovskii, Aleksandr, *V. A. Zhukovskii: Poeziia chuvstva i serdechnogo voobrazheniia* (Petrograd, 1918).

Viazemskii, Petr, *Stikhotvoreniia* (Leningrad, 1986).

Vickery, Walter, *M. Iu. Lermontov: His Life and Work* (Munich, 2001).

Vinitskii, Il'ia, *Dom tolkovatelia: Poeticheskaia semantika i istoricheskoe voobrazhenie V. A. Zhukovskogo* (Moscow, 2006).

Vinokur, Grigorii, *Filologicheskie issledovaniia: Lingvistika i poetika* (Moscow, 1990).

Vladimov, Georgii, *Vernyi Ruslan: Istoriia karaul'noi sobaki* (Frankfurt am Main, 1975).

Volgina, Arina, "Iosif Brodskii / Joseph Brodsky," *Voprosy literatury* 3 (2005): 186–219.

Volkov, Solomon, *Conversations with Joseph Brodsky: A Poet's Journey Through the Twentieth Century*, trans. Marian Schwartz (New York, 1998).

Voloshin, Maksimilian, *Sobranie sochinenii*, ed. V. P. Kupchenko and A. V. Lavrova (Moscow, 2000–2003).

Vvedenskii, Aleksandr, *Polnoe sobranie sochinenii v dvukh tomakh* (Moscow, 1993).

Wachtel, Andrew, "The Youngest Archaists: Kutik, Sedakova, Kibirov, Parshchikov," in *Rereading Russian Poetry*, ed. Stephanie Sandler, 270–86 (New Haven, Conn., 1999).

Wachtel, Michael, *The Cambridge Introduction to Russian Poetry* (Cambridge, Eng., 2004).

———, *The Development of Russian Verse: Meter and Its Meanings* (Cambridge, Eng., 1998).

———, "Joseph Brodsky chitaet Iosifa Brodskogo: "Chast' rechi i poetika perevoda," in *Sub Rosa: Koszonto konyv Lena Szilard tiszteletere*, ed. Denise Atanaszova-Szokolova, Anna Han, and A. Hollós, 594–603 (Budapest, 2005).

———, *Russian Symbolism and Literary Tradition: Goethe, Novalis, and the Poetics of Viacheslav Ivanov* (Madison, Wis., 1994).

Wackenroder, Wilhelm, and Ludwig Tieck, *Confessions and Fantasies*, trans. Mary Hurst Schubert (University Park, Pa., 1971).

Waldrop, Rosemarie, *Against Language? Dissatisfaction with Language as Theme and as Impulse Towards Experiments in Twentieth Century Poetry* (Paris, 1971).

Wanner, Adrian, "Russian Minimalist Prose: Generic Antecedents to Daniil Kharms's 'Sluchai,'" *Slavic and East European Journal* 45, no. 3 (2001): 451–72.

The Way of a Pilgrim, and The Pilgrim Continues His Way, trans. R. M. French, intro. Faith Annette Sand (Pasadena, Calif., 1989).

Weissbort, Daniel, ed., *Translating Poetry: The Double Labyrinth* (Iowa City, 1989).

Wellek, René, "The New Nihilism in Literary Studies," in *Aesthetics and the Literature of Ideas: Essays in Honor of A. Owen Aldridge,* ed. François Jost, asst. Melvin J. Friedman, 77–88 (Newark, N.J., 1990).

Weststeijn, Willem, "'The Thought of You Is Going Away . . .' 'Mysl' o tebe udaliaetsia, kak razzhalovannaia prisluga,'" in *Joseph Brodsky: The Art of a Poem,* ed. Lev Loseff and Valentina Polukhina, 177–90 (New York, 1999).

———, "Timur Kibirov," in *Neo-Formalist Papers: Contributions to the Silver Jubilee Conference to Mark 25 Years of the Neo-Formalist Circle,* ed. Joe Andrew and Robert Reid, 269–81 (Amsterdam, 1998).

Wigzell, Faith., ed. and intro., *Russian Writers on Russian Writers,* intro. Robin Aizlewood (Oxford, 1994).

Williams, David-Antoine, *Defending Poetry: Art and Ethics in Joseph Brodsky, Seamus Heaney, and Geoffrey Hill* (Oxford, 2010).

Wittgenstein, Ludwig, *Tractatus Logico-Philosophicus,* trans. D. Pears and B. McGuinness, intro. Bertrand Russell (London, 1961).

Wolosky, Shira, *Language Mysticism: The Negative Way of Language in Eliot, Beckett, and Celan* (Stanford, Calif., 1995).

———, "An 'Other' Negative Theology: On Derrida's "How to Avoid Speaking: Denials," *Poetics Today* 19, no. 2 (Summer 1998): 261–80.

Woolf, Virginia, *The Waves* (London, 1992).

Wordsworth, William, *The Complete Poetical Works of William Wordsworth* (Boston, 1904).

———, *Prose Writings of Wordsworth,* sel., ed., and intro. William Knight (London, 1893).

Yeats, William Butler, *The Poems of W. B. Yeats* (New York, 1983).

Zenkovskii, Serge, ed., trans., and intro., *Medieval Russia's Epics, Chronicles, and Tales* (New York, 1963).

Zhakkar (Jaccard), Zhan F., *Daniil Kharms i konets russkogo avant-garda* (St. Petersburg, 1995).

Zhirmunskii, Viktor, *Nemetskii romantizm i sovremennaia mistika* (St. Petersburg, 1914).

———, *Voprosy teorii literatury: Stat'i 1916–1926* (The Hague, Neth., 1962).

Zholkovskii, Aleksandr, *Bluzhdaiushchie sny i drugie raboty* (Moscow, 1994).

———, "'Ia vas liubil . . .' Brodskogo: Interteksty, invarianty, tematika i struktura," in *Poetika Brodskogo: Sbornik statei,* ed. Lev Losev, 38–62 (Tenafly, N.J.).

———, *Izbrannye stat'i o russkoi poezii: Invarianty, struktury, strategii, interteksty* (Moscow, 2005).

Zhukovskii, Vasilii, *Sobranie sochinenii v 4 tomakh* (Moscow, 1959–60).

Zubova, Liudmila, *Sovremennaia russkaia poeziia v kontekste istorii iazyka* (Moscow, 2000).

Index

About the Author

Sofya Khagi is an assistant professor in the Department of Slavic Languages and Literatures at the University of Michigan.